To Sharon,
Best wishes,
Karina Wetherbee
8-06

The Minefield of Memories

a memoir

Told by Alf Tieze

Written by

Karina Wetherbee

authorHOUSE

1663 LIBERTY DRIVE, SUITE 200
BLOOMINGTON, INDIANA 47403
(800) 839-8640
www.authorhouse.com

First published by AuthorHouse 03/31/04

ISBN: 1-4140-5485-8 (e)
ISBN: 1-4184-1408-5 (sc)

Library of Congress Control Number: 2004091014

Printed in the United States of America
Bloomington, Indiana

This book is printed on acid-free paper.

ACKNOWLEDGMENTS:

I am very grateful for the support my family has given me throughout this process: my husband, Charles, always the voice of reason, and my three children, Tristan, Sebastian, and Tessa, who reminded me that a child's perspective on the world is truly unique.

Thank you to my mother, Sunni, for providing priceless assistance with editing. Thank you to Myriam Avalos-Teie, Korine Fujiwara, Cameron Bennett, Janine and Tim Degitz, Monika Brown, Richard and Lorna Hutchinson, Roland Kiessling, Lee Massaro and Erik Tieze for keeping me motivated with their consistent eagerness for the next chapter.

Thank you to Doug and Nancy Bachtel for their encouragement and for supporting my father through the arduous task of revisiting his past. Thank you to Hank Parker for his enthusiasm for the book and for bringing it to the attention of so many others, through his book club. Thank you to Bob Craig, whom I have always admired for his own story of survival.

Finally, thank you to my father, who opened his very soul to me throughout this process. Thank you, Dad, for trusting me with this task.

To my Dad, whose strength of spirit is immeasurable.
His story will touch anyone who has ever longed for a place
and a time that are gone forever. May the telling of it bring him some
peace.

In Memory of Oma and Opa, who guided my father
through the perils of a turbulent world; he will
never forget their invaluable gifts of love and loyalty.

In Memory of Gerle, who will never be forgotten.
In Honor of those friends and family for whom my father is still searching.

AUTHOR'S NOTE:

I have written this story on behalf of my father, Alf Tieze. Beyond merely surviving World War II, he has navigated the minefield of his memories. While purging the very corners of his heart, and recording his thoughts in copious piles of notes, my father has emerged on the other side, stronger and more able to face his past. I hope that by lending him a voice with which to more deeply express these memories, I have honored his experiences and the lives of those who touched his world in so many ways.

INTRODUCTION

This story is a series of memories emblazoned in my mind as a child, whose world, like that of many, was thrown asunder during one of the most turbulent and horrific times in modern European history... W.W.II. It revolves around my boyhood home, that special place in a child's heart that is the axis of his life. This place called home changes dramatically in the course of a lifetime, but the line connecting each person to his roots remains, though sometimes vague and unrecognizable. Not all critical memories need be formed by an event as dramatic and destructive as war. Often, it is the more subtle occurrences... a shared moment with a stranger, an unexplained distance between members of a family, a series of pieces in a puzzle that never seem to fit. These shadows, these cloaked deceptions that veil reality can be as significant in a child's life as an overtly traumatic experience such as war, with the loss of innocence that inevitably accompanies it.

Time erases many scars. The passing of decades helps to heal a place of its history, but there are some scars that never completely disappear. The memories of a child who was scared, hungry, cold, and alone linger on.

Thus, a person's childhood home is a very powerful potion. Reacquainting oneself with a special place from one's childhood can conjure up very vivid memories of previously forgotten gems from one's store of experiences. Sights, smells, even tastes can be recalled simply by being there in the place one once called home.

If anyone would have told me that thirty-three years later I would be returning to my beautiful hometown as an American citizen, reunited with my sister, herself a German citizen living in Croatia, after so many years of turmoil, grief, and horror beyond which any child should ever have to experience; I would have said that person had been reading too many fairy tales. But, reality often writes a more gripping tale.

My hometown is nestled in the famous mountainous regions of Sudetenland, once a part of the mighty Austro-Hungarian empire. Germans and Austrians have settled these valleys and mountains for a thousand years, making a people who are very tenacious and hardy to survive in a region much coveted by neighboring lands. Germany lines the largest part of this forbidding region, enveloping it on three sides. Poland, Hungary, and Austria also claim borders with it. The area subsequently became part of Czechoslovakia, made up of Bohemia, Moravia, and Slovakia.

The inhabitants were determined souls who survived by taming the stubborn rocky soil and who built their many small villages among the wild forests and rushing streams of this picturesque land. Small industries even managed to find their way into the area, with my city, Jagerndorf (now Krnov) finding its niche in the textile industry. The production of fine wool and linens helped support a population of approximately 20,000 people. The city bustled with many workers and teemed with activity as continuously steaming chimneys dotted the skyline.

Yet, at the same time, there remained a rural feel to the land, as inhabitants honored their ancestors' abilities to cultivate the rolling hills into prolific gardens and orchards, and to nurture and tend the fine timber forests.

Two scenic rivers flowed through the city, the Black Oppa and the Gold Oppa, both bringing mysterious ancient glacial waters from the "AltVater Geberge" (Old Father Mountain Range), a region made magical by the many fairy tales with their origins in those high alpine valleys. The icy mountain waters flowed down the Gold Oppa, on the east side of which sat our house. This smaller river soon merged with the larger Black Oppa and eventually found its way to the mighty Oder River, which formed the natural border between Germany and Poland.

Our house, its two stories lined with white stucco not unlike its neighbors, belonged to my grandparents and lay a mere fifty meters from the tall ornate bridge which spanned the Gold Oppa. Across this ran the main road leading from the German border, which was about three kilometers to the east. It was not until later in my childhood that the significance of this line between the two nations became apparent. W.W.II brought Sudetenland into the forefront with its face quickly changing as Hitler and his ferocious greed swept over the peaceful cities as a blanket of darkness covered most of Europe, all but smothering the diverse lifeblood of its people.

It was this proximity to Germany that came to rule the fates of so many souls in my valley and beyond. It was upon this narrow, seldom-traveled road that wound through my hometown that my life changed in a way I never imagined possible... and it is a change I am amazed I survived.

Map of region (pre-war)

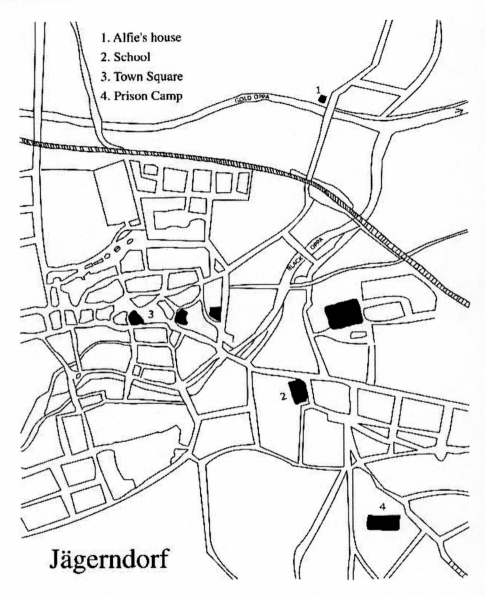

1. Alfie's house
2. School
3. Town Square
4. Prison Camp

Jägerndorf

Map of Jagendorf

Pre-war Jagerndorf

CHAPTER 1

The radio crackled loudly. The soft cadence of music that had been filling the room stopped. In its place boomed the familiar announcer's somber voice. My grandmother, who had been kneading dough at the table, paused, her gaze transfixed on the dial of the machine. She gasped, a slight shudder rippling across her hunched shoulders. Her anxious eyes flitted about the room, resting finally on mine. She forced a smile. Soon, the punctuated thumps of the dough upon the counter returned.

The news issuing from the radio had been increasingly disturbing of late, at least to my grandparents. I deciphered little from the endless reports. Food-rationing and murmurs of the "Anschluss" meant nothing to me; my mind was occupied with things nearer to home…

"Bye, Bye, Gerle!"

"Remember to find some more twine for our raft!" shouted Gerle behind me as I ran home, with the sun skimming across the tops of the trees along the river, signaling supper time. The warm summer air tempted me to return to the riverbank, but my grandmother insisted on scrubbed hands at the dinner table, so I had to hurry…

It was 1938 and I had been six since March. As most small boys, I enjoyed the countless joys of water play on a hot summer day. My friends and I passed many full hours down by the river near my house. The soft sandy bank under the bridge created a very secret, peaceful world for

4

us away from the bustle of the road overhead and the prying eyes of the neighborhood girls.

Today, Gerle and I had spent the day in this favorite spot of ours, filling the time as only youngsters can. Gerle was a half-year younger than I and quite a bit smaller, but his size betrayed his energy; he was very wiry and always eager for lively adventures. He lived only two streets from my house, so the bridge was a good place for us to meet to begin our daily forages along the riverbank.

The neighborhood also had several other boys whom we regularly included in our games. Otto (Otti) and his younger brother, Kurt, lived next door, their house separated from mine by a small fenced garden. Otti and I had spent many hours climbing over the fence between our yards to pick fruit. I went for the sweet dark blackberries drooping in tangled bunches along the hedgerow, and Otti was tempted by the shiny transparent red and gold currents that massed on bushes near our side of the fence. My small dog, Waldi, would jump about, barking wildly at the base of the fence, regretting all the while his short stature and his inability to scale the wooden fence after me. Waldi was a regular participant in all our activities and a willing accomplice in any mischief.

We toured the neighborhood joined by the many young boys who lived within a short distance of our home. Gunter and his four-year old brother, Walter, lived five houses up the road. Yet another boy, Franz, lived across the street from Gunter. Together, we liked to climb the trees in Franz's parents' small orchard and pick the plump ripe plums that threatened to drop to the grassy ground with the slightest tickling breeze. We would then run to sit in the shade of their small greenhouse to eat the sweet dripping fruit.

The river water was cool and refreshing as we washed the sticky purple juice from our chins and elbows before beginning our latest game along the river. We built canals and small ponds in the fine gravel banks that lined the water's shallow edge. In the crystal clear water that magnified the sandy golden bottom, we could see the glistening scales of the fish while they scattered as we tried to chase them into our traps.

More often, though, we retrieved gnarled driftwood, which had been swept into the cool shadows beneath the strong stone base of the bridge as the water crept its way downstream after the spring thaw. This was always a treasure-trove for us, as the wood made fine boats for our many races.

Gerle and I had challenged the other boys to a final race the next day, but we wanted to perfect our boat, and twine would be just the thing. My mind was full of the following day's plans while I dashed home to wash for supper. Upon reaching the wrought iron gate, I paused to watch a small gray bird alight on a branch of the tall lilac bush that sat near the entrance to the yard. I reached down and gathered into a pile a few small branches that lay under some leaves near the fence. I was hoping to use one for a mast for tomorrow's raft. As I opened the gate, the sounds of the factory steam whistle echoed over the valley, marking the hour of the evening shift change. I quickly rubbed my hands on my grubby shorts, sending a fine dust drifting through the deepening amber light.

The sound of splashing and gurgling water made me tuck my filthy hands into my pockets as I peered over the gate. Leaning over the pump in the yard was my Uncle Alois, his arms moving slowly up and down as the water sloshed into a battered metal bucket. As the bucket filled, he shifted uncomfortably from foot to foot, favoring his right leg.

My uncle had been born under unfortunate circumstances. His mother— my grandmother—had suffered from measles while pregnant with him, her eldest child. He was deaf and had never been able to speak, though he did his best to communicate with garbled mutterings and waving arms. Whatever movement his arms had, his legs lacked. He was partially paralyzed on one side of his body, which caused him to drag his right foot as he walked. I was fond of my uncle, with whom I shared one of the two small bedrooms on the first floor of my grandparents' house. Often, kids who did not know the family would taunt and tease him as they watched him lurch around the yard, following behind my grandfather while he puttered in his garden. But, once my friends became familiar with my uncle's peculiar mannerisms, they also grew to like him, with his welcome smile and his willingness to help anyone who needed a hand.

I lifted the latch on the gate and wandered into the yard, waving a hello to Uncle Alois. He greeted me with his familiar smile, only slightly concealed behind smoke circling from his ever-present pipe. His arm stopped pumping and he groaned slightly as he eased the heavy bucket down to his side and turned back toward the house. I ran ahead to open the door, the very full bucket being too heavy for me to carry. Waldi trotted beside me, his tongue lolling wearily from his mouth. It had been a busy day.

The coolness of the room made my skin tingle as I held the door wide to allow my uncle to pass, the bucket bumping against his body as his useless leg dragged along behind. He smiled again in thanks and headed through the door to the right into the kitchen. The evening light was turning slightly rosy as it glimmered through the glass that made up the walls of the entryway. Latching the door behind me, I savored the feeling of the cool wooden floor on the soles of my dusty bare feet. Curling my toes pleasantly, I followed my uncle into the kitchen. I waited as he poured some of the clear water into the bowl sitting on the sideboard and then I began to wash my hands of the day's dirt. The rest of the water was left in the bucket and placed in the sink for the few dishes we would use for our supper.

While I was drying my hands on the coarse linen towel that hung on a hook on the sideboard my grandmother entered the room with a small bundle of firewood in her well-worn arms. She crossed to a square iron door in the wall, which she opened with her free hand. She placed several of the smaller pieces of wood into the smoldering orange and blue flames. This access door opened into an oven that was really quite large and very useful. Called a Kachelofen, it existed mainly in the next room, the sitting-room. It was a very large forest-green ceramic oven with many cubicles and shelves. The oven provided the majority of the heat for the house and it was a fine place for warming shoes and drying clothes, as shelves further from the source of the heat were perfectly suited for these tasks. The fire inside was started through the door my grandmother had just opened.

"Show me your hands, Alfie." she said, as I walked over to her with my palms out for her to inspect. "Please call outside to your Opa that his supper will be cold if he doesn't come soon." I returned to the entry porch room and poked my head out the door.

"Opa, supper time!" I called. There was a muffled response from around the corner of the house, so I knew my grandfather had heard me. I trotted back across the cool floor and entered the kitchen. Uncle Alois ambled over to the table and sat down, stretching his stiff leg out with a long sigh, his eyes rolling slightly up to the ceiling with a look of relief to be sitting at last.

With the smells of Oma's fragrant cooking beginning to waft through the room, I realized how hungry the day's play had made me. Gerle, the other boys, and I had been so busy with our games at the river that now lunch seemed a very distant memory. I carried my cup of milk to the table and sat down.

The clatter of the front door echoed through the house and shortly after Opa walked in, rubbing his hands together in an expectant sort of way. Clearly, his gardening had also gotten the better of his day and left him as ravenous as I was. He crossed over to the washbasin and I watched his broad, only slightly stooped, shoulders shake as he began to scrub the black earth from beneath his nails. His gray hair lay limply damp on the nape of his sunburned neck. It had been a fine warm day, and as always, Opa had spent most of it outdoors. Turning, he ran his damp hands along his upper lip where a thick Kaiser-style mustache framed his strong mouth. He was very proud of this mustache, with its graceful curl, and he often caressed it during thoughtful moments.

"Are the cherries almost ripe?" Oma asked. "I want to make a cake for dessert on Sunday."

"You might need to do a plum one instead if you want it for this weekend." replied Opa. "The cherries need some more time." Opa's trees were the prized possessions in his bountiful garden. He tended them and cared for them as though they were wayward children in need of continuous vigilance. There were apple trees, cherry trees, plums, and pears. If one of the goats wandered too close to a tree there would be quite an uproar as Opa and Uncle Alois protected their precious buds from the four-legged interlopers.

"There should be a good crop of beans this summer, if the weather stays as fine as it has been the last few days." Opa said to my grandmother. My grandfather liked nothing better than to spend the day tending his many trees and flowers and defending his rows of vegetables from the many small creatures that also made their homes along the quiet river. Opa was retired, so his time was his own, but the many demands of his fields and gardens kept him busy throughout the day.

As a younger man he had worked for the postal bureau as a supervisor. Respect from his colleagues had enabled him to pull some strings for my dad to get his job with the postal rail services. This meant my father was away much of the time, traveling to many faraway cities as part of the demands of his job.

"How has my little Alfie's day been?" Opa asked in his rich voice. He walked over to me and tousled my hair with his large gentle hand.

"Great, Opa! Though, Gerle and I need to finish our raft in the morning. Can I have a small piece of that twine that you use to tie up your peas?" I asked, with a grin on my face, knowing full well he would agree. He was never one to discourage my desire to build things. Opa nodded, lowering himself into his chair at the head of the old kitchen table.

"Remind me in the morning, Alfie. I need some myself to tie up the beans. They are starting to run all over the place. You can help me first before you play." He blinked eagerly as Oma placed a platter in the center of the table and thrust a large spoon down into the fragrant contents... potatoes with chives and butter. Opa smiled at Uncle Alois as he watched him stare hungrily after Oma as she returned to the stove to bring the bowl of goulash that would be heaped over the potatoes, with its gravy filling the plate like a thick rich soup. After she set the bowl down, she reached for the potatoes and began spooning large piles onto Opa's plate.

"I need you to feed the rabbits after supper, Alfie, before you get ready for bed." Oma said to me while ladling the deep russet-colored goulash over Opa's potatoes. She then did the same for Uncle Alois before I received my plateful of the perfectly cooled meal. A long loaf of soft white bread with a crispy crust was placed before us next, though only after Oma had blessed it with the mark of the cross on the underside. Our prayers and words of thanks for our daily bread followed.

Meals were always very pleasant with my family. My grandmother was a very good cook and took great care in creating delicious meals out of limited provisions. Uncle Alois usually had a good story to tell, in his stylized manner of grunts, as well as elaborate mime with his hands. To earn a few coins he often helped the town undertaker with the grim job of prepping the body for burial. His stories often involved much gesticulating with his arms and morbid facial contortions, though usually barely concealing a grin and a twinkle in his eyes, as he acted out the day's victim's particular demise. I was utterly fascinated and my attention usually encouraged him to be more imaginative the next time.

That evening, though, a more somber topic was at hand. My mother was working longer hours at the textile mill; workers were needed for an increase in production as demand for woolens for the coming winter mounted with the numerous changes happening across Europe. I understood little of the reasons for my mother's long absences, but knew that even while she was at home I would see very little of her. She and my father lived upstairs in my grandfather's house. It had been that way for as long as I could remember. I had always shared a room with my uncle and rarely spent time on the floor above.

When mother was at home she would spend her time upstairs reading or knitting frilly pink garments. I often wondered how she could bear to sew at home after spending her entire day working with fabrics. Now, it sounded like her work at the factory might take her away from home even more, though I almost doubt I would have noticed the difference. My mother's place in my world was very unusual, looking back. Though, at the time my, life was rich and I was dearly loved and fussed over by my grandparents, so I didn't feel the missing mother-child bond. I had never experienced it with her; so it was difficult to crave what I had never had.

My grandparents filled in for my father most of the time, as well. He spent many weeks, even months, traveling with his job. When he did return from a trip mother kept him to herself most of the time. But, I did get to hear stories of the many cities through which his job took him. Some evenings he would talk of the sights in Vienna, Innsbruck, Warsaw, and even faraway Rome. They meant little to me as places on a map, merely as more destinations for my imagination and my twig boats as they floated away down the Gold Oppa. Father may have liked to be nearer to home, but work was work... and that was getting harder to find, Opa said.

While I helped Oma clear the plates from the table, Uncle Alois filled his pipe with sweet tobacco and stretched back in his chair with his hands behind his head, gazing up at the ceiling. The sounds of contentment filled the room as we felt our hunger ebb away. Oma's efforts to reach cups off a high shelf made her gasp slightly, a sound that paired well with Uncle Alois's short puffs on his pipe. The effect left the room feeling rather dreamy and thick, its opulence punctuated only by the loud metronymic ticking of the old grandfather clock in the next room.

Oma brought cups to the table, placed them around, and returned to the stove for the kettle. Tea made from the blossoms of Opa's linden trees completed a pleasant day. "There are plenty of today's carrot tops and rotted turnips on the compost pile for you to take to the rabbits." my grandfather said to me as we walked out the door together to begin the evening's chores. I was getting old enough to help in small ways around the garden and the animal shed. Opa wandered back around the corner of the house to resume his daily inspection of the trees. I headed out the gate, walking toward the shed to get the bucket for the rabbits' share of the garden's castoffs. Otti, from next door, was waiting for me.

He shook his blond bangs from his eyes and glanced around in a conspiratorial way. "The girls say they have a boat ready for tomorrow's race. Should we let them join?"

"Which girls?" I asked.

"Oh, only Edith, and Hanni, and her gang." he replied, his lip clenched between his teeth as he nervously awaited my answer. I frowned. It was always with great reluctance that we included the girls in our games; but I was eager, nonetheless, to have more teams to beat with our raft, in which I had the utmost confidence.

"OK, but tell them not until after lunch. I have to help Opa in the morning." I didn't want to admit to Otti that Gerle and I wanted time to test the boat first. I waved goodbye to Otti as he headed down the road to tell the good news to Edith.

I completed my evening chores just as the sun began to take a definite dip behind the low hills that cradled our city while it eased itself to sleep in its quiet hollow. In the morning there would be a fine dew covering the meadows as the sun slowly woke up and bathed the church spires and house gables with a soft caress of warm summer light. I wandered back into the yard, reluctant to let the day end, but knowing I still needed to brush my teeth and dress for bed.

The sounds of gentle music met my ears upon reaching the door and I knew I would find Oma and Uncle Alois sitting near the old radio to hear accounts of the day's events. Although my uncle could not actually appreciate the full function of the radio, he enjoyed the peaceful scene that surrounded it each evening.

Standing in the cool darkness of the hallway, I smiled, thankful that there were no more reports of the unsettled world to shatter the calm of that moment.

Alfie's house from bridge over
Gold Oppa River

CHAPTER 2

Feeding the chickens was my first morning duty. I had grown accustomed to the old red rooster waking me as the sun crept up over the trees. Long shadows stretched across the shimmering river, caressing the sparkling ripples as they slipped silently away. The river seemed to whisper to me through my window to come play in its cold fresh water, still black in the shadows of the trees that bordered it. I hurried out into the early sunshine. The ducks and the chickens were already waiting for me outside in the yard; the rooster was herding them in circles, possessively.

I finished tending to the hungry chickens and made my way back inside to remind Opa about the promised twine. My hunger that had so quickly been abated the evening before had returned. The time would come when I would go far longer between meals, but for now I needed only enter the warm inviting kitchen to have my needs satisfied.

There was a thick piece of the previous evening's loaf of bread sitting on the table. The sound of the whistling kettle filled the room as I sidled up to the table next to my grandfather, who was spreading golden currant jelly onto a crisp piece of toast.

"Good morning, Opa." I said. I turned to glance at Oma, who had just entered the room with her arms full of clean linens for the washstand. She dropped them next to the brimming pitcher and bowl and hastened to rescue the kettle, its steam issuing madly from the spout. I crossed the room, wrapped my tiny arms around her warm body, and hugged her tightly.

"Alfie, be careful, I have the hot kettle here!" she said sharply, but there was a sweet smile on her face and she pecked me lightly on the cheek, wrapping her free arm around my shoulders. I watched her make a fresh pot of tea, then sat down in my usual chair.

"Are you still tying up those beans this morning?" I asked my grandfather casually, in case he had forgotten his promise.

"You can help me with them straight away after you eat your breakfast." he replied. "Then I will have some twine for you." He paused to take a bite of the toast, which was beginning to drip jelly across his thumb. "Alfie," he said, when he had finished chewing, "School will be starting in a few days and you need to be ready. Oma will find you a slate and chalk while she is at the market today."

Opa had spoken several times throughout the summer about the coming fall and the great world that would open for me upon beginning first grade. It had all felt so far away, with the days stretching before me in a seemingly endless sea of adventures. Time had lingered on the very hot breath of summer, barely moving, while I had spent my time watching rafts drift down the river and clouds shifting and swirling to create ethereal impressions of dragons and pirate ships.

My friends and I had talked a few times about the upcoming changes in our routines, but it had held little real significance. I felt a shiver of excitement, more than slightly mingled with fear, as I thought of the imposing building that would soon be my school. At least I was safe in the knowledge that all my friends would be starting, as well, and we would still be together.

But, today my mind could not wander too far from the big event at hand. I quickly ate my bread and tea, eager to join Gerle and show him the treasures I would contribute to our winning boat. I followed Opa out to his vegetable garden, which lay beyond the small road that headed into town. We nodded a greeting to a tired-looking man who was pedaling his bike along the road; he was most likely heading to another long day of work at the mill.

The sun was already warming the morning nicely; it would be a hot one. Opa had brought with him a small spool of string, which he cut with a bone penknife from his pocket. He handed me a few strands of twine and showed me how to tie the long lanky beans to the sticks that were spaced evenly along the neat rows. My small fingers fumbled with the knots; I was not used to tying things too well yet, having spent so much time barefoot— shoe laces were for church. We finished fairly quickly and Opa awarded me with not only a nice bit of twine, but a fresh plum off a nearby tree, as well. I ate the sweet dark fruit and walked back to the yard to wash my hands at the pump.

Gerle waved to me from the river bank, so I ran down to meet him, having first gathered up the handful of lilac branches I had set aside the previous day. "Did your Opa give you some string, Alfie?" he asked, rather breathlessly, having just jogged over from his home a few streets away. His sandy brown hair already lay damp on his forehead. The heat was starting to rise. The cool river was going to be a good place to spend the day, one of the last free days of summer.

I handed the twine to Gerle, who immediately set about scraping it against a sharp rock to tear off a suitable piece. After a few minutes he had managed to slice five similarly sized pieces of twine, which he handed to me, throwing the remaining ball onto a rock.

"We need to get these sticks to lay together very tightly." I instructed, always enjoying the role of engineer. "Then we can twist the twine around the pieces... sort of weave them together." We spread out the sticks, selecting the straightest ones. After much haggling as to which way the twine should go, we hoisted a small mast onto our completed raft, which measured about a foot long.

We tried the boat a few times in the shallow water at the edge of the river, and each time it began to drift quickly along with the ripples of the gentle eddies along the bank, only twisting slightly with the motion of the water. It looked like we would have a fairly competitive boat and we grew eager for our friends to arrive. They were not due until after lunch, so we whiled away the morning trying to catch frogs and fish in the cool shade under the bridge.

"I'll see you back here after lunch." I said to Gerle, who was hiding the boat under a bush to keep it safe from any prying eyes.

"Bring some lemonade if you can. We will need it." he answered. We both headed off to our houses for a quick bite, knowing we were too excited to eat much on such a hot day.

I ate so little and so quickly that Oma was sure I was ill. "This bright sun is making you dizzy, Alfie. Maybe you should wait until later to go back out. Your face is all flushed and red."

"Oh, leave him be, Julie! He is fine... aren't you, Alfie? Just a little excited for his afternoon plans, eh?" Opa said, winking.

"Here are your things for school, Alfie." Oma said, ignoring Opa's comments and placing before me a clean gray slate and a small box of thin strips of new chalk. "Mind you don't break those all to pieces." she said, frowning with the thought of the new costs of school supplies. "And try not to shuffle your feet through the dirt all the way to school. We want your shoes to last through the winter." Oma bustled out of the kitchen, leaving me wondering what had put her into such a temper.

As if reading my thoughts, Opa said, "Your Oma is just concerned with the difficulty she had shopping today. There seemed to be much less to buy at the market. That paired with the news…" His voice trailed off and he, too, turned to go out the door. "Oh, good luck with your raft. Hope you win, Alfie."

I headed back out to the river, quickly forgetting the somber mood of my family. The riverbank was practically swarming with boys; the girls had not yet arrived. Gerle motioned to me, his hands clutching our raft as though it were a precious jewel. "Franz thinks we should start the boats at the bridge and run them all the way to the big tree at the bend. We need to pick someone to hold them all back with a board till we yell start. Otti went to get one from his papa." Someone would have to stand in the water behind the boats, with the board bracing them back so the race would be fair.

There was noise from the bridge as a few faces peered over. The girls had arrived. It was time to begin. Otti was back with a long white board. "Just don't get it wet" his father had said. Otti just shrugged, saying it would be dry by the time he returned it. We grinned, and all agreed it would be Otti who would hold the board. None of us wanted to face the wrath of his father—the board was sure to get soaked.

Edith and Hanni had brought several other girls with them, adding three boats to the race. The river would see much activity today. Hanni shared a boat with Dorle, a girl from the next street over, and Edith was paired with Gretel, a pretty girl with long blond braids. Inge, the oldest, had a boat all to herself, and she boasted endlessly to all who would listen that she had spent days designing it.

Otti waded out to the middle of the river, the water coming only to his knees. We each delivered our entries to the wooden starting line, which he held out in the water perpendicular to the bank. We all clambered for the best view as, on Gunter's count of three, Otti raised the board, and the boats, all seven of them, were set free.

Inge's boat promptly sank, which sent Otti into fits of hysterics, laughing so hard he fell over, drenching himself and the board entirely. Upon this, Otti's little brother, Kurt, began laughing as well, until he realized their boat was stuck in a small whirlpool and was spinning hopelessly around in circles.

The rest of us ran along the bank, shouting and laughing, watching the progress of the remaining boats. This proved to be difficult as we were often unsure which boat belonged to whom. It became clear after only a few feet that the race would be down to three boats: Edith's and Gretel's, Franz's, and ours.

The boats were just approaching the large tree that marked the finish line when Otti, soaked from head to toe, ran through the river, splashing water to all sides. He was determined to preside over the end of the race as well as the beginning. He arrived in time to declare Franz's boat the winner, followed closely by Gerle's and mine, leaving the girls to take a not-too-distant third. There was a loud cheering from all, mostly due to Otti's fine performance. Inge even managed a smile, though somewhat halfheartedly.

We spent the rest of the afternoon sharing the lemonade and some cherries that Franz had brought. When we weren't lying on the cool grass, we were splashing through the inviting water, all of us determined to have this special day continue. We talked little of the coming change. Monday we would all be starting school, but we still had two days left to enjoy being free.

It was fall and I had been attending school for three weeks. My day began even earlier. After my morning chores, I had a two kilometer walk to the school house. I did not mind, though. The walk was a pleasant one, at least for now. The weather was still warm and the meadows and yards were full of the rich hues of autumn. Also, it was a chance to visit with my friends, since we all walked together. We would meet at the corner of the bridge, the dawn still chilly, and we would set off briskly, carrying our satchels over our shoulders. The neighborhood girls would be there, too, though they walked slightly behind, giggling amongst themselves.

The boys and girls had separate classes, and in fact separate buildings. A third building housed a gymnasium, which was shared by all the students. School began at 8 o'clock and by the time the bell rang at 3 o'clock we were eager to head home for a few hours of play, having spent most of the day at our seats. Each child had his or her own chair with an attached desk, the lid of which could flip up to reach a storage space. In the upper right hand corner there was a small inkwell with a wooden lid. These somber rows of desks constituted our world for the better part of each weekday, so our restless minds and limbs learned to relish any moment of freedom.

Gerle, Otti, and I were just coming out of the last class of the day, when the bell rang shrilly behind us. We ran down the flight of stone stairs that flanked the building, eager to be away. It was Friday. We had two days ahead of us, already filled with adventures planned during moments when our minds had been sent wandering, with the teacher's voice droning on and soon becoming a mere buzzing in the ear.

The walk home was often a long one; it was rarely completed in a straight line. We found many reasons to stop along the way, our favorite detour being the railroad tracks that ran parallel to and about five hundred meters from the river. There was something about the pencil straight lines of the tracks disappearing into the distance or curving around a hill into the unknown that excited us.

Our ambling steps would usually lead us to the secret fort we had made from an old tarp Opa had given us. This was an area we guarded fiercely from the girls. Usually, we posted one of the younger boys, Kurt or Walter, on guard duty to lookout for any infiltrators into our camp. The unlucky one on duty was always provided with apples to help keep him from getting too restless and neglecting his duties. It was not unheard of that the girls spoke to each other of running away from lobbed apple cores.

Finally, we reached the bridge, that point for all of us where our lives connected for moments during the day. Each of us waved to the other, knowing the farewell would be brief, and knowing that we would be back in the same spot in the morning, secure in the fact that we would always be together.

CHAPTER 3

It was potato harvest time. Gerle and I had agreed to meet Saturday morning as soon as we had both completed our chores. This was a special time of year for us. The earth gave forth its reward for all the season's toil, and the fields blazed with a light that seemed to come from within. The hay grew high and rolled in undulating waves, beckoning to swallows as they soared and swooped above the seas of gold.

I woke early; the rooster seemed eager for his breakfast. His crowing had anticipated the sun's climb into the sky; a beautiful autumn day was promised. After a hasty meal, I completed my chores, greeted my grandparents and Uncle Alois with a gentle kiss on the cheek, and ran off to the bridge. Gerle had not yet arrived. "His rooster must still be asleep." I thought. I sat on the riverbank where it curved under the flared base of the bridge's stone pillar, and I watched the many trees drop their leaves, gifts of color to the clear water below.

I heard activity on the road above and stood up for a closer look. An elderly man, wearing a dark green sweater and a felt hat with a feather protruding jauntily out the back of it, was walking to town. He was followed by a mule pulling a small wooden cart piled high with potatoes and squash. The hooves of the mule made a pleasant sound upon the narrow road, punctuating the quiet morning air. As I waved a greeting, to which the man responded with a cock of his hat, Gerle came around the corner from the next street, skipping lightly and eating an apple.

Gerle and I enjoyed a quiet time by the river while he finished his apple and we waited for the world around us to wake. Dust was starting to rise from some of the fields adjacent to the road, my grandfather's included. The potatoes needed to be gathered and the soil turned over with the heavy iron plow. We knew the fun would begin later in the day when the dust would settle and we could scavenge for forgotten potatoes.

Otti, Gunter, Franz, and the others joined us after lunch and we ran among the overturned rows of Opa's field, gathering all the potatoes we could carry. Back on the sandy riverbank, Gunter made a small fire surrounded by round rocks we had collected from the river.

Otti, who had been across the road cutting willow branches to hold in the fire, trotted down the bank to us and said, "The girls will be coming in a minute. Edith promised to bring some cottage cheese, so I said it was ok."

There was a murmur of uncertainty, as few of us wanted the perfect scene tainted by the inclusion of the girls, but the prospect of condiments for our roasted potatoes won out.

"Here we are, Otti!" a voice called from above. We looked up to see Edith, Hanni, and Gretel. True to her word, Edith had brought the promised cheese and she had also brought a small shaker of salt. "Mama said this would make them taste better." Edith said, handing the contributions to Franz, who set them on a flat rock near the fire. The girls found places on the soft sand and sat down cross-legged to await the coming treat.

The potatoes sizzled and popped as the skin shrank and cracked in the hot coals. Eager faces peered out of the lengthening light, the autumn day slipping earlier towards twilight. Silence fell, as anticipation for the seasonal snack mounted.

"I think they are ready." said Franz, grabbing the poker he had brought from home and jabbing it into one of the larger potatoes to test the doneness. "Here, Gunter. Set it there on the rock to cool first. Oh, we need something to spread the cheese. Alfie, can you see if your Oma will give you a knife to use."

I soon returned with the knife. "I want it washed and back in the drawer when you are through. Don't go leaving it lying in the sand." Oma had said. All the potatoes had been removed from the coals and were cooling on the rocks that rimmed the fire.

Gunter carefully picked up his, tossed it a few times from hand to hand, blowing on it, and picked up the knife to cut into the perfectly crisp golden skin. Steam rose from the fissure as Gunter continued to blow on the potato, his hands blackened from the soot of the fire. We all followed suit, taking turns with the knife and sending billows of steam into the air.

We spent a fine afternoon, eating our fill of the delicious salted potatoes lathered with cottage cheese. We spoke of our times at our new school, snow fort plans for the coming winter, and other matters of equal importance. When the whistle from the mill sounded, we all poured handfuls of water onto the flames, washed our sooty hands and faces in the now cold water, and headed our separate ways.

I wandered slowly toward the gate and the warm lights of the house, meeting Opa as he came from the field across the road. "I can see by your face that you ate half my field of potatoes!" Opa said, smiling and sliding his hand across my shoulder as we continued together toward the gate.

A vague rumbling noise sounded behind us and we turned to peer into the rapidly fading light. Echoing over the valley appeared a small airplane, black against the gray sky of the approaching night. It crossed over the city a few times, then flew off over the hill, its roar fading as quickly as it had come.

"Let's get inside, Alfie." Opa said, his voice tight. He fumbled hastily at the gate, turning to look back in the direction the plane had gone, a look of concern on his lined face.

That evening on the radio there was continued news of the coming "Anschluss", which Opa explained to me as the taking over of our country by our neighbor, Germany. I did not understand how this could have happened, though my grandfather didn't seem prepared to elaborate.

The next morning I entered the kitchen to find my grandparents deep in conversation. "... hundreds of them, littering and floating everywhere!" Opa said, holding up several small slips of paper. He glanced at one, then crossed over to the fire, opened the door, and thrust the bunch of paper, all but one, into the flame, which licked at the fresh fuel eagerly.

"What does this all mean, Reinhard? What is going to happen?" Oma asked, kneading her hands around the dish towel she was holding.

"I don't know. We'll have to wait and see." Opa replied. "Meanwhile, I've got work to do." His eye caught mine and he stretched out his arms to me in a warm hug. "See how many of these you can collect today, Alfie." he said, holding up the remaining scrap of paper. His eyes looked searchingly into mine, his mouth wearing a forced smile. He placed his hands on my shoulders, shook his head slightly, and headed out the door.

The entire city had been blanketed during the night with leaflets, dropped from the airplane we had seen circling overhead. They proclaimed Germany would be annexing Austria as part of the newly formed German Reich. Posters had appeared during the night as well, plastering almost every upright surface in the city. The announcement read: "All citizens required to assemble at the Town Hall square, Tuesday morning, 10 A.M. Prompt attendance is necessary. All students need not report to school until further notice."

Oma shuffled around the kitchen for awhile in a distracted fashion, then told me to stay with Opa. She was heading to church, she said. Oma found great solace in her faith and spent much of her time at the old stone Catholic church on the square.

I found Opa outside in his orchard, plucking ripe apples off a heavily laden tree. Handing me one, he said, "Did your Oma go already, then?" I nodded, my mouth full of the juicy sweetness of the apple. "I will tell your uncle to keep an eye out for you. I need to go out, too. I will be at your Uncle Fritz's tavern, if Oma asks." Opa said, hoisting the heavy basket of shiny red apples to take to the cellar.

Uncle Fritz was my father's brother. He lived near the center of town and was the proprietor of a popular tavern on the main road near the square. Opa often spent an evening or two a week there, playing cards and reminiscing with his World War I buddies. But, I knew Sunday was not one of his usual days, and I had a sinking feeling that this visit had something to do with the leaflets, flashing glaringly white and foreign as they drifted among the beautiful muted colors of autumn.

My mind traveled to my father, who was still away with the train in some far off city. Perhaps, he was even moving down a track littered with papers similar to the ones coating the fields around our town. I knew that if he had been home he would be with Opa at the tavern, talking in hushed voices in the smoke-filled room.

It seemed that everywhere I turned that day the talk was of war and the possibility of it spreading to our valley. It all felt so unreal to me; our peaceful city, nestled in its ancient valley, didn't seem like the sort of place to brew a war.

That evening Mother made a rare appearance in the kitchen downstairs. I gave her a quick hug; anything more felt unnatural. She acknowledged my greeting with a weak smile and pulled back quickly, her hands tugging restlessly at the pockets of her faded blue apron. She approached Oma, who was busy at the stove tending a pot of delicious smelling stew, the scent of which was making my mouth water. A hot plum cake, with its golden streusel topping, sat cooling on the counter.

"I'm worried sick about Joseph, Mutti. They say at the mill that train cars are being confiscated for... other uses." my mother said, haltingly.

"He'll be fine. We will all be fine." my grandmother replied, shortly. She turned to look at my tired mother, who had been working extra shifts at the factory for a couple months and the strain was beginning to show. Her face was pale and drawn, and there were dark circles framing her eyes. "You go take a warm soak. Get some rest. You need to take care of yourself... in your condition." Oma said, with raised eyebrows that sent a message I could not understand. My mother glanced unsmilingly at me, waved to Uncle Alois, who had just entered to wash his hands, and soon I heard her labored footfalls on the stairs in the hall.

Tuesday morning came and the sun rose warmly against an azure blue sky. It was a perfect fall day, the air crisp and refreshing, the breeze sufficient to give a slight chill. Opa entered the kitchen early, eager to rake together the hay while the sky was clear. He had told me the night before that we would need to be out early to get the hay gathered, due to the Assembly later in the square. I asked no questions, sensing my grandfather's unease with the subject.

We ate our toast silently as we made our way across the road, which was already unusually crowded with people heading into the city's center. Everyone was walking in small groups, huddled closely, talking quietly but fervently amongst themselves. We greeted several familiar faces, crossed the road, and immediately set to work. Opa handed me a rake and instructed me to move along beside him, pulling together any hay his larger rake might miss.

We were making good time, in spite of frequent stops to mop sweat from our brows. The welcome breeze was no longer sufficient to cool us beneath the brilliant sun. The crowds on the road had swelled over the couple hours we had spent in the field. Occasionally, a fellow would wave. Opa merely nodded back, too intent on his haste to do more.

"It is nearly time, Reinhard. You better get moving! Today is the Anschluss. We must all be on time." called a voice from across the field, which was now buzzing with bees and grasshoppers that we had stirred up in the sweet warm hay.

"We are coming!" Opa shouted back, looking vexed. I wasn't sure if he was upset about not finishing or about the summons itself. He shook his head, sweat dripping down across his brow, which today showed lines of worry I had never seen before. Turning to me and leaning on his rake, he said, "We will just finish this last row and then we will go." His eyes flickered up for a brief instance to meet mine, and I saw what looked like dread, before he quickly turned his face and moved away along the row.

A loud rumble met our ears as we made our way past the railroad crossing near the center of town. Opa's hand rested firmly on my shoulder, and he made big strides, now intent on being on time. I was so busy keeping pace that I didn't notice the source of the noise until we were upon it. Traffic unusual to our peaceful town was filling the streets. Large trucks, each filled with stiffly uniformed soldiers piled in their backs, bumped along the cobbled streets. These were followed by more trucks carrying cannons, as well as by cumbersome tanks that looked abnormally large on the narrow streets.

My mouth hung open as the sights filled my range of vision. Everywhere was a sea of green and gray, the colors of camouflage and military might. After the tanks had thundered by, the rhythmic sound of marching feet echoed against the stone dwellings that lined the main road. From around the corner appeared columns of hundreds and hundreds of soldiers, some wearing the intimidating black uniform of the soon-to-be-familiar SS troops. More of these troops lined the sidewalks, which were already filled to overflowing with spectators and townspeople. People were pushing and shoving as they made their way to the town square, which before now had always seemed so large, yet now felt tight and oppressive.

I bumped up against Opa's arm, while I hastened to tuck my small hand into his. I could feel the tension in the muscles of his arm as his fingers closed tightly over mine. My ears were ringing with the jumble of sounds, so different from the sigh of the tickling breeze that had cooled my brow for most of the morning.

Several marching bands were competing for prominence, their pounding drums shaking the window panes of the nearby shops. The air was no longer crisp with the smells of molding leaves and ripe apples, instead, it was heavy with putrid billows of exhaust and the sweat of too many bodies.

The tanks continued to roll down the narrow streets until they had formed a circle around the large cobbled plaza in front of the town hall. It was then that I noticed the flags, bold in their newness against the old stone facades. They all were variations of the same image: graphic white circles filling a blood-red flag like a bull's eye, in the middle of which was the symbol of the new German Reich, the fanged swastika. Others, more banners than flags, were black, long, and narrow, and were draped from the eaves of the buildings. They were so long they grazed the sills of the doorways. They, too, bore the rigid red lines of the swastika. These huge flags dominated every window sill around the square, leaving no doubt as to who's day this was.

Pulling my eyes away from the jagged shape on the flags, I held even more tightly to Opa, placing both my hands in his one, as we entered the sea of people massed in the space between the tanks. Since we had been one of the last to arrive, we were forced to stand with our backs against several large picture windows of a small shop. I glanced over my shoulder into the shadows of the store, whose doors were securely locked for the occasion. A delicate vase containing one red rose caught my eye. The window seemed so quiet and dark compared to the chaos in the space just before me.

People were standing so closely together that I had to keep shuffling my feet to avoid being trodden upon. If it had not been for Opa's reassuring hand around mine, I would have been lost in the tunnels of tall bodies before me, all pushing for a better view. All I could see were people's backs, pressing uncomfortably closer as the crowd continued to swell.

Shadows passed across the sky, deepening the gloom of my small space in the crowd. Formations of airplanes, similar to the one we had seen in the evening a few days before, roared overhead. I wanted to cover my ears, but I feared losing the safety of Opa's grasp.

High above, through the rows of people, I could see a balcony on the third floor of the Town Hall. More uniformed men, this time officers, their many medals glinting in the bright sun, crowded the small space of the alcove. Each wore a red band around the left arm, emblazoned with the same symbol as the flags, a symbol we learned quickly never to ignore... the swastika, its points projecting out like the deadly knives of a lumberjack's saw.

Suddenly, a roar of noise rose up from the soldiers, followed quickly by a second wave from the spectators. "Sieg Heil! Sieg Heil!" sounded the cry. The noise subsided as quickly as it has risen. I shook with fear and my eyes were smarting from the unfamiliar smells that continued to swarm up around me. A drone of talking drifted out over the crowd from the balcony beyond, carried by a speaker too small and distant to reach everyone's ears.

As the speeches continued, my legs grew tired, and thirst from the long morning in the dusty field became unbearable. "Opa, when will this be over? I have to pee." I grimaced, pulling on Opa's shirt. I knew Uncle Fritz's tavern was just a couple blocks away. Perhaps, I could be back before anyone noticed... Opa shook his head quickly and clutched my hand more tightly.

"It will be over soon, Alfie." The look in his eyes told me the matter was settled; I must wait.

A murmur began to ripple through the crowd. "The Fuhrer! Look, up there! Sieg Heil! Sieg Heil!" The noise rose to a crescendo as everyone took up the refrain, their arms quickly rising in a stiff salute.

Opa nudged me in the back, yelling, "You better put your hand up too, Alfie, or we'll be in trouble. No, the other one, the other one! Look, Alfie, like mine." He winked at my startled face and raised his arm also. It trembled slightly, already tired from the day's exertions.

I tore my eyes from Opa's face and glanced back at the central balcony, my arm already aching in the unnatural position. Flanked by the officers stood a small man, dressed in a belted black leather coat with a hat obscuring his eyes. "The Fuhrer, the Fuhrer! It is Adolf Hitler!" hummed voices all around me.

My arm began to burn, as the blood flowed slowly away from my raised fingertips. I longed to flop it to my side and give it a good shake. Finally, its heaviness became overwhelming and I lowered it, raising my left arm, instead. I sighed, the feeling returning to my fingers. At once, a tall man dressed in a black uniform materialized in front of me, his hand on his belt. He barked something unrecognizable at me, showering me with angry spit from his twisted mouth. Opa grabbed my right arm and returned it to the painful position from which I had rescued it. He urged, "Come, Alfie, leave it up. It will all be over soon."

My whole body trembled, a mixture of anger, fear, and humiliation being only part of it; I still needed to go to the bathroom. The uniformed man had melted back into the crowd; it had engulfing him like a wave obscuring a grain of sand on the beach. But, I suddenly noticed how many of the uniforms surrounded us, and this only served to double the weight of my arm, causing tears to well in my eyes. Through these tears, which I tried desperately to blink away, I looked back again to the man on the balcony, only now noticing a razor blade mustache above his thin lip, which spread into a cruel line as he bellowed to the crowd, his fist waving angrily in the hazy air above him.

Alfie in Opa's Garden

CHAPTER 4

The assembly on the plaza finally ended, though only after much fanfare and more ostentatious presentations of military invincibility. The crowd had been worked into a frenzy. People were shouting and pushing, completely mesmerized, some in awe and some in fear, by the powerful words of the man on the balcony. I was finally allowed to put my hand down; it now tingled painfully from the lack of blood, and I swayed on my tired feet, realizing for the first time how long it had been since the pitiful piece of toast so many hours before.

I was dancing in place with such a pained look on my face and clutching my crotch that Opa reluctantly gave me permission to run ahead. The crowd was still lurching unpredictably, like an angry swarm of bees. Opa clearly feared I would be trampled, though it was only two short blocks to the tavern, and I was quite familiar with the way. For the first time that day, it served me well to be small. I dodged and slithered my way through the diverging crowd, my whole mind focused on the coming relief, as I neared the latrine in the back of the hallway at Uncle Fritz's tavern.

I emerged shortly after, once again able to focus on how hungry and thirsty I was. I followed Opa to the back room of the restaurant. There, some familiar faces were already seated at a large corner table, which was big enough to accommodate a dozen people, with its built-in benches around three sides. This room was usually reserved for special guests of my uncle's and it served as a welcome calm after the pressing noise and stress of the morning's events.

The delicately decorated wrought iron sign which hung above the table was swinging with the motion of the thick smoky air, and the seated men shifted upon the bench to make room for the newcomers. The sign was an invitation for those special guests of the proprietor to use this reserved table, set aside strictly for that purpose.

"Where is Oma?" a voice behind me asked. "Opa, did she come with you?" My Aunt Sofie had a full tray in one hand and a wet wash rag in the other, having just cleared a table for the people now straggling in, hungry for lunch.

"She came separately. I'm sure she is with Alois. They might just head home. Or perhaps she will stop off at the church… I wouldn't expect her, Sofie." replied Opa, putting an arm around me as he sat down on the bench.

"Could you find a little something for Alfie here, Sofie? We had a small breakfast and it has been a big day."

Sofie smiled, nodding, and she took my hand. Her kind face was glistening from the steady exertion in the overcrowded room, but her eyes were calm as she gazed down at me.

"Go on, Alfie, then you can play." Opa said, nudging me gently in the back. He watched me until I reached the door to the kitchen, then his head bent low toward the fellow next to him and they began talking. I followed Aunt Sofie eagerly, the smell from the kitchen rekindling my briefly forgotten hunger.

I sat at a small low table in the corner of the bustling kitchen, watching the progress of many heaped plates as they made their way through the swinging doors into the crowded dining room. Aunt Sofie reappeared after several minutes and set before me a plate piled with some rye bread, soft cheese, and slices of fragrant sausage. "Eat up, Alfie! Then you can join your cousins in the back room. I think your Opa might be here awhile." she said, handing me a fork and a napkin.

The delicious food settled my rumbling stomach and my mind began to wander as I thought back to the morning in the square. Everything around me, once so familiar, appeared to me now in a new, more ominous light, forever clouded by the images of the forces of destruction: the tanks and guns, the yells, and stomping feet… the fever of war. The events in the plaza had been the first glimpse of a world that existed outside my safe and ordered universe. It was as though I had breached an impregnable wall and was peering into a garden filled with nothing but alien plants—vicious carnivorous ones.

I sat for several minutes, growing slightly sleepy in the hot kitchen. The steady bustle of the small kitchen staff blurred into an indistinct noise, and I suddenly longed to lean my head against the chair for a nap. A pot clattered loudly as Uncle Fritz's voice called through the door with orders to bring more beer. Returning to the moment, I eased myself out of my chair and I retraced my steps to the room where Opa sat with his friends.

The old men were now deeply engrossed in conversation, in groups of two or three, all discussing the somber, world-altering events of the day. The sweet smoke from their pipes hung thickly over their heads as it drifted blue around the lamps that hung low over the table. Plates were pushed back, steins pulled forward, beer flowing in a steady stream.

"Well, the army is impressive!" said one cynical voice from the corner.

"The Kaiser would have matched it, given a chance. Though, no one is asking my opinion." grunted a surly fellow, his brows furrowed. He twisted his beer stein in his leathery hands. The talk continued in this vein, the men generally lamenting the day Sudetenland had become a province beholden to Czechoslovakia—not to mention the forces beyond—and turning its back on the beloved Kaiser in his "Schloss" in Vienna.

"Well, the Kaiser certainly offered better waltzing music than this lot!" chuckled another. The laughter rose as more beer was passed around and the mood lightened considerably.

I wandered by the table where they sat, Opa winking at me as I passed, and I made my way into the large dance hall, dark except for the long autumn light streaming in through the latticed windows. In the far corner a couple of my cousins and their friends were building a house out of some cards. They whispered in hushed voices and then squealed in laughter as the carefully balanced cards tumbled down in a heap. With an unexplainable chill, I shuddered at the sight of the fabricated home crumbling into ruins.

"Alfie, come here." motioned Traudl, one of my cousins. "You have a go." I shook my head, instead crawling beneath the large black grand piano that sat in the opposite corner. Traudl got up, followed by Lisel and Gerdi, two other girls whom I had met once before, though I was unsure of their relation to me, if any.

The piano was covered by a large white linen cloth, the slightly dusty edge of which was just skimming the floor. Traudl lifted the cloth and peered under, her bright blue eyes shining with merriment. "Great tent! Can we play?" she asked. She did not wait for an answer but crawled in beside me, holding up the drape for the others to follow. We spent awhile playing fort, and then tag, making the darkness under the piano the safe zone.

That is where Opa found me, a couple hours later, when it was time to go home… curled up and asleep in the safe zone.

School had started again, and for this I was grateful. The colder weather made it harder to be outside and I missed the daily contact with my friends, though Oma and I spent some fine afternoons by the fire as the rain pattered against the windows. She had made several apple strudels, filled with plump raisins and walnuts, and we had sat sipping tea and drying fragrant cherry pits on the hot ceramic tile of the Kachelofen. The cherry pits would then be sewn into small linen bags, which could be heated in one of the stove's cubicles and taken up to bed in the winter to warm cold feet. The smell of the roasted stones was deep and organic and mixed well with the fragrant smell of the still-cooling strudel. Oma hummed a melody from her favorite operetta, one I had often heard on the radio… at least before the news of the war blanketed most of the airwaves.

There had been many changes since the assembly in the square. The coins Uncle Alois brought back from his job at the morgue were German "Reichsmarks" now, and his tales of people in their last moments of life didn't seem so funny anymore. Many of my friends' fathers and uncles had been called to German military duty, so we dreaded what news Uncle Alois might someday bring home.

Autumn gave way to winter and the days grew shorter. I was thankful I had heeded my grandmother and gone lightly on my shoes, as the snow came early and fell deeply. With the pale evening light fading quickly to darkness, we spent increasing amounts of time in the kitchen, the warmest and most inviting room in the house. Meals were simple: dark bread with a slice of cheese or ham, and hot milk from our own goats.

Oma would sit sewing, singing me her favorite songs, or telling me fairy tales from our tattered copies of Brothers Grimm and Hans Christian Anderson. Often, I would crawl under the kitchen table, pour out my wooden blocks—the ones Opa had sanded into many smooth shapes for me, and I would build houses and castles… fit for a Kaiser, I thought.

Opa spent more and more of the evening hours by the radio, the grave reports issuing forth continuously. The German Reich was moving east with its legions of troops, steadily conquering our people… while stealthily destroying another. As the war drew ever closer, my grandparents became increasingly concerned about my father; he was still away with his job.

Mother was considerably more withdrawn and irritable. The slightest noise I made in the yard would cause her to yell down to me from the window, "Alfie! Stop that racket this instant!", as she slammed the shutters.

The cold squeeze of winter did little to limit my time outdoors with my friends. Of course, we each had chores to do; we were getting older and an increased responsibility came along with that privilege. Along with my duty of tending to the chickens, now nestled in the cozy shed, I was given the job of feeding the goats. They would nip at my hat and collar, more interested in my clothing than the dry brittle hay I raked into their pens.

On one such day, I woke to a bitter cold morning. But, the icy sun soon climbed up over the dark hills, casting them with a blue tinge, and spreading a carpet of glistening diamonds across the newly fallen snow. I hurried through my chores, a cloud of frosty breath curling above me as my cold fingers fumbled to close the latch on the door of the goats' pen.

I was eager for the day to begin in earnest; Gerle and the others would be meeting me at the bridge for a fun-filled day in the snow. I ran to the back of the shed and dragged out my sled, its runners biting into my already cold fingers. I hurried to the bridge. The sled bumped against my shins as my feet sank into the deep sugary snow. Fritz and Gunter were already there, whooping and laughing as their sleds cut icy grooves down the riverbank.

There had been much debate as to the day's activity. Gerle had insisted we continue our unfinished hockey game from a few days prior. "Alfie, Otti, and I were up by two when we quit! That's why you don't want to finish." he told Gunter, who only shook his head.

"I want to try out my sled. Papa sharpened the blades. It should go like a shot!" Gunter replied. We all had sleds, long ones made from strong, yet flexible, strips of wood, each strip ending in a graceful curl at the head of the sled. The sharp metal blades ran the length of the sled and, if kept clean and free of rust, they would fly like the wind.

Gerle and Otti acquiesced and ran to get their own sleds, while I joined Franz and Gunter with mine. I was eager to keep moving; the cold was seeping into my bones and tightening my nostrils with its arctic bite.

"Hi there! How's the track?" I called to them, plodding clumsily toward them along the slippery bank. Waldi trotted behind me, occasionally veering out of my tracks to bury his muzzle into some forgotten rabbit hole. His face would emerge, free of any prize rabbit, but blanketed with a coating of snow crystals and his enthusiasm fully intact.

"It is really fast now, Alfie! Give it a try." replied Franz, sending clouds of breath into the air as he smiled. I prepared my sled and was about to push off when Gerle and Otti came around the corner of the bridge. I nodded a greeting and pushed off, the cold air taking my breath away. The runners slid effortlessly across the well-defined track and I shot out across the river, twisting in an arc on the clear ice, before slamming into the deep soft snow on the opposite bank.

Cheers of laughter went up as I dug myself out of the snow and made my way back to the top of the hill where the boys were lined up to take their turns. Walter and Kurt had arrived, and being younger, would be sharing a sled. Waldi scurried about, barking furiously at each sled as it slid down the bank in a billow of fine powder.

We spent several hours in this fashion and soon became unaware of the icy temperatures, our bodies warmed by the exertion of the game. I watched Gerle slide down and make a magnificent spin on the ice and then I readied myself for another run. I picked up speed quickly and even bounced slightly when I hit the flat surface of the ice. The bank of snow zoomed nearer and I closed my eyes for impact… but, it never came. Instead, I heard a loud pop and I was plunged, eyes still closed, into the frigid water of the river.

Instantly, my clothes turned as stiff as cardboard. I struggled to regain my footing and to drag my sodden self out of the water. Laughter and gasps greeted me as I crawled out of the hole, hauling my sled behind me. No one spoke; they just looked at me with their mouths hanging open, watching the icicles form on my hair. I limped quickly to my yard, still dragging the sled, which I managed to prop up against the fence before my shivering arm could drop it.

Oma was at the pump, but she forgot her task upon seeing an iced boy with hair sticking up in every direction, already heavily laden with frost. Her hand clutched her throat, but no words came out. She simply grabbed me, began pulling at my crisp clothing, and headed me toward the wash house. Once inside, she found her words. "What were you thinking, swimming on a day like today?! You boys had to pick the coldest day of the winter to fool around on the river." She bustled to and fro, having set me down on a bench in the corner, a towel wrapped over my shoulders.

She made a fire under the large copper kettle and I waited, desperate to peel off my clothes, which were clutching at my skin like icy tendrils. Baths were a rare occurrence, usually only once a week, but Oma insisted I climb into the steaming water, and she pushed me down until it almost covered my ears. After a long soak, in which I regained the feeling of my trembling, tingling limbs, I climbed out. Oma stood ready with a thick towel.

"There, you look almost human again. I thought you were Jack Frost for a moment!" she said, smiling and giving me a tight hug. I sat huddled on the bench, thickly wrapped in the towel, my body finally warm under its plush covering. Oma's voice was muffled as I pulled the towel completely over my head, the light now glowing pink through the deep red cloth.

"Dry off and I'll get you some clothes, Alfie. We've warmed you on the outside; now let's warm you up on the inside, too. When you are done getting dressed, come inside for some tea." Oma said, pulling back my towel to look into my eyes. She rubbed my wet hair with the towel and placed it back over my head. "I want you to stay in for the rest of the day so you don't get sick." she said, before she left the washroom carrying my frozen clothes. I could hear her humming as she made her way back to the house.

Winter finally released its grip on the valley and I managed to endure it without another dip in the river. Temperatures began to rise; the earth woke up and the air responded by rustling gently through the newborn leaves like the caress of a loving mother. It was May, 1939. I had turned seven in March while winter still reigned.

Now, my friends and I found any excuse to be outdoors. The walks to school were once again a pleasure. My shoes had even survived the winter, though surely I would grow out of them soon… now that I was older, I thought.

News had come from my father. He was still with the rail service, though he had had word that he might be transferred to work with the army supply trains. It was much better news than that of many of our friends, whose loved-ones were being sent to the front in increasingly alarming numbers.

Mother had withdrawn even more, if that were at all possible. I still saw her rarely, but I had noticed how pale and tired she looked most of the time. She walked slowly, the stairs being a particular burden for her. I assumed she was concerned for my father, as well as continually tired from her long hours of work. Oma told me that Mother was sick and needed her rest.

One night I awoke, pulled the blankets closer under my chin… the window was open a crack… and I heard voices. They seemed to come from afar, my mind too sleepy to focus. There was also an occasional thumping on the floor overhead, but not enough to keep me awake. The soft breeze brushed across my face, lulling me back to sleep.

The kitchen was empty the following morning; even Uncle Alois had come and gone, his cup and plate already dry by the sink. I walked to the door, opened it a crack, and peered out. The sound of birds twittering in the bushes along the fence was the only movement discernible in the early morning air. Fresh pale leaves rustled slightly as I made my way to the wash room behind the house.

Only then did I hear my grandmother's exasperated voice. "Oh dear, how will I ever get these all clean?" she said to herself. I heard her scrubbing on some laundry over the wash tub and I opened the door slowly.

"Good morning, Oma." I said, crossing to her side and glancing in the bucket. A pile of soiled bed sheets, stained red, were lying in the frothy hot water. Oma brushed a few stray hairs out of her hot face with her arm, and turned her head to me, her arms still holding the sheets under the water.

"There was a surprise visit by someone last night, Alfie!" Oma said with a tired smile, her hands finally releasing the soapy laundry and rising, instead, to rest on my shoulders. I tried to ignore the wetness from her soapy fingers as it soaked through my shirt, while I stared, puzzled into her excited eyes. "Last night the stork was here and brought you a baby sister!"

My mouth dropped open and I stepped back, dark patches forming on my shoulders where her wet hands had been. I had heard noises last night— that, I remembered… but a stork? My sister, Gertraud was born that night. The date was May 14, 1939.

CHAPTER 5

Another year had come and gone; the arrival of my baby sister eclipsed all other events for our family. Father made a visit home, though only long enough to admire the color of little Gerti's eyes. "I need to check if they are the same as mine." he said, winking. He had news to tell of conditions deteriorating all over Europe. Food was becoming more scarce; Adolf Hitler was moving his massive forces both East and West. Father had received word that his job with the rail service would now be under the jurisdiction of the Reich and military supplies would be the primary freight. His visit was as brief as all the others, but worse still, we did not know how long it would be until his next one.

Meanwhile, Mother was fiercely protective of the baby. Gerti grew quickly, but I soon realized it would be a long time before she could join me on the riverbank. I quickly lost interest in her faint inarticulate gurgles, which relieved my mother greatly, as my presence near the baby seemed to irritate her. "Alfie, don't walk so close to the crib, I don't want you to bump it!" she often said.

Gerti grew, and with her grew the distance between my mother and myself. All her time home from work was absorbed by the baby, which even at the time seemed strange, as I never remembered being fussed over like Gerti was. Oma sensed my unease, and she tried to satiate the void my mother's indifference had created—an indifference I hadn't been aware of until I saw her loving attentions directed towards my sister.

But, being only seven and reminded daily of the love I did receive from Opa and Oma, I soon adjusted to my new place in the family. The lack of attention from my mother had never really affected my life anyway, so I moved on.

School absorbed most of my time; my second year began, and with it came the excitement of new adventures. Like most youngsters, gym was my favorite part of the day. My friends were all with me on the same soccer team and we spent many fun hours dribbling Otti's old black soccer ball between us.

It was a warm Friday afternoon. The tawny light of a splendid autumn day was casting rosy tints onto our flushed faces as we made our way home from school. We were having our daily bout with Otti's soccer ball on the narrow road that wound its way from our school house toward home. We reached the main road and were surprised to hear the loud echo of many voices reverberating off the stucco houses that lined the road. It was unusual to hear so much activity in this area of the town, the most common noises being that of horses' hooves and clucking chickens.

"What can that be about?" Fritz asked. I shrugged and tugged my satchel higher up onto my arm. It had swung to the ground as I had aimed a mighty kick at the dusty soccer ball. Otti grabbed the ball quickly in his arms. He pushed his hair out of his eyes and, grinning, he said, "Let's go see!" He ran ahead to the side of a large stone house, the corner of which was partly hidden by an ungainly bush. We all looked at each other, then ran after Otti, piling under the bush behind him with such force that we almost pushed him into the street.

As we peered around the corner, a new sound met our ears, a sound which reminded me of that horrible day almost a year before in the square. There came a great rumbling noise from further down the street; the cause of which was still out of sight. But, I knew what we would see before it appeared… and I saw from the looks on my friends' faces that they knew, too.

Perhaps one hundred meters away the road disappeared from view on the horizon, where the cobbles rose slightly and then dipped beyond. The voices grew louder and shifted almost imperceptibly from an echo pulsing in some indistinct place, to a clear sound, very present and near.

Several lines of soldiers appeared, almost as if they had sprung up out of the road itself, and they were marching our way. We shuffled and wrestled with each other to move further beneath the protection of the branches. It seemed important not to be seen, although I doubt none of us really knew why. The soldiers were almost parallel to us, the sound of their shuffling feet and their muffled voices blending together into a solid drone.

"No, Otti!" Franz cried, pulling Otti back as he tried to peek out for a closer look.

It was not necessary, as Otti's head shot back almost instantly. He turned his anxious face to us and said, "Tanks! Lots of them! Let's get out of here!"

"No, it will be better if we stay put." whispered Gunter, his hoarse voice barely audible over the approaching roar of the tanks. We crawled in even deeper beneath the bush, which was thankfully large and dense, and we stared out at the mass of bodies that were passing only feet from our hiding place. After several dozen rows of darkly-clad soldiers had passed us, we knew by the intensifying noise and smell that the tanks would be approaching next. With a thrill of fear and excitement, I peered out at the massive gray machines as they lurched and crawled their way along the street. Gerle was huddled directly in front of me and I watched as his small shoulders began to tremble slightly.

Finally, after five more tanks and four jeeps fluttering flags brandishing the now familiar symbol of the Reich passed, we were able to step out from our cramped spot under the bush. We brushed the leaves and dust out of our hair and gazed, stunned, into each other's eyes.

"Papa said we might see some soldiers sometime soon." said Franz, picking a small branch out of his sock. "There is fighting in the East. I guess that's where they are going."

Gerle shook his head, as if he were shaking the image from his mind and replied, "What do you think would have happened if they had seen us?"

"Probably nothing." answered Franz bravely, though he was frowning. "Except having to salute again." My stomach lurched as I remembered my anger and embarrassment at the assembly when the officer had abruptly insisted I return my arm to its agonizing position. I was happy we had avoided having to repeat that experience.

We continued home without any further incident. All of us were quieter, the soccer ball having been forgotten, remaining instead in Otti's arms, clutched tightly like a security blanket. Peace had returned. The buzzing of the flies and bees in the fields resonated louder as the noise of the army faded, its footprint already moving through some other quiet town. We reached the bridge, none of us speaking much.

"Maybe I'll see you out after chores." Gerle said to me as we waved to each other. He headed back toward his street, and I turned toward my gate and my home.

By the time winter arrived, sending the geese flying south early, we had become familiar with the sight and sounds of troops on our city's streets. They never lingered, but passed in ever-increasing numbers to some unseen battlefield beyond. The unusually cold winter also brought with it food-rationing. For the first time, I understood limits on the things I had always taken for granted. Those who had small plots of crops fared better than those inhabitants of the city's center, where gardens were more scenic than functional.

This meant Opa, Uncle Alois, and I had more work to do around the yard. Oma managed to transform the abundance of crops into a variety of delicious meals, so at times we almost forgot that there were empty shelves at the store.

The proximity of the war could not be entirely ignored, though. The many men and women, my mother included, who worked for the textile mills, found their labors increased significantly. The need for woolen hats and mittens for the German army on the icy Russian front demanded many more hours of backbreaking work out of the already exhausted workforce.

Even the elderly were put to work. The Allied army was conducting regular bombings of cities all over Europe, so the need arose to protect the civilians from possible similar occurrences in our town. As a result, air-raid drills began on a regular basis. Veterans from World War I, some of them crippled or partially blind, became block wardens to assist in the organizing of sections of the city.

The thoughts of all those in our community, young and old, therefore, were fixed on the shadow that loomed ever closer. Yet, in the midst of it all, life continued. It had no choice.

During the dark winter months I spent most of my evenings with my nose in a book, drifting off to faraway lands and better times. Reading captivated my fancy of the unknown, enlivened in me by my father's many stories of foreign cities and exotic peoples. The wonderful tales by Karl

May were my favorite. The American Wild West was a culture so alien to my own; it created a timely escape from the insecurities of the unstable world in which I found myself so unwillingly placed.

The boys and I would draw from the never-ending spring of inspiration found in our fanciful books of America, that wondrous land across the vast Atlantic. Our world suddenly became full of red canyons and mesas, herds of cattle as far as the eye could see, or tepees surrounding a campfire on a dusty prairie. We split into teams of cowboys and Indians and spent many fine hours forgetting the threatening war. We played hide-and-seek in the nearby woods, ambushing each other from behind the large dark oaks. We forgot for a brief instant, that somewhere, not far away, a similar scenario was playing out, but it was anything but a game.

It was 1942, and I was ten years old, that time in a boy's childhood, when he begins to feel closer to being a man than ever before. This feeling of maturity was reinforced by the fact that some neighborhood boys and girls, only slightly older than myself, were being sent to youth training camps, also known as "Hitler Youth Corps". Some came back with fascinating stories of the intense training they had received.

My friends and I listened intently, longing to join in, until the stories began to change. We soon learned that most of the young boys would not be returning, but would instead be heading straight to the front lines. They had gone away children and would return… if they returned at all, as men. The young girls were sent to different households as hired help or were obligated to become factory workers… all to assist in the war effort.

In the evenings, I would try to read by the Kachelofen, its warmth permeating the dimly lit room like a gentle hug of summer air. The radio was constantly on, making reading a lesson in concentration. In spite of the noise, the warm kitchen was much more inviting than my dark chilly room. With my book forgotten on my knee, I found myself listening to the reports of the victorious German troops as they marched East, through the Balkan countries, onward toward Russia, and westward as well.

It was early spring, 1943, and I awoke to the dull sound of the ever-present radio echoing through the wall, against which my bed stood. I pulled my pajamas off over my head and tucked them under my pillow. My shirt

sleeves had recently become shorter; my arms were beginning to stretch…
I was nearly eleven.

I found Oma in the kitchen, standing with her hand on a broom
handle, its job long since forgotten. Oma was staring at the radio with a
furrowed brow, her hands twisting the neglected broom around on the floor.
The voice on the radio was listing the latest changes in the rationing of food.
Each citizen was now to receive 100 grams of meat per week, the equivalent
of only one slice of sausage.

The announcement was broken by the arrival of Opa, his hands
clutching a small basket of fawn-colored eggs. We were still managing to
eat fairly well, in spite of the continually tightening food restrictions. The
hens provided a regular supply of eggs, and the goats gave a steady stream
of milk. Our fall harvest had been plentiful; the cellar was stocked with
potatoes, onions, carrots and turnips. Our animal shed housed several goats
and the two pigs that Opa raised every year. Opa had generously given some
of our chickens to acquaintances in the city, replacing my friend the rooster
with his young offspring.

"I need some seeds for the cabbages, Alfie. Can you get some when
you go to the co-op this morning?" Opa asked, placing the eggs gently on
the table. Oma had been roused out of her inactivity by Opa's entrance and
was completing her task of sweeping. A light cloud of dust swirled aimlessly
in the sunlight that was shining in through the window above the sink.

"After you eat your breakfast, Alfie, and finish your chores, come
get me out back. I'll be washing the linens. You'll need to get the money and
I might add a few things to the list." Oma said, handing me a small scrap
of paper with several hastily scrawled items on it. I completed my chores
quickly, wanting to get my errands done so I could meet the boys by the
bridge, as promised.

I hastened out the gate, having first retrieved a large woven basket
and the money from Oma. "Please get some sugar, too, Alfie. As much as
she'll let you have."

The store sat a short distance toward the heart of town. The walk
was a pleasant one on such a warm spring day. I squinted my eyes against
the bright March sun, longing to be running through the cool woods, instead
of treading the dusty road.

The road had become increasingly crowded of late. Occasionally, a
truck loaded with soldiers would jolt by, sending me into the ditch until the

dust would settle. I had lost my fear of the activity on the road. It had grown too constant to cause much concern. It had become more of a nuisance than anything else.

I reached the store, a small establishment we had frequented for years. Sun beat on my back as I moved aside, holding the door, while I watched an old lady step out, her head shaking in disgust at the meager amounts of food her precious money had been able to buy.

"Gruss Gott!" I said, cheerfully, to the familiar lady behind the counter.

She was facing the wall behind her, having returned a loaf of uncut bread to a high shelf. Upon hearing my voice, she whirled around, her broad face turning slightly purple, and she yelled, "Out! Get out!" Seeing my shocked face, she added, her voice still bristling with anger, "Read what it says... the sign on the door!"

I stumbled backward, fumbling for the handle of the door, my eyes locked on her livid face, my body trembling with fear. I retreated to the warm sidewalk and only then did I notice a small brass plaque, which had previously eluded my attention.

It read, "Our greeting is: Heil Hitler!"

My eyes rested on those words for several moments as I paused to let my racing heart settle. I stepped back into the store, my slightly sweaty fingers slipping on the smooth metal handle of the door.

I approached the counter, behind which the plump lady still stood, her eyes now moving over some papers she had on the surface in front of her. She seemed to be pretending I was not there, which only served to make me more nervous. I found my voice, which emerged from my throat as a croaky whisper. "Heil Hitler!" I mouthed. She merely grunted, turning her still blazing eyes upon me. "Heil Hitler!" I said in a slightly more audible voice. The look in her eyes softened only slightly at my success; but I approached the counter with my hand tightly clutching Oma's list, ready to be finished.

She filled my order, though going rather stingy, I thought, on the sugar. I remained quiet throughout the transaction until it was time to make my exit. I was afraid of what to say, wondering, with a returned pounding of the heart, what the proper farewell should be. She saved me the trouble, though, and shooed me with her hand, as she said curtly. "Don't you forget the next time! You hear me?"

I ran home as quickly as I could manage; even the meager ration of sugar made the basket heavy. I scowled to myself as I thought about how the horrid lady had barked at me. She had always been so friendly.

I met Opa at the gate. He was mopping his sweating brow with a blue handkerchief; the sun had grown unusually warm for a spring day. He noticed my solemn face and asked, "Did you get my seeds all right, Alfie? Did she give you everything on Oma's list?" I dug to the bottom of the basket and extracted the cabbage seeds, placing them in Opa's outstretched hand, which was dirty from his long morning in the garden. "Everything ok?" Opa continued, placing his free hand on my shoulder. I swung the basket to the ground and leaned against the gate, crossing my thin arms over my chest.

Upon hearing what had transpired at the co-op, Opa sadly shook his head, his mustache sagging slightly as he frowned. "I wouldn't worry, Alfie. Everyone is just very edgy these days, what with the war getting worse each month." He managed a weak smile and added, "Oma has fixed a lovely lunch for you. She'll be happy to see you were able to get so much sugar. Someone's birthday is coming up soon, isn't it?" He gave me a knowing wink and bustled off with the bag of seeds.

I hoisted the heavy basket, barely relieved of its weight without the bag of seeds, and made my way inside. Oma was sitting at the table, folding towels and looking tired. The radio was on, the sound breaking the monotony of the rhythmic clock in the sitting room. She glanced up when I entered and smiled a weary smile, pulling her fine white hair away from her temples, which were slightly damp with the heat of the room.

"What did you manage to get?" she asked, as she reached for the basket. I placed the contents one by one on the table, lining the precious purchases up like a row of trophies. I almost felt as though they were, having been won at great peril to my own pride. "Well, she seems to not have too much sugar on hand. This should do, though, yes?" Oma said, half to herself as much as to me. She stood up, moaning slightly at some unseen ache in her much-toiled back. She crossed to the cupboard, into which she thrust the sack of sugar and the packages of salt and herbs.

I remained standing, my mind struggling with the decision of whether to confide in Oma about my experience at the store. She seemed to sense that something was troubling me, for she turned back to me and enveloped me in a warm hug, whispering in my ear, "Alfie, what's on your mind, dear?"

She listened patiently as I told her, a pained look forming across her gentle face, and only when I was finished, did she answer. "We are living in a time unlike that of any other we have known, Alfie. Don't worry... some people just change when something has unsettled their world. It is hard to tell just who people really are at times like these. Best not talk too much about such things to your friends—at least with the situation as it is right now. Someone is always listening. Remember that, Alfie... someone is always listening."

Her voice broke off with a slight tremor and she passed her hand over her brow. I was sure I saw the trace of a shadow flutter across her ordinarily cheerful eyes. "Just continue to be the big helper that you have been, Alfie, and we will get through all this just fine.... don't worry." She gave me another long hug, clinging rather tightly this time, before she walked out of the room. I could hear her tired legs slowly dragging her up the stairs to Mother's and Father's room; Gerti had woken from her nap and was crying out for her.

My little sister had grown a great deal, and she was now three years old, but she still napped once a day. This was a relief to my grandmother, as the constant care of such a young child was exhausting for her, though she took great pleasure in finally having a girl around.

My mother was rarely home. The pool of able-bodied laborers had decreased sharply; the front was claiming most of the men. When my mother was at home, she hovered over Gerti, screaming at me when the slightest frown or tear appeared on my sister's face. This, paired with the fact that Gerti was still too young to be a true adventurer, led me to limit my time with her.

My mother's absence was only eclipsed by my father's lack of presence in our lives. It had been a couple years since I had actually seen him, and letters rarely came. Thus, his face began to fade in my mind. His position on the army supply trains took him all the way to the border with Russia. We prayed the trains never traveled too close to the front.

The wind howled around the eaves; the snow swirled up to meet the stars for a dance in the darkness. It was nearly Christmas, and the latest air raid drill was nearly over. We sat in a small circle in the cellar, our tired faces lit eerily by a flickering oil lamp resting on a dusty crate. Gerti was huddled on Mother's knee, her face buried in Mother's robe. The noise was always the hardest on Gerti, being the littlest, but it also posed a unique problem for Uncle Alois.

Since he was deaf, he had to rely on Opa to alert him to the siren, which blared very loudly over the city. He would try to amuse us by covering his ears tightly with his hands, in mock disgust at the awful noise, as we all made our way solemnly down the dim narrow stairs. My mother would glare at me, a tight frown pinching her face, while I tried to muffle my laughter behind my hand.

This time Father was with us, standing removed in a corner, his foot propped up on a box. He was home for a brief Christmas visit. We had only received word a few days before he arrived. Mother was angry she had to work so much; she found little time to see him. Gerti hid behind Mother's robe, unsure of this strange face, despite her mother's urgings to go to Papa.

Father seemed removed, possibly resigned to the sad fact that his children hardly knew him. His exhaustion was mapped all over his haggard face. He had no more stories of beautiful cities to tell. In fact, he didn't want to talk at all about what he had seen in the unstable world beyond our home.

The all clear siren sounded, Gerti's pale face finally emerged from Mother's robe, and we gathered ourselves up for the return to the surface. I tapped Uncle Alois on the shoulder; his head had fallen against the wall and he was snoring. He covered his ears again with his hands and winked, with a quizzical look in his eye. I shook my head and pointed to Oma, who was already mounting the stairs.

We returned to the kitchen, the radio still blaring to the empty room; it had been left on in our haste. Oma picked up her cooking where she had left off; she seemed unaffected by the interruption. Having her son home had put a bit of the old twinkle back in her eyes. She was planning a special meal for the following night, Christmas Eve.

December, 24, 1943, dawned clear and cold. The wind had died down during the night, though it had left small drifts of snow against the frosted doors and windowpanes. Oma was up early, busy with her preparations for that evening. She hummed merrily as I poured myself a cup of tea and bundled myself up in my woolen coat and mittens to head out into the brisk air to feed the animals. The shed smelled sweet and pungent, with the animals packed in, their feet crushing the fresh hay as I forked it into their stalls.

By the time I returned to the house Mother had already left for work. She would be back in the afternoon; she was one of the lucky ones to have a shorter shift for the holiday. Mother was happier than I had seen her in a long time. The separation from Father had never pleased her, and she was grateful he could be there for this special occasion. Oma appreciated the extra hands to keep Gerti occupied; she had great plans for a real Christmas feast.

That evening we sat around the old kitchen table, the radio pouring forth music for a welcome change. Oma had prepared some baked sole, something procured as a result of the chickens donated to friends of Opa. Opa had butchered one of the rabbits, its crispy brown skin covered in one of Oma's special gravies. There were two cakes, plum and walnut, both gone in a matter of minutes. Opa brought out the brandy, the occasion warranting a memorable toast.

Time slipped sideways; the candles dripped slowly on to Oma's clean linen, the one embroidered with delicate roses at its borders. My eyes grew heavy as I surveyed the warm kitchen—my whole family gathered around the cozy table laden with delicious foods, my sister finally trusting Father enough to sit on his lap, her blond braids lying flat against his chest, my mother finally smiling… though I noticed not at me, never at me… Oma holding Opa's rough hand in her soft one, Uncle Alois puffing contentedly at his pipe. Life was good.

Father had to leave early the next morning; he had received his draft papers—he was going to the Eastern Front. Mother sobbed on his shoulder as she clung to him, willing him to stay. Standing at the front gate, we watched his tall lean frame diminish into the distance… and I couldn't help but wonder whether I would ever see him again.

CHAPTER 6

The morning dawned clear and cold. New Year's Day, 1944, had come and gone without much ado in our house; reasons for celebration were becoming harder to find. I crawled out from beneath my feather blanket, reluctant to begin the day. School had resumed, and I was not looking forward to the cold walk.

When I wandered into the invitingly cozy kitchen, the usual reports were emanating from the radio. I leaned against the Kachelofen's smooth surface, letting the warmth seep through my still chilly clothes. I listened for a few minutes to the radio announcer telling of "… the victorious German army successfully capturing many important cities and much valuable land in between." All reports stated the war was going very well… though our food supplies consistently hinted otherwise.

I completed my breakfast, thankful for the wonderful provisions our small plots of land provided, then I hurried through my chores, eager to keep moving on the bitterly cold day.

I returned to the warm kitchen, kissed Oma and Opa hastily, waved to Uncle Alois, and headed to the bridge to meet the boys for the walk to school. Gerle was already waiting, hopping up and down in his effort to keep warm, his shoes inadequate against the wet snow. Gerle had grown significantly in the last few months, though most of us still towered over him. But he seemed determined to try to catch up, his appetite proving too much for the available food. Otti, Franz, and the others soon joined us, including Gretel, who still had beautiful long blond braids and bright blue eyes, the sight of which often caused some of the older boys to blush and stumble over their feet.

Gretel was very somber that morning and, when pressed, she revealed that her older brother, Karl, had been ordered to the front in an anti aircraft battalion. It occurred to me as I listened that he probably had been on the train with my father—the boys heading off to fight alongside the men. Once again we each whispered our own private thanks for being under the fourteen year old age limit.

We reached school slightly wet, having had to walk in the ditch part of the way. The road had been swarming with troops heading methodically eastward, each soldier's face blank, masking his own thoughts of what tomorrow might bring.

The school room bustled with the overflow of bodies that had become essential since the first of the month. Classes were now doubled up, with almost fifty students per teacher. It had been necessary to combine several grades; many teachers had been sent to work in the defense industry or to the front itself.

Everyone bustled quickly to a seat; desks at the back were at a premium—the teacher's piercing eyes rarely reached that far. Today we began on a note that had become increasingly part of our day during the rapidly expanding war. The teacher asked us all to stand, gesturing solemnly toward a small boy near the front of the class, whose mousy brown hair barely concealed his red puffy eyes. The teacher's voice rose over the room, and ours soon joined, some quavering slightly. We sang a heart wrenching lament for our classmate who had learned his father would not be returning from the front lines. I couldn't help but wonder who we would be singing it for next. I was sure Gretel's thoughts would be running along on the same vein as mine, with her class likely singing this morning also.

The day inched along, the room stuffy from so many steamy damp woolens. The drone of the the teacher's voice seemed to reach me in slow motion, as it got lost in the thick somber atmosphere that hung over our heads. It was a relief to step out through the heavy wooden doors and feel the biting January air on our faces.

We headed home, tired from the busy day in the crowded room, where we had to strain to hear the teacher's words. We reached the corner with the main street and Gerle pulled on my sleeve. He stopped and pointed his slender finger toward a large poster that had been roughly tacked to a lamp pole. The image showed an ominous black shadow of a figure on a deep red background, beneath which read the words, "Feind Hort Mit!" (The enemy is listening).

Gerle frowned and said, "What do you think that means? Who is supposed to be listening?" Franz shrugged. Gunter shook his head and continued off down the road, the rest of us following, not bothering to try to answer Gerle's question... not sure if we even could. I remembered my grandmother's words—her warning to keep quiet, even to my friends. I lingered to stare at the picture, emblazoned clearly with the rigid image of the swastika. A sharp shiver traveled up my spin. Shaking it away, I ran to catch up with my friends.

After I had completed my chores and school work for the day, Gerle joined us for a couple of hours before bedtime and we enjoyed a quiet time by the warm stove playing chess on the old wooden set that had been hand carved by Opa. The troubles of the world seemed very distant, almost forgotten, our warm room successfully closing out the darkness and its potential evils.

The windows were covered with thick black drapes, part of the new mandatory blackouts that had become an aspect of our evening routine. The block wardens would patrol, checking for any escaping light, and it was rumored that if even a twinkle of light was spotted, the inhabitants could be turned in as traitors to the Reich. Even the military vehicles had covered headlights, except for narrow slits across each beam, giving the dark shapes of the slowly lumbering trucks an eerie, ghostly appearance.

Long after Gerle had stumbled home in the dark, thankfully aided by a crescent moon and a sky full of stars, we headed to our own beds and sank into thick billowing comforters, Oma's fragrant cherry pits warming our toes.

It must have been at least midnight, when that sound I had learned to associate with fear pierced the air throughout the sleeping city. This time the sirens were not a drill. We stumbled to the basement cellar door, only after I had poked and prodded Uncle Alois fiercely to rouse him. The adrenaline that coursed through my veins swept the sleepiness instantly from my foggy brain, and I held Oma's arm steady while she lumbered down the steep narrow steps. Mother and my sister followed, Gerti whimpering sleepily on

Mother's shoulder. Opa followed shortly, carrying the radio he had grabbed from the kitchen table.

A crackling noise filled the cellar, assaulting my buzzing ears, as I strained to listen for the all-clear siren, which seemed a long time in coming. Opa had turned on the radio and was busily twisting the knob to search for an accurate report of the situation. Finally, a man's voice quivered into tune, the sirens audible in the background even through the radio airwaves. Allied bombers were flying heavy bombing missions east of Jagerndorf, hitting targets like munition factories and supply railways. I caught the mention of Gleiwitz and Warsaw, names familiar to me from Father's wonderful travel stories.

I began to feel restless; the all-clear would surely be given soon—those cities were far enough away. I went to sit on the stairs, ready to be the first one to head up when it was over. My ears listened so intently; every sound was suddenly magnified. Gerti sat crying softly on Mother's lap, Mother's hands were running gently through her hair. Oma's eyes were closed and her mouth was barely moving, though I knew she was muttering a prayer. Uncle Alois had fallen back to sleep, his head drooping onto his chest, which rose and fell peacefully. Opa continued to chase the reports across the dial of the radio, each station supplying another version of events.

As my mind began to dull again with weariness, a new sound rose out of the distance—one I had heard only once before, when the leaflets had been dropped—a time that now seemed so long ago. A deep muffled drone entered my sleepy brain and caused me to sit bolt upright. I strained my ears to hear it again, though suddenly it was gone. Thinking the power of suggestion was ruling my senses, I shook my head slightly, as if to expel the troublesome thoughts from my mind, then I slowly eased my body back against the wall.

I heard it again, this time louder. "Opa, listen!" I stammered, my voice hoarse from sleep. I waved my arms, gesturing for him to turn off the radio, which he immediately did, trusting to my young ears not to be fooled.

The heavy resonant sound had increased. Even Gerti had heard it. She had stopped crying. Her pale face was contorted with fear, her eyes fixed on the ceiling, as if willing the planes away. For it was clear there was not only one, but several.

Soon, the noise we had never heard before but had all been dreading for months, began. A shrill whine pierced the night air, the cold amplifying the terrible sound. Then, came the throbbing jolts and echoes throughout the earth around us as the bombs impacted. The pounding continued constantly, some feeble and distant, others thunderous and near.

After what seemed like hours, though it was probably only several minutes, the hum of the engines grew louder as the planes approached closer to the house. I held my breath, waiting for the inevitable… but it never came. The planes headed off over the hills, their sonorous roar quickly fading into my subconscious, to resurface on another unforeseen day.

The silence that followed was almost as unbearable as the terror of the bombing itself; it seemed like forever before the all-clear was given. The only sounds that interfered with the eerie calm were my sister's stifled sobs and the whisper of the dust settling after its unexpected disturbance.

The morning dawned brilliantly, as though in defiance of the horrors man had inflicted on the earth just hours before. Billows of black smoke hung over the valley in small clusters, barely moving in the calm air.

I met the boys as usual near the bridge; everyone was very bleary eyed from the lack of sleep. We headed off, talking little, each of us still in shock from the events during the hours before daybreak. As we neared the center of town we noticed that the largest smoke cloud hung over the railway station. It seemed obvious that it had been an intended target, which reminded me of the intermittent radio reports of the bombings on other cities. I wondered if our factories had been hit as well, aware with a start that my mother had been lucky to have been at home.

School went by in a blur, though a very slow one. The teachers seemed to sense that attention spans were not at their optimum level, and they therefore went slightly easier on the workload. This might have also been due to their own self-preservation, as most of them looked as tired as we did.

After school, adventuresome Otti leading the way, we all went to inspect the damage. We left the side street of the school and headed for the train station, the source of the smoke we had seen that morning. The main street was dotted with large craters, nearly blocking the entire roadway, though nothing other than foot traffic was present now. Large chunks of earth and paving stones had been hurled about, leaving a thick layer of dust coating the nearby bushes.

A crowd of people was gathered outside a row of three houses. Each had sustained significant damage, due to its proximity to the trains and to the main road, a regular thoroughfare for the German troops to the front in the East. Smoke was still rising from the smoldering ruins of the buildings, the roofs of which were now below eye level. One home had had its front blown off, giving the cold winter wind an invitation to dance among the elegant furniture. The delicate sofas were still draped with lace, though blackened now by the ashes blowing from the house next door.

"It is a pity for Frau B." said one voice from the crowd, "Both her husband and eldest son left for the Front on the last train. Just she and the little ones, now. They will probably have to move in with her mother."

"Oh dear!" said another. Similar conversations swirled around us as we turned and made our way grimly back toward home, grateful that we would each have a bed to sleep in that night.

It was nearly summer. Vacation from school was upon us… and we still had a roof over our heads. During the long dreary months of late winter and early spring, we endured several more nights like the first. Air raid drills were no longer necessary; we were getting more practice than we cared to with the real thing. I longed for fresh summer air; too many nights in the cold damp cellar had lead me to crave the arrival of warm weather even more fervently.

Now, the leaves were open to bursting; it had been a beautiful spring. This pleased Opa a great deal. The fair temperatures increased the chances of a good crop, which would prove vital due to the heavy food rationing. Also, Opa had other plans to help add to our stores of food not covered by the restrictions.

Every summer he and I traveled to my relatives' farm in the next valley, higher up in the mountains near the source of the beautiful Gold Oppa River that passed in front of our house. We would travel by train, Oma staying home to care for Gerti and the animals. The farm was near Opa's birthplace, a picturesque village fit for a fairy tale.

Opa and I stepped off the train that morning into a brilliant sunshine, softened perfectly by a gentle breeze. We had enjoyed the brief ride, though it had been a shock to see bomb craters and damaged houses along the way;

the scope of the Allied bombing raids seemed to be quite unforgiving. The train station where we alighted was untouched by the war, except for the occasional sad parting between loved ones and a soldier.

We hoisted our small rucksacks, laden only with a sweater for cooler weather, a toothbrush, and some snacks. Opa set out in front, his strong hand gripped tightly around a long walking stick that he had lovingly carved for himself. We left the bustle of the station, and soon only the steam whistle of the departing train pierced the silence of the day as we headed down the road toward my great aunt's farm. The smell of sweet honeysuckle and phlox drifted across the road, which quickly left the village and wound steadily upward, between carefully tended fields and mysterious pine forests.

Darting among the bushes lining the road was a multitude of twittering birds, all of them looking for succulent bits to take back to their offspring. Lost in the pleasures of the fine morning, the bees were too heavy with intoxicating nectar and golden pollen to bother moving out of the way of the excited birds.

"Look carefully, Alfie. Somewhere around here, if I remember correctly, is a nice patch of blackberries. I promised your Oma I would look." Opa said, as he wandered near the edge of the road. He pulled back branches, squinting with tired eyes into the dappled undergrowth beyond.

I crossed to the opposite side of the narrow road and peered carefully into the shadows under the trees. I wanted to be the first to spot such a valuable treasure. I knew Oma would create a dessert memorable enough to talk about all summer. After some time of walking thus in silence, I spotted the familiar dark berries massed on dense bushes that framed a small clear stream. The water was bitter cold as my boot slipped off the moss-covered rock, my greedy fingers already reaching for the first mouthful.

"Opa, here! Lots of them! Over here!" I shouted, standing tall and waving my arm over my head, so my grandfather could see me under the dark trees.

"Good job, Alfie! You get the first piece of the pie, I think." Opa said, smiling, as he slowly made his way through the tangles and bushes that lined the little hollow in which I stood. I grinned in turn and we went to work, filling two buckets Opa had had tied to the side of his rucksack. After an hour of steady picking… and thankfully, not as steady nibbling, we managed to fill both buckets with plump juicy ripe blackberries.

"Well, we should get a move on, Alfie, but not before I check out some mushrooms I spotted just before I heard you call." said Opa. He covered the buckets and retied them to the rucksack with his purple stained fingers. We scrambled back up to the road, which was now basking in the midday sun, and we crossed over to the opposite bank, where Opa pointed to a dark cluster under a large tree. Beautiful golden mushrooms, their skins smooth and unmarked, were growing in abundance, as mushrooms will do after a spring of opulent rain.

"What do you think, Alfie? Eh? Not bad for one stretch of road." Opa said, pulling off his rucksack to retrieve a burlap bag in which to house the latest treasure. I smiled in answer and bent down near the mushrooms. I inhaled deeply, allowing the fragrant combination of moldering earth and newborn life, those primal essences of eternity, to penetrate my senses.

"Make sure you pick them all the way from the base, with a little twist. That way you won't break apart the cap." Opa opened his small penknife and sliced a mushroom off near the ground and flipped it over. The dark pungent underbelly looked as soft as velvet and as delicate as lace. "Be careful putting them in the sack; we don't want creamed mushroom soup yet!" Opa said, laughing merrily at his own wit.

We filled the sack as close to bursting as we dared, wanting to deliver as many intact mushrooms as possible to Oma the following day. Then, we resumed our journey down the road.

The walk continued to be pleasant, although I was eager to arrive; the blackberries had tricked my empty stomach for only a brief while. I knew my great aunt always had wonderful home baked breads and cakes, and the thought of what lay ahead made my stomach rumble. We rounded a thick grove of tall spruce trees and saw that Tante Marie was busy in her garden, a swarm of chickens and ducks pecking busily near her feet.

She waved as she spotted us and wiped her hands on her apron. The farm dogs came to greet us first, their tails wagging in anticipation of new playmates. "Hi, Reinhard, you are later than I was expecting!" Tante Marie called from near the door, where she began busily working the pump to fill a large bucket with cool water.

"We made a few detours!" answered Opa, holding up his mushroom-filled sack for her to see.

"Ah, it is a good year for those, I imagine. I must head out for some myself soon. Things are growing so fast this year; I need all the time I can get just to keep up." She glanced down at me, smiling, and said, "You have grown again, Alfie! Good gracious!" She tousled my hair with her damp hand and turned toward the house, handing Opa the bucket to carry.

The house was a very cozy two-story farm house, though the eaves hung so near the ground, it appeared as if there were only one level. It had always reminded me of the gingerbread house in "Hansel and Gretel", with its upstairs windows set in so deeply to the roof I could barely see the sky.

The kitchen functioned in the same role as ours; it was the room lived in most of the time. A large Kachelofen dominated the space and saw much use during the longer winter months. The animals benefited from the heat of the house, even adding to it as well, as a door in the hall opened directly to the barn. It was a very symbiotic relationship amongst all residents, warmth and security being provided from both sides.

As we walked into the refreshingly cool and dimly lit room, I could tell Tante Marie had been baking; my wish had been granted. A beautiful marble coffee cake sat on the farmer's table, the long pine planks of which were stained and polished to a fine gloss. Next to the cake sat a pitcher of fresh milk from the old cow who now ambled outside near the abundant garden.

The room was permeated with an aura of calm and order, reflecting a simple life untarnished with fear and uncertainty, those symptoms which had become, of late, so much a part of our lives. After a hearty lunch, my plate brimming with all the good things from the farm: homemade sausage, goat cheese, snap peas and asparagus, and fresh rye bread, I left Tante Marie and Opa to their conversation and I wandered outside.

Opa found me several hours later, perched in a small tree, where I sat watching the orange summer sun sink below the tall dark hills of the narrow valley. We spent an equally pleasant evening, for once spared the ominous news on the radio, and I tumbled, very tired, into the narrow feather bed under the eaves. My eyelids grew heavy with the day's pleasant memories filling my head, and I watched the moon trace a brilliant silver line along the delicate leaves dancing in the breeze outside my small window.

The fond memories of that pleasant excursion filled my thoughts many times during the rest of the summer, most of which paled in comparison. The demands of the war were now encompassing even our young lives. Eligible students were required to report for some kind of summer work.

We would receive no pay, as it was all done as service to the Reich and the Fatherland.

Gerle, Otti, Gunter and I spent each day for several weeks wandering about the forests surrounding our valley in search of selected plants, which would be dried and packaged as tea for use by the soldiers at the ever-expanding Front. This was almost enjoyable, as we found plenty of opportunity for mischief during our rambles through the dense wild woods.

The tea-hunting looked like an even more enviable pursuit when we were instructed that we would move on to bug-hunting. The Allied planes had broadened their means of destruction by infesting the area with potato beetles, known for their ravenous appetite for tubers. We spent hours searching for the striped brown potato-loving pests, crushing them between rocks or drowning them in buckets submerged in the river.

The war was on everyone's mind. The news from the German radio stations supported the theory that the Reich was winning the war, although the scope and severity of the rumored horrors of the fighting placed doubt and fear in the minds of most. But, few admitted it, as this would have been seen as a betrayal to the Reich. "Someone is always listening…" became Oma's mantra, so we kept our eyes and ears open and our mouths shut.

After another sleepless night due to further bombings, we awoke to the news, one early August day that one of the Allied planes had crashed into the hills nearby. I had barely started on my morning toast, after stumbling wearily through my chores, when Gerle burst into the kitchen and placed a fond peck on my grandmother's cheek before sitting down opposite me at the table.

"Did you hear the news this morning?" Gerle asked, breathless after his early morning dash from his house. I nodded, still chewing. Gerle looked disappointed that he would not be the bearer of such exciting information. It appeared that the pilot and crew of the crashed plane had ejected before impact and had been captured not too far from our own village. "They believe they are British soldiers." whispered Gerle, glancing sideways at Oma, who was busy washing dishes and who seemed too absorbed in her singing to notice our conversation. "They are housing them right here in town. Guess where?" he asked, his face showing the delight at being able to deliver a bombshell this time. I shrugged. "At the brickyard!"

Our latest duty for the Fatherland involved carting bricks from one station of production in the vast brickyard, to the next. We had been at it for only a few days, but I already knew that I preferred hunting for beetles and tea leaves, both less backbreaking work.

Gerle waited for me to finish my breakfast, then we both gave a kiss to Oma, who handed us each a sandwich for our lunch. "You stay away from any trouble today, boys. Just keep your minds on your work… and Alfie, come straight home afterwards. Opa needs your help in the fields." She waved gently to us while we greeted Opa who was just coming in the door.

"Did Oma tell you I want a hand today, Alfie? Your uncle was needed again at the morgue." Opa said, looking suddenly exhausted and grim. The need for a bigger store of food had taken a toll on my grandfather, who undertook work that would have tired a much younger man. "Have a good day, Alfie. You too, Gerle." Opa nodded to us.

"Thanks, Opa. I'll be back in time to help. Bye!" I said. I opened the door for Gerle and we headed off to work.

By the end of the week, all my friends were working in the same brickyard, which was only a short walk from my house; so we treated the walk to work the same as that for school and met every morning at the bridge.

It was a sweltering hazy day, and we shuffled through the gates of the bustling yards, each scrambling for a spot in the shade as we waited in line for our gloves and our carts. The leather gloves, although thick and stiff, were worn away quickly because we handled hundreds off sharp-edged bricks every hour. Our job was fairly straightforward; we had to move wet, newly formed bricks out into the sun to dry on long narrow shelves. Once the bricks were dry, which generally took several days, we were responsible for returning them to the large hot kilns where they would be fired. The third phase consisted of moving the hard, cooling bricks back out to the shelves for curing. All in all, the process was slow, with us, in effect, moving the same bricks three times. But, the demand was so great that we rarely sat down.

It was during our brief lunch hour that we finally had a chance to talk about what had been on our minds all morning—the British prisoners who resided on the other side of a tall barbed wire fence. It was apparent that the prisoners had been immediately put to work, doing the unpleasantly hot job of tending the fires in the kilns. It was noon in August and the air in the yard was thick and stagnant with an ochre dust, which settled in our hair and filled our nostrils and ran in small rivers down our sweating necks as we hoisted brick after brick into the hot sun.

"Can you imagine how hot they must be?" asked Franz, jabbing with his thumb over his shoulder at the British crewmen loading opaque lumps of coal into the brilliant orange and blue flames of the fires.

"Who cares!" mumbled Gunter, through crumbs from his sandwich. "It was mighty unpleasant down in our cellars when they were dropping bombs on us!" He scowled and brushed the back of his hand over his sweaty brow, smearing it with a wide stripe of orange dust.

"I just thought…" continued Franz, looking sheepishly from face to face. Most of us were too hungry and too hot to bother answering.

"They have it better than most, don't you think?" ventured Otti, glancing quickly at Gunter, who continued to frown at the prisoners through the fence as he gnawed on his crust of bread. "I mean, imagine what prisoners captured nearer to the front lines have to do."

"Yeah," added Gerle. "Look at that lot." he said, gesturing with his chin to several of the men on a break from their work. They were engrossed in a card game with two German guards, whose guns were slung over their shoulders as the game progressed into liveliness. These guards were on injured leave from the front lines and seemed surprised at their good luck. This relatively easy duty was a vast improvement from the conditions that had lead to their wounds.

War, at that moment, seemed so complex to me. These men might have faced each other over a barren smoking wasteland, willing the other one to fire first, and praying that their own bullet would win the duel. Yet, here they sat, drinking beer and sharing cigarettes, fighting another battle… a battle against boredom and loneliness, leading them to reach out to the closest source of humanity, the enemy.

We all paused for a moment, each absorbed in his own thoughts and imaginings of what it must be like where many of our fathers and brothers and uncles were spending that same hot day… perhaps as prisoners playing cards with the Russians.

CHAPTER 7

For the first time ever we were ready to leave summer vacation behind. It had breezed by, though not through careless use of our time, as we would have preferred, but through intense labor that tested our new adolescent stamina. School served as a release from the monotonous routine of the brickyards.

Yet with this turning of the seasons came the harvest, another pull on our free time. The river had all but ceased to be a place of amusement, though it often served as a symbol of better times, and Gerle and I stubbornly continued to meet by its russet banks. The leaves of the trees above drifted slowly down as ever before, not bothering to be hurried by any threat of war or change. We raced sticks just as we had when we were six, but more often we would simply relax on the bank in the fragrant grass, which was already dappled with musty golden and red leaves. We longed to lie idle, to wait with our hands folded behind our heads until the perfect cloud dragon would form in the brilliant blue sky, but there was rarely time to linger.

Opa was forced to stop working in the fields at dusk, as any kind of lights would be spotted from above. Everyday after school I would meet him in the yard. I would find him taking a brief rest on a stool, where he sat leaning his tired graying head against the rough stucco of the house. There he would wait, only barely raising his heavy eyelids to the sound of my footfall outside the gate, until I returned from placing my satchel in my room. He then would drag himself off the stool and we would slowly wander back out to the fields for more work.

The wonderful growing season had yielded an abundance of food for both ourselves and our small herd of animals, on whom we were relying more and more. We would be well provided for the winter food rationing, and as Opa believed, whatever else might be in store.

It was Friday. School that day had been a somber affair; the songs of lament, increasing by the day, seemed to tarnish all sense of purpose among both teachers and students. It was a relief to all when the bell finally rang, and each of us hurried out, eager to leave the heavy fog of sadness and despair that hung over the room.

Oma had informed me as I left for school that Otti and his younger brother, Kurt, would be spending the afternoon at our house. Their mother was now working at the textile factory and their father was with everyone else's father... on some unknown battlefield far away.

The city was sullen and empty, its lifeblood having been sucked out of it. All able-bodied men had been sent to the Eastern Front. The factories were filled with women who worked until their bones ached, their eyes failed, and their lungs filled with the cold and foul air of the dark and dank factory rooms.

As a token tribute to those deemed unusable by the Reich—the old men and the boys under fourteen, like myself—had been labeled, "Volksturm" (home guard), and we were now relegated to patrolling the desolate, crater-marked streets, or to carrying out other tasks deemed necessary for the service to the Fatherland.

Today, though, we were anxious to head straight home, where Opa had promised us an hour of play before we needed to help him in the fields. We chatted merrily, reinvigorated in the clear air and fresh sunshine of the beautiful afternoon.

The main street of our town still bustled with activity that was lacking elsewhere. The now daily troop movement was underway as we reached the end of the street that met the main road.

We no longer hid when faced with the disruption of military machines on the road. It had become such a part of our daily walk to and from school. Yet, the uncomfortable feeling in the pit of my stomach returned each time. Today, that feeling almost welled into my throat, as I turned away in surprise and revulsion at the sights before us.

Sweating emaciated horses lurched wearily by, each pulling a large wooden wagon, which was painted with a bold red cross on its side. The wagons were filled with men who looked worse than the poor beasts who bore them westward. For that was where they were going. These were the soldiers who had been so badly wounded that they could not be healed by the field doctors closer to the fighting. Instead, they were heading for longer stays in hospital wards from which many of them might never walk away. The men were piled uncomfortably into the overcrowded wagons, their gaunt faces framing eyes dull and sunken from the countless horrors they had seen.

We stood without speaking, our eyes fixed on the last of the wagons as they lumbered slowly away into the dying sun. Its rays shone on the faces of the wounded men, casting their thin faces into a ghastly relief. Every once and awhile we could hear a moan rise from one of the wagons, as the horses navigated around the dips and hollows in the bombed out road. In making the roads increasingly impassable, the Allied bombers had been careful to remind even the defeated soldiers of their presence.

That Saturday was a warm day reminiscent of midsummer. Opa had rewarded our hard work the previous evening with a free day to enjoy the fine weather, as he himself wanted to do. He headed off early toward town, where I knew he would spend the day at my uncle's tavern playing cards with his friends, as they discussed their own unbeatable solutions for winning the war.

I chose to linger in bed. Uncle Alois could be heard whistling to himself as he sat outside in the warm morning sun, smoking his pipe under the pretense of painting the trim around the windows. I could hear his stool rock slightly as he leaned it up against the side of the house, and I guessed that he would soon be snoring blissfully, the paintbrush forgotten in the bucket at his feet.

The sound of Oma's singing in the kitchen and her gentle voice patiently answering Gerti's constant questions finally won the battle with the inertia that was trying to overtake my brain. I stumbled out of bed, and after a quick trip to the washroom, I made my way into the sunny kitchen. I was surprised to find Gerle sharing a piece of toast with my sister, her small fingers reaching toward him eagerly as he tore her off another sticky piece.

"Morning, sleepyhead!" muttered Gerle, his mouth full of toast and honey.

"Good morning, Alfie. Looks like you took Opa at his word when he said you could have the day free." said Oma, her eyes twinkling. She was very fond of Gerle and had obviously been enjoying his company; it seemed to have put her in a fine mood.

"What are you doing here, Gerle?" I asked curiously, my hand reaching for a piece of toast from the pile on the table.

"Gunter thought we could play in the forest today. I said we would all meet him at the bridge at nine. That's pretty soon, I think, Alfie, so hurry up!" Gerle said, all of this rushing out like a freight train, seemingly eager to be off.

"Don't forget your chores first, Alfie. Gerti can feed the chickens. But, you do the rest, please." Oma said, managing to give me both a stern look and an indulgent wink.

We finished up our quick breakfast, sharing every other bite with my ravenous sister, her fingers now growing very sticky from the over abundance of honey on each small piece. We grabbed a jug of water, a small loaf of bread, and some dried sausage. Throwing them all hastily in my rucksack, we headed out the door, anxious not to waste a single moment of that precious day. I let Gerle go on ahead, while I bolted through my chores, suffering a small kick from the goat in my haste to milk her quickly.

My friends found me rubbing my sore shoulder as I made my way at a trot down to the bridge. After a hearty laugh at my expense, we headed off, ready for what promised to be a day to remember.

As we walked, Gunter informed us of his plan for the day. There were two large cherry trees high up on the hillside not far from the town. The branches of these old trees spread out like long delicate fingers, as if preparing to embrace the first passerby in an attempt to get much needed attention. The woods had fallen into neglect; the war had taken up so much of everyone's time, no one cared to wander as far for their firewood as they once had.

Gunter was convinced that these forgotten trees held succulent deep red cherries, ours for the taking. I thought for a moment about returning to my family with enough cherries for one of Oma's delicious cakes. My mouth watered in anticipation. I could see that I was not the only one who was fantasizing about being the hero delivering such a delicious find to one's hungry family.

We agreed to follow Gunter, who led us along a narrow pathway lined with tall grasses and overgrown bushes. The forest had once been tended by a local forester, a grumpy and grizzled old man who was believed to have been the one who had grafted the old trees from hybrid branches many years before. This personal attachment, it was rumored, had led him to guard his adopted realm with the greatest possessiveness.

We walked quietly along the path, winding and interrupted from its lack of use. We felt confident that we would meet no one that day; the forest had obviously been forgotten as the great shadow of the war grew ever larger. After a short walk, during which we climbed slowly higher up the gradual hillside, we came upon the big mythical trees. They were covered with thick heavy clusters of dark cherries, so ripe they were nearly black. There were so many, the air itself exhaled with the heady perfume of the opaque jewels as glorious to us as clusters of garnets.

In a matter of seconds the six of us had all climbed the two trees, where we hung like monkeys from the stout branches and ate the juicy cherries till our chins dripped with the pulp, and the ground beneath was littered with pits and stems. When we had eaten our fill, Otti had the clever idea that he could stuff the front of his shirt with cherries and take all the more home to his mother. We snorted and laughed at the sight of him, his shirt puffed out like a sail and already staining with the deep burgundy juice. We soon forgot where we were, intoxicated by the intense sweetness of the overripe cherries, and we all began to emulate Otti, clearly convinced it was a brilliant plan.

Gunter and his brother Walter had scampered to the top most branches of one of the trees, causing its already heavily laden branches to sway dangerously above the rest of us.

"Hey, you're knocking cherries on my head, Walter! Stop it!" yelled Gerle, as he squinted up into the crackling and rustling branches that hid the two boys overhead.

"Relax, Gerle, I'll move over. Hang....!" Walter replied, his voice muffled quickly.

"Shhhh! Quiet! Shhh! Someone's coming!" hissed Gunter, whose hand was now clamped tightly over his struggling brother's mouth.

65

We all cocked our ears, trying to hold as still as possible in the swaying branches, our hands clasped to our shirt fronts, sticky with the hordes of cherries filling them. Faintly, but clearly growing quickly louder, we could hear the sounds of several dogs barking.

"Who do you think it is?" asked Franz, his eyes peering anxiously through the tangle of brambles and bushes that lined the glade in which the trees stood.

As if in answer, came a man's rough voice, slightly thick with breathlessness. "Hey, hey! I see you! You get out of my trees, you little trouble makers! Go get them, boys!" We began to scramble down as quickly as we could manage upon hearing the dogs urged thus into action.

As my feet thumped to the ground, I heard a loud crack from above. Walter's branch had snapped in his haste to extricate himself from the dense foliage, and his body plunged rapidly through the leaves, bouncing and snapping off branches on his descent. He fell with a loud thud, flat on his back, inches from my feet, where he lay gasping, his eyes bulging with the shock of the impact. Cherries fell all around us like hail, bouncing off our heads like rubber pellets.

"Walter! Are you okay?" cried his brother, as Gunter all but slid the remainder of the way down the trunk of the tree. Gerle, Franz, and Otti had reached my side, their hair full of leaves and dark cherry stains from their quick exit from the tree.

"I'm OK." gasped Walter, his voice croaking with effort. "Just got the wind knocked out of me. Give me a minute."

"We can't! He's coming!" shouted Franz, who was already grabbing Walter's hand and pulling. The sound of the dogs was now closer; we had only minutes to make our retreat. Gunter had reached the ground, which was now littered with the disturbed cherries, and the undergrowth was growing slippery with the squashed fruit.

"Move!" Gunter hissed. He grabbed Walter's other hand and dragged his stunned brother to his feet. Franz and Gunter hoisted Walter's resisting arms over their shoulders and we followed hastily as they half carried, half dragged him down the too narrow path. We immediately veered off the difficult way and struck out, instead, through the thick and scratchy underbrush. The dogs were still barking somewhere behind us, though they had given up pursuit.

We stumbled out of the forest, wheezing with the exertion of our rapid descent down the hill. I had a stitch in my side, which I kneaded with my fingers, only then noticing that my shoulder was also sporting a hearty bruise from the goat's well aimed kick earlier that morning.

We didn't halt or talk much until we reached the bridge, though occasional moans issued from Walter, who hobbled along, obviously still in significant pain. We eased our aching bodies down to the very edge of the water and spread out like tipped over scarecrows along the soft grassy bank.

Gerle remained standing, a quizzical look on his small face, as he stared at each of us in turn. The corners of his mouth started to twitch, his shoulders began to shake, and soon he was laughing so hard that cherries were falling out of his loosened shirt tails.

Otti looked quickly up at Gerle and said,"What is so funny? I'm going to be in deep trouble with this stained shirt. My mother is already going on at me about how badly I treat my clothes. Look at it!" He held out the shirt front, allowing the cherries beneath to roll into his lap. He frowned and said, "We do look a frightful mess. I think I lost half my cherries on the way back." He turned to Walter, who was lying very still on the grass, his arm over his eyes, "Are you all right, Walter?"

All heads turned toward Walter's soft voice, as he started to speak, "I'm a little sore, but…" his voice broke suddenly and laughter replaced it. "… But, that was great. Did you see how fast I got out of that tree? I bet it was a record!" He grinned and chuckled more softly, clutching his ribs tightly.

The mood lightened considerably, and we all began to take stock of the cherries we had managed to save during the great escape. My shirt was not as full as some of the others, but it also had been spared some of the heaviest staining, for which I was exceedingly grateful. I was not looking forward to Oma's disappointment and anger at ruining such a fine shirt.

We spent the rest of the day in a more peaceful fashion, washing our sticky bodies in the icy late summer water. Walter sat out while we played a long game of soccer on the grass near the river. None of us wanted the day to end, and none wanted to face the consequences of the clever cherry transporting idea of Otti's. (His shirt was stained more than everyone's.) I secretly hoped that my acquisition of so many fine ripe cherries would distract Oma from the laundry chore ahead.

Oma didn't disappoint; she did make a cake to rival all those that had gone before. Or, perhaps it was the fact the cherries had been so valiantly earned that made that cake the finest in years. The success of the day was barely dimmed by the long hour that evening that I spent scrubbing my shirt clean with lye in the cold wash house after dark. The stars still shone as brightly and the silence still reigned as sweetly. It had been a day to remember.

A voice was calling inside my head, "Time to get up, Alfie. We need to go soon." I tried desperately to ignore it. Hadn't I just put my head on the pillow? The prior evening had been a late one; we had roasted potatoes that we had spent the day gathering with Opa. It had been a rather celebratory feast. The harvest was done and our cellar was well-stocked for even the harshest winter. Opa had relied on my aid like never before. He was exhausted from his months of continuous work to keep up with the aggressively growing crop.

"It's not a bad problem to have, though, Alfie. A lot of people don't have a garden to help them make it through the winter." Opa had said.

"Get up, Alfie!" came Oma's voice again, her gentle hands firmly shaking my shoulders.

My eyes opened reluctantly; Oma's face quivered into focus.

"It's almost time to go to church, Alfie. You need to get up now." Oma said, brushing my hair gently out of my sleepy eyes.

"OK, I'll be right there." I answered, my voice sounding raspy and thick inside my throbbing head. My throat felt dry and tight from the smoke from the fire and my hair still smelled of the soot. It took me several minutes until I was able to rouse myself enough to face the bustle in the kitchen.

Oma hated to be late to Mass on Sundays, although she had been going almost daily now. My grandmother's days were very full, yet her time at church had become increasingly vital to her. She had made sure that I had my place as an altar boy, and she also insisted that I sing in the church choir. One of her biggest dreams was to someday see me singing in the fine tall cathedrals in Vienna. I didn't mind accompanying her once a week, though I shuddered every time I had to don the long red robes, with their tall white collars and their tight white cuffs. I felt they were something more suitable for Hanni or Edith, or even my sister, but certainly not for us boys. In defiance some of us would keep our pockets beneath our robes stuffed with rocks and sticks, in a secretly rebellious effort to assert our masculinity. Admittedly, most mornings I would have preferred playing, or on that morning in particular… sleeping.

One of the finest parts of our morning at church came after the service was completed and we had slowly made our way down the aisle and out into the sunshine. Every Sunday, Oma would take me around the corner near the large textile factories, their tall grim facades casting a dense shadow on the dirty street running along side them. Around another corner was a large stone synagogue, its roan-colored dome dominating the peaceful street. Across the street from the temple was a grand two story villa, very old and very beautiful, its large shuttered windows lined with carefully tended flower boxes full of colorful red geraniums.

On the street level of the villa there were several apartments, all occupied by the many Jewish elders who owned the bustling shops that ran up and down the main street not far behind the synagogue. The shops were always filled with delicious smelling foods and carefully crafted treasures, which the shopkeepers procured from all over the world.

Above the apartments in the villa, in a large flat that ran the whole length and breadth of the upper floor, lived an old widow, Frau Kreuzinger. Her husband had once owned the textile mill that ran the entire distance of the street not far from her house. She lived alone now, and she was often in need of assistance, as she used a walker and rarely left her home. For many years we had been visiting her each Sunday and I had become very fond of her; I even called her Tante (Aunt).

The autumn day had dawned cold and clear, the bite of winter already in the air. From Frau Kreuzinger's high living room windows I could see the backside of our church, its tall spires framed elegantly by the old trees in her carefully tended walled garden. The leaves were long since gone from the trees—a strong wind had brought down the last stubborn ones during the night.

I sat on the elegant couch, my feet firmly planted on the floor, and my back uncertain of where to rest. The fabric was stiff and uncomfortable and I was afraid of soiling the pale coloring of the lace that rested on its arms. I could hear Tante Kreuzinger and Oma talking in the kitchen, their voices occasionally dropping to whispers, though I could not make out the words anyway. The old bell on the church, along with all the other bells in the city, had just finished chiming the noon hour and my ears were still ringing with the low booming sound.

Tante Kreuzinger's voice grew louder as she entered the room, talking over her shoulder as she came. "That's very sweet of you, Julie, dear. I appreciate all your help." Oma often cooked and cleaned for the old widow, as her walker made it difficult for her to tend to all her own needs.

Tante Kreuzinger greeted me with a warm smile and she made her way over to a large faded burgundy chair opposite me. She moaned slightly as she sat down, saying, "These old bones, Alfie. I don't know what I would do without your Oma's help." Her wrinkled hands trembled slightly as she pushed away her walker and eased herself more comfortably into her favorite chair. "Help yourself to some of those cookies, Alfie. I made them just for you." I helped myself to a delicious raspberry cookie covered with wisps of powdered sugar.

"Tell me all about school, Alfie. What are you boys up to these days?" She smiled, her eyes twinkling warmly beneath the white bun that was coiled neatly upon the top of her head.

She listened carefully as I related some of the week's happenings to her; I even recited a poem learned several days earlier in school. As I finished, Oma entered the room, which was quiet except for my halting voice as I tried to make my way through the last few verses of my brief presentation.

"That was very good, Alfie. You have always been such a bright boy." Tante Kreuzinger said, resting her soft delicate hand on my arm and squeezing slightly.

"Alfie, one more cookie, and that's all. I want you to save room for lunch. Move over and let me sit too." Oma said. She was carrying a small tray upon which clattered two flowery cups and a delicately curved tea pot, which steamed slightly with its fragrant contents.

"May I use the restroom, Tante Kreuzinger?" I asked, as I stood up to make room for Oma to set the tray on the small table near the couch.

"Certainly, dear. You know where it is." Tante Kreuzinger answered, her frail finger pointing shakily down the narrow hall.

Strange though it may seem, this was always one of my favorite parts of the visit. The villa was equipped with a small, but rare, indoor toilet, much unlike the rustic one in our washroom across the backyard of the house. The bathroom was narrow and lit only by a tiny rectangle window, its glass frosted slightly, set high into the wall. The walls were covered with wallpaper decorated with large billowing yellow roses, and although it was slightly faded, it made for one of the most elegant bathrooms I had ever set foot in.

The main focus of my fascination, though, sat against the far wall— a small porcelain bowl, with its tank high up on the wall under the window. From the tank above, which was perched on a long thin pipe, there hung a golden chain with a porcelain ball at the very end, also covered in yellow roses. Oma had shown me how to pull on the thin chain, which would send water gushing noisily through the pipe on the wall behind the bowl. I had often thought how nice it would be to have one of those toilets to use during the cold winter nights, rather than my cracked chamber pot under my bed. Instead, I had to be content with my weekly chance to use Tante Kreuzinger's, and I usually made sure I drank an extra glass of milk in order to guarantee myself a visit.

The winter weather had come early that year, although it was still only the beginning of November. Walks to school were very unpleasant, with many of our shoes now thin at the soles. The stores were all but empty, even if Opa and Oma had not been reluctant to spend money on anything but the absolute essentials. Besides, we now had another mouth to feed; Gerle had moved in with us at the end of October.

I had secretly been thrilled, though I remained reserved, as Gerle was shocked and disturbed at his sudden homelessness. His father, of course, had been gone for quite awhile with the rest of the eligible men, sent to the East to fight the Russians. Oma had said, simply, that Gerle's mother had not been to work for several days at the mill, according to my mother, and there was no sign of her anywhere. It was not unheard of that someone had gone missing in those uncertain times, but the resources to find people were not in place. So, Gerle became an orphan, and my grandparents did not hesitate for a moment to bring him into our family.

Uncle Alois was pleased to move across the hall to the spare room, perhaps relieved not to have me shake him awake each morning as soon as the rooster crowed. Gerle moved in and became the little brother I had always wanted, and I felt more grown up than ever before. The extra bed against the opposite wall became Gerle's, and late at night, when the skies had all darkened and the black drapes had been hung across the windows,

I could hear the muffled sobs of my dear little friend as he pined for his mother and father, unsure of where they were or if he would ever see them again. For several weeks he woke with his large brown eyes red and swollen from lack of sleep and lack of spirit. Finally, the tears dried up and the pain sank more deeply and profoundly into his gentle soul, only flickering occasionally to the surface.

Several weeks later, on a surprisingly mild autumn Saturday, Opa came into the kitchen carrying his old rucksack, and I knew an adventure was in store for the day. Oma had already decided that Gerle would spend the day with her, helping in the yard and kitchen, and receiving, she added, "… a little time to himself. He needs some space right now, and perhaps he can help me in the bargain." Gerle seemed pleased with this arrangement, even before hearing Opa's plans for the day.

"Uncle Johann told me last summer that he would have something for me to pick up in the fall. So, today, Alfie, is the day we go. We leave on the train in an hour."

"What are you getting from him, Opa?" I asked, my curiosity rising. I glanced over at Gerle, who sat across the table, quietly sipping some steaming tea. Gerle simply shrugged, and I looked back at my grandfather.

"Never you mind. You'll find out soon enough, Alfie. It's only a short train ride, but we best be off. Bye, Julie. Enjoy your day, Gerle." Opa added, rumpling Gerle's already untidy brown hair, and smiling broadly. "Save some of whatever you bake with Oma for us." Gerle smiled in response and looked over at Oma, who winked at him and gave him a loving smile. Oma had tried very hard to make Gerle feel at home and included, and Gerle finally seemed to be responding. There was always room in Oma's heart for another child to love.

I waved to Gerle, kissed Oma on the cheek, and I headed out the door to meet Opa in the yard, where he was checking on the goats. We left for the train station, my curiosity on the rise once more. Trips with Opa always brought enjoyment, and I never turned down the chance to travel on the train. The ride was a short one, into the village of Olbersdorf, a small hamlet cradled in the tight palm of the wild mountains. Here, my great uncle, Johann, owned a small sawmill and wood shop, and he would often help Opa with repairs to plows and the various other wooden tools that occasionally needed mending.

"What does Uncle Johann have for you, Opa? What's he fixing?" I asked, my patience slipping as we neared the small station tucked among the tall dark pines.

"Oh, you are an eager one today, aren't you, Alfie? You will see soon enough. I'm sure you will agree it was worth the trip." replied Opa, winking at me. He flung the rucksack over his shoulder as the train lurched to a stop in front of the platform. It was a short walk to Uncle Johann's shop, which was good; the tantalizingly warm weather of the morning had disappeared and in its place a cold drizzle was beginning to fall. The breeze now carried a sharp edge to it.

We hastened to his large wooden door, which was set into a small building with long gray diagonal slats of wood running the length of the facade. Uncle Johann answered our knocks and he welcomed us both with hearty hugs and slaps on the shoulders. We followed his ample form through the dark hall and into the large workshop, where the air hung thick with the smell of sawdust and pitch.

"Well, Alfie, I think I made them just the right size for how much you've grown since I last saw you." said Uncle Johann, his breath wheezing laboriously out of his large body. Noticing my puzzled expression, he added, "Oh... I see we have a little surprise going here, Reinhard. Excellent! I'll just go get them, shall I?" He smiled broadly, his eyes all but disappearing in the folds on his merry face as the smile grew into a chuckle. He squeezed behind a long workbench, grunting slightly, and he began to rummage noisily behind a pile of scrap lumber, all sizes of which were leaning against the wall.

"Ah, here they are!" he exclaimed, with apparent mirth at being able to reveal a secret. "What do you think, Alfie?" He made his way around the table with what, in the dim light of the dusty room, looked like two long ordinary boards. It wasn't until he thrust them toward me that I noticed the delicate curve at the tip of each and realized that they were skis. My mouth fell open as I glanced rapidly from the beautiful shiny boards, each with a leather strap for the boot, to my grandfather, who was smiling in delight, and finally to my Uncle Johann, who was all but trembling with the anticipation of my reaction.

I swallowed quickly, realizing I still had my mouth open, and I stammered, "These are for me? Really for me? Wow, Opa, they are great! Thank you! Thank you, Uncle Johann!" I grasped the skis in one hand, trying to make space for a quick hug to Opa and Uncle Johann, and it nearly sent the cumbersome pieces toppling to the floor. They were tall, but perfect; I could just reach the tips with my fingers.

"A perfect fit." declared Opa, slapping me heartily on the shoulders.

"A little practice and you'll be flying down the hill!" said Uncle Johann gleefully, his delight causing me to smile even more broadly than I had been.

Uncle Johann coughed, then became all business, taking the skis out of my hands and laying them gently, bottom sides up, on the workbench. "They are made out of hickory, Alfie, and should last you a long time, as long as you take care of them." He reached for a small wooden box on the shelf behind him and showed me how to rub pine tar and wax on the smooth pale bottoms, creating the ideal surface for skimming rapidly across the snow.

After insisting I take several containers of the strong smelling tubes of tar and wax, we joined Uncle Johann in the back room for a brief lunch, which passed in a blur, as my mind already had me speeding down the hills around town, the envy of all my friends.

That night, after a late dinner, our train having been delayed by heavy troop movement across the tracks, Gerle and I admired the sleek long skis. We each agreed that we would share them; I was determined to ease Gerle's transition into our family. I had heard Oma tell Opa that Gerle had perked up a bit during the day, and he had even shared an amusing story by the fire with her and Uncle Alois. Now, he seemed almost as excited as I was about the coming winter and all the new thrills we could have on our wonderful skis.

As we lay in our warm beds, comforters tucked up to our chins to keep out the winter chill that was already creeping into the room, we could hear Oma's and Opa's hushed voices in the hall.

"She said that if we want more food stamps we need to turn over two more chickens to the food department." came Oma's worried voice, cracking slightly in her effort to keep it low.

"Well, we will do what we have to, Julie. We are better off than many. Also, Uncle Johann gave me a side of ham. That will last for a few weeks. We'll be fine." Opa's soothing voice answered.

Wondering if he had heard, I glanced over to Gerle's dark form, his face barely visible in the darkness. The light from the hallway was casting a pale glow across the top half of his face, and I saw that his eyes were closed tightly, but I noticed a small shimmer of a tear as it rolled across his nose. It fell, soaking into his already damp pillow.

Several days later, after school, Gunter herded us all together at the bridge, and he hushed us quickly with his hands, looking over his shoulders at the girls who were gathered on the opposite side of the road. "I have an idea...." he said, his voice sinking to almost nothing as Edith walked by our huddle, heading home for the day. "I have an old bicycle inner tube. I thought we could have some fun with it." Gunter continued, his mischievous eyes twinkling in the cold winter light.

We spent the next hour fashioning a few crude sling shots out of some tough hazelnut branches. They were cut into small "Y" shapes, and we tied them with pieces of the old inner tube from Gunter's rusty bike. Each section of inner tube cradled a piece of leather tongue from some of Walter's old shoes. This made a perfect hollow for the ammunition, which we found in the abundance of small smooth rocks lining the icy banks of the river.

Otti retrieved a board, this time promising it had not been stolen from his father, and we propped it against a tree and took turns testing our aim on the crude target.

Several of the girls had remained on the bridge overhead, their laughter ringing loudly against the stone pillars that flanked the river. Our enjoyment at shooting at the idle target soon waned. Franz picked a handful of wet cold sand from the very edge of the water, and let it fly from his dripping slingshot. The wad of sand flew true, landing on the backs and legs of the girls who were leaning against the rail of the bridge.

Soon the air was filled with the screams of the girls and our laughter and hoots of released boredom. The one-sided battle was over quickly; the girls had not remained as targets for long. With their cries and angry words hanging where they had stood, the fun faded immediately, as we quickly realized we would all be in trouble if word got back to our families about our actions.

"Hanni's going to squeal. I just know it." murmured Walter, his head between his hands. We tried to push the thoughts of punishment from our minds with a game of soccer, but it ended early as our hearts were burdened with the impending admonition.

Finally, when the light had faded to a gray blue and the cold brought on by the rising twilight began to creep into our bones, we had no choice but to head to our homes to deal with any possible consequences. Opa met me as soon as I walked in the door, his thick mustache quivering with anger. He grabbed me by the neck with his strong hands and whipped me sharply across my rear end.

Gerle managed to escape with a severe talking to by Oma, but I think he was just as crushed as I. Maybe he would have felt more like a real part of the family if Opa had dealt with him, too.

Gerle and I ate a very rushed meal, hardly tasting the delicious bread dumplings covered in rich cream sauce, or the tender rabbit roast, one of our last of the season. We ate with our eyes on our plates, our faces burning with shame and embarrassment, before we returned outdoors to willingly complete the many evening chores.

The next morning on route to school, the girls marched ahead in a very tight group, their faces set with smug satisfaction at the knowledge of the harsh punishments each of us had received. Franz faced many cold shoulders that day, as some of us remembered all too well his eagerness in releasing the first disastrous shot. Our alliance ran too deeply, though, to remain angry at him for long, and we found ourselves back at the bridge that evening planning new adventures together.

CHAPTER 8

Winter had swept into the valley, leaving no patch of ground untouched by its tendrils of frost. Steam rose from the muzzles of the goats as they huddled closely in their stalls, and their milk frothed hotly in the frigid morning air.

It was the beginning of December, 1944, and news from all mouths was grim. Everyone's cellars were packed as high as could be managed, yet the sense of need of the basic necessities pervaded; rationing had been tightened even further.

The radio insisted that the war was well in hand; the rationing was merely a cautionary measure and any potential relocation of civilians would be temporary and brief. In the midst of the stress and worry, time continued on, and occasional pleasures could still be found.

Gerle and I filled every free moment at the frozen riverbank with the new skis, grateful for the early snowfall. Anticipation among our friends grew as we approached the holiday, aware that we would be embarking on our first class excursion away from home. Not long after I had received my skis, our teacher had announced a week long field trip to the mountains for some skiing and other snow activities.

Opa and Oma had consented, though Oma rather reluctantly, and Gerle and I eagerly began to mark the days on the small calendar that hung in the kitchen. The long afternoons by the river had produced many sore muscles as we struggled to learn the basics of staying upright on the skis Uncle Johann had given me.

We had spent the whole evening after dinner in the shed with Opa, carefully making sure the skis were in optimum condition for the trip, which would commence the following day. Oma fussed endlessly over our rucksacks, concerned we had not packed enough warm socks and sweaters. Finally, the drapes were pulled over the dark windows and the world was shut out. Oma insisted on early bed for both of us, and we didn't argue. We were ready to have the morning arrive.

The day dawned gray and damp, though fresh snow had fallen during the night, giving the city a clean blanket of white. The train station swarmed with bleary-eyed boys and their nervous parents, as everyone hurried to stuff forgotten rolls of socks and extra tubes of ski wax into their bulging rucksacks. Oma spent several minutes explaining to me about the importance of obeying the teachers and the need to get enough sleep each night. She was still fussing as Opa pulled her gently by the hand away from the billows of steam, which issued from the train as it began to inch slowly out of the station.

"They'll be fine, Julie." I heard my grandfather say, raising a hand in farewell, while we looked on from the large windows, which were already steaming up with the press of so many bodies. Gerle and I quickly settled ourselves in seats near the middle of the train, and Otti, Gunter, and Franz joined us soon after.

We passed several hours in pleasant games, as well as heated discussions regarding the proper technique for stopping while on skis. The houses began to thin and the snow piled more deeply along the banks that skirted the winding tracks leading into the high country.

My mind wandered. I had grown tired of the endless suggestions as to the ideal combination of wax and tar that would enhance the speed of the descent down the slope, and I leaned my head against the cool metal window sill, my eyes following a drop of condensation as it traced a path slowly down the glass.

The snow had begun to fall heavily and the wind blew clumps of ice off the dark pines in a shower of white. My mind suddenly jumped to my father, as startled, I realized sadly, that he would be spending this evening and many to come somewhere far away in a similar storm trying to stay warm. For a moment, I felt guilty for yearning to get out into the cold and the snow, but the lurch of the train and the whoops and laughter of the boys pushed the grim thoughts away.

The train slowed several times, waiting for unseen delays further down the snowy track, but it finally inched its way into the small open railway station, a mere hut on the edge of a dense forest. We exited hastily, anxious to stretch our legs and begin our adventures. Soon the teachers had us marching in lines… like soldiers, I couldn't help thinking, although a great deal less orderly, as each boy had to carry his own long pair of skis over his shoulder.

We headed through the narrow streets of the small village towards a long low building, which was the youth hostel, our first home away from home. My mind went back to my father several times on that trip, but each time more self-indulgently, as I wondered if our conditions were more similar to his than I had thought on the train. We found ourselves housed in a large dimly lit room, with rows upon rows of narrow bunks covered with old dusty straw. The room was not heated, and even if it had been it would not have held warmth for long, as the walls were full of small cracks through which the wind whistled shrilly.

After several hours out in the snow, we reluctantly settled ourselves into our bunks, thankful Oma had insisted on the extra sweaters. Despite the cold, most boys fell asleep quickly, though the teachers had to demand silence on occasion.

I awoke to the dull light of morning creeping in through the long narrow windows that ran the full length of the building. I immediately noticed my breath curling up toward the dark ceiling. "Oh, good grief!" came Otti's shivering voice, and I peered over my bunk. He stood in the corner, his hand tapping a small bucket full of water, and he slowly lifted a thin sheet of ice off the trembling surface.

"The sooner we get moving, the sooner we warm up, boys." came the muffled voice of our teacher from beneath his sweater, as he pulled a second one over his rumpled hair, his glasses catching on the collar and clattering to the cold floor.

Breakfast was sparse, though sufficient for our moods, as no one wanted to linger long in the cold room. We tumbled out the door, each boy eager to be the first one on the hill looming closely over the low roof of the hostel. Gerle and I had agreed that we would take turns on the skis, the other watching from the row of benches that ran beneath the windows of the building.

Skiing on the larger hill was nothing like our early attempts on the river bank, and it took many spills and soakings in the deep snow before we grew confident enough to go very quickly. Uncle Johann's magic concoction of ski treatments never failed me, and the week's end had us well learned in the basic pleasures of skiing. All our free time was spent out of the gloomy cold youth hostel, as it was the dark quiet hours of night into which thoughts of home would creep.

Lying shivering in my damp bunk, I often thought of how it would feel to be like Gerle and not have a family to return to, and then I reminded myself that we were his family now, and we would be heading home to our own warm beds soon.

After our return, the holidays ended without much fanfare, though we managed a fine feast from our last pig, which Opa had butchered out by the animal shed, the stain of its steaming blood standing out blazingly red against the brilliant white snow. Oma managed, from our meager supplies, to create many delicious cakes, pies, and marmalades. The time passed pleasantly enough. My sister joined us at almost every meal, though we rarely saw my mother.

January, 1945, began for us as so many years had. The walk to school was as cold as ever, the classroom just as depressed, as the teachers droned through their notes, glaring at anyone who whispered or squirmed. The feared rod lay threateningly on the edge of the teacher's large desk, ready to leave a deep red mark on the knuckles of any boy who stepped out of line. Any serious mischief would result in more extreme punishment, with the rod being used on the naked backside of the poor fellow who had been so bold as to take the chance.

Twice a week we braced ourselves for our most dreaded class, which came at the hands of our music teacher, a severe-looking Hungarian man with deep-set dark eyes. The eyes were all but hidden beneath bushy dark eyebrows that loomed fearsomely over his long hooked nose. He always arrived minutes after the bell rang, as though he relished the tension the wait created. He would storm in, carrying an old wooden violin case under his arm, and a scowl already firmly embedded beneath his angry glare.

He made it a practice to jab a few boys in the back with the end of the instrument case as he swept quickly past, roaring, "Silencium!" Whoever had been unfortunate enough to sit near the door cowered with dread and fear of being the latest victim of his seemingly random wrath.

We had managed to reach his classroom earlier than usual one day, and we waited nervously to initiate a daring plan of Gunter's devising. Part of our teacher's daily routine included the brandishing of the punishing stick and smacking it firmly several times across the surface of his large oak desk, as he shouted, "Silencium! Silencium!", several times until the stillness was sufficiently to his liking. This rod was made from a long thin reed, strong enough to bear the handling it received on a daily basis, yet light and hollow from end to end.

Gunter shuffled us all in silently, twitching with excitement at his devilish plan, which he had waited until that moment to reveal. "Otti, give me your knife! Come on, hurry!" he said, gesturing frantically with one hand as he reached for the rod with the other. His eyes glanced anxiously at the door. Franz and Gerle gasped, and Gerle backed up slightly, shaking his head, clearly convinced this plan would bring trouble.

Otti, his face clouded with suspicion, reached into his pocket and quickly handed Gunter a small gray pocketknife, which Gunter opened with fumbling fingers. We stood, our mouths gaping in disbelief at Gunter's bravery, and we watched him slowly and carefully slice a small, almost invisible line in one end of the rod. He shoved the knife back into Otti's hand and hurried to the side of the desk where a large inkwell sat, its rim coated with thick dried black ink. He placed the open end of the rod into the ink and set the other newly sliced end into his mouth and began to inhale.

His eyebrows raised, his face turned red, and his eyes crossed slightly as he carefully marked the progress of the ink up into the rod. When he felt it was sufficiently full, he wiped the ends carefully on the underside of his shirt and gently placed the ink-filled rod precisely in the spot where he had found it.

The rest of us had remained silent during Gunter's operation, partly stunned at his brilliance and partly shocked at his audaciousness. Sounds in the hallway signaled us to promptly take our seats. The door rattled fiercely as our teacher stormed in.

"Silencium! Right now! Silencium!" he bellowed, as he slammed the door, his violin case for once, safely tucked under the arm towards the wall. He marched to the platform at the front of class, placed the violin case gently on a shelf against the wall behind him, and turned around to face us with a firm searching stare.

Every boy's face was set with a dogged determination not to reveal anything out of the ordinary, though my knees trembled beneath my desk and my heart pounded in my chest, until I was sure he could hear it and would single me out with his piercing eyes.

An almost imperceptible gasp came from Gerle as the teacher reached for the rod. Roaring, "Silencium!", one final time, he raised it above his head and brought it down with a terrible crash against the surface of the desk. A sudden explosion of thousands of tiny little black drops issued from the end of his rod as the ink splattered out, leaving a line of dots across the length of the ceiling as well as on the startled faces of the boys who had chosen seats in line with the teacher's aim.

The laughter erupted almost as explosively as the ink had, and our teacher stood in disbelief for several moments before dropping the ink-coated rod onto his desk. His hands went to his hips and I stifled a final chuckle as he stepped off the platform and began to prowl silently between the rows of desks, taking in every terrified face with his probing dark eyes.

"Whoever was responsible for that little… foolery," he whispered scathingly, his eyes darting from boy to boy, "… will be sure to be properly punished. And… I will find out who did it. I promise you that." He turned suddenly on his heel and walked almost leisurely back to his spot behind the desk, apparently convinced he had struck enough fear into our hearts. "Now take out your slates. Immediately!"

It was during lunch that we were told we would be remaining after school to receive punishment for the event that had taken place in the music class that morning. We stood in a small huddle, our shoulders bunched together as we tried to figure how our involvement had been revealed.

The music professor entered the classroom shortly after the last bell rang, the pleasure at having caught us written all over his smirking face. He beckoned us all forward to a long bench beneath the window. One by one he lashed our bare bottoms with the long thin rod, its tip still coated with the sticky black ink. My eyes continued to smart as I limped out the door behind my friends, each of us certain that we had all kept our secret, though also equally uncertain of who had given us away.

Several days later, our backsides still sore from our punishment, we made our way slowly home through the frosty January afternoon. The main road intersected the train tracks half way home from school, and it was here that we often turned our path in the direction of the rails. Today, though, the gates were down, signaling an oncoming train. At times we tried to rush the gates, ignoring the yells and rude gestures of the station attendant, but the memories of our latest brush with authority caused us to wait.

As we paused for the slowly lumbering supply train to pass, undoubtedly on its way to the Russian Front, my eyes fell on another engine resting a short distance away on a side track. The engine was idling restlessly, frothy steam issuing from beneath its wheels. It was attached to several cars, each surrounded by four or five German soldiers. Their bayonet tipped guns were leaning over their shoulders and they strolled back and forth alongside the cars.

Also along this side track was a loading ramp with its top edge raised to the level of the floor of the train cars bordering it. The last narrow car in the row had apparently just been loaded, for I saw two soldiers drawing a large iron bar through some clamps along the sliding door in the side of the train. As I watched the door seal shut I noticed a blurred movement slightly higher within a row of narrow slat windows. I gasped in shock, realizing that the movement had been a face, and I shuddered with an inexplicable revulsion to find that hands were starting to reach out through the small openings.

The activity from the people in the car increased suddenly, as though in a last scramble for freedom. I heard a child's muffled cry and a small voice sobbing, "Mutti, where are we going?"

I could not hear the response, though I desperately wanted to, as a similar question was forming on my lips. "Where are those people going?" I asked. The boys gathered around me, their eyes also drawn to the horrible images before us.

"Are they Russian soldiers?" asked Otti softly, his face filled with uncertainty.

"Don't be silly, Otti. There are babies and women in there! Can't you hear their voices?" replied Gunter, his voice dropping slightly so as to not be heard by the soldiers. This was unlikely though, as the noise from inside the cars had reached quite a din, and the soldiers were yelling fiercely to the

83

unfortunate occupants to silence themselves. Their guns were now pointed ominously at the high slats, where the fear-filled faces were gathered.

Gerle turned his back suddenly, and I could hear his shaky whisper, as he said, seemingly to himself, "It will be so cold! How can they do that?" The slow train soon passed and the gates opened. A bell clanged shrilly over the desperate voices in the train and we remained, though the road was now clear. My feet wanted to run away from what I was seeing, yet at the same time, I felt rooted to the spot, unable to take my eyes off the jumble of hands grasping at the air through the holes, nor to cover my ears against the frightened sobs of the children.

"Let's get out of here." murmured Franz nervously from behind me. I glanced one last time at the train and noticed one of the soldiers looking straight at us. He moved as if to head our way and this jerked us out of our bewilderment. We hastened across the tracks and headed down the road. Peering quickly over my shoulder, I saw that the soldier had turned back to the train and he was thrusting the sharp point of his bayonet into one of the windows of the last car.

"Look!" I said, grabbing Gerle's shoulder and pointing surreptitiously with my finger. Gerle turned reluctantly to see, then turned back quickly, his face pale and set. He said nothing, but sped up, determined to reach home more quickly.

We headed straight into the kitchen, which was warm with Oma's fine cooking, though the smell of the food made my stomach turn slightly. Echoes of the cries from the train were still reverberating in my head. Oma noticed we were both sullen and not speaking. She tapped her wooden spoon on the rim of the large stew pot on the stove, wiped her hands on her apron, and said, "What's wrong boys? Something happen at school?" She moved to the table and sat down, her eyes full of concern. Gerle and I looked at each other, neither of us sure how to describe what we had seen.

"We saw something…" began Gerle, his voicing trailing off as he looked at me imploringly.

I glanced at Gerle, then said to Oma, "There was a train sitting on the side track at the crossing… with people on it… and, and well… they were crying. Children too, Oma. What does it mean? Where were they being taken?"

Oma stood abruptly and crossed herself silently, tears filling her startled eyes. Her hand grasped the back of the chair as if she were about to fall, and in a faltering voice she said, "I'm sorry you saw that, boys. So sorry...."

"Oma...." I ventured. "Please, what was it all about?"

She looked at us for several moments without speaking, though I knew she was debating how much to tell us. "Well, Alfie, Opa said he's seen a few of those trains going in the last few days.... They are all headed to a town called... uh, Auschwitz, I think is what Opa said. People are being... relocated, that's all... yes." She shook her head, fighting with her own thoughts, and she continued, "It's best not to talk about it any more, dear. Though, there will probably be more; the front has moved a little closer, I guess. Moving people, that's what it is, dear... moving people. It's the war." She brushed her trembling hand across her brow, which was now slightly damp with perspiration, though the room was not particularly hot. "Now go wash up for supper, you two... and get your Uncle Alois and your sister. Opa's eating at your uncle's tonight."

Several days later we were passing the same train tracks and noticed the cars were gone. No sign of them remained. Instinct warned of devious activity, but the time for questions had faded. We spoke little of the events we had witnessed, though all our minds drew inward, and we crossed the rails without looking back.

We began to chat again lightly and were rounding the final turn before our house, when something caused me to look up. I became aware of a figure in the distance standing near the side of the road. As we slowly approached, the figure began to move quickly toward us, and I realized, with an unexplainable sinking feeling, that it was my grandmother.

Her hand was clutched at her throat and her eyes were filled with tears. At that moment, it felt as though my stomach had fallen into my shoes. I knew. I knew before she had even reached us. I had been anticipating this moment for a long time; the cold wind had been carrying it ever westward, from battlefields far away.

"It's your father, Alfie. He's dead... We just got the news. Oh, Alfie, I'm so sorry." She collapsed against my small shoulders, her warm arms enveloping me in a tight hug.

The boys around us shifted uneasily as Oma sobbed against my shoulder, her tears hot against my cold face. My throat tightened with the effort to contain the tears that were pricking at the corners of my eyes, and I gasped at the cold air. My arms stretched around the poor figure of my dear grandmother, and I held her like never before.

With a look from Gerle, the others moved on, leaving Oma and me standing together on the empty road. The biting January wind whistled around our ears, as if it still had more messages to send, only pausing for a moment before it roared off to someone else's mother. We walked slowly home, Oma never releasing my hand. We met Opa at the gate, where he joined us in another hug.

"He died several months ago, Alfie. We only just got the letter now." Opa said, his brow tight with emotion. "From what I heard at the tavern, there will probably be a letter for Gerle soon too, though don't say anything to him yet."

The next morning at school the voices rose in song for me, though they felt very far away; the blood pounded in my ears as I, once again, fought against the lump in my throat. I had hardly slept the night before, acknowledging a grief so deep that the tears would not flow. Now, all eyes were upon me, as the sorrowful verses of my friends and companions reminded me of my loss. I had been right that Christmas morning, as I watched my father walk away… I would never see him again.

It was Sunday; the clattering church bells returned me to the present, where I sat in the pew next to my grandmother and sister. The voices rose slowly as people began to file out of the church. Yet I remained, reluctant to let the world enter into my somber thoughts. Oma sat motionless also, equally transfixed by some thoughts of her own. It wasn't until moments later, as she crossed herself slowly, that she seemed aware again of her surroundings, or of Gerti's little hand pulling on her sleeve.

My sister was now five and her blond braids framed a round sweet face. It was a face that always spread into a smile at the sight of me, though we didn't see each other often. Now, she was staring silently up into Oma's sad eyes and tugging gently on my grandmother's arm.

Oma started and raised her hand gently to Gerti's cheek. "We'll go now, child. I am sure Frau Kreuzinger will have some nice cookies for you both. You sat very quietly, Gerti. I'm proud of you." she said sweetly.

We eased ourselves up from the hard benches and followed the crowd into the breezy morning. Nodding quietly to several parishioners, we moved off around the corner towards the synagogue and Frau Kreuzinger's villa. My mouth watered for the sweet cookies she would serve, and I tried to remember something from the last few months of school to fend off her questioning. We had not been to visit her for so long, and I was sure she would expect me to talk, or worse, to sing.

My eyes were on the ground, following a crack in the sidewalk, when I heard Oma gasp, and felt her hand clutch tightly at my shoulder. I glanced up quickly and my jaw dropped. My gaze traveled across the beautiful square to the synagogue, now only a battered shell with smashed out windows and rough boards nailed across its once grand double doors. Several pigeons flew noisily out of one of the gaping holes in the wall, making me jump.

"What's happened, Oma?" I croaked, my words buried in disbelief at what I was seeing.

"What's wrong, Oma?" I heard Gerti's small voice say from the other side of my grandmother.

Oma said nothing, but pulled us quickly along, her eyes fixed straight ahead to the spot where the street turned to the row of villas. As we passed the doors, I saw the hastily scrawled image of the swastika painted across the boards. Beneath were the words, "No Trespassing. Violators will be punished."

Oma pulled us even faster, and as we turned the corner, I caught her words, barely audible, "Please, dear God, please… no!" She let out a small wail, dropped our hands, and ran the remaining length of the deserted sidewalk, her fingers clutching her face. I stumbled over an upended window box, its black dirt spilling helplessly onto the bricks.

I followed after Oma, my hand grasping Gerti's as I went. The elegant front windows were dark, their lace curtains hanging limply and torn as they rustled in the unforgiving wind. A crude sign hung on the beautifully carved wooden door, and its meaning was the same as before. No one remained inside. No one could enter.

My grandmother slumped against the wall, weeping silently into her hands, before raising her eyes with a sudden look of panic. She peered nervously up and down the street, her face laced with fear—the primal fear of a hunted deer. She brushed the tears quickly away, and grabbing the hand of my startled sister, she beckoned me to follow. "Quickly now!" her broken voice pleaded. "We mustn't be seen here. I'll explain at home. Hurry up Gerti, dear!"

That night over dinner, Opa explained to us that the German army was "relocating" people of certain classifications, and Jewish citizens were among those being moved. Where Frau Kreuzinger and the others had gone, he really didn't know, but "… most probably west, boys. The front is getting closer. We may have to move ourselves." He sighed, his eyes full of anxiety and an emptiness that had been there since the tragic word of my father had arrived.

Opa had brought his own news from his now daily visit to the tavern. Many of the shops that lined the main street were closed; the shop keepers were too anxious to keep them open. People fearing the proximity of the war had packed up and headed to live with relatives in the small mountain villages west of the city. Word had come that several cousins and other relations had also perished on the front, but it was the death of Uncle Leo, Opa's brother's son, that seemed to disturb my grandfather the most.

"I just can't explain it, Julie. It makes no sense, and I don't like it." Opa said sadly, shaking his head slowly, his eyes fixed on his plate of untouched potatoes.

"What is it, Reinhard?" ventured Oma, resting her gentle hand on Opa's arm.

"Well…" Opa said, pausing to look between Gerle, Gerti and me, as a muscle tightened behind his mustache. "Well, I am not sure if what I heard is correct… but, Leo was shot by German soldiers… not the Russians." Oma gasped, her hand going up to her mouth, which dropped open in disbelief and confusion. She began to speak, but Opa continued, "I know. It makes no sense, except for something Fritz said, which might be part of it. Leo's fiancee, Sophie… sweet girl… do you remember meeting her that time at the tavern?"

Oma nodded, a puzzled look on her face, apparently uncertain what this all had to do with Leo's death, and Opa said, "It seems Sophie was Jewish… so, it's possible…" He paused, shaking his head emphatically, his hands kneading his tired legs. "No, Fritz is probably wrong. None of it makes sense, Julie. That's all… none of it. But, I do know that all this news on the radio is ridiculous! 'The war is going well', ach… ridiculous." Opa stood suddenly, bumping the table in his haste, and he headed out of the room, "Ridiculous! It really is…" The door slammed loudly as Opa's voice passed out into the night.

I lay awake that night, my sleep disturbed by troubled thoughts and haunting images, as I tried to fathom the depths of the changes that had flooded so quickly into my previously peaceful world. I tried to push away the dark lurid shadows of the soldiers with their rifles, as they aimed them at my uncle's head, then I buried my own head under the pillow to stifle what my mind was preparing for next.

I lay still, forcing my racing brain to focus on something pleasant, and I finally felt my thoughts lose out, as my body slipped slowly into restless slumber. Moments later I was jerked awake, filled with momentary anxiety, until I realized the sound I thought I had heard was something else. No droning airplanes had roused me, rather a subtle, yet distinct shuffling noise had wormed its way into my unsettled dreams. I remained in bed for several minutes, my ears straining to identify the sound. Finally, my curiosity got the better of me and I threw back the thick covers and strode across the cold floor to the window, which was heavily covered with a coarse blanket.

I carefully pulled the corner of the blanket up, and I was forced to blink several times, as my eyes adjusted to the brightness of the full moon. It illuminated the bridge and road with a blinding blue light. I rubbed my eyes slowly, allowing them to adjust to the contrast, then peered back out, this time taking in the dappled shadows of the trees and bushes along the riverbank, and the black form of the bridge looming nearby.

Dark shapes were moving slowly along the road, heading westward. As my eyes continued to adjust to the light cast by the moon, I noticed each shape was the figure of a man… a soldier. Though, from the looks of them, not all were German. There were some, though… many of them, with rifles, herding long columns of staggering haggard-looking prisoners toward the town and beyond. The lines of dark shapes massed like a swarm of locusts, undulating recklessly along the road until my eye lost them amongst the trees.

Each head was bent forward; each man's step seemed labored. Only the armed Germans moved with any sense of purpose or ease, surrounding the captured Russians like a python slowly closing in on its prey. Every once and awhile a man would stumble or slow, and the python would strike, thudding the man in the back of the head or the shoulder with the butt of a black rifle.

I watched, transfixed, until the shapes began to blur and my head began to nod, and still the lines kept coming. I settled the blanket securely back into place, and ran back to bed, burying my cold nose into the deep folds of the goose feathers. My eyes drifted closed; the rhythmic treads of the thousands of feet blended with the sounds of my own breath, as it slowed finally into rest.

Early the next morning, I awoke with the memory of the night's visions lodged firmly in my mind, and I ran to the window to check the road. It lay still and calm, hardly similar to the bustle of the previous night. Upon the settled dust walked a solitary young woman, wearily making her way home from a long shift at the factory.

"What are you looking at?" came Gerle's sleepy voice from across the room, his rumpled head protruding from beneath the deep covers.

"I saw Russians last night! Hundreds of them. Right out there!" I exclaimed, pointing to the undisturbed line of the road, where it curved up into the hills around the town.

"What? What do you mean, Russians?"

I explained as best I could, reminding a doubtful Gerle that I had had only the light of the moon by which to see. But, my emphatic assurances that what I had seen had been real were unnecessary, as a new blur began to form on the horizon. We hurried through breakfast and ran to the bridge, our hearts thumping with the thrill of what we were about to see.

"Does this mean the war is over?" came Walter's words from the sidewalk behind us, as he trotted over to our sides.

"I doubt it. We would have heard. The radio didn't mention anything this morning." said Gunter, wandering up behind his brother. His hands fumbled with the straps on his rucksack, which had recklessly been thrown over his shoulder in his haste to leave his house.

We stood near Opa's fence, which ran along one section of the sidewalk, and we waited while the long line of men shuffled by. The gaze of each man lingered aimlessly on us, his unseeing eyes faraway with some comforting memory of his homeland. Our mouths hung open at the sight of their filthy shriveled bodies. Their cheeks were wasted to hollow pits from lack of food, and their clothes hung limply over protruding bones. Most of the men wore burlap sacks tied around what remained of their tattered shoes, in a hopeless attempt to keep out the snow and cold.

A scuffle to our left pulled us out of the trance, and we gaped sideways to see several of the prisoners dive out of line and lunge themselves toward Opa's compost heap, which was piled up against the rails of the fence. It was littered with old rotten beets, potato peels, and eggshells, all mixed in with the frozen rich humus and mildewed leaves.

The men only had seconds to grab at a few blackened pieces of lettuce before three German guards materialized out of nowhere. With fierce snarls of rage, they raised their rifle butts high in the air. The sides of the starving men's heads were met with thunderous cracks from the weapons as they bashed into their skulls.

"Move it! Get back in line! Now!!" pierced the rabid screeches of the guards, their guns quivering eagerly over their heads, ready to strike again. The men staggered and crawled their way back to the road, their weary comrades struggling to pull the bloodied and crumpled bodies to their feet. Bleeding from what was left of their mouths and noses, they dragged themselves along slowly, occasionally aided slyly by their fellow prisoners.

Meanwhile, the guards had melted back into the mass of bodies. The stench of illness and filth now rose thickly into the cold January air, causing us to hurry on. We stepped quickly over the growing pools of blood in the trampled snow, desperate to put distance between ourselves and the horrors and brutality we had just witnessed.

Several mornings later I awoke to the same shuffling sound, and upon reaching the road, I was not surprised to see another long column of wasted bodies advancing slowly westward. This time, fewer guards surrounded the pathetic rows of prisoners, who staggered three abreast. None seemed in any condition to escape, even if they had wanted to.

Otti, Gerle, and I watched with throats clenched, as two men struggled weakly, all but dragging a wounded third. He was a pale young man with straw-colored hair, though it was matted with blackened patches of dried blood. His vivid blue eyes pierced through me like a twisting knife before the men hobbled painfully onward.

My gaze was wrenched away from his pleading eyes, as I felt a gentle touch on my arm. I spun around, fearing the presence of an angry guard. Instead, a ragged, dark-haired man was tapping my arm with a dented and dirty tin can, and he stuttered, almost wordlessly, in fragmented German, "Water! Please.... water!"

I glanced nervously around and I heard Gerle next to me whisper, "No, Alfie! You can't help him... the guards!" I felt the blood rush into my ears as anger and determination coursed through me. I grabbed the can, slid quickly down the icy bank to the river at the edge of the bridge, and tipped the container into a shallow dent in the ice, through which a tiny stream of frigid mountain water was trickling. The cup filled to half, before the angle began to spill the rest out. I turned and scrambled back to the road, where the prisoner still stood, wobbling uncertainly on his cloth-wrapped feet.

Nodding my head, I reached the icy can forward, emboldened by the thirsty longing in the man's eyes. Suddenly, a movement in the corner of my vision caused me to start. A large guard, the murderous end of his rifle aiming at my face, lunged across the narrow space on the side walk. With spit gathering at the corner of his twisted mouth, he snarled, "You pig! Helping the Enemy!! Get out of here!" His hand met my arm with a hard smack, and the can toppled to the frozen ground, its water fading quickly into the snow. I turned aside and squeezed my eyes shut, waiting for the blow of his rifle on my head, just as I had seen in my dreams. But the guard moved off, yelling and kicking at the poor soul who's only crime had been a parched throat.

I sank back against the fence, its hard rails giving me an oddly reassuring comfort in the small of my shaking back, and I forced down the angry sobs welling deep in my gut.

"Are you ok, Alfie?" whispered Gerle at my shoulder, and I struggled to stand upright, my mind tormented with the unfairness of it all. What was wrong with giving a thirsty man some water? I didn't understand. My mind landed on my father again, as I wondered, with a shudder, if any Russian peasant, another innocent passenger on the runaway engine of war, had tried to help ease his suffering... I wondered, bitterly, if he had even had time to suffer before he died.

I nodded shakily, and we started down the road to school, though I wished for nothing more than to crawl back into my warm bed, close my heavy curtain, and shut myself away from the horrors and the mindless inequities of the world.

All that day I struggled with the longing to run into Oma's warm reassuring arms and to pour my worries and fears out to her. But, then the image of her sweet face would pass before my eyes, as I imagined it contorting with sadness and pain at all we had been forced to see, and at all that was happening that we couldn't see. I decided she didn't need more burdens to bear; her heart was already so terribly troubled with its own grief. The pain of losing her son was still clear in her eyes, where the twinkle had all but gone out. Her visits to church had increased even more and the songs, which had been so much a part of her nature, had dried up. I would simply have to bear my fears like a man... after all, I was twelve.

Finally, it happened; the reality of the troubles elsewhere reached our city, our home where we always expected to be safe. Many large weathered posters were stuck on walls and fences throughout the city, proclaiming that all women with children under ten years of age were required to assemble on the town square. The memories of the terrible hours spent standing on that plaza still haunted me, and I was glad I would not be required to attend... until I was told by Opa that the women and children would be shipped off to the west... to a place far away from the advancing front.

My sister wept bitterly as she clutched at Oma's skirts; she was clearly afraid to face whatever seemed to be making her mother so nervous. Preparations for their hasty departure had gone on all day, and I felt awkwardly detached. My mother was leaving. "I should care more, shouldn't I?" I thought. I knew I would miss my sister, though our lives had always taken different paths from each other. But, I had never been close to my mother, and though this had troubled me on occasion, I couldn't force an attachment that I had never experienced.

With a sinking heart, I sensed the same from her, as they readied their small bundles at the gate, preparing to head to town with Opa. Tears rolled down my mother's face, and she looked imploringly at Oma. It looked as if she were willing my grandmother to have some control over the orders handed down by the Reich. But, when her eyes turned to me, there was no more emotion than when she had said farewell to Gerle. They turned to leave, and I watched my mother's slight frame diminish. My heart was already missing my sweet little sister, whose small hand wiggled in a timid wave, and her fearful eyes touched on my face once more.

"Bye, Alfie!" she called, her voice cracking with effort. "Bye, Oma. Bye, Gerle!"

"We'll see you soon, Gerti, I promise." I called after her, though I was unsure of my own words. She turned quickly, grabbing Opa's free hand with her other one, and the three of them faded slowly into the distance. I held tightly to Oma's hand. She cried piteously with her face buried in her apron, her heart once again plunged into sadness.

CHAPTER 9

The world seemed to be drifting away without us; being left behind was difficult. Oma spent most mornings in church. Services had been limited. Many members had fled westward, away from the menacing shadow of war in the East. February drifted aimlessly into March, though it felt as though there would never be a spring again. The city was nearly empty; school had been canceled indefinitely... teachers and students had stopped attending. Gunter and Walter had left with their family, heading west with the growing lines of refugees that now filled the road both day and night. I turned thirteen without much fanfare, as my grandparents and I were simply grateful that I was still under the fourteen year old cut off for mandatory service.

It was the middle of April, 1945, and the sun rose as ever before. Yet, the world seemed to sense that it had no more use for the sun's nurturing powers. It no longer held any warmth, and the light seemed to pale against the many troubled faces. Smiles were forced; laughter rarely rang true. The shadow loomed ominously over the valley like a great black thunder cloud threatening to burst. Everyone waited, but for what... none of us knew.

The news that Opa had hinted at finally reached our lonely street, where most of the houses sat vacant. Word arrived that Gerle's father had indeed perished on the front, and Gerle sank into a deep fog upon hearing what he had long feared. There had been no word from his mother for many months and he seemed resigned that he was destined to remain an orphan.

Gerle's love for Oma and Opa grew more apparent as the threat of the war moved closer. They had become as much a source of security for him as they were for me.

When Oma managed to drag herself out of her deep moods of sadness and helplessness, she worked in frantic fits of activity. A readied pile of necessities sat heaped by the door in preparation for the call to move west. The city had all but emptied, with only handfuls of families, most of them already incomplete, remaining.

Oma and Opa waited anxiously for word of where my mother and Gerti had gone, but reports were sketchy at best, and their sources unreliable. The city seemed unnatural without the cries of young children, their laughter ringing out over the school yards. All those under ten were gone; as were all those over fourteen. Only Gerle, Otti, and I remained of our group of friends—boys we had known our entire lives; they had all left the shrinking city. Every day the road was filled with the mass of humanity affected by the war. It was an odd sight... and a disturbing sight.

A wave of refugees passed one morning, following closely on the heels of stumbling and moaning Russian prisoners, their eyes filled with the vacant look of defeat and resignation. Creaking wagons woke me from a restless slumber shortly after the arrival of dawn, the rooster having long since provided us with one of our last meals of meat.

I pulled aside the thick blanket with reticence and peered out. All the world seemed to be passing by. Dust hovered thickly over the road, as carts and wagons overflowed its sides. Each vehicle was surrounded by whatever that household had been able to grab in haste. For some this included the entire contents of their barns; cows, horses, and oxen straggled along behind, complaining loudly to their masters. Chickens, ducks, and pigs wrenched around in cages along side pale frightened children, as they huddled together for warmth. The mornings were still frosty, though the trees were already thick with pale green shoots.

Behind the wagons came the unlucky ones, those who had only their own feet to carry them away from the horrors creeping ever westward. Shoulders were hunched under heavy parcels or young children, too small to manage the long journey any other way.

I jumped to find Gerle at my shoulder. He had been standing silently at my side for several minutes, but I had been too absorbed in the sights passing before my eyes; I had not noticed him until he muttered a strained sigh. I turned to look into his small face, framed as always by his rumpled brown hair, and I saw that his eyes were rimmed with tears. He whispered, "Do you think she is out there somewhere, like they are… on a road somewhere?" I knew he meant his mother, though it could have easily been my mother or Gerti he was referring to.

"We can only hope they are somewhere safe… all of them. We'll be ok with Oma and Opa, Gerle. We really will. They will always take care of us… both of us." He looked at me, his wide brown eyes filling with an intensity I'd never seen before. The tears were gone. He nodded slowly and walked from the room.

Gerle and I finished a quiet breakfast alone in the kitchen. Oma and Opa were both out in the barn, tending to various chores, and Uncle Alois was gathering sticks by the river for kindling. The clock ticked loudly against the silence of the room. The quiet was occasionally broken by a bellow from a passing cow or the squeal of a disgruntled pig as it shifted in its tight cage atop a bumping wagon.

A loud shout rang out, causing me to dribble tea down my chin. Gerle and I darted our eyes toward the door. "What was that?" I coughed, hastily wiping my chin with my sleeve.

"I don't know. Let's go look!" answered Gerle, the dogged determination returning to his eyes. We pushed back our chairs, and grabbing pieces of toast, we headed out the door to find the source of the noise, which had intensified. Opa and Oma were just coming from the side of the house as we approached the gate, and I noticed Uncle Alois gesturing madly in our direction from where he stood by the road, which still bustled thickly with people.

Oma gave a loud cry. She ran with her skirts tucked up about her knees toward the road and Uncle Alois. Gerle looked at me and shrugged, and we headed out the gate. Opa met us and we wandered together through the dew-covered grass to the small mass of people huddling on the side of the road. "What's going on, Opa?" I asked, tugging at his sleeve, as he strode quickly toward Oma.

"It's some of our relatives, Alfie, from Bratsch. It looks like they've been ordered to head west." Opa replied morosely, his hand resting on Gerle's shoulder as we stepped near the crowd.

"Julie, it was terrible! We hardly had time to pack anything. Don't wait until it's too late!" insisted an aunt I recognized vaguely from many years before, though the name escaped my mind as I focused on her disturbing words. Behind her on the road stood a large hay wagon pulled by two reluctant cows. Tethered to the rear of the wagon, which was piled high with household necessities, walked four goats, one of whom nibbled contentedly on the fraying rope tied to its collar.

"Stay with us for awhile. Maybe you don't have to go so far." coaxed Oma, holding her cousin's shoulder. "Things can't be that bad yet." she added, as though the words would will away the threat.

A shudder went through my aunt's plump frame, and she exclaimed, "God, no! We will try to go as far west as possible, and you should too, Julie." She paused to look at Gerle and me, and leaning in more closely, she whispered, "We hear the Russians are doing terrible things to the women." She nodded knowingly, acknowledging Oma's startled gasp. "Get Julie and the children out of here, Reinhard!" she said fiercely, turning her intense gaze on to my grandfather.

Oma whimpered slightly, put one hand over her mouth, and she grabbed Opa's hand with the other, clenching it so tightly, he winced.

My aunt continued, her words tumbling forth in a frenzied stream. "We had to leave most of our livestock, Julie. There wasn't time. Bombs were falling everywhere. Things were burning!… Oh, it was terrible!" She sobbed loudly, tears streaking her dusty face. "I just want to get away. The front is breaking up. Your orders will come any day now."

As if to emphasize her point, a Red Cross wagon lumbered noisily by, loaded with wounded German soldiers. Some had bloodied bandages circling their heads, others had shattered or missing limbs. All were pale and thin, their traumatized eyes vacant with pain and hopelessness.

I found myself inching closer to Gerle, where he stood sheltered beneath Opa's arm. I glanced into his face; it read like a mirror of all the fear and sense of foreboding that I felt at that moment.

Oma lunged forward suddenly to envelope her cousin in a tight hug and Opa urged us forward to do the same. After several minutes of awkward but heartfelt farewells, in which Oma tearfully promised her cousin that we would seek them out as soon as we headed west, we stepped away from the road and watched the cumbersome wagon squeeze its way into the never-ending caravan of despair.

"We will be ready when the orders come, Julie. I promise you we will not stay longer than is safe." said Opa, his arm clenching Oma's shaking shoulders as she leaned her head against his chest and wept. We watched the familiar faces blur into the sea of anonymity, then we turned sadly toward the house, each of us absorbed in thoughts of what was to come… or what had once been, but had been lost, perhaps forever.

That evening, as winter's last remnants penetrated deeper into the valley, the sky loomed crimson over the eastern mountain ridges, and continuous tremors, as deep and as rolling as thunder, could be heard echoing out of the darkness.

The next morning dawned cool and clear. An eerie silence hung over the city, as if it sat in anticipation of some expected visitor. There no longer were women walking to work in the factory, as all the owners, most of them Jewish, had been shipped out on the many trains that had halted only long enough to load them up. There no longer were stores for townspeople to frequent; all of main street lay boarded up or forgotten. There no longer was school to call the children forth each day into the streets; no children remained to attend.

Otti met us at the gate, his eyes wide with strain, as he told us, "We are going today. In a few minutes… just wanted to say good-bye." His voice cracked, and we reached across the void and held him in a quick three-way hug, each of our faces taking on an embarrassed tinge of pink.

"Take care, Otti. We'll see you back here when we return… when it's all over." I muttered. I raised my hand in a wave, then I dropped it suddenly to my side, I shuffling my feet uncertainly. Otti met my stare with a slight smile, and he shrugged.

Gerle voiced what we had all been thinking, "We will all come back won't we? This will all still be here… right? Right?" His dark eyes swept across the house and the garden, as though desperate to imprint every corner of it into his memory. He moved through the gate and reached his hand out to Otti, who grasped it tightly in his own and gave it a terse shake, before Gerle stepped back, his thin shoulders squared in a dogged attempt at stoicism.

"Well, we are off on an adventure, I guess. See you!" smiled Otti, his good-humour rarely suppressed for long, and he headed back toward his family, who were already waiting on the road.

"An adventure…" muttered Gerle, as he lifted the latch slowly on the gate and returned to my side. "… I wonder. Alfie, I have an idea. It shouldn't take us very long… and there would be plenty there for the taking." His words trailed off, but his thoughts were clearly racing on ahead. He glanced toward the house, where Oma and Opa were working in the kitchen and the cellar.

Oma had been frantic to pack all necessaries, and she had enlisted Uncle Alois to comb the vacant rooms upstairs for any personal items of my mother's and father's that she might want to include in the bundles which were mounting quickly near the door.

"Gerle, what's your idea? I don't understand. What do you want to do?" I demanded, testily, puzzled at Gerle's mood.

"Your mother has a bike, right?" he asked, his eyes still on the house. "Where is it?"

"It's in the shed. Why?… What's your plan, Gerle?"

"It can't be too far to Bratsch, can it? I was there once with my uncle. How long would it take us? Just think of the food we would find in your aunt's cellar, and she has loads of chickens, right? I didn't see them on the wagon. Did you?" Gerle's thoughts finally tumbled out, as though he could hold them back no longer. I simply stared, running his startling words through my mind again just to be sure I had heard him correctly.

"Are you kidding? Go back there? You heard what she was saying… the front…" Words failed me. I pictured the empty farm, nestled against the hillside as I remembered it, with dozens of fat chickens and the roosters… several of them, who ruled the coop. "I'll run in and get some bread and water." I said suddenly. "Give me a minute." I turned to go inside, but Gerle grabbed my arm.

"Don't tell them. Just say we are going to play at the fountain… or something." he insisted, his eyes burning with a fire I had never seen before. "I'll get the bike. Meet you at the back; we'll circle around."

I raced inside, my heart thumping against my chest, and I felt my palms bead with sweat, though the house was not very warm. Oma was in her room, packing some clothes and mumbling to herself. She barely raised her head from her work as I rushed to the door, muttering incoherently about lunch at the fountain and a soccer game in the field. She waved her hand from the depths of the closet and said only, "Be careful, Alfie. Don't go too far."

"Bye, Oma. We'll see you at dinner. I'm going." But, she didn't hear my answer; she was already humming and busily folding forgotten items, so I turned and left.

Gerle was waiting for me behind the tall branches of the lilac bush outside the gate. The bike was leaning against the fence, hidden from the house. I grabbed the handle bars, which were slightly rusty from age, and I eased the bike through the ruts in the path left from spring's first rains. We slowly traversed the back lane, the bike bumping beneath my hands as I pushed it before me. The rear tire was soft to the touch, though I felt it would hold enough air for the short journey.

"Why don't you climb up on back. I don't know if you can reach the pedals." I said, as we approached the main road.

"I can't. I tried it in the shed. By summer, I should be able to, though. Then you'll have to ride back here." answered Gerle, his face breaking into a shaky grin.

We set off, Gerle holding on to my sides as he teetered on the small luggage rack behind me. My own feet struggled to grip the distant pedals with my toes. From what we remembered, Gerle and I had determined that it could be no more than five kilometers to my aunt's farm. We noticed, only slightly concerned, that the road, which the day before had been crowded with refugees and soldiers, was now empty. But, I told myself, it was better than meeting the eyes of so many forlorn people.

Occasionally, we would pass an overturned cart, its wheel rims bent and twisted where it had been dragged from the road to clear the path. After several minutes of clumsy pedaling, we reached the outskirts of the first small village, and the smell hit us before we saw its origin. Over the desolate square hung plumes of smoke, the tendrils drifting like crooked fingers among the skeletal remains of the town. We wobbled slowly through the center, surrounded on both sides by smoldering ruins of houses and blackened trees and wagons.

My stomach lurched slightly as the repulsive smell pricked at my nostrils, and I could hear Gerle making gulping sounds behind me as he tried vainly to breath through his mouth. We cleared the town quickly; it was very small and nothing had hindered our progress. Suddenly, upon rounding a clump of trees, the source of the stench became apparent.

Gerle nearly upset the bike as he leaned to one side and retched into the dirt road. My throat tightened convulsively as I forced the bile downward in my effort to remain upright.

The bloated corpse of an old man was protruding from a small bomb crater; the bottom half of his body was missing. His lifeless face was frozen in a silent scream, recording the dreadful moment when his limbs had been wrenched apart and life wrestled from his grasp. I pressed my eyes shut, trusting to fate to guide me in a straight line as I shot past the horrific sight. But, when I opened them, I was met with similar scenes.

Blocking half the road lay two crumpled horses, their rigid bodies still harnessed to a broken wagon. I pedaled more quickly, trying desperately to escape from the nightmare we had unwittingly entered. I swerved recklessly through the maze of destruction, nearly colliding with an army jeep. Steam issued from its dented hood, over which two German soldiers were limply draped, their eyes glassy and cold.

"Should we turn around, Gerle?" I stuttered, wiping my pale lips on my sleeve, in an attempt to suppress the nauseous feeling creeping into my mouth.

"No!" Gerle said hastily. "It can't be far now, right? They've already been through here. There is nothing left... nothing. No one here to shoot at...." He coughed.

"... Except us." I thought, as I reluctantly forced my aching limbs to pedal onward. The back tire was creaking slightly as the air hissed slowly out of it, and the weight of Gerle, small as he was, put a drag on the rear of the bike, slowing me down.

The distended white belly of a dead cow glared up at me from a ditch, the warm sun reflecting off its smooth abdomen as if it were glass. I shook my head slightly in an effort to fend off the swirling feeling that was beginning to creep up my body, and I leaned forward, more eager than ever to reach our goal.

We followed the last small meadow bordering the path that lead to my aunt's farm and I had to stop for a rest. I needed to gather myself together for what we might find when we got there. We sat on a large rock near the road, careful to sit far away from the gruesome masses of bodies, some of which were already swarming with the spring's first flies.

"Look at that." exclaimed Gerle, pointing through the immature leaves to the crest of the hill. What stood there had once been a landmark I looked for whenever we had visited my aunt's farm. It was a windmill, so large that the blades seemed to slice the sky as they moved languidly in a circle. The dramatic wooden structure had always evoked images of Hans Brinker and his skates, and it had made me dream of the land of tulips and dikes.

I raised my aching neck off my bent knees and peered after Gerle's finger. A nightmare had replaced my dream. The windmill's huge wooden spokes were shooting yellow and orange flames into the pale sky, as the heavy wood filled with sparks, the wind spreading them quickly.

"We better finish this. Let's go." I said, groaning as I got to my feet. We started off again, the flames from the windmill now audibly crackling behind us. We eased the weary bike into the narrow lane that ran between some thin evergreens as it curved upward toward the farm.

A deep drone, persistent as a mosquito, yet infinitely more terrifying, reached us through the sparse trees. Gerle and I simultaneously leapt from the bike, sending its rickety pedals spinning.

We dropped behind a tree and huddled tightly against its pungent sharp needles. The plane roared closer and the sound filled my head with the images seen along the road. I closed my eyes in an effort to rid my mind of the horrors.

Slowly opening them, I noticed Gerle was pulling back a branch of a delicate balsam tree behind him. We peered anxiously through the narrow gap to the dark shape slowly zigzagging toward us against the sky. Suddenly, sparks blasted from the wings of the plane and we realized, with panic sending waves of adrenaline through our static limbs, that it was firing at a spot not much further along the road from where we had veered off.

There was an audible gulp from Gerle, as he wet his lips and whispered, "Do you think it saw us? God, Alfie... we were on that road!"

I shook my head, too stunned to speak, and I squeezed myself further into the branches, heedless of the prodding needles. After several moments, which seemed to last an eternity, we watched the plane bank quickly to the right and turn, before it finally rose steeply into the sky and disappeared over the distant ridge to the east.

We waited, neither of us ready to raise his head into the open... until we realized we couldn't linger... the plane could return at any moment.

My mouth had gone dry. Sweat was pouring off my forehead, giving me a chill, as a sudden breeze whipped through the trees. We pushed the bike toward the farm, which revealed itself immediately around the next bend. The yard would have been tidy, but for the fragments of roof shingles that were scattered among the fresh shoots of grass. The wooden fence in front of the house lay toppled and askew, begrudgingly relinquishing its guard on the haven within.

A creaking met our ears, and I jumped, grabbing Gerle's arm, before I realized the sound had come from the shutters, most of which were hanging lopsided on their hinges.

"Wow. It looks awful." said Gerle, wrinkling his nose. "… But, it doesn't seem to have been hit."

"I know. Strange…." I replied, puzzled. A shrill whistle of mortar fire interrupted our words, and the resulting impact shook the ground. Another shutter tipped noisily off its remaining hinges and clattered to the ground. One mystery explained.

"That was close… Quick! Hide!" I hissed, and I pushed Gerle down onto the damp ground, allowing the bike to topple sideways again in my haste to follow him. There was a loud roar as a jeep being driven at full throttle thundered along the road, just visible through the thin trees. The German soldiers, their Nazi flag whipping frantically in the wind, were too preoccupied by the persistent rumbling behind them to take any notice of our trembling bodies as we tried to flatten ourselves behind several shriveled bushes.

One soldier seated in the back of the jeep turned toward the rear and raised an enormous bazooka over his strong shoulder. He fired. We covered our heads with our hands, burying our noses into the moist soil, which was slightly crusted with old snow. The ground shook again as the shot landed, but the jeep hurtled on westward toward our town.

"We better hurry. That was close!" I groaned, rubbing black clumps of earth from my nose. I stood up and gestured toward the barn, which was half hidden behind the house. "Come on. Let's see what's left in there."

Gerle followed, brushing dead leaves and twigs from his clothes, and peering nervously over his shoulder back towards the road. As we rounded the corner of the house we were startled by a sudden blur of movement at our feet. Chuckling nervously at our own skittishness, we followed the hen into the barnyard.

Several more fat chickens ambled complacently about the yard, pecking carelessly at unseen morsels in the dirt. None of them seemed concerned by the ominous rumbles that were slowly encompassing the valley; the war was merely passing them by. A goat and two cows peered out at us from the stable doors and we threw them some hay, their bins long since empty.

"Should we open the doors… so they can get out?" asked Gerle, his hand on the latch, as he glanced in my direction.

"I don't think so. What if my aunt comes back in a few days and they are gone. I don't know." I answered, raising my hand to his.

Gerle persisted, not removing his hand, and said, "They'll die in there before they might return. We can't leave them."

"… Ok." I said, after a long pause during which the cow's soft muzzle rubbed against my extended hand, as if to reinforce Gerle's plea. "… Ok."

Gerle opened the door and nudged the three animals out, then propped the door open with a rock. "It's still cold at night. They might need shelter." he insisted, seeing my surprised face. The goat seemed pleased at his new freedom, but the cows returned to the cozy sanctuary of their stall and continued to chew their cud, their large brown eyes looking at us with enviable indifference.

We turned our attention to the barn. It stood next to the remnants of a feed bin, which was still smoldering from being hit by some stray fire. The rancid blue smoke stung our eyes and filled our noses as we crossed the yard to the large barn doors. I reached to lift the heavy lever barring the door, but Gerle grabbed my arm and pointed, "Look at him! I haven't seen that fine a bird in a long time!" A large rooster strutted across the muddy barnyard, his sleek auburn feathers glistening as he pulsed his large chest forward and cocked his noble head high and low.

"Let's get him!" I cried. "He'll make a feast!" My mouth began to water as I imagined the many delicious meals Oma could stretch out of one succulent chicken. We trotted after the rooster, his long tail feathers flitting tantalizingly out of reach as he headed through a small opening in the barn door. I heard the gurgles and clucks of many hens as they greeted their mate, so I grabbed a large stone and jammed it tightly against the hole.

Gerle, already keen to my plan, added several more rocks until the opening was completely sealed. We returned to the large doors and eased them open slightly, allowing just enough room to squeeze in; we did not want to allow our prize rooster a means of escape.

The barn smelled sweet and dry. The hay was piled deeply around us and flies buzzed thickly, almost muffling the distant sounds of the raging battle. We inched slowly forward, giving our eyes a chance to adjust to the dim light filtering into the vast interior. Several chickens scratched aimlessly at the hard dirt floor; others ruffled noisily in the mounds of hay around us.

The shrill whine of a shell hissed over the barn, making the hairs on the back of my neck bristle in fear. The reverberating impact of the bombs came from the west, meaning we would have to pass whatever had been hit on our way home. My mouth watered again, this time with returned nausea as I remembered the appalling smells and the horrific sights of the morning. I began to think, perhaps, that we had entered into more of an adventure than we had bargained for. Gerle shuffled nervously in the straw, his eyes wide and terrified in the subdued light.

"That was close, Alfie." Gerle said, as he ran his hands through his hair. He began peering around eagerly for the rooster. "Let's get him and get out of here!"

We tiptoed carefully around the cluttered barn, peering into the dark corners for signs of our prey.

"There he is!" I yelled, dashing after the streaking red tail as the great rooster ran nimbly past me and under a large hay wagon. Gerle crawled quickly and deftly after him, but he emerged on the other side empty-handed and cursing. Feathers and dust danced everywhere, making my nose twitch and my eyes water.

"He's up there now!" Gerle called from across the wagon and we both scrambled up the piles of hay, which teetered precariously with the unexpected activity. But when we reached the high hayloft, the rooster tricked us again and fluttered back down to the dirt, cackling insolently at our nerve.

"He's getting away!" I cried, watching the rooster's dark shape disappear through a previously hidden crack in the barn wall. "Come on!" I insisted to Gerle. He followed me, both of us slithering down the heaps of hay like a slide. I reached the large back doors, which were wide enough to allow the big hay wagon easy berth.

As I tried to raise the heavy wooden board where it hung at eye-level across the massive iron brackets, another discharge of mortar fire sent us cowering—this time it had been closer.

Amidst the noise and chaos, we had lost our prize. The rooster had fled to the brambles and branches of an old hedgerow, so we turned our attention to the hens still scouring the bare yard for feed.

"Let's just finish this. I want to get out of here. Try that one, Alfie." said Gerle, in a voice laced with anxiety.

I turned my head to where Gerle pointed, saying, "What?... Oh, yeah, that one... ok. But, look, Gerle." It was my turn to point. Across the narrow valley rose puffs of dark smoke, drifting in sinuous arcs above several green tanks, their long guns swiveling slowly to and fro in search of a target. Every few seconds thunder would erupt from the barrels and more billows of acrid smoke would join in the swirl of clouds above. The rumbles echoed off the hillsides and rattled what was left of the windows on the house.

"Are those... ours?" asked Gerle.

I shook my head. "I don't think so. Let's get that chicken and get out of here. Now!" I dove at the nearest hen, stifling its squawk with a tight squeeze. I handed the squirming chicken to Gerle, who held it close to his body as he averted his head, pinching his eyes closed.

"Ready? It's ok, Gerle, I've done this before for Oma. It's ok." I urged, as I took the thin sinewy neck in my hand and twisted. The cackles ceased, though the tremors in the hen's limbs continued for several seconds as death seeped in slowly. Gerle dropped the motionless hen into the empty pocket of the rucksack, as I ran, back bent, after another fleeing pair.

We caught two more, and I made fast work of trundling them into the rucksack; my nerves were now racing with fear. The tanks were closer, and their sights would eventually land on us, as they slowly bounced and rolled their way across the landscape toward what was left of the village... and us.

"That's enough, Gerle. We have to leave. You take the bag!" I said. I flung him the rucksack, which was now dripping with the blood of the last chicken, whose neck I had completely severed in my haste.

I grabbed the bike, still lying by the bushes where we had left it. The tire was completely flat. The rim creaked in protest at the exertion, but I pedaled furiously down the short lane and through the village, barely aware of the carnage that enveloped us on both sides, though the smell had intensified with the midday heat.

107

Upon leaving the smoldering village behind, the road began to slope slightly downward, which eased the strain on the tire. But, the increased speed made it difficult to avoid the large craters that had appeared in the road—new since we had first set out.

"Isn't that the jeep we saw earlier?" shouted Gerle, pointing to an overturned vehicle in the ditch. Four dead soldiers lay sprawled across the remnants of the big gun that we had seen one of them using. The young soldier's stiff hands were still clamped tightly around the barrel, as if willing it to avenge his death.

I raced on, my shins cramping with the effort of reaching the pedals. Finally, the bridge loomed in the distance, and I skidded into the small lane along the fence, dropping the useless bike at the gate. I doubled up with exhaustion, my breath coming in great gasps, before I heard Gerle saying, "Alfie… something is wrong here. It is too quiet. Listen!" I raised my head from my knees and held my breath. I strained my ears for any sound of activity… but, beyond my labored breaths there was nothing but the soft wind stirring the budding branches along the river, and the distant rumble of the advancing Russian tanks.

"They must be inside." I said, trying to sound confident, though my insides had turned to ice as the unthinkable crossed my mind. We wandered into the house. Not a sound could be heard except for the ticking of the old grandfather clock.

"Oma, we're back! Opa? …. Uncle Alo…!" I yelled. "What am I doing? Uncle Alois can't hear me." I thought, my insides taking another tumble, as the sweat burst forth on my forehead. "Oma? Where are you?"

Gerle wandered into the kitchen, and I headed for the upstairs, hoping they were merely out of earshot. I mounted the stairs slowly, though I heard no creaking floor boards or muffled voices above me, and I knew in my heart I would find no one.

"Alfie! Come here! Oh, my God… come here!" came Gerle's frantic yells, his voice shrill and high with panic. I bolted into the kitchen and found Gerle standing by the table holding a small slip of paper toward me, his eyes filling with tears. His lip trembled, and he brushed the back of his dirty and blood-encrusted hand across his shadowed eyes, saying, "Oh, my God, Alfie… they've gone!"

I grabbed the paper from Gerle, my eyes widening with shock. The room began to swirl around me, the panic rising uncontrollably through my tired body.

On the torn paper were the hastily scrawled words:

"We were ordered by the armed forces to evacuate at once. We tried to wait for you, but they wouldn't let us. We are worried sick about you. Where are you? We will try to locate you. Get out of town, boys. It is not safe. They are coming! There is a little money under our mattress—take it. Stay safe! Love you and God Bless! Oma and Opa."

I let the note flutter slowly to the floor, and turning to Gerle, I grabbed him in a tight hug, and we wept bitterly for what we had lost, knowing we only had each other... brothers, now, in the truest sense of the word.

CHAPTER 10

The rest of the day was a blur of tantalizingly familiar sights of security: the leisurely flowing clear water of the river, the sounds of our ducks along the banks. The riverside was now thick with fresh green moss, cradling the newborn ducklings in softness. The day lengthened, enhancing the play of the bright afternoon sun on the tall church steeples throughout the city, the bells silenced with the absence of their ringers.

All these reminders of normalcy were tainted devilishly by the twisting fear and despair gripping our hearts. Tears fell unhindered as we longed for the return of the guardians of our uncertain futures. We had been so confident that Oma and Opa would help us forge a path through all life's troubles.

The stillness in the house seemed to smother us, the sounds of distant explosions only accentuating our isolation. Fear of being found led us to remain huddled in the kitchen, moving only to sneak to the washroom when nature called.

"We must not be seen, Gerle." I said earnestly, several hours later. We were rummaging through the cupboards for bread and cheese, though neither of us felt too hungry.

"What should we do, Alfie? Should we try to follow or stay put?" asked Gerle, his forehead furrowed with concern.

"I think it will be easier for Opa and Oma to find us if we stay here… though we have to make sure no one else finds us first." I answered, nerves tingling again with the memories of the morning. "But, let's do something about those chickens… we didn't go through all that for nothing."

Our rucksack had remained in a heap under the kitchen table where Gerle had dropped it upon discovery of the note. A small pool of dried blood circled it, and the carcasses dripped heavy clots as we removed them from the stained sack.

"Go get some water, Gerle." I said, as I carried the two limp birds to the sink. "I'll start plucking them. We need to wash this rucksack... we may still need it." Gerle grabbed the familiar bucket from beneath the sink and headed for the door. Startled at our own carelessness, I yelled after him, "Gerle, be quick and stay low. We don't want to be seen!"

I watched Gerle's hunched shoulders pause, his hand resting on the doorknob. He replied, "Believe me, I don't have to be reminded." He took a deep breath, as if fortifying his nerves, then he opened the door slowly. He glanced out carefully, and crouching with the bucket against his chest, he ran out the door, leaving it open for a quick return with the heavy water.

Returning to the sink where I began to pluck the hens, I realized how bloody and filthy I still was. "We will need more water." I said to myself, and I started to rip golden feathers from the first bird. Gerle's ragged breath became louder as he returned hastily with the heavy bucket sloshing against his stained pants.

"Here, you do the next one. That is not fun! Now that I know what might be out there—it's creepy!" he groaned. He brought the bucket to the sink and I helped him ease it into place next to the growing mound of feathers. "How are we going to cook the chickens?" he asked, rubbing his wet, but still dirty hands on his shirt... we were both painfully aware Oma was not there to reprimand him.

"We better not have a fire in the daylight... and only as small as we can manage when its dark, I guess. No one is supposed to be here, remember..." I said. "No one." The smoke from any of the houses could prove deadly, and we were eager to remain unseen. I continued, "Let's check out what Oma has in the cellar and the attic. We need to know how much food we have, then we will know how long we can last... as long as we keep hidden, Gerle... that's the main thing."

"I know, Alfie, I know... I saw those things today, too, you know! Now, let's get busy." replied Gerle, gruffly.

We left the chickens to drain in the sink and opened the cellar door. As we stood staring into the shadows, now containing nothing more ominous than potatoes and turnips, I remembered all too well the many distant hours passed below when the terrifying sound of the planes overhead first ripped through our dreams.

Now, no one was here to sound an alarm... there was nothing to warn us of what might be coming. In the morning we had seen what had happened to the unfortunate people who hadn't had a chance to see what terror was lurking to the east. We knew a bit of what they had not known, nonetheless, a feeling of helplessness swarmed through my body, and I grabbed the door for support.

After a quick inspection of Oma's ample stores of food, we headed toward the stairs and the attic in the eaves. Passing my mother's and father's room, I hesitated for a moment, my mind briefly picturing my sweet sister's tearstained face as she waved goodbye to me. And I remembered, too, the sullen formal farewell my mother had reserved for me. A sudden wave of hollow guilt flowed over me as I realized that I missed my grandparents more than I did my own mother.

"Come on, Alfie. It's almost night. I want to look out the window before it gets too dark." muttered Gerle, gently, obviously sensing the subtle disturbance in my mood. He placed his hand on my arm, and I followed him up the creaking stairs to the attic, where small narrow shelves were piled with jars of marmalades and sacks of dried fruits.

We slowly folded back an inch of the thick blanket covering the small dusty window and peered out into the gathering shadows. The sun was now low over the glistening river. All seemed calm and normal... except for the rows of Russian tanks waiting in an undulating line along the hillside to the east, laid out in neat rows such as a child might make with his toys.

To the west, just visible from our position at the window, we noticed a cluster of activity that we hoped came from the Germans; we were not ready to believe we were utterly abandoned. Aware suddenly of the significance of the positions of the two opposing forces, with us in the middle, I shivered. With icy panic rising through my body, I realized for the first time the gravity of our situation... we were alone in "no man's land", between two massive armies.

The first night passed without much event, though the sadness and loneliness filled the void of darkness like a heavy block of ice sitting on my heart. Terrible sounds echoed over the valley and a red glow of fire rimmed the black curtain covering the window, as the valley erupted in a constant hail of gunfire. We had cooked the fat birds slowly over a tiny fire, determined not to focus anyone's aim on our house.

We slept late, exhausted from the previous day's experiences and worn out from a sleepless night. In the deep shadows of night, the house had felt as though it were filled with every horror we could imagine. Creaks and groans of the walls and the trees—once normal sounds—had been transformed in our distressed minds into something unidentifiable, yet unmistakably evil.

"What about the animals?" asked Gerle the next morning at a breakfast consisting of spoonfuls of marmalade. "Do you think Oma and Opa took any of them? Should we go look? It would be nice to get some milk."

"Well, I guess we can sneak out there after this. We need some water anyway." I replied, yawning widely, and stretching my still filthy hands above my head. "I could do with a wash. No offense... but you could too." I managed, grinning, before another yawn swallowed my words.

"Wait until we tell Otti and Gunter and the gang." giggled Gerle, purple marmalade dribbling down his chin. "They won't believe it. This is just like camping... well, almost. I guess more like cowboys hiding from cattle rustlers."

A loud whine hissed across the valley at that moment, followed on its heels by a tremendous explosion. The house shook. Clattering sounds could be heard from overhead, as some part of the roof succumbed to the unwelcome attention.

Gerle's mouth hung open, his spoon still deep in the jar of blackberry jam. His wide eyes traveled to the ceiling, as if expecting it to fall at any moment.

I felt equally unsure of what the situation was, but I stood up and headed for the stairs, saying hoarsely, "Come on. Let's go up and see what happened."

Gerle grabbed my arm as we reached the door, and with a voice broken with anxiety said, "You don't think it's burning, do you? Like the windmill?"

"Only one way to be sure. We can't just sit here and not know." I replied, squaring my shoulders and dashing to the stairs, before I lost my nerve.

We inched our way toward the attic door, and I placed my ear against the rough wooden surface, grateful for its cool touch, and I listened. "I don't hear anything. I think it's all right." I whispered. I slowly turned the knob. Warm spring light of a morning well along met our eyes as we pushed the door carefully ajar. It caught and jolted against some obstruction, so I peeked around and noticed a narrow shelf had fallen against the door. I glanced up and saw the sky, visible as scattered vignettes across the pocketed roof.

"The roof must have been hit by parts of the bomb. There is no fire." I told Gerle, as I pushed and squeezed my way through the small gap. "Look! Here are some pieces of it, I think." I said, holding up several twisted shards of metal.

"We can see more now, Alfie, though I guess we better stay low so no one sees us." said Gerle, crouching down and crossing to one of the larger holes open to the sky. "I wonder who holds the rail lines." he muttered, peering westward towards the disappearing tracks.

"You wait here, Alfie. I'm going to go out and look around." Gerle said suddenly. "There is stuff lying in the yard. I want to know what it is."

"Are you crazy, Gerle?" I gasped. "Look at what they did to our house when they weren't aiming at it!"

"Oh, it's no worse than getting the water yesterday… besides I have to pee." he answered briskly, brushing past me in his haste to get downstairs. "You keep a look out."

The Germans, we guessed, still held the western side of the river, as firing erupted from there toward the east whenever heavy tank activity could be seen on the far hillside.

As I waited anxiously for Gerle to return, I scanned the distant hills trying to see where the hidden enemies swarmed. A slight movement caught my eye near the road, and an instant burst of gunfire chased the form. It was a bedraggled and terrified dog. It ran, tail tightly coiled between its legs, under a bush and to temporary safety.

My heart began to pound as I envisioned Gerle creeping around low to the ground just like the unfortunate dog, and I headed for the stairs, desperate to retrieve my friend. A pounding of feet echoed up the stairwell, and I leaned against the wall into the shadow, suddenly afraid of who it might be. Then, I heard the frantic whispers of Gerle's welcome voice. "Alfie! Alfie! Are you still up there? Did you see that? They tried to shoot that dog… A dog, Alfie!"

Gerle burst through the door, his face bathed in sweat and dust, his eyes wide with anxiety. In his arms he carried several metal objects, one of which he handed to me, saying, "Here! Binoculars—just lying there by the road, and they are not broken. They must have dropped from some jeep." I grabbed the heavy green binoculars and stared in disbelief at what else Gerle had to present.

"Is that a....?" I murmured, breathlessly. "... A bazooka?"

Gerle nodded. "The boys will never believe this one!", he cried, his lips twitching into an unsteady grin, as he held it up for me to see.

"I don't know if we should have that here, Gerle... What if it goes off?"

"Oh, it won't, Alfie. Besides there were many more; no one will miss this one. There is an overturned supply truck down there, right next to the bridge. We should go back tomorrow." he said, thrusting his treasure into a rubble-filled corner.

We spent the day in the attic, marveling at our position in the middle of the chaos that swarmed around us. Several times we heard German jeep patrols rumble by on the otherwise deserted strip of road, which now resembled a military junkyard. We were forced to the cellar twice when the Russian tanks shelled very close to the house, and the attic began to feel exposed with the sunlight streaming in through the ragged openings in the roof.

The shafts of sunlight, too pure in their juxtaposition to the sights spread out below us, lit the dust, which drifted in eddies and swirls as it was caught in the gusts of wind created by the blasts of artillery nearby. The whole world seemed to be at once stagnant and alive, as if teetering on the brink of a shrouded precipice. We felt as if we were waiting for something... something yet unknown to the world. We knew we were somewhere we didn't belong... we were having our adventure.

The enemy was near, almost upon us, and my mind landed upon, of all things, Oma's beautiful china neatly displayed in a carved cabinet in the front room. A sudden anger engulfed me, and I ran from the attic, determined to leave nothing of value for the Russians to pillage.

"What are you doing?" Gerle yelled, following closely, as I leapt down the stairs three at a time.

"I'll be damned if they get a thing out of this house!" I cried, tearing open the glass door of the cupboard. I paused, breathing deeply. I stared at Gerle, my eyes gleaming with reckless emotion. "They will not get Oma's things. Not if I can help it!"

Gerle's eyes widened with shock as he watched me reach into the tidy cupboard and extract one of Oma's favorite bone china cups. I fingered it gently, remembering many shared conversations with Oma over fragrant tea, then I grasped it tightly, and hurled it against the opposite wall.

"Yes!" Gerle cried, suddenly caught up in the mood. He crouched, peering about the room, and his eyes landed on the crystal chandelier swaying gently on the ceiling. He grinned at me, and clambering onto a chair, he leapt wildly toward the light, grasping its delicate flutes with his outstretched hands. He crashed to the floor, pulling the entire light, as well as a thick layer of dust, with him.

Angry, defiant adrenaline flooded my veins, and I proceeded to empty Oma's china cupboard. Soon, there was a scattered heap of cups, mingling dangerously with broken slivers of crystal and clumps of ceiling plaster.

After our bold show of emotion, we stumbled into the kitchen, laughing nervously, amazed at our own nerve. We wandered about looking for food for several minutes, the stress ebbing slowly away. Our sparse lunch was interrupted by the threatening drone of a Russian fighter plane as it roared toward us from the east, and before we had reached the cellar door, it had begun bombarding the rooftops at random. The thick earth walls did little to muffle the loud sounds of impact, as machine gun fire and small shells pierced the houses along our street, ours included.

We huddled in the corner of the cellar furthest from the stairs, our heads buried in our arms, clenching our teeth in fear. The roars of the engine shook the house, sending new clouds of dust to dance in the attic among the rays of sunlight, increasing with every new hole.

An eerie silence followed, and my mind jumped to the dog, wondering if he had found a way to survive, or if he had succumbed to the madness now enveloping our city.

"Do you think we can go back up, Alfie?" Gerle asked, raising his dusty head from his bent knees and staring at me through the darkness. Before I could answer, new gunfire could be heard, this time from the west;

the Germans were firing back, though the aircraft had already disappeared into the next valley.

That day and several others passed in a similar fashion. We felt bravest in the morning, trusting that the beautiful sunlight of spring could not be blasted out of existence like all else had been. We foraged carefully along the road, always with ears cocked at the first sign of trouble, and we would crawl along the fence on our bellies, convinced we were invisible. Fence planks could be easily pried loose, and we traversed several yards in this fashion, hunting through gardens for spring's first vegetables and berries.

The nights were gladly left behind each morning, as the hours of darkness seemed to amplify all sounds of the battle, which raged now continuously. Unable to sleep, my mind drifted to all those we had lost: my grandparents, my mother and sister, our friends—would we ever see any of them again... would we ever see anyone at all? The tears welled in my eyes, my throat tightened until it hurt, but I knew I couldn't allow the tears to flow. I would not be able to contain the flood. Instead, I forced my mind into a shadowed calm, and I willed the anguish in my heart into a painful dormancy, and finally a shallow sleep followed.

As we waited for something to happen, so too, it seemed, did the opposing armies. The railroad siding, which many months before had held the train cars where the Jews had cried and begged for mercy, now was lined with dozens of spotless and unused "Tiger Panzer" tanks. Several German guards patrolled them on occasion, yet none were moved, as they apparently lacked fuel, a commodity much in demand.

One morning, while dawn was barely toying with the day, we lounged in our beds, reluctant to allow the ominous sounds of troop activity in the town to invade our dreams. My visions of a glorious summer sun dancing on the river were suddenly interrupted by a tremendous crash at the door.

"What! Wha... Alfie!" yelled Gerle, his voice laced with fear. Three dark figures loomed in the doorway, the silhouettes of long rifles aimed at our heads.

"Hands up!" roared an angry voice.

The figures began to take on the shape of German soldiers as our eyes adjusted to the sudden light in the room. Gerle and I flung our hands in the air, though every fiber of my being longed to dive beneath the thick covers and shut out whatever might be coming.

"What the hell are you doing here?" barked the first soldier, his vivid blue eyes wide with fury. He jabbed his rifle eagerly forward, clearly accustomed to firing first. A slight whimper rose from Gerle, who was returning the soldier's intense stare with a terrified one of his own. The two other soldiers left the room and could be heard storming about the house, checking for other inhabitants.

I ran my tongue over my suddenly parched lips and muttered, "We, uh, we got left behind…" I glanced into his livid face, surprised that he was very young. He had blond hair and a face still scarred with pimples. I continued, "We got left behind when our family left… we live here." I shivered suddenly, as another wave of fear swept over me upon realizing that I might very well die in my own bed.

"Ach, let them alone. They are just boys. Put that gun away, Tomas. Look at them… they'll wet themselves!" chortled the second soldier, who had returned and was now leaning on the door frame, holding a jar of Oma's blackberry preserves. With his gun tucked awkwardly under his arm, he grunted slightly, finally opening the lid and its wax ring with a slight pop. He continued, grinning obscenely, between slurped mouthfuls of the sticky jam, "You two need to come with us. This is no place for kids… or for anyone else, in fact."

We sat, stunned, glancing from the soldiers to each other, unsure of what to do. "Hurry up! We don't have all day, boys. There's a war on… better that we found you than the Russians. They would not have been so easy on you. Get your things, so we can get out of here. Now!" he continued, his jovial demeanor rapidly vanishing. I jumped out of bed, unconvinced that I had to leave the only home I had ever known. I could see a similar uncertainty in Gerle's eyes, which continued to travel ceaselessly from face to face, yearning for an answer, a guarantee that all would be well.

I pulled my rumpled clothes on over my thin pajamas, aware in the back of my mind that I might be grateful for them later. Gerle, who had scampered into the kitchen, returned with the rucksack, which was now finally dry, although still slightly stained with dried russet blood.

"I've put in some apples from the cellar and some of the last bread. Should we take anything else, Alfie?" Gerle whispered, glancing about him nervously. Although the soldiers were clearly aware of the relative wealth of food in the house, Gerle seemed reluctant to betray the fruits of Oma's and Opa's labors to the strangers.

"Grab a jar of preserves. Maybe we can trade it for something." I answered, as I watched the soldiers rummage eagerly through Oma's tidy cupboards, tipping jars and scattering linens in their hunt for something edible. I bit back a surge of anger, reminding myself that these men were not the enemy.

"Come on! Let's go." said the smooth-faced soldier, his face red with rising impatience. "You've held us up long enough." He flung the door open and strode out, his rifle aimed menacingly before him. "All this trouble for a couple of kids. What were they thinking?" his loud voice grumbled from outside. I strode slowly after him, pausing for a last glance behind me at the door.

Several cupboard doors were creaking loudly on bent hinges, and the sun was now shining in on the heaps of shattered china we had left in the sitting room. I shook my head sadly.

"Come on, Alfie. We better go. Let's grab the bike." Gerle whispered at my shoulder, and I backed reluctantly out the door, closing in firmly behind me. That seemed important to me suddenly, to shut the door properly just as Oma and Opa had left it.

"We won't cross at the bridge. Come this way. Follow closely, boys." said the second soldier. He was a broad shouldered man with black hair already receding across his forehead. "How long were you boys there alone?" he asked, good-naturedly. The young blond soldier grunted slightly as he brushed past us, apparently disapproving of his comrade's friendliness towards us.

"We spent about four or five days, I guess." muttered Gerle, as he moved away from the grumpy soldier with his eager gun, and closer to the friendly one. "I've lost track of time a little." he continued, sheepishly.

Spread out before us was the river, enveloped in an early morning fog, making the gurgles and murmurs of the clear water more distant and unclear. My shoes were already wet from the thick dew coating the sweet smelling grass as we splashed through the cold water. It was running high with the spring run-off from the snow in the mountains. The bike creaked and wobbled as I pushed it along next to me, and I received several sideways glances from the three men.

"Are you sure you want to bring that thing? It's seems pretty useless." sniggered the third soldier, who had been quietly watching until this time.

"It's all we have, and we, uh… we've used it before." I answered, my voice faltering as I struggled up the sodden bank with the bike wobbling more than ever.

"Suit yourself. But better not let it slow you down." he replied. He wandered slightly ahead, his hand gripping his rifle more tightly. "The fools will be wanting to drag their entire house next time." he muttered, shaking his head.

They led us quietly through some bushes and across the narrow meadow for about three hundred meters until we emerged in a small clearing which butted up to the raised plateau of the railroad. Several long but shallow trenches dropped away before us, each piled high on three sides with brown sand bags. The existing bluff on which the rails ran created an added defense, making the digging of trenches a less tedious affair. Only a handful of men were in the bunker. Some were relaxing in a manner of repose only those used to harsh conditions could enjoy. Others were fingering long rows of machine gun clips, sorting them and stowing them in metal boxes, dozens of which were piled high against the tall sand bags.

As we approached the bunker, I eased my rickety bike down to the ground, not wanting to let it clatter into the eerie stillness surrounding the soldiers as they stared up at us in disbelief.

"What the hell are those kids doing here? Get them out of here!" snarled a dirty-looking officer glaring from behind the sand bags. "What do you think you kids were doing over there? That's just shy of the Russian side now… are you crazy?" he cried, his eyes wide.

"We didn't know, …. uh, sir. We were left behind when our grandparents left. That was our house we were in." I stammered in response. After a pause, I continued, "Are the Russians really in the town, sir?"

"Yes they are—parts of it at least, and they will be here soon too, I think." His gaze turned to the soldiers filing in around us and he added, "We are heading west tomorrow. Orders came in while you were gone, men. We need to get these two out of here then, too." He glanced at us. "You understand, boys? You can't stay here."

Gerle nodded fervently, and after another look toward my house and the rows of tanks in the distance, just visible through the fog still draped over the deserted city, I nodded too.

"Here, boys." said the older soldier. He thrust some small tin cups and a couple crusts of stale bread towards us. "You can't live forever on your Mama's jam—though, it was good." he continued, smiling kindly. "Real army rations for you, boys. Then, you can help us get some of these boxes moved." he muttered, his mouth full of bread.

Gerle and I took the food: thin soup with several scraps of vegetables floating in it, and the bread, and picking a corner not already claimed by the soldiers, we ate in silence. The men soon forgot our presence, as the demands of the retreat—for that was what it was—occupied their full attention.

"What would the boys say now, eh, Alfie? We are getting more of an adventure than we bargained for." whispered Gerle, his face hovering above his cup. The shakiness in his voice betrayed his brave words, and I sighed in relief... not for the first time, for having my friend near.

We hovered in the corner for several hours, whispering quietly between ourselves, until the officer beckoned us towards him with a hasty flick of his finger. We glanced quickly at each other, then rose slowly, our limbs stiff from being cramped beneath us. We weaved our way through the crowd of soldiers to his side.

"See those boxes there... the ones behind you." he said, pointing. "Those are the ones we need you to move. All along there..." He gestured with his other hand toward the opposite end of the trench where a sand bag covered tunnel led to the next trench. "... until you get to the last trench. Stack them against the far wall. That's where the machine gun positions are. Ok? If you do it well, there will be another meal in it for you." he said, matter-of-factly. Then, he moved on, already delegating other tasks to the men around him. We stared at the pile of boxes destined to provide us with several hours of unwelcome activity.

"It's like being back in the brick yard." I muttered, angrily, kicking the sand beneath my dusty shoes.

"Yeah, but this time the guns are closer." replied Gerle, with a grimace, as he hoisted the first box. "Whoa! This is heavy. Did he say all of them? This will take us all day." he groaned, twisting awkwardly in the cramped space and staggering toward the tunnel at the far end.

I followed soon after, grateful for my small stature. I was glad not to have to stoop to clear the ceiling as I lugged the large metal box, loaded with newly sorted machine gun clips, through the tunnel.

Hours later we slumped against the cool sandy wall of the bunker, our faces drenched in sweat, and our clothes covered in dust and grass.

"Here boys. Good job!" said our soldier friend, handing us a canteen and a green cloth bundle. "Here's some water… and some more bread. We have a little bacon, but it's only supposed to be for the officers. But, since you are kids, there's some for you, too. It's only a little, mind you, and there's no more where that came from, but… anyway. Then, try to get some sleep. You need to leave with the rest of us in the morning. We will point you in the right direction, then you better get moving as quickly as you can… head west. Ok?"

Gerle and I nodded dumbly, too tired to speak, and too eager to eat our sparse rations; my stomach rumbled noisily. We tore the bread into two pieces, both of which were small, and we pulled from the cloth the chunk of dried bacon. After several attempts, I managed to tear it into fairly equal parts, and giving one to Gerle, I began to gnaw my half. We guzzled the water gratefully, aware all the while that the salty bacon would only make us crave more.

With the night came more loud shelling and bombardments of the town. The noise that had reached a plateau during the day intensified as the cover of darkness encouraged the Russians to increase their activity. Gerle and I no longer had the blanket-covered windows to give us a sense of security from the chaos. The sky was lit with an alarming array of colors. Closing our eyes did little to keep out the flashes of light, which left threatening black shadows looming on the insides of our eyelids.

We huddled together in our corner, taking turns using our rucksack as a pillow behind our backs. The mild spring breeze toyed with our hair, mocking our pathetic attempts at sleep. Around us in the trench the sounds of a war still raging decreased our chances of easing into a state of calm, meaning we woke before dawn with stiff backs and necks and droopy eyes.

Several hours later, a loud commotion through the tunnels set everyone stirring. An uniformed officer, his clothes yet unsoiled, strode into the bunker, surveying the men like items in a store window, laid out for inspection and criticism. The soldiers stood silently to one side, none of them anxious to approach the lieutenant, a tall thin man with piercing gray eyes.

Those eyes traveled along the faces of the men, assessing them to their very souls. Then, they crept slowly over to rest on us in the corner, where we were trying to blend into the sandy wall.

"Who was the idiot who invited children into this bunker?!" he roared, spit flicking into the face of the nearest soldier, who responded with nothing more than a blink.

"Sir, they were found in the town... in a deserted house... their own house. Somehow... they were left behind." replied the officer, now eyeing us with renewed curiosity, as he tried to puzzle out why we had been not been able to evacuate with the rest of our family. Gerle muttered something under his breath, clearly realizing at the same moment as I, that the lieutenant might not look too kindly on our foraging adventures that had led to us being left behind in the first place.

As I hastily mulled over a series of possible plausible excuses in my head, the lieutenant barked orders to the men to pack up and head out. The bunker was to be vacated; all personnel were to move west to new positions. Gerle and I looked at each other, both of us clearly relieved to be apparently forgotten on the fringe, when we realized that the lieutenant was gazing at us with a somber expression on his thin stark face.

"You two will have to get out of here, as well. You can't go with us, though. We will not have children on the front lines. Now, better get moving and head west as quickly and quietly as you can. Since this is your town you should understand my directions. Head along the cemetery wall by the park, then catch the main street at that end where it skirts the train station. Stay clear of the middle of town and keep your eyes on the sky. Do you understand?" his deep voice rattled at us. It finally calmed and his gray eyes softened slightly, as he continued, "You can look for news of your folk in one of the villages west of here. Best of luck to you. Remember, move quickly... they are coming."

"Thank you, sir." I muttered, uncertainly, as I handed the lumpy rucksack to Gerle, who flung it over his slight shoulders, and we began to climb the sand bags which formed slim stairs at one end of the trench.

"Hey, boy!" came a voice behind me, as I neared the top. "Catch!" Our defender from the previous day tossed a crust of bread my way, and I managed to snatch it out of the air before it landed in the disturbed earth around the pit.

"Thanks." I said, smiling slightly.

"Just head west boys, and you'll be fine…. You'll be fine." he said, before he turned to load his gun with new clips.

My bike seemed to protest more loudly since its run through the river the day before; the rear tire was now entirely flat, and the front one was beginning to soften, as well. We traversed the meadow towards the cemetery, hoping to meet up with the path near its tall concrete wall without being seen by the Russian spotters. Several German soldiers marched ahead of us, their packs heavy with equipment and food for the evacuation of the area.

We crossed the road that led to our school, and I glanced toward the massive building, stark and gloomy now with its broken windows. I recalled, bitterly, the many fun times shared with my friends, who were now scattered somewhere along the road westward. Would we find them? Would we find anyone we knew? …. What had I done to deserve being left alone in the middle of a war?

Gerle's muttering from the small luggage rack behind me returned my despondent thoughts to the present. He said, "Alfie, can we stop for a second? My rear end hurts." I eased the bike to a halt, pulling it under the large branches of a tree so we would not be exposed to the enemy. "How far are we going to have to go on this thing?" he complained, rubbing his backside roughly. "Let me try to pedal again."

I dismounted and he climbed on, but the bike immediately began to tip; his legs simply were not long enough. He leapt off, grumbling to himself in an undertone.

"We really better keep moving, Gerle." I said, reluctant to raise his hackles any further, as I sympathized with his situation. My bottom was beginning to hurt, too… but at least I had the padded seat.

We continued past the cemetery, noticing with sinking hearts that even it had not been spared. Several small craters had blasted apart gravestones and flattened some of the old trees. The aura of melancholic peace and solitude had been shattered; in its place had been raised a monument of ironic indifference. Even in the slumber of death, war found a way to destroy.

"Who would fire on a cemetery?" Gerle asked, incredulously.

"I suppose they were aiming at the train station… it's just around the corner." We clattered slowly around the edge of the tall wall and eased our bike to a halt at the pedestrian bridge that traversed the tracks. The train station had been spared the heaviest damage, from what we could see, but we hastened away, carrying the bike across the bridge. We feared the next strike could prove on target, with us standing dead center.

Loud rumbles and sporadic machine gun fire reminded us that the armies were on the move and speed was vital. For the first time in my life I was pleased to turn my back on my home. My family was out there somewhere and I had to find them... I had to know if they were still alive.

In the span of several days, the innocent pleasures of my life had been eclipsed by the vital challenges of seeking an improbable reunion with my family, and the unlikely reality of my own ultimate survival in this new harsh world.

CHAPTER 11

Once free of the town, I pedaled along the road as quickly as I felt the bike was able. It shimmied and creaked viciously and several times threatened to die in the ditch. We soon discarded the tattered remnants of the rubber tire, hoping the crooked rim would hold.

We continued onward, determined to put as much distance as possible between ourselves and the fighting. We soon reached a tiny outlying village, one familiar to me from happier days, when my sister and I would travel to visit our other grandmother. Gerle now squirmed on the luggage rack that had cradled my much smaller sister for the short ride; but now we had an endless road ahead of us. Anything beyond this point would be unfamiliar to both Gerle and me; neither of us had ever ventured so far before.

The village was deserted and silent, except for the crackling of flames from small fires, proof that we had not yet escaped the reach of the enemy. Empty cavernous windows stared out at us, jagged glass framing the dark interiors.

"I'm tired, Gerle. My grandmother's house is around the corner. Let's stop there for the night. I can't go any further today." I moaned, shifting my sore bottom on the narrow seat.

"Oh! I thought you would never stop. I need to use the bathroom. Do you think your grandmother's house is open?" Gerle replied.

"Well, if it's not, it hardly matters if we break a window to get in, does it? Look at this place. Besides, she would be glad that we were able to shelter here." I answered, hoping we would not have to test her generosity.

A loud motor roared suddenly behind us. I veered into a narrow ditch to avoid the jeep thundering westward. It was loaded with German soldiers, too intent on their orders to pay us any attention.

"That was close!" cried Gerle. He had taken a tumble when the bike had lurched off the side of the road, and he was now pushing himself shakily to his feet, brushing the weeds from his clothes. "Oh well, I just as soon walk from here, Alfie. How much farther?"

"It's right around the next curve, off to the right. I'll walk, too—my rear end doesn't feel so great either."

"Here, I'll push it for a change." Gerle insisted, taking the handle bars from me and shoving the bike forward. "It would be great if there is some food in her cupboards. I'm starving."

The fence bordering my grandmother's yard didn't appear damaged, and I was pleased to see the house also looked untouched. We eased the gate open and propped the bike near it... ready for a quick exit, if necessary. We headed for the door, which was framed elegantly in budding roses. I turned the knob slowly and was thrilled to discover that it opened.

"Great! A place to sleep tonight. Let's hope soldiers leave us alone this time." I said, and I pushed the door slowly open. The interior was dim, as thick curtains still hung over the windows. "They must have left at night. The drapes were never lifted." I whispered, peering into the gloom.

"Let's find the kitchen." said Gerle, from behind me. "Do you remember where it is?" he continued, stepping past me.

"Yeah, go straight ahead, then left. I can check the cellar if we don't find anything in the cupboards. Here, we need a little light." I said. I raised one of the dark curtains onto its hook, allowing the late afternoon sun to penetrate into the shadows of the room. Dust swirled and sparkled in the long arms of the light, as I led the way to the back of the house. "Let's just remember to close that. We don't want any more surprises." I muttered. "It looks like they have been gone awhile. It's really dusty in here. Grandma was always very tidy."

The kitchen smelled foul. Moldy cheese and rotten eggs sat in a box on the counter, packed as if for travel, but forgotten. A mouse scurried under the table as we disturbed the thick dust on the floor. "Whew! It smells awful! Let's get those eggs out of here." said Gerle in a muffled voice, pressing his hand over his nose.

I grabbed the box and carried it to the back door, which was locked. I opened it with the large key that dangled loosely from the keyhole, and I set the reeking food on the step.

"Looks like she took her animals with her. She didn't have many. Just a couple of hens, but it would have been nice to have some fresh eggs." I turned back toward the kitchen and noticed Gerle had already begun rummaging through drawers and cupboards. "Find anything?" I asked.

"Well, this bread is green, so that's no good." he grimaced. "But these jars have some apricots in them, I think. And there was some landjaeger in the cupboard." He grinned, holding up several narrow strips of dried sausage, perfect for surviving long storage.

"Great, I'm hungry! But first I want to get us some water. Hand me that bucket." I returned to the small backyard and worked the pump, which had grown stiff and lazy from its lack of use. After several attempts I managed a thin trickle of gritty water, before it began to flow evenly and gushed, gurgling, into the small bucket.

We nibbled silently on the meager fare, which stuck in our tightened throats, as we each thought sadly of what lay ahead. "Do you really think we will find them, Alfie?" Gerle asked, with his mouth full of juicy apricots.

"I don't know, but let's head out early tomorrow. I don't want those tanks following us." I replied. I yawned and stretched my arms over my head. "I'm so tired, Gerle. If we have to keep moving all day tomorrow, I want to go to sleep." I looked around, noticing the dark staircase disappearing into the growing shadows, and I decided the couch would be sufficient for me. "Maybe it would be better if we slept down here, Gerle… in case we have to leave quickly."

Exhaustion reigned, and after a quick wash with the cold water, we curled up at opposite ends of the narrow couch and fell asleep instantly. The day's exertions and the constant fear coursing through our bodies had left a shallow reserve of energy, and we yearned for a peaceful night. Aside from sporadic distant rumbles and noisy caravans of retreating troops speeding through the tiny village, we enjoyed an uneventful sleep.

Morning found us sore, but rested, and eager to put the war behind us. We loaded our rucksack with several potatoes we had found in the cellar, and we retrieved our bike from the yard. I groaned as I climbed onto the seat, aware that one night was not enough to heal my aching muscles.

"Watch the bumps today, Alfie, if you can. This seat back here is awful." Gerle complained, clinging to my sides as I careened around a large pit in the road.

"Sorry, Gerle. I'm doing the best I can. This thing is hard to maneuver with the flat tire. It keeps wanting to pull in different directions." I lumbered to a sudden stop, climbed off and removed the pathetic remains of the last tire. "There, it was only slowing us down, anyway." I sighed.

The day continued in a similar vein, with Gerle muttering complaints, and with me apologizing meekly, until my own woes finally left me grumpy and less sympathetic. The hungry rumbles in our stomachs kept our tempers short, and we looked constantly for any sources of food. Spring was really too new to expect much from the many gardens and fields we passed, yet we surveyed each one expectantly for any hint of the year's first crop.

We were forced to make an early lunch stop. The road had begun to swarm with the faster moving vehicles leading the retreat. The handful of wrinkled potatoes did little to squelch our hunger pangs, even with Oma's precious marmalade coating them. While we sat in a ditch and ate, a bedraggled group of soldiers slowly made its way east. None of them seemed too eager to be the ones chosen to represent the last stand on the front with the Russians.

The road became increasingly littered with the destruction of the far-reaching guns of the Russian artillery. Burning supply vehicles spewed caustic black smoke into the pristine blue sky, and birds flying overhead in their pursuit of insects swerved recklessly to avoid the fearful heat. Parallel to the road beautiful streams rippled and cascaded over moss covered rocks, but they were strewn with animal cadavers, their bellies bloated and their decaying entrails swarming with flies and maggots. Attempts to bomb the bridges spanning these scenic streams had luckily landed off their marked target, leaving the evacuation route momentarily passable.

As I viewed the clear stream riddled with corpses, I regretted our previous eagerness for water. Overwhelming thirst had emboldened us to drink from the stream, where it had gurgled temptingly close to a curve in the road.

"Great. Now we are probably going to get sick." muttered Gerle morosely, as we averted our eyes from the disturbing sights. "Just keep moving, Alfie. There must be some place soon that is all right." I knew he hoped that meant finding my grandparents, but in actuality we had found no one at all… no one but fleeing soldiers, many wounded and maimed beyond caring, all of them too preoccupied to bother with two wandering boys.

Both of us were a sorry sight: dirty, hungry, and very tired. Evening arrived quickly. We had been on the move all day, with barely a rest, and nothing but morsels for food, yet we had covered only a short distance. The bike protested at every turn, but it valiantly held together as my throbbing legs pushed us slowly further west… into the unknown.

"Where are we going to sleep tonight, Alfie? I don't think we are anywhere near a town, but I can't sit here much longer." Gerle moaned, his thin legs dangling limply to the sides of the wobbling bike. At midday he had experienced the runs, and now he cursed under his breath about the water we had drunk the day before.

"Well, I am pretty ready to stop too, Gerle. I guess it is warm enough to sleep in one of those haystacks." I pointed quickly with my hand, eager to keep a grip on the stubborn bike; it took any chance available to head into a ditch. We were in a rolling valley, intersected several times by narrower valleys that led up into the fabled mountains of the region. Haystacks, brittle and brown from neglect, had been forgotten in the fields, now already overgrowing with weeds and wildflowers. Farmers had never had a chance to bring the sweet hay inside their barns during the winter; the threat of war had deemed it unnecessary. But, the haystacks were a welcome and homely sight for our tired eyes, and we made our way slowly to one slightly set back from the road.

I hid the bike under the hay, in case the Russians were advancing faster than we feared. I burrowed eagerly into the rich smelling hay. It tickled and poked through my clothes, but I barely felt it. I stretched out in the warm embrace of the field's produce and stared up at the slowly dimming sky. The rumbles were distant now, though an occasional blast of artillery lit up the sky to the east.

A whimper from the ditch reminded me of my friend's misery, and I eased myself reluctantly to my feet and grabbed some broad leafed weeds to take to Gerle.

"Here, Gerle… you might need these." I said, as I tossed them at his hunched form, before backing away and returning to the haystack.

"Thanks, Alfie." replied Gerle in a weak voice, and my heart clenched at the sound of it. I knew of no way else to help him, except to get us both to my grandparents in any way I could manage.

Gerle returned, pale and trembling, and he flopped down beside me. I stared at him, my forehead furrowed with worry. "I should find us some clean water. I bet there is a stream in those woods over there." I said, motioning with my head. "It would be clean—it's not near the road." Gerle looked at me nervously. "I promise to check the banks for anything first. Ok?"

Gerle nodded quickly, though anxiety rippled across his ashen face at the thought of more possible taints on the mountain streams. Our thirst had been mounting throughout the day, with only one stop at a village pump to satisfy it.

I wandered toward the woods, which were still and dark in the rapidly approaching dusk. The coolness of the trees embraced me as I stepped on the thin brown pine needles that blanketed the edge of the forest. Small animals squeaked and twittered in the dying light as they settled down, or roused themselves, for the evening. A momentary, but welcome, sense of calm descended upon me. The sounds of the battle became muffled in the soft breeze and inviting murmurs of a forest yet unaffected by the horrors swirling around it.

The trickle of a tiny stream seemed amplified in the stillness of the trees, and I tiptoed towards it, hesitant to disturb the welcome haven. The stream was clear, and it seemed to bubble directly from the rocks, so I leaned close and let the water play across my hot and dirty face. The water's chill sent shivers throughout my body. I allowed myself to succumb to thirst, and I eagerly drank my fill.

I closed my eyes, gulping the water, which was so cold it made my head ache. The taste was pure and untainted and I felt confident no harm would come of it. I rinsed the apricot jar carefully and filled it thoroughly before capping it. Then, I sadly turned my back on my newly discovered island of calm, knowing Gerle lay suffering by the road.

As I retraced my steps across the field, now golden in the dying sun, I reminded myself to return in the morning to fill the jar again for the ride. Fresh water might continue to be difficult to find.

Gerle remained where I had left him, moaning and shaking, his back against the haystack. His damp hair was thick with strands of hay as he rolled his head from side to side with the pains in his abdomen.

"I brought you some water, Gerle. Here, drink some. I had some already... you go ahead. Have all you want. I can fill it up again." I insisted,

131

noticing his questioning stare, as he continued to groan and clutch his stomach. "You really need to drink, Gerle. Tomorrow we will find some food... but, now we at least have good water." I paused as I knelt, and I gently placed the jar to his lips. "Go ahead, Gerle. You have to."

Gerle suddenly grabbed the jar from my hands, splashing water on his shirt as he tipped it towards his mouth. He drank deeply, pausing only for breath, then he finally emptied the jar. "Thanks, Alfie... thanks a lot." he gasped and smiled meekly, leaning further into the cradle of hay.

"I'll go fill it again before it gets dark. Then we can get some more in the morning. I'll be right back." I returned several minutes later to find Gerle in a fitful sleep. I piled some hay loosely over his shivering frame, and I eased myself into the stack next to him.

At that moment, a row of jeeps roared by, though Gerle only stirred slightly in his sleep. I burrowed more deeply into the hay, anxious to remain hidden from whatever might be moving on the road during the night. Drowsiness tickled at my eyes, and they drooped and sagged with utter weariness, yet my mind remained sharp, thinking ahead to what tomorrow might bring. My exhausted body finally triumphed and I fell into a deep sleep, one so profound that not a single ripple of a dream disturbed its surface.

Morning arrived suddenly, with birds twittering and fluttering overhead. The serious preparations of nest-building were underway and the stiff strands of hay tempted the many eager pairs. I sat up slowly and ran my fingers through my gnarled hair. I glanced at Gerle and was pleased to see that he remained asleep under the comforting blanket of the hay. His face was beaded with sweat, though he slept peacefully.

I carefully removed the hay from my clothes and grabbed the apricot jar, which was now empty. Stretching my cramped limbs, I scurried to the woods to catch the fresh morning water. The field was filled with dew-laden flowers, some with their petals still folded in sleep in spite of the attentions of the butterflies fluttering teasingly among them. The woods hummed with activity, the squirrels scampering busily to and fro in the tall pines above my head.

The stream greeted me eagerly; it bubbled merrily between the small pebbles lining its shallow banks. I drank deeply, trying, in vain, to fill the throbbing void of hunger in the pit of my stomach. The water did little to remove the emptiness, but it tasted sweet and cold, waking me quickly.

With the jar freshly filled, I returned to Gerle, who was beginning to stir from his rest.

"How are you feeling, Gerle? Here... some more water." I said, handing him the jar.

He reached up, squinting into the rising sun, and he took the jar, though this time he drank more slowly. "I feel a little better. I actually slept. I'm not looking forward to getting back on that bike, though...." he said, then pausing, his head cocked slightly, "What's that?" he mumbled suddenly, turning his head toward the road. I looked in time to see a cloud of dust swirling beyond the tall trees at a point where the road curved away into a slight hollow.

"We better hide, Gerle. Quickly! Get back in the hay!" I whispered. I flung myself head first into the hollow my body had left. I felt Gerle throwing hay on me, then settling himself into hiding too. Stifling a sneeze brought on by the mustiness of the hay, I peeked out and risked a glance at the road. A throbbing engine roared loudly as a large truck sputtered past, its back filled with wounded men sprawled recklessly among hastily retrieved artillery and weapons. The pale faces were drawn tightly across emaciated bodies, their eyes deep pools of emptiness.

After we were certain the road was clear, we trundled the ailing bike to the edge of the ditch and climbed on.

"Oh! I wish we could move fast enough walking." moaned Gerle, twisting and turning on his small luggage rack in a vain attempt to find comfort.

"We will try to take more breaks today, ok?" I answered, raising my sore legs above the pedals to push the bike forward. Both wheels now wobbled thoroughly on their rims, the useless rubber entirely gone.

We continued westward in silence, though Gerle coughed and groaned several times, obviously still experiencing pains in his stomach. Another tiny village soon filled the narrow horizon, as I pedaled the bike higher into the mountains. We looked eagerly for any working pump and settled on a small house at the far edge of town.

"You fill it up, Gerle." I said, handing him the jar. "I'm going to look inside to see if there is any food." I headed for the door, no qualms this time about entering someone's house uninvited. The unlocked door guarded an interior as gloomy and dusty as my grandmother's had been, though it lacked the smell of rotting food. I opened every cupboard in the old kitchen

133

and found nothing, but the small cellar yielded several wrinkled apples and a jar of pickles.

I met Gerle at the door. He was wiping his sweaty forehead. I could tell by his pale face that his stomach was still ailing him. "Are you all right?" I asked, hesitantly.

"I'm ok, I guess." replied Gerle. "Just wish I had never had that water. Let's try to stick to pumps instead of streams from now on, ok?" I nodded, and we commenced to eating the apples, seeds and all, deciding to save the pickles for lunch.

The sun climbed slowly higher into the spring sky. The weather was mild and crisp, as if tempting us to stop and play, but I began to wonder if we would ever play again. Instead, it seemed we were destined to inch our way throughout the country searching for our family, while also trying to dodge the tightening snare of the war.

Nearing yet another small village, the traffic on the road increased suddenly. We were surprised to see several large Red Cross tents clustered in the pristine central square, almost concealing a round stone fountain that bubbled and splashed pleasantly.

"What do you think, Gerle? Should we stop and see if there is any food… or maybe news of people from our town?" I asked. "At the very least we can have a drink of water." I was breathless, partly from my attempts at pedaling us up the increasingly mountainous terrain, and partly from my excitement at finally seeing someone besides the soulless faces of the defeated soldiers.

"Good idea, Alfie! I'm very hungry, and maybe they know something about the evacuation." replied Gerle. "Stop here. I need to get off. There's a latrine." He groaned and scrambled quickly to the rickety wooden shack near the tent, while I waited, unsure of whom to approach first. Several uniformed men and women moved quietly among a handful of German soldiers, most of whom had bandages wrapped around their heads or crutches under their arms.

A small cluster of men peered eagerly at a tattered notice board tacked crookedly to one of the tent braces. I was deciding that this would be our best chance at news when Gerle returned, tapping me from behind on the shoulder. "What do you think? Over there first?" I pointed with my chin. "… or something to eat." I asked.

"I think we should try to find some food, Alfie. I feel pretty empty… you know, because…" his pale face darkened momentarily with color, his eyes darting toward the latrine.

"Sure, that's fine." I answered, anxious to change the subject. We leaned the bike against the fountain and washed our dusty hands and faces in the cool refreshing water, then we approached a group of men lined up near a broad table. The table had clearly been dragged from a nearby home, and it had been set up bordering a small fire above which a steaming pot of soup boiled. We fell in line behind the men, finally convinced our attempts at a meal would be rewarded.

"That smells really good, Alfie. I am so hungry. They better not turn us away!" Gerle whispered vehemently in my ear. We sidled slowly forward with the throng of men, all as visibly excited about the chances of food as we were.

The man in front of us shuffled silently toward the large lady who was manning the cooking pot. She hoisted the vast ladle with her broad hand and scooped the thin, yet savory-smelling soup into a tin cup and placed it into his outstretched hands. He leaned toward his meal, cradling it between his filthy fingers as he quickly wandered off, clearly not wanting to wait for it to cool.

We approached the table, loath to meet the cook's intense gaze, in the fear that we would be denied food. But with nothing more than a slightly raised eyebrow, she handed Gerle a cup, after she surprised us by topping it off to almost overflowing.

Her curiosity surfaced finally after handing me my own full cup, and she said, "What are you boys doing here? You should be long gone. This is no place for children. Where are your folks?"

"Thank you." I said, taking the hot cup and almost scorching myself as it was so full. "We got left behind. Have there been many refugees through here?"

Her eyes softened, and she glanced from my face to Gerle's with a growing look of pity. "You go over to that tent. They would be the ones to ask… if they know anything at all."

"Thank you." Gerle said, between gulps of hot soup.

"You go check with the hospital tent, son. You are looking pretty pale."

135

Gerle sloshed his soup across his dusty shirt, and nodded with a startled look on his face. "Come back here before you leave and I might have a crust of bread for you two." she said, winking kindly, her broad mouth breaking into a grin. "Go on." She returned to her ladle, and not a moment too soon, as the next man in line looked ready to burst with hunger.

"Well, why don't you go over there, Gerle..." I said, pointing to the tent with a large Red Cross emblazoned on its dingy green canvas, "... and I'll check for any news." Gerle nodded, though looking as if he would rather head back to the latrine. But, he shuffled slowly toward the large tent, outside which a dozen men were lying or half-reclining in the grass, all wounded in some capacity. I stared after my dear friend, his discomfort visible in his walk and the tilt of his head, and I hoped nothing too serious would be discovered.

I turned toward the huddle of uniforms near the placard on the tent pole and jostled my way through toward the front.

"What do you need, kid?" rasped a deep voice behind me. I turned to face a large man in a dark uniform, the red band of the swastika visible on his arm. His eyes reflected the tone of his voice, all business, with no extraneous emotions.

"Um... my frie... my brother and I got left behind when the orders to evacuate came. We are looking for our family. Would there maybe be any news of them here... uh... sir?"

"What city are you from?" he asked, in the same gravely detached tone, as he worked a smoldering cigarette in a hand at his hip.

"Jagerndorf... sir."

"Well, let's see." He squinted slightly and scratched at the day old stubble on his chin. Then, he turned to the post, on which was tacked a lengthy list, apparently a record of some refugee caravans that had passed along this route. "Jagerndorf... Jager..." he muttered, his voice deepening to a growl as his finger traced a line down the soiled paper, the cigarette scattering ashes as it went along for the ride. "Well, a fairly large group from your area seems to have passed through, but it doesn't say where they were sent from here." His cold gaze fell on my face, now visibly fallen with the useless news. "Your best bet is to keep heading west, son. That's where everyone is being sent."

136

I thought I felt his tone soften slightly at these last words, but the dismissive gesture with his cigarette-laden hand convinced me that it had most likely been imagined. "Thank you, sir, anyway... for your help."

Gerle was leaning against the cement pillar of the fountain, taking advantage of its meager shade, when I returned.

"Well...?" we both said together.

"Go ahead." I insisted, sitting down next to my friend.

"The nurse said I most likely have dysentery." Gerle said quietly. Then frowning, he added, "You'll probably get it too. She said almost every soldier who passes through here has it."

"What do we do about it?" I gasped, feeling my skin crawl at the thought of the coming illness.

"Watch what you eat and drink, she said... as if we didn't already know that!" Gerle snorted, darkly.

Minutes later we were swallowing the last of the small scraps of bread the kind cook had been able to spare for us. Her words rang in my ears as I pedaled awkwardly westward out of the village. "I hope you find your family, my dear. The wide world is no place to be alone... especially now. Good luck."

CHAPTER 12

Several days had passed, and my backside felt numb yet sore at the same time from countless hours of chafing against the rough seat of the bike. My short legs were stiff and throbbing, with occasional sharp pains shooting through my thighs and knees. Gerle continued to suffer from dysentery and I found myself beginning to make frequent stops at the side of the road, as well.

The world became increasingly foreign to us. The mountains we had always admired from a great distance now lay behind us. It seemed as though we had tackled the very spine of the world, leading us into territories yet unknown, just as had the fabled explorers of the American West, those I had so greatly admired in my childhood books.

It seemed increasingly doubtful that such an unfamiliar and unwelcoming road could indeed lead us to my grandparents, yet we knew there was no other direction to go but onward.

We had encountered more army field stations, each one swarming with German soldiers completely drained of spirit and energy. Many had unwillingly left limbs in some doctor's crude surgical tent near the front, and they now faced a future of spreading gangrene and foul illness.

Our attempts at news achieved only scattered stories and few facts; all was utter chaos. On barn doors along the country roads we found hastily scrawled notes, most simply listing names and addresses of people being sought. Wind-torn strips of weathered paper contained snatches of lives lost or displaced. People seeking neighbors, loved ones, and friends had tacked these pleas for information on every upright surface.

Suddenly, the sense of the enormity of our search seemed overwhelming. Thousands of homeless individuals were on the move, meaning our questions to Red Cross personnel were often met with blank stares and muttered apologies. There were simply too many refugees to account for them all.

What made the situation even more alarmingly disturbing was that we had yet to see any of the wandering caravans of the desperate souls who had scribbled their heartfelt entreaties on every pole and tree. Where had all these people gone? How had we gotten so far behind? If we could not find them... how did we really expect to find my grandparents?

After days of fretting thus and continually inching further away from home, we reached the only sign of promise after almost a week of constant moving. In the first village west of the mountains, with which I was eager to be finished, the officers manning the Red Cross station finally gave us some useful news. They insisted that the latest refugee group, a fairly large one from the east, had been directed on to the town of Maerisch-Schoenberg, another day's journey across a lateral mountain range.

With the first glimmers of hope, we packed our rucksack with the crusts of bread donated by the mobile kitchen and headed in the direction pointed out by the officers. The prospect of scaling another mountain pass weighed heavily on my mind, as now I too suffered from the symptoms of dysentery. We were hungry, cold, and tired, and beneath the layers of grime coating our faces we flashed cheeks both pale with fear and flushed with fever.

As the village slowly fell away into the valley below us, I voiced my hopes to Gerle. "What if we really do find them, Gerle? We can finally get rid of this infernal bike."

"Well, Alfie, I don't think we will make it today. Look... the sun is almost down; we should find a place to sleep. I don't feel so well." The skin on the back of my neck crawled with the thought of Gerle being sick on the rack behind me, but the thought of more uphill pedaling in the morning convinced me to press on.

"Let's just try to make the top. This doesn't seem like too high of a pass. Plus, the man said it could be traveled in a day... so it can't be too far." Just to emphasize my eagerness to continue I pressed harder with my aching legs, and I managed several extra lurches forward before I sank back into my slow, but steady, plod up the mountain road.

We neared the top as the sun began to dip into the west, casting a soothing flush of orange across the horizon. A shiver ran up my spine as I turned my gaze to the east and realized that a deeper crimson glow emanated from beyond the eastern hills, rivaling the setting sun's splendor. Only knowing the cause kept me from admiring the unnaturally colored sky. Sonorous thumps and rumbles drifted through the damp evening air, adding unwelcome disturbances to the quiet fields and woods ready to sleep for the night.

Gerle gasped and sobbed behind me as we finally pulled the bike to the side of the road. He lurched off instantly, clearly unable to hold in the meager contents of his abused stomach any longer. He stumbled into the dark ditch, retching loudly between heaving breaths and angry sobs, as his body struggled to rid itself of the unseen enemy gradually tearing it apart.

I turned my gaze away from my friend, lest I feel the urge to join him; I had been fighting the waves of nausea since the morning. Several German jeeps were parked neatly near the summit of the narrow road, silhouetted against the deepening tinge of the approaching twilight. Soldiers milled quietly about, unconcerned by our presence, the glowing ends of their cigarettes visible like tiny fireflies against the dense shadows of the trees.

The calm scene settled my nerves, though my knees felt weak, and my body still trembled with fever and chills. Gerle crawled, coughing, from the ditch behind me and said, "Alfie, do you think there is any water left in that jar?" His voice shook with emotion and weariness, and he staggered slowly to his unstable feet.

"There might be a few sips, Gerle… that's all. But, I'll ask them for some if you need more." pointing toward the soldiers. "… or maybe there is a spring around here somewhere… being up this high." I pulled the jar from our few belongings in the filthy and torn pocket of the rucksack, and I handed it to Gerle, who drank deeply, remembering only at the last moment that I had not had any water, either.

"Sorry, Alfie… I forgot it is all we have. I'll go get more. You try to find us a place to sleep. I'll be right back." He staggered away, his clothes hanging loosely along his bony shoulders. I pulled the bike into the ditch, avoiding the spot visited by Gerle, and I headed into the small field in search of a dry haystack.

The morning had welcomed us with a brief drizzle, leaving a damp sheen on the roads, finally cutting the billowing dust of the many military convoys. But, the rain had also set us up for an uncomfortable night, as the hay seemed to hold the water in its core like a porous sponge.

I pulled the hay apart to let the air dry the inner layers, but then gave up as I realized the air was too damp to have any positive effect. My legs wobbled fiercely and convinced me that a wet bed was the least of my worries for that evening, so I flopped myself down into the thick hay.

Gerle returned with the jar full of water, and grinning weakly, said, "Sometimes it pays to look sick. They were really nice… gave me this piece of cheese, too." He handed me the jar; it was beaded with drops of water, so tempting to my parched mouth that I longed to slurp every bit of moisture that trickled in a cool line into my hand. Instead, I took a long deep drink and capped the jar, conscious of the need to save some of the precious fluid.

"Here." said Gerle, handing me a small piece of the cheese. "They didn't give me much. I don't think they had much to spare." He leaned back against the hay, grimaced suddenly, and bolted forward again. "This just tops it off, doesn't it? Wet! Ah, I'm too tired to care. Good night, Alfie."

"Good night, Gerle."

I ate my cheese in silence, taking small nibbles and slowly chewing each tiny piece to extend the flavor, hoping my empty stomach would be tricked into settling for the long night.

I drifted on the edge of sleep for several minutes until my body finally succumbed to the world of dreams, where the war always seemed so far away.

Our fevers heightened during the night, and morning passed unnoticed as we both drifted in and out of restless sleep. The sounds of the jeeps rumbling to an early start did little to rouse us, though Gerle muttered softly to himself, "There goes the cheese…", as he lolled senselessly in the damp hay, his face beaded with sweat.

The cramps in my stomach had also increased during the hours before the dawn, and I found myself crawling toward the ditch several times to try to eliminate the contaminates. My lips stuck together like two pieces of sandpaper being rubbed against each other, and the few sips of water that could be spared from the jar did little to alleviate the dryness.

The sun was high in the sky before either of us was strong enough to rouse himself, and I felt relieved that I had insisted we continue to the top of the pass. I didn't think I could have managed any hills in my condition; it seemed it was going to be enough of a challenge to focus my bleary eyes on the road for the descent.

The bike wobbled more severely than ever, and I began to worry if it would hold together for the rest of the trip. I kept to a controlled speed, pleased my legs were to be spared some effort, as we rolled awkwardly down into the valley of Maerisch-Schoenberg. A low mist hung over the rooftops, thin church spires piercing the veil of white.

A weathered sign marked with the symbol of the Red Cross hung on a large tree near the road at the base of the long pass. It consisted simply of a faded red arrow pointing toward town. We followed several such signs, excited at the prospects of seeing people other than soldiers. On the outskirts of town I eased the bike to a stop in front of a small Red Cross tent.

"Well, here we go." muttered Gerle, after sucking air in through gritted teeth. He seemed as worried about what we might find… or not find, as I was.

"I'm sure they will have some information. There are a lot more people here. That's promising." I answered, determined to remain positive. I was right. Bedraggled individuals milled about, clearly refugees unfamiliar with the town. Their clothes were dirty and ragged, their belongings as minimal as ours.

Children clung closely to their parents, eyes wide with curiosity mingled with fear. A thin line of these men and women waited patiently in the sun for a turn at the Red Cross refugee registration center. We glanced momentarily at each other then fell into places at the end of the slowly moving line.

My eyes darted across the many faces, all unfamiliar to me, though I hoped a glimmer in someone's eyes would stimulate some recognition. Gerle pivoted around also, clearly scanning the crowd for anyone we might know. Tongues foreign to us could be heard in small groups throughout the line. It was obvious this town had become the holding center for people from as far away as Poland and the Ukraine. An officer passed along the line handing clip boards with forms and pens to each adult, expediting only slightly the wait in the hot sun.

The officer reached us and after only a glance continued past us, assuming we belonged to the woman standing adjacent. Gerle cleared his throat carefully. Our mouths were so parched that words slipped out in a shallow rasp, and he said boldly, "Excuse me, sir! I think we need two of those." The man paused and ran his steady eyes up and across our filthy bodies, then turned toward the women in front of us.

"Are these boys with you?" he asked, clearly not ready to take Gerle's words for fact. The woman trembled visibly and muttered something incomprehensible, while the man shook his head in disgust and rested his probing eyes back on Gerle. "Where are your families?" he asked tonelessly, flickering his eyes momentarily onto me.

"We were left behind when the evacuation orders were given in our town. We have been traveling on our own... but we are looking for our family." Gerle said quickly, before pausing for a breath. "May we fill out a form?" he asked, his gaze surprisingly steady and firm. The man's eyes flared suddenly with anger at Gerle's impertinent questions, then they dulled again as he thrust two clip boards into our chests. He strode off, distributing more to the people in line behind us, obviously already adding us into the blur of nameless faces he had to tolerate throughout a long day.

We answered the questions on the form to the best of our ability. It was mostly a request for information, so people could be properly categorized by region and thus prioritized as to placement in refugee holding camps.

After a long wait we reached the low desk in front of the tent and were subjected to further scrutiny and questions about our missing guardians. Finally, we were directed to a nearby camp, housed in the local school building. We headed off eagerly, desperate for a meal and some potable water, not to mention a dry bed.

The town was in chaos. Litter and waste filled the gutters and no one seemed to move with a purpose. We rode the old bike across narrow bumpy cobblestone streets to find the school gymnasium. We rounded several corners, each clogged with people, most of them women and children. It dawned on me, with sadness, that many of these families lacked a father.

We located the building easily. It was a tall two story structure made of huge gray stones and ornate brickwork, and it dominated an entire corner of a block. When it had bustled with students, it must have been a truly impressive sight. Now, though, its grandeur was somewhat diminished.

The musty hallway was packed with reclining bodies, making the air stuffy and foul, and vacant faces covered with several layers of grime stared up at us from among the moaning and whining children. We followed the dank tunnel to the camp director's office, once the headquarters of the school superintendent.

"What do you want?" barked a large sweaty man from a rickety black chair. The chair creaked dangerously as it swiveled laboriously beneath his bulk behind a massive oak desk. Spread out upon the dusty surface were numerous forms similar to the ones we had completed.

"Um…" I began, eager to repay Gerle for his efforts with the man in the information line. "Um… we need a place to stay, and we are looking for our family. Can I… uh, give you their names?" I asked, nervously. As soon as I had begun speaking, his face had commenced to contorting into deep folds and an intimidating scowl erupted across its fleshy surface.

"Silence! I'll ask the questions!" he spat, his jowls trembling violently.

After many minutes of uncomfortable grilling by the unpleasant man, we were told, much to our horror, to report to separate floors, as the director insisted none of the spaces could handle another two bodies.

"But… we arrived here together. We need to be together." I pleaded, anxious to maintain my link with Gerle, the only remaining constant in my life. Gerle looked equally distressed at the prospect of being separated, but the intimidating bulk of the large man convinced him to keep his mouth shut.

Gerle was ordered to bunk with a large family of many children and he quickly slipped into anonymity among the rowdy throng of offspring. I wandered dejectedly down a long hall and up a flight of dark stairs until I found myself in a narrow room with about sixty people, all hovering around their small bunks waiting for the evening meal. Only one unclaimed bed remained in the room, and I made my way to it, placing the sagging rucksack on the thin moldy blanket.

The family immediately surrounding me took it into their heads that I was someone to be ignored and at best, tolerated. They had traveled a great distance and seemed well settled in their dominance of the room, so I was immediately relegated to the role of outcast.

The first evening meal was a difficult moment. Hunger boiled fiercely in my stomach, but the parents of the family made it clear that their five children were to receive food before I was even to be considered. The exhaustion from so many days on the move, and the growing feeling of the illness coursing slowly through my body left little room for a struggle of wills, so I waited patiently until all others had been served.

I washed my grimy face and hands and did my best to brush the largest spots of soil from my clothes, which had covered my weary body for almost a week.

The next morning I searched out Gerle and together we returned to the director's office in hopes of altering our living situation. This time a stern horse-faced lady sat in the chair, from where she perused the hundreds of forms spread out over the wide desk. She sat silently for a moment, carefully arranging the papers into neat piles.

"I'm sorry. There is nothing I can do about your bunks. There is just not any available space. Need I remind you that this is not a hotel... you should be grateful you have a bed at all." she sneered, her eyes boring into mine above her narrow glasses, which were perched precariously on her long nose. "I see from your form that you are trying to locate your guardians." she continued, shuffling several papers in front of her on the cluttered desk. "I will check with the records of the latest convoys of registered refugees and let you know soon what I find out. Now, that's all I have for you. Go on." Her tone was dismissive and her eyes had returned to their examination of the piles in front of her, so we backed silently from the room.

Time inched slowly forward; as always, waiting was torture. It was the beginning of May, 1945, and spring was in full force. Gerle and I spent as little time as possible in the drab smelly halls of the school. It was painful to see our own suffering reflected in the many somber faces surrounding us. It seemed as though all human misery and despair dwelled in the eyes of the small children. And, any hope was dismissed when gazing upon the wise, life-hardened faces of the elderly, some decorated veterans of the previous Great War.

Gerle and I were summoned to the director's office two days later. We hurried along the crowded hallway, our palms sweaty with the anticipation of the possible news.

"Your grandparents and an uncle, I believe, are registered in another camp across the city, but the director there has informed us that they are entirely full... they have no space for you." the director told us in a flat tone.

145

He seemed unconcerned that our faces fell miserably at the news. Surely, we hadn't come this far to be turned away from our own family?

"If we find out anything else, we will let you know." he continued, his hand gesturing a farewell, as he turned back to his work. His frown widened and he raised his gaze to us once more. "Don't think about going to see them, either. This town has been placed under a curfew. You are to stay put..." He paused dramatically, "... or suffer the consequences."

We shuffled quietly from the office and leaned against the wall. Angry tears welled into my eyes, but I blinked them stubbornly away, determined to maintain the calm that our new situation required.

"How can they do that?" Gerle hissed angrily, slamming his fist into the grimy wall and wincing with pain.

"We will just have to wait. At least we know they are all right." I sighed, though I hardly felt cheered at my own words.

The next two days continued thus; the hours were nothing but interminable fights against boredom. Finally, an afternoon came when I was surprised by yet another summons from the office. I hurried along the hall, wondering what terrible turn of events could have required my presence again.

"Ah, there you are." The brisk gruff words came as soon as I opened the door. "Your mother and sister have been located. Here's the address. You may go see them if you like, just check out with the warden at the door." The man's eyes pinched slightly at the corners in what I imagined was his first true smile towards me those entire few days.

"My mother? Are you sure?" I gasped. "Thank you sir." I added quickly, noticing that the wrinkles around the eyes had faded suddenly, at what he must have read as my ingratitude. Then, I remembered his previous threatening words. "But, sir, the curfew..." I stammered.

He handed me a small slip of paper and dismissed me promptly, telling me first that the door wardens could give me directions. I would have to be back for the more rigid six o'clock curfew, and if I was checking out, it would have to wait until tomorrow. Clearly, the curfew was nebulous, especially if there seemed to be a chance that the burden of another individual on the system would be eliminated. The opportunity to get me out of the overtaxed camp network was enough to run the risk.

I ran to tell Gerle, because even though he had not received permission to leave, I knew his fate was still tied up with mine.

"That's wonderful, Alfie! It never occurred to me they might be here, too." he gushed. "I'm going to bed now. I don't feel so well, but tell me in the morning... so I know what time we are getting out of here." He waved to me from the dark doorway of his large crowded bunk room, and I hastened to the front entrance. I noticed with only a slightly sinking heart that my bike had been snatched from its spot against the tall wrought iron gate. But, at that moment, the joy of soon seeing some of my family eclipsed any other disappointment.

The wardens kindly directed me along some winding streets, all of which were crowded with refugees and townspeople, though neither group seemed too happy about mingling with the other. Wagons, many with blankets draped from their sides as makeshift tents, blocked some of the side streets. Oxen or cows, most still harnessed to their heavy yokes, stood eating leisurely from heaps of hay piled in the street. Goats, pigs, and other livestock were everywhere and the stench was terrible; manure mingled with human waste was oozing among the cobblestones.

Confirming the directions at several corners, I finally reached a tall three-story house, one of a long row set back slightly from the filthy street. My heart leapt into my throat at the excitement of seeing my mother's and sister's faces again, and I took the broad stone front steps two at a time in spite of the pains in my thighs.

I had been told that they were in an apartment on the third floor. So, after allowing my eyes to adjust to the dim interior of the narrow entryway, which was lit sparsely by a dusty light filtering in through a few thin strips of pale glass coated with grime, I tiptoed up the stairs, wondering at the conditions in which my mother and sister now lived. The reek of stale boiled cabbage pricked at my nose, but my mouth watered nonetheless, as I had decided to skip the skimpy evening meal at the camp in hopes of a grander one with my family.

My mind raced with planned words of greeting and with long cherished dreams of finally being reunited. A joyous laughter erupted from my lungs as I gasped to a halt outside the door. I had realized, with a start, that my sister would be turning six in almost two weeks, on the 14th of May. More importantly, we would be seeing each other for the first time in four months.

A soft glowing light was emanating through the frosted glass of the door, the only one on the landing. A small brass bell was set in the wall, so I twisted it firmly several time. A dull pounding echoed in my ears, as muffled voices murmured in response to the shrill peals of the summons.

I hopped in place, clutching my hands to my chest, which had grown tight with emotion at the thought that I would finally be having a home again. As I reached again nervously for the bell, a shadow loomed beyond the door, and it was pulled slowly open. My mother stood in the doorway, her hair framed beautifully by the halo of light coming from a small lamp behind her.

"Hi Mutti!" I croaked, my voice trapped in the gripping depths of my constricted throat. My eyes darted to a small shape clutching tightly to my mother's faded apron, and I recognized my sister's blond braids before her face darted into hiding in the folds of my mother's dress.

As my gaze returned to Mother's face I was startled to see along side the expected signs of shock, a look of anger twisting its way across her shadowed eyes.

"What are you doing here?" she spat curtly. She fumbled at her side with a trembling hand, pushing my sister further behind her skirts.

The reunion I had been expecting was replaced suddenly by harsh and spiteful rejection, and it hit me like a tree branch across my face. I could hear my sister's sobs gathering slowly in my mother's apron.

"Mutti… Gerti, I'm here…. and Gerle, too. We…"

"You can't stay here. There is no room." my mother interrupted, angry red blotches appearing on her otherwise pale cheeks. Her eyes darted to the floor, as if unable to meet my anguished stare. No smile or other sign of delight at seeing me touched her face; indeed, it remained stone cold and detached.

My ears hummed in disbelief and the muscles in my face twitched with shock. I backed slowly toward the top of the stairs, my hand groping for the railing. I continued to look pleadingly into my mother's down turned eyes.

"Mutti?" I whispered.

But, she began to close the door, uttering one more time that there was no room. Behind her, my sister's sobs had turned into gulped versions of my name.

Somehow, I managed to find the street, though I remembered nothing of the descent down the narrow stairs. Gerti's pleas had become loud wails of, "Alfie! Alfieeeee! Mutti, please!", but my mother never bothered to call me back up, as my heart yearned for her to do. My eyes were glazed with a layer of tears, though I desperately willed them not to trace a track down my pale feverished cheek. I stumbled away from the building, leaving the front door ajar. My sister's stifled yells followed me down the street, as I headed back to the only home I had left... the refugee camp.

The night stretched long and dark before me, as I lay awake in my bunk, praying for the tears to come so the pain would release its grip on my heart. Those tears never came. In their place through the darkness echoed waves of panicky whispers that the front had been broken and the Russians were coming.

CHAPTER 13

I spent the night returning sadly in my mind to a lifetime of rejection and ambivalence from my mother. Yet, I could find nothing to explain the treatment at her hands that evening. Aimless guilt at what I should have done differently during my childhood swarmed through my dreams, and I awoke the next morning, my head throbbing with anxiety. The weight of the world and a feeling of responsibility for the horrors around me pressed heavily on my weakened shoulders.

Gerle sympathized as I knew no one else could. It heartened me to remember that he had also suffered the unexplainable loss of his mother. We were linked by our shared childhood, and now even more deeply, by our shared miseries.

But, there remained little time to become overwhelmed by my mother's surprising and inexplicable treatment of me. Rumors spread like wild fire; panic was not far behind. The massive and, word had it, brutal Russian army was sweeping like an uncontrollable flood across the eastern reaches of Europe. There was a sense of inevitability among the refugees and the townsfolk. Authorities had ordered no one could leave… there was no place left to go.

The powerful Allies were heading quickly across Austria, and the once invincible German army was on the run, with fewer places open to it. The lines holding the Russians had collapsed, though Goebbels made it clear on the radio that victory was at hand, and that peace and prosperity would return to the Fatherland.

Gerle and I listened to the frantic ravings of the German leaders, who were clearly speaking as though trapped in a corner, with little hope of escape, yet refusing to admit that the end was near. In contrast, the word on the street was painfully clear; the war would soon be over, and Germany and those countries lorded over by its previously indestructible military machine, now faced immediate futures of squalor, starvation, and despair. The promised Fatherland had been a smoke screen, a false front for a power hungry leadership.

But away from the war room and the barracks, life in the camp was a daily challenge not to lose heart. Simply surviving to wake another day became each person's paramount goal. It took effort to remind ourselves that luck was with us—to have a roof over our heads and even limited food in our stomachs was a rare gift indeed.

Nonetheless, miseries abounded. The outhouses reeked no less foully, knowing we were alive to use them. The nose stung constantly as the body tried to fend off the overwhelming stench.

The filth had emboldened a population of disease-laden rats, their pellet-like feces coating every flat surface. Sickness of every form hung like an invisible toxic cloud over the sleeping rooms. Hacking, bloody coughs of tuberculosis and moans of dysentery reverberated off the lice infested walls. Mold grew thickly in the damp air of the dark rooms, providing optimal conditions for the infestation of many varieties of parasites.

We never felt clean. Bathing was nonexistent, as water, both clean and tainted, was a highly coveted commodity. Food also became scarce. A mobile kitchen had been erected in the school yard, yet there was little to prepare. Many of the livestock Gerle and I had seen on our first day in town were quickly butchered and distributed in a thin soup. But, so many mouths meant empty stomachs every night.

The large rooms were filled with disconsolate people. Rudderless children screamed, cried, and whimpered to their mothers, many of whom lay sweating and sick upon filthy bunks. Fear was visible on every face, the rumor of the coming storm feeding its fire. The citywide curfew had been tightened for everyone's protection, and anyone spotted on the street would be eliminated without question.

My heart yearned for my grandparents, who, I knew, remained in the camp on the other side of town. I began each night in silent anguish, my mind filled with the thought of not being able to reach them, though they were so near. I imagined that they must have believed Gerle and I had died somewhere near home, and it tore my heart open not to be able to ease my grandmother's pain.

As I drifted each night to sleep, Oma's kind face swam into view, her lips, usually so ready to smile, twisted into a tormented fervent prayer, her hands knotting tightly against her heaving bosom.

On one such sleepless night the sky exploded with vigorous impacts, as the weakening flood wall holding the Russians back finally burst. The windows up and down the length of the school building shattered with a deafening clatter that left the ears ringing. Several tremendous bombs had landed in the front yard of the camp.

Everyone tumbled out of bed screaming. The long anticipated arrival of the enemy was upon us all, yet none were truly prepared for the level of panic that swarmed instantaneously through the crowded rooms. People massed to the doors, trampling each other to escape to the cellars. A booming voice echoed throughout the building as the camp director pleaded through his loud speaker for everyone to remain calm and head carefully down the narrow stairs.

The halls were dark and clogged with dust stirred by the jolts and jitters of the old stone building. Its very foundation seemed to be in jeopardy. What products of man's ingenuity could withstand the rabid product of man's hatred? Suddenly, it felt as though we were hiding within walls that were no more protective than a net. They were coming, and we were trapped.

Desperate to find Gerle, I groped my way gingerly behind a small elderly lady, who muttered continually under her breath that she had to go home to feed her chickens. She stopped halfway along the crowded hall and turned to face the throng of refugees pushing their way heedlessly towards safety. Her eyes were wide and blank and the light of several hoisted candles danced eerily across her shocked face.

My mind jumped to my grandmother, who, if alive, might be wandering alone in a similar state of confusion. I took her wilted hand in mine and coaxed her forward, mindful to keep her moving as quickly as possible. The terrified mob behind us threatened to level us in its haste.

The cellars were pitch black except for weak puddles of candlelight around which huddled groups of sobbing families. Ghastly shadows danced on the flaking mortar walls as the candles spat and flickered in the stale air.

I searched the down-turned faces and finally found Gerle leaning against a brick arch at the end of the long room.

"Alfie! I'm so glad you found me. I thought you had been trampled up there. I actually saw someone step on a fallen child and not stop!"

"I'm all right, Gerle. Are you?"

"I guess so... Alfie, I'm scared. They say the Russians are almost here."

"I know. I heard that, too. We will just try to stay together, ok, Gerle... Promise me... we will try to stay together!" Suddenly this seemed the only anchor I had left. The stifling heat of the cramped space began to make my head swim and unpleasant waves of nausea began to swirl their way up my throat. I gulped frantically at the thick air, forcing myself to remain calm, and I threw myself into a heap next to my friend.

A renewed wave of frightened screams erupted following another series of massive bombs that pounded very close to the school. Sand and crumbling mortar drizzled in a fine white dust onto the upturned faces, as the rumbling outside intensified.

My nose tingled with the smell of fear, so vivid that it crackled into the stillness. Everyone sank into a terrified silence. Only the sound of whimpers from the children could be heard as they buried their faces into their mothers' skirts. The pale light of the fading candles flickered, sending menacing shadows looming onto the nearby walls. The candles soon took on gruesome gargoyle-like shapes, as the wax dripped ceaselessly away through the night. No one wanted to allow the darkness to reign—the light seemed the only thing keeping the ravenous rats at bay.

Food and water were limited, though few except the children felt well enough to eat. The smell of urine and vomit swirled amidst the dust, which soon became deep enough to accept a footprint.

The noise never ceased, and time soon flattened into an unmeasureable continuum. Hours inches painfully along, the rumbles of our stomachs seemingly blurring with the rumbles of the incessant bombs.

It was mid morning when we finally surfaced into a wasteland of twisted metal and crumbling bricks. Glass littered the open hallways, allowing the light spring breeze to whistle down the corridors. No one spoke. Disbelief at the destructive power of the bombs made words inadequate. People roamed to and fro, stumbling, unseeing, over small bundles of personal items and shifting piles of bricks.

Near the front of the old building a vast jagged hole gaped into the street beyond. All that remained was a heap of bricks and timbers, covered in a sparkling sheen of deadly glass shards.

Several bombs had left craters in the middle of the street, spewing destructive shrapnel in all directions. The wall of the building across the street also had a broad section blown open and its contents had been thrown recklessly about the dark interior.

As the dust cleared and the bright light filtered into the broad street, it became apparent that the Russians had been trying to destroy supply stores. The building opposite the school was piled with wooden crates of various food items, all waiting to be shipped to the German soldiers on the now broken Eastern Front. Rows and rows of boxes, neatly stacked to the ceiling, stretched the length of the building. The crates nearest the blasted wall had crashed to the floor, shattering their wooden frames, and spilling the contents to the ground.

The significance of the proximity of the camp to such a building seemed to dawn on the camp director at that moment. He hollered hoarsely, through a frayed kerchief tightly pressed to his nose, for everyone to return to the cellar immediately. The Russians would surely be continuing their bombing missions on such vital supply sources.

But the street seemed calm, almost eerily so, and most people felt reluctant to leave the sunlit room. The mild spring breeze had the effect of easing the traumatized minds of everyone too long in the dark. Also, most faces were turned longingly toward the tempting array of edibles, all of which had been so long denied.

A loud angry sob broke the relative silence, which was punctuated only by the hoarsely barked orders of the director, whose words fell mostly on deaf ears. A pale young woman, her long auburn hair laying in filthy lice-covered tangles against her thin face, clenched her tiny infant to her shriveled breasts, and cried, "Look!... Look at all that food just sitting there... and we have been starving here for so long. I have no milk left for my baby!" she screamed. Her baby writhed uncomfortably in her mother's tightening grasp. "That food should be ours! It should be..." Her voice broke off with a whimper as her child began to cry pitifully. The unfortunate mother buried her head against the baby's soft cheek.

The breeze struck my face suddenly, rippling my hair; I was standing very close to the wide chasm in the side of the school. My mind seemed instantly cleared of the fog enveloping it since the long night in the wretched cellar. My heart began to pound into my throat as I considered what I had to do. I leaned against the crumbling brick wall, scraping my hand on the jagged edge of the opening, and I peered carefully down the length of the smoke-filled street.

Then, without a second thought, and knowing I had only seconds, I propelled myself over the heap of uneven rubble. I dashed headlong toward the opening of the food-filled warehouse. The air rushed into my throbbing ears as I reached the middle of the street. Suddenly, rapid stabs of machine gun fire echoed against the tall stone buildings. Red clay roof tiles showered onto my head, as the bullets ricocheted overhead.

A fit of energy hidden somewhere deep in my otherwise deprived body burst forth from my aching legs and propelled me across the rest of the street. I dove into the gaping hole, only then mindful of the yells and screams of the stunned onlookers in the camp. I thought I heard Gerle's frantic voice yell my name, when, upon realizing what I had just done, the rush of adrenaline once again filled my ears, blocking out all sound.

My lungs were heaving with the sudden strain, and I bent over with my hands on my knees, gasping for breath. I peered around the dim room from beneath my damp bangs, sweat dripping with a sting into my eyes.

Large boxes rose before me, all of them labeled with coded numbers, yet I was sure each one contained some sort of food. Most were still sealed shut, except the several dozen that had toppled in the explosion. I tiptoed deeper into the gloom and gasped, my eyes resting on several massive rounds of cheese, each the diameter of an ox cart wheel. Piled in a long row behind the cheese were metal pails neatly labeled with different flavors of marmalade.

The pounding in my ears had subsided, but my mouth watered with the sudden presence of such riches. My stomach rumbled noisily in anticipation as I considered my selection... finally, the sweet tooth in me triumphed. I grabbed a pail of preserves and was startled at its weight, yet I managed to hoist one more under my other arm.

Shifting the pails uncomfortably, I wormed my way between the rows of crates. It was only upon slowly approached the obliterated wall that I was conscious, once again, of the people yelling from across the perilous street.

"Come on! Be careful! Quickly!...." the anxious voices cried.

I adjusted the slippery metal pails under each arm and closed my eyes for just a moment. I took a deep breath, trying hard not to remember the sounds of the bullets. The instant my eyes opened I dashed forward, the sunlight catching me hotly on the forehead, sending up blotches of shadows before my startled eyes.

At once, bullets ripped across the rooftops above me again. The sides of the buildings erupted in a shower of debris, as chunks of stone, brick, and glass were dislodged upon my bobbing head. I felt a stinging thud on the nape of my neck and a warm sensation, as something sticky oozed slowly down my back.

Tiny pricks of light danced in front of my eyes and everything blurred before me. Suddenly, the weight of the pails seemed overwhelming; my fingers were beginning to tingle. With a last surge of determination, I stumbled the rest of the way across the street. Debris was scattered dangerously in my path, but I managed to skid my way to the opening, thrusting the heavy pails into outstretched hands.

I staggered to my knees, finally overcome by my brazen adventure. The yells of the women became fierce as they moved away into a huddle, tightly surrounding the new bearers of the precious marmalade. I glanced sadly towards the cluster of writhing bodies and knew that I would not be rewarded with even a taste of my hard earned treasure.

"Alfie! Are you all right? I can't believe you did that!" gasped Gerle, rushing to my side.

"You should at least get some, Gerle." I sighed. "You need it more than I do."

"Never mind, Alfie. You are just lucky you didn't get hurt."

I leaned against the dusty brick wall, only then aware of a pain in my neck. I reached up with my fingers and touched a damp gash. Bringing my hand away, it was covered with blood.

"Oh my God! You are bleeding!" a woman's shrill cry rang out above the squabbling din.

"It's ok. Really... I'm all right." I muttered, dimly. I felt slightly numb and a bit dizzy, though the pain seemed to be fading slightly. My stomach rumbled angrily with its lost chance at a meal, so I closed my eyes and tried to block out the sounds of the last of the marmalade being consumed.

Gerle had moved away, inching closer to the throng of ladies and old men, yet clearly reluctant to enter the rabid fray. I turned my head toward the opening in the wall and noticed that the street had once more descended into a dusty calm. I twisted my head back and forth several more times, aware, with a vague flicker of triumph, that the pain was subsiding.

I eased myself quietly to my feet and once more blindly dashed into the open air, this time determined to score myself... and Gerle... even a small morsel of something.

Everything erupted as before; clearly the snipers had been waiting for further activity. Bedlam once again rained down around me, as rubble crashed to the cobblestones at my feet. Yet the angle of fire seemed to be hampering my assailants from achieving a clear shot. This heartened me greatly, and I scampered to the relative safety of the warehouse.

This time, I steered clear of the heavy pails of preserves, instead making my way towards the vast wheels of cheese. After gaping around into the dark corners for several moments, I grabbed a rusty garden spade, which stood against a crate of canned beans. I thrust it deeply into the pungent rind of the moldy cheese.

Large chunks of the foul-smelling green skin crumbled onto the floor and I bent over, thrusting any small pieces into my fraying pockets. I hacked another square piece from the wheel and tossed some brittle scraps into my watering mouth. I retched in revulsion as the strong acrid taste swirled across my shocked taste buds. I forced the cheese down my parched throat, knowing I might receive none upon returning to the others. I hoisted the remaining large piece onto my shoulder in preparation for my return dash.

I cleared the street quickly, this time barely aware of the chaos around me. The frustrated enemy continued the assault on his very stubborn... and lucky target.

I watched with detached interest as the mob fell upon me again, wrestling the cheese from my hands and tearing it into crumbling shards before it even hit the floor. Gerle, once again, was at my side, shaking his head in disbelief at my boldness... or perhaps, foolishness. I beckoned him closer, glancing over his shoulder at the crowd, all of whom had completely forgotten about my existence.

"Here... I saved this for you. But, watch out. It's pretty foul." I said quietly, handing him several small lumps of cheese in my cupped hand.

"Well, anyway… I guess it's better than nothing, though I really would have liked to have had some of that marmalade."

"Thanks, Alfie. Don't do that again… really. But, thanks." replied Gerle, grinning broadly.

"I won't. Don't worry." I answered, gently massaging the tender spot on my neck, which was growing increasingly stiff. For a moment I stared at Gerle, realizing that his smile, once so ready and genuine, now seemed foreign and out of place on his sad and gaunt face. The smile faded quickly and turned to a grimace as he forced himself to consume the wretched cheese.

That afternoon brought more heavy shelling, this time extensive enough to cause worry that the building would collapse under the strain of the repeated impacts on nearby targets. Gerle and I sat with the crowds of terrified people in the loathsome cellar, our shapes fading into thickening waves of dust that burned our dry throats. The candlelight served only as a reminder that other souls existed who shared in our misery. But, it also exposed the rats, now more bold, as they scurried across people's outstretched limbs.

Then, as suddenly as it had begun, the shelling ceased. Another hour was allowed to pass before anyone felt ready to lead the crowd upstairs. We were not sure if we would emerge under a roof… or if we would emerge at all. Finally, the air became so thick with the shifting dust, that the camp director, his mouth muffled behind his faded handkerchief, mumbled hoarsely, "Maybe it is all over. You two come with me." He gestured to a pair of old men and edged slowly over the debris littering the stairway.

Gerle and I fell in closely behind the three of them, anxious to fill our lungs with fresher air. The men staggered slowly up the narrow flight of stairs. They placed each foot deliberately and carefully; an encounter with unstable rubble in the dark would have led to a nasty tumble. Sobbing and coughing bodies pressed in behind us as everyone's desire to vacate the stifling depths of the school increased.

The director paused in the darkness at the door, took a deep breath, and pushed it open. It caught only slightly, and the director let out his held breath and stepped into the long hallway. Sporadic shells were still streaking overhead, their distant impacts leaving all of us jumpy.

Most people lumbered back to the large gymnasium, which was now even more exposed to the outside. The air, though still heavy with debris, felt sweet and refreshing to our oppressed lungs, and we sat as close to the open wall as we dared.

The two men singled out by the director followed him down the hallway, clearly intent upon inspecting the damage from the bombs. I watched as one elderly man gingerly stepped across some shattered glass and tiptoed cautiously up the crumbling stairs.

Gerle and I rose and headed down the wide entry hall toward the front doors, both of which were blasted completely off their hinges. Broken glass crunched gratingly under our thin shoes, threatening at every step to imbed itself into our feet.

The heavy smell of fire filled the street and we covered our noses with our sleeves to protect our lungs from yet another assault. As we slowly advanced toward what was left of the door, a tremendous crash followed by a terrifyingly loud explosion knocked us off our feet. A lobbed grenade had ripped through the upper level.

We scrambled on our knees toward a massive oak desk that sat in the hallway, and only slightly mindful of the glass, we slithered under its protective bulk.

As the echoes of the explosion faded, a new sound met our ears. The man who had set off to inspect the upstairs now screamed in terror and agony, "Help! Help! Please... I've been hit! Oh, God! Help me!"

We stumbled back toward the broken stairway, climbing over fallen beams and toppled furniture. A shaft of sunlight glared upon our upturned faces as we rushed up the remnant of the stairs. We found the man in a heap near the top. He rolled back and forth among the debris, clutching his right leg amidst a growing pool of blood, which was congealing rapidly in the settling dust.

"We need some help up here!" Gerle yelled, panic rising in his voice. Some large shrapnel had ripped through the man's heel and had torn off the shoe and his foot completely. Only a dripping stump remained. Charred shoe leather and torn flesh were scattered among the bloody mess. His frantic motions suddenly stopped and he lay still, though anguished moans continued to disturb his ragged breathing.

We turned our eyes away and several voices approached slowly from beneath us. "Up here! Quickly!" croaked Gerle, then he doubled over with a fit of coughing. The new smell of gunpowder from the exploded grenade left us struggling to breathe, as we considered how best to help the poor man.

The possibility of another rogue grenade pressing on our minds, we comforted the man as best we could as the director and two other men half dragged and half carried him through the rubble strewn hallways to the cellar, where most of the people now sat sobbing. The narrow stairway proved difficult, and the man had slipped into unconsciousness by the time we eased him onto a dust-covered blanket on the floor.

Women rose and hovered closely, gasping and crying at the sight of the old fellow's terrible injury. As murmurs of the incident spread throughout the gloom, two women approached, their hands already tearing strips from their filthy aprons to try to bind his wound. Precious water was splashed on blood-soaked blankets, in a desperate attempt to clean the poor man's slashed and bruised face and arms.

I watched as a young girl, no older than myself, assisted her mother in tending the old man, wrapping what remained of his leg with cloth torn from her flowered apron. Her hands fumbled uncertainly, and she tried to hide her horrified eyes behind her blond braids. My mind traveled to Gretel, my young classmate who had disappeared into the grand tapestry of the war. Where was she? Had she survived the bombings? Was she, too, being called upon to do duties beyond her years?

The girl and her mother never left the man's side, even after the candles had sputtered their last breaths, and the rest of us had determined to steal several moments of sleep. All the while, the man's limbs lay slack and his eyes inert, and his breathing grew increasingly shallow. Yet, the old soldier's heart continued to struggle on, his labored breathing barely audible in the terrifying darkness. Around him, people settled down into another long vigil that promised to stretch through the entire night.

The next morning, May 8th, 1945, we again staggered up into the light of day, lured out by the eerie stillness that had descended over the city during the protracted hours before the dawn. Several people too weak to move remained below, lying on blankets near the old man who had not even whimpered during the night. He remained in a glistening pool of his own congealing blood, its putrid stench wrapping around every particle of dust that drifted through the room. I found myself wondering if he would ever emerge alive from the cellar. Possibly, he had already passed on.

We stumbled into the gymnasium, all of us clenching our empty stomachs, most fighting both illness and hunger. A loud yell erupted from the direction of the front office, and soon the director came thundering down the long hallway, heedless of the piles of brick and shattered furniture in his path.

"The war is over!!" he shrieked, his voice catching with emotion and strain. "It is over! The radio said so… the Red Army has taken the city and many others. The Allies have won!" He paused to gasp, then continued, more subdued; he seemed to notice, finally, all the terrified faces staring back at him. "The Russians have the city… They are here."

"No!" Gerle muttered at my side, and the fear in that single word was echoed many times over throughout the room. This was it. The moment had come. We were to face the feared Russians.

"Oma…! Opa…! Please stay safe!" I pleaded silently and I slumped sadly against my friend's shaking shoulders.

CHAPTER 14

The rest of the day was spent in silence and despair. Most people wandered fearfully around the demolished camp with glazed eyes. No hope remained. The shock of the bombings and the anticipation of the coming enemy only served to overwhelm the terrified clusters of families, most of whom suffered already from severe hunger and illness.

The women huddled in tight circles, far from their children's' innocent ears. They warned each other, in frantic whispers, to stay clear of the rumored abuses of the Russian soldiers. But, they knew, as they hoped, that there was no place to escape the anticipated horrors; the city had been entirely overrun.

Most of us spent our time sleeping in filthy corners of the toppled remnants of the school rooms. Places that were amply distanced from the stench of the outhouses were highly prized and a fierce pecking order decided control.

The lavatories had once been neatly housed in a small shack across the yard at the back of the main school building. The four toilets, mere holes on a wooden platform, were enclosed behind ornately carved wooden doors, yet the nearby bombings had left the doors only partly intact. Whatever privacy had been lost was negligible, as any fresh air was applauded. Once each day, one of the elders would take a shovel full of lime from its bag behind the shed and pour it into the stinking holes, but the effect was far from satisfactory.

The air further away from the outhouse was not much better. The unattended bodies of those unlucky souls who had braved the streets during the bombings—thankfully myself not included—remained where they had fallen. Also, animal carcasses were everywhere, mostly dogs and horses; no one had yet commenced to eating those.

The serious lack of food hung like a cloud over the heads of all those remaining in the camp. The gaping warehouse loomed temptingly from across the street, but the director insisted everyone stay within the grounds of the school, as the Russians could arrive at any moment. No one wanted to be discovered alone on a street with the fabled enemy.

As the camp helplessly awaited its fate, my heart ached with the desire to discover the whereabouts of my grandparents. I lamented each night the chasm my mother had formed between my sister and me. I longed to pull Gerti's soft blond braid and hear her tinkling laughter as I tickled her, but instead I was forced to pray that she was even alive. The bombing had been thorough and unforgiving.

To ponder the fates of my loved ones meant to live in agony. Gerle suffered similarly, as well. The location of his mother was even more of a mystery, and he was faced with a lifetime of questions regarding what had led to her disappearance.

Thus, we pined in silence; each aware of the other's fears and grief, yet aware that any comforting words would sound hollow.

Each morning dawned with more uncertainty. Czech partisans, along with the Russian troops, controlled the area, and beatings became a regular occurrence for anyone who ventured too far into the street. The coarse brutality of the victors only increased the misery of the wayward people, who clung to the crumbling school building like a life raft.

On one such morning, as I waited for Gerle to emerge from his bunk in another room, I huddled in a quiet corner whispering with several other children. The mothers were ensconced at the other end of the long room sleepily discussing their hopeful futures.

A loud crash echoed from the hallway. All voices ceased and terrified eyes turned to the door.

An indistinguishable jumble of slurred speech, in a tongue I did not understand, sounded in the hallway, and a large group of very young soldiers crashed through the door. Faces, with features slightly Eastern and distinctively foreign, darkened the morning light pouring into the room. The men were filthy and covered in sweat, and all of them were bald, their hair gone to protect against lice. They were obviously drunk with both liquor and victory, and they peered leeringly around at the frightened faces. Their own faces red with intoxication and laughter, the men stumbled and lurched into the room. Each soldier had one hand cradling an empty or sloshing vodka bottle and the other, a loaded machine gun.

As their greatest fears materialized before them, the women began to scream and cry, many yelling for their children to hide under the bunks. The children responded with cries of anguish and pleads for their mothers to hold them. Yet, the women remained clustered at the opposite end of the long narrow space, reluctant to stand out in front of the men who gazed at them with eyes so full of lust.

One soldier belched loudly and crashed his unfinished bottle to the floor, where the vodka scoured a clean path through the layers of dust and rubble. He muttered something under his breath, like an oath, then swept suddenly across the room and grabbed the nearest body. To my horror, I realized that it was the young girl who had come so valiantly to the aid of the old man in the basement. She barely had a moment to utter a startled cry when the soldier shoved her roughly onto a nearby bed. She shrieked horribly, her cries echoed by most of the women in the place. Several women tried to approach but were pushed forcefully back by the other soldiers. One, the girl's mother, fell to the floor in a faint, but the others felt too frightened to go to her aid.

A terrifying tension filled the room, with realization dawning in everyone's mind as to what was about to happen. From my sheltered perspective, I was still aware that a young life was about to be violated. The girl's older sister threw herself behind a blanket, which had been hung against a bunk for privacy. She sobbed into the cloth, clutching her ears against the heart-wrenching sounds of her sister's clothes being torn from her pinned body. The girl was thin… too thin, and fair, except where bruises were already welling up from the soldier's tight grip. Only the faintest signs of womanhood were visible, but the sight of her innocent flesh seemed to stir the man to a desperate fury.

I squeezed my eyes shut, knowing instinctively that what was coming next was what women feared above all else. A smooth dark face, so young he had scarcely a whisker, the man held the girl easily; her kicks measuring as nothing more than a slight ripple in his fantasies. He frantically opened the front of his trousers with his free hand and leapt onto her frail limbs, sending new screams of pain and fear from the girl's hoarse lungs.

The other soldiers, now yelling in delight and encouragement, poked and prodded at the occupied man. The primitive urge to follow his lead coursed through their lusty veins. Hardly had the man retreated from the girl's writhing form, a dazed smile on his flushed face, and buttoning his pants as he backed away, when I noticed brilliantly red blood pooling rapidly between the poor girl's legs.

The men slapped each other heartily on the backs, clearly reveling in their sport of stealing the innocence of a refugee girl. Just as quickly, another man took the first one's place and the screaming, though more feeble now, began again. It soon subsided completely, though, as the girl slipped into shock, her body going limp. Finally, a sharp crack echoed among the heavy groans and thrusts of the second soldier. The girl's head had smashed at an odd angle into the wall.

"Close your eyes, my children." a mother sobbed quietly. Yet few were able; the horrors were too close.

Several more men expended their pent up energies upon the child, leaving her body thrown grotesquely across the bloody mattress, its straw spilling out the sides. But, her voice had gone silent, the life finally torn from her limbs. Yet, the men persisted, not caring that her soul no longer dwelled in her body. This remained sufficient for their horrid needs until it grew cold.

Sobs and moans filled the air, now taut with the pants and gasps of the spent men. An hysterical woman, a tattered scarf barely hiding a haggard but pretty face, leapt up with a scream, her mind undone by the pure evil of the invaders. She flung herself forward, pounding her white knuckled fists into the tight shoulders of the first young man.

"You bastard! You killed her! You bastard!" she screamed, flailing her arms wildly into the figures slowly massing around her. Several of the soldiers grabbed her arms, still laughing and joking, and others began punching every exposed surface of her body. Seconds later her muffled cries ceased and her bleeding and bruised body slumped to the floor.

Immediately the men tore at her clothes like animals, and her eyes flew open, filled with the anguished realization that she was to share the fate of the girl. Soon they were scrambling to pile on her, just as they had done with the other. Her screams faded to moans and whimpers, but her wide eyes traveled pleadingly around the room and blood trickled slowly from her gaping mouth.

People backed away; now the cost of aiding someone had become all too clear. Faces were hidden in hands or averted. A broad, middle-aged woman, her hair in a disheveled bun, spat defiantly onto the back of one soldier. He turned to her with a sneer. She gasped, covered her mouth with her trembling hands, and began to back away. He raised the butt of his black machine gun and drove it with a hollow thud into the side of her skull. She, too, crumpled to the floor.

The men's hunger for the women seemed unabating, and several more were raped before the men finally stormed out, grabbing two untouched mothers to take with them for their future urges. The screams of the women could be heard clearly as they were dragged into the street, only to be met there by the enthusiastic yells of more soldiers.

The air was thick with the aftermath of the brutal attacks. The women who had been spared tried to comfort those who had been hurt, and several children cried out for the mothers who had been taken. The body of the young girl remained sprawled across the rumpled bed, her lifeless eyes staring blankly at the ceiling. Her clothes were in bloody shreds around the room and her torso and legs were covered with blotches of ugly bruises and caked blood.

Her sister emerged slowly from her hiding place, trembling uncontrollably, shimmering tears streaking down her pale face. She jumped in terror as her mother's gentle arms encircled her from behind in a comforting embrace. The mother's head was bruised and bleeding; she had been flung against a bunk frame before the men had taken their turns with her. These two survivors clung to each other and wept... wept for the brutal end to their loved one's short life.

Gerle and I found each other as soon as the noise of the soldiers disappeared around the corner of the block. Gripping my arm tightly, Gerle related similarly horrific stories of attacks in his bunk room.

The body of the girl was carried carefully out to the school yard, where it was covered with a spare blanket. Leaning heavily upon one another, the mother and surviving daughter followed silently behind the somber procession. The tears flowed unchecked, and the sun slanted its long amber rays in a last caress of farewell upon the girl's still face.

Gerle and I remained in the doorway, unwilling to disturb the intimate moment of the two women as they hunched over the body, their arms lovingly entwined around each other in a mutual attempt to ease the other's pain. Soon, the shoulders of the mother began to tremble and she raised an anguished face skyward, her bloody and swollen lips mouthing a fervent prayer earnestly towards heaven.

Gerle's voice quavered violently as he whispered through clenched teeth, "That could be what happened to my mother, Alfie... it really could be." He brushed the back of his hand quickly across his shadowed eyes and turned his head slightly away, fighting for control of his words. "Will I ever see her again? I never even got to say goodbye, Alfie... not even a goodbye." He coughed.

"At least you didn't have to see what those two saw today, Gerle." I said, gesturing with my chin. "That's something... But I know what you mean. It is terrible not knowing." My mind jumped to my grandparents. Had they experienced similar scenes in their camp? Had they survived? Was old age enough to protect a woman from such a fate?

I desperately wanted to run away from the horrible visions crowding into my head... run away to somewhere safe and peaceful... a time long since forgotten. My mind jumped suddenly to the sound of cool water splashing among the rocks on the riverbank at home, the fish darting playfully away from our traps, the laughter of my friends in a better time. Now, it was my turn to hide a quivering lip against the back of my hand.

A sickly calm descended over the camp. Crowds of local partisans were keeping the throngs of unruly troops temporarily at bay. Skirmishes flared up briefly along the streets, making any chance of escape a daring proposition. Conditions in the camp deteriorated rapidly. Many of the women needed medical help; some had sustained injuries severe enough to keep them motionless on their bunks.

Food grew scarcer by the day, though the first hot meal of the long week came as the field kitchen was once again able to be used. The bombings had made it impossible for any cooking to take place; we had been surviving on infrequent cans of cold food for many days. The anticipated hot meal consisted of a small cup of watery potato broth, but the first sip was the most pleasant sensation we had experienced in a long time.

We felt hungry all the time, our energy sapped so low that we did little more than lie around in the school yard, waiting eagerly for the next meager serving. I would dream of Oma's delicious food, all heaped abundantly in bowls around a peaceful table with my family—memories of a time when every breath I took wasn't laced with fear and sadness.

As did nearly everyone in camp, we still suffered from the symptoms of dysentery, yet Gerle and I fought the urge as long as we could so we wouldn't have to face the horrible outhouse. Its odor now ruled the camp. Fresh air was only a memory. When the wind shifted, the stench of human excrement was replaced by that of rotting bodies in the street.

As awful as the war had been, the few days following the 8th were the most miserable we had experienced. We felt cheated… cheated by our leaders, cheated by our country… but most of all cheated by humanity. This was not how it was meant to be… or was it?

The sun rose as ever before, warming the fetid air as it wafted heavily over everyone's down-turned and despairing faces. We knew we were supposed to be getting on with our lives. The war was over, yet we felt as trapped as ever.

It was the morning of the 13th of May, and the war had officially been over for almost a week. The camp director summoned me to his office, where he sat in his chair, the desk in shards at his feet. His fleshy face no longer looked threatening. He seemed to have lost his will, or his desire, to intimidate the inhabitants of the camp. Large circles ringed his eyes, which were red from lack of sleep and filled with a despondency that I could only imagine was caused by the very hopelessness of our predicament.

"I'm sorry to tell you this, my boy…" he started, his forehead creased with sadness, "… but we have received word that there was some… activity at the address of your mother and sister. You are being given permission to go… in fact, it is imperative that you do so. You must speak to no one on the way, and you must take the most direct route there. Do not be gone long." he concluded, in a rush.

"What is wrong, sir? Do you know… I mean, what has happened there?" I asked, fearfully.

"I don't know, son… I don't know. My sources just told me that you are needed there… right away. Go, now." he finished rapidly, dismissing me with his averted eyes.

"Can my friend go with me?" I asked suddenly, thinking company might make whatever I might find easier to bare.

"No, just you." he replied curtly, not raising his eyes, which remained focused on a rumpled pile of papers lying in his lap. "And remember, stay out of sight."

I scurried quickly back to Gerle, who lay dozing on his bunk, the straw matted and foul under his torn blanket.

"Good luck, Alfie. I hope everything is all right." he answered, upon hearing my situation. "Just be careful, Alfie... You know what they are capable of."

I raised my eyes to his face at these words. I swept the racing thoughts to the back of my mind and hastened out of the room. I was desperate to aid my mother in any way necessary... in spite of everything, she was my mother.

I turned and retraced my steps to the front of the building, where I peeked out cautiously. The sun was just rising over the narrow buildings that butted up against the street. Dust hung in the air above small fires that continued to smolder deep beneath some of the ruins. But, other than distant voices, and an occasional child's cry, I was alone in the eerie silence.

I headed off as quickly as I could, painfully aware that I had eaten no breakfast, until I reminded myself that I hadn't had any for several days. I checked around each corner with caution before I hurried onward. My heart raced with the thought that my mother finally needed me... she finally wanted me near.

Each street seemed longer than on my last excursion. Nothing looked as it had before. Every other building was demolished, their twisted frames leaning threateningly into the rubble-filled street. I climbed over roof tiles and broken glass, which crumbled noisily beneath my worn shoes, as well as bricks and mortar, and long beams of timber, which had stood reasonably straight since the Middle Ages. Now it all lay in ruins, to be piled up and thrown away to make way for another generation... just as the poor souls who had lost their lives in the terrible war would someday be forgotten... and all for what?

After what seemed like hours, I turned into the street where my mother's narrow townhouse apartment stood and I increased my pace to a trot. I saw several women standing near the broad stone steps that lead to the door, which as now swinging recklessly off its hinges. They turned as

169

I approached, their conversation ceasing, and they looked at me in silence, some with their eyes full of tears.

It was then that I noticed the broken windows and toppled tree limbs, and the smoke drifting slowly out of the courtyard to the side of the house. I glanced at the nearest woman, with questions clearly visible on my pained face, yet she merely pointed around the back, saying quietly, "She's out there." I glanced once more at their quiet faces, then hurried around the side of the house to the walled garden beyond.

As soon as I entered the sheltered garden, now strewn with debris, I heard the crying. My little sister's sobs pierced the still air, sending chills along my spine. "Mama! Mama! I want my Mama!"

"Gerti!" I cried, hurrying forward. I stumbled to a halt. Her red tearstained face turned toward me from where she knelt next to a grotesquely crumpled body. It was my mother.

"Oh, God! What happened, Gerti?" I gasped, as I flung my arms around my sister's shaking shoulders, her sobs uncontrollable against my chest. Her tiny hands clutched at my ragged shirt, plucking frantically at the dusty folds. Small stains of blood began to rise on the fabric of my shirt… my mother's blood. I looked over Gerti's head and was overwhelmed by the sight before me.

Dried blood covered Mother's beautiful face, now pale as a porcelain doll's, and her eyes were rolled back into her head, revealing only the whites. Her clothes lay across her in shreds, barely covering a badly bruised body caked in blood. She lay in a twisted position, her head contorted unnaturally on her shoulders.

Gerti whimpered again against my shirt, pleading softly, "Mama! Mama!" I stroked her hair, soft as I had remembered it, and I stared in disbelief at what was left of my mother. My throat was tight with the desire to scream, but my sister's presence made me bite my tongue in a desperate attempt to suppress my feelings.

I glanced upward toward a balcony, one of several that lined the shared garden, and I noticed small faces of children where they peeked curiously through the slats of the railing. Behind them women whispered in their ears, pulling them gently by their shoulders, until they disappeared into the dark rooms within.

There was a crunching of footsteps behind me. The lady who had spoken to me in the front of the building was stepping carefully along a path now thick with broken glass. She pulled Gerti gently to her feet and led us, with one hand on each of our shoulders, toward her first floor flat. I glanced over my shoulder once more at my mother's body, hoping it had all been a cruel nightmare, but the twisted shape remained, her back bent slightly backwards.

"Now, you just sit here, honey." the woman said quietly to my sister, easing her into a plush chair. Then, she gestured to me to follow her into the kitchen. My sister curled herself into a small ball, her filthy bare feet tucked tightly up under her hole-filled dress. Her eyes traced a line on the rug below her as she hiccuped her sobs absently.

"What happened?" I demanded, as soon as we rounded the corner from my sister. The woman paused to stare into my eyes, clearly working over in her mind just how much to tell me, when I continued, "Please... Tell me everything. I need to know how my mother died." I found myself shaking at these words, the thought that she was really gone finally surfacing. I fought to keep my eyes level and my voice controlled, while we continued along the narrow hall into the kitchen.

"I'll tell you, but first let's get you and your sister some tea and bread. You look like you could use some food.... and your sister, she hasn't been eating properly for weeks." she answered firmly, but kindly.

She bustled silently for several minutes, so I peered around the corner at my sister, who remained as we had left her. After Gerti was settled with her tea and bread, generously covered with precious jam, we returned to the kitchen, away from my sister's ears.

"Well, it started last night." the lady began sadly, her hands wrapping nervously around a towel hanging from her apron pocket. "A large group of soldiers, clearly reeling from too much to drink, stormed in here late last night." Her voice shook slightly and she blinked sullenly, then she continued, "They tore through the houses, looking for women... and did things to them that you wouldn't understand."

"I think I do, ma'am." I interrupted in a whisper. From the look on my face, she seemed to realize that I did know more than a boy my age should. "Some soldiers visited our camp, as well." I finished, the heat rising into my face with sudden anger upon recalling the horrors I had seen. Thus, I acknowledged to myself for the first time that this was also what had happened to my mother.

"Well," she muttered, clearing her throat. "Most of the soldiers got very... rough with some of the women... a few of us were spared, God willing, though not many. They even went after some of the children... not your sister!" she added quickly, as I started. "But, your sister did see things no one should ever have to see, but she will be all right... in time. Give her time. She's lucky to have you."

I dragged my hands through my hair, noticing for the first time some crusted drops of blood on my arms where I had held my sister... my mother's blood, passed on to me from my sister, who had clutched my mother's lifeless body in a desperate attempt to revive her.

"... She fought back..." the woman's soft voice continued, breaking into my thoughts. "... That's why they were so rough with her. But, she couldn't hold off all of them... and they all seemed to want her." She shifted her eyes toward the window, which looked out over the trees shading my mother's body in the grass below.

"I think they threw her off the balcony when they were... done." she said quickly, as if anticipating my next question.

I closed my eyes and asked, "Was she... was she dead... already?"

"I don't think so." came the answer. "But if it helps at all, I think she died quickly. I think she must have broken her neck." There was a long pause, then she cleared her throat and continued, "You should have your tea now. A truck will be coming shortly to... collect her. I'm sorry." she finished, placing her hand on my shoulder.

"Collect her?" I asked, grimacing. "Where do they take her?"

"Where they take all of them, dear... where they take all of them. Say your goodbyes now." she answered, shaking her head sadly.

I sat next to Gerti, who remained huddled in a ball, and I ate my bread, angry with myself for not enjoying the delicious jam more.

A loud crashing in the street jolted us back to the moment, and Gerti began to whimper again. I wrapped my free arm around her shoulders, noticing sadly how her bones poked through her thin dress.

"The truck is here, dears. Time to go." said the lady and she opened the door to the courtyard.

Gerti grabbed my hand tightly in hers, her nails digging into my knuckles, as she tried to keep me from heading back to our mother. I pulled her gently along and emerged in the garden just as two large sour-faced men wandered around the corner and strode casually across the debris covered grass to my mother.

They were both wearing gloves and long rubber aprons, and I couldn't help but think that they looked like butchers. They peered at my mother as though she were nothing more than a troublesome sack of grain they had been ordered to move. They hoisted her twisted body with little regard, and her head fell limply backward where the bones were crumbled.

They trundled her through the narrow side alley, unconcerned when her hanging hand caught on the wrought iron gate. One man propped her head against his protruding belly, and flung her hand back onto her exposed chest, before marching out to the wagon. I followed closely, with Gerti dragging reluctantly on my arm, and the men's voices reached my ears as they rounded the corner, "She was a looker. Pity we didn't get here sooner." They sniggered and jostled with their load to the rear of the wagon.

It was open and revealed a mass of jumbled bodies, many with severed limbs; all encrusted with thousands of flies. The sun beat down on them, sending the stale sweet smell of death into our faces.

The gentle muzzles of two black horses turned to gaze placidly at us, from where they stood harnessed to the ghastly load. The men approached the wagon's open back, and swinging my mother wildly back and forth, they heaved her body onto the top of the pile. The disturbance sent the flies swarming into a dense cloud, before they settled eagerly back down to their morbid feast.

Gerti snapped suddenly out of her trance at the sight of her mother's pale face on the pile of bodies, and she screamed, "Mama! Mama! Noooo! No! Mama! Come back!" I grabbed her shoulders to restrain her, for she seemed ready to throw herself onto the wagon. I held her closely, burying her eyes into the grimy folds of my shirt.

The men strolled languidly to their seats at the front of the wagon, tapped the horses gently with the reins, and the wagon lurched forward. The bodies shifted horribly and blood dripped from above the axle of the groaning load.

I took Gerti by the hand and started to follow along beside the slowly creaking wagon. It stopped suddenly and one of the men jumped off. He strode over to me and shoved me roughly in the chest with his gloved hand. I stumbled backwards, falling into the dusty road, and my sister toppled on top of me. The man snarled, "Get out of here, you little whelps! … Or we will throw both of you on top, as well!"

I stared, openmouthed at the horrid man, watching him stomp back to his place on the wagon. He glanced angrily over his shoulder, making sure I remained firmly seated in the dust.

Gerti screamed and sobbed, her small fists pounding into her face, and she tore at her braids in grief. The wagon continued on its gruesome rounds, and I could only gape in farewell at the figure that had been my mother, where she lay tossed like an old rag in the trash.

Hate seared through my veins, and I picked myself up from the street, clenching my fists at my side in an effort not to run after the retreating wagon. Soon, only the sounds of the creaking wheels and the clopping of the horses' hooves could be heard from afar, and my sister and I stood hand in hand, alone in the dusty street.

It occurred to me suddenly, with a somber clarity, that the next day, May 14th, 1945, would be Mother's Day… which was also the day we would have to celebrate my sister turning six… alone.

CHAPTER 15

The wagon, the only coffin my mother would ever have, was followed by a whirling veil of dust; it eddied and swirled in the silence, before settling in a heavy layer on the street. Gerti and I remained frozen to the spot. Our world had been shattered cruelly before us, and hope for the future seemed impossible.

I felt a gentle touch on my shoulder and I turned to see the kind lady standing near me, her eyes trained on the bend in the street.

"She would have wanted you to be strong for your sister." she said softly.

"I'm not so sure about that." I found myself thinking, but instead, I said, "Yes, I will take her with me."

"If you explain at the camp, perhaps they will let you go to your grandparents—the war is over now, after all. Soon you will all be going home... everything will be ok. Don't you worry, dear." she whispered, placing her hand again on my slumped shoulder.

She twined the handles of a small satchel between my fingers, saying, "Here are Gerti's things. There are not many—just a hairbrush and a dress. There is also a watch... I believe it was your father's. It was among your mother's belongings."

"Thank you. Thank you for your kindness... and for taking care of Gerti like you did." I muttered, my voice catching as I suppressed a sigh. "We better get back. I wasn't supposed to be gone so long."

She smiled sweetly and shook my outstretched hand. "Good luck, dear. Good luck to both of you." she said, ruffling Gerti's hair, which hung in messy braids against her tearstained face. Gerti boldly attempted a smile, but her mouth twisted uncontrollably downward, and she sobbed quietly into my shirt.

"Come on, Gerti." I said softly. "Let's go. Gerle will be so happy to see you." I added, eager to cheer her up. "Goodbye, and thank you again." I said to the lady. I turned away, my hand guiding my sister gently forward by her shoulders, her face still buried deeply under my arm.

The walk back to camp filled me with a fear that had been latent on my first journey. I had seen, once again, the potential cruelty of humanity, and this abandonment of hope unnerved me. I jumped at every sign of activity, benign or otherwise. Gerti clung tightly to me the entire way. Her eyes were wide with fear and awe at the once beautiful city, its splendor now crushed into rubble beneath our feet.

I stumbled along, still in shock from seeing my mother lying in her own blood. Yet, I remained in grateful disbelief that I was reunited with my sister. I was determined to not let anything destroy her life in such a fashion again. I was all she had to protect her from the vortex of chaos swirling around us.

We reached the camp unhindered. From the street-side the school looked as if its roof would fall in at any moment; it was so full of holes. But inside it continued to swarm with the crowds of hungry despairing people, all of whom were aware that this was the best shelter they would find for miles.

I proceeded immediately to the director's office, where I found him rummaging through more piles of papers, each one of which represented some poor person's fate. He looked up quickly, the sides of his mouth pulling into a tight crease at the sight of my sister.

"I see." he said, curtly. "I'm sorry, son... your mother?..." he queried. I nodded my head silently, not yet ready to explain the details.

"Can my sister stay here, sir... please?" I asked, keeping my gaze level on his face. Gerti grabbed tightly onto my arm, hiding her grimy face behind my back.

Well, we really are at our limit here... even with, you know..." I knew he was referring to the girl who had died in the bunk room, as well as the others, but I persisted as if I had not heard him.

"Please, sir. She can sleep in my bunk with me. She won't take up a lot of room. I'm... I'm all she has now." I finished, my voice trembling slightly, the heat of desperation putting color into my otherwise pale face.

"I'm sorry, but there just isn't room. But..." he continued, raising his hand up, as I attempted to interrupt. "Let me finish! But... we have made arrangements for you and your sister, and that boy..."

"Gerle..." I coaxed.

"Yes, Gerle... to join your grandparents and uncle in their camp. From there you will be returned home, as soon as there is a train available." he said. "I don't want you out too late, so best get your friend and get going. Mind you, it is the same rules as before. Go quickly. Here are the directions. Stay off the main roads." he added, handing me a small wrinkled piece of paper. "... The victors will not look too kindly upon Germans they encounter in the streets. Especially your sister." he added, knowingly. "So stay clear of everyone." he finished bitterly.

My heart leapt with mingled relief and fear as I grabbed the paper from his outstretched hand and managed a hasty, "Thank you!", before I hauled Gerti out of the room to look for Gerle.

Outside the door I leaned gratefully against the wall, my head spinning with a mixture of emotions. "We are going home, Gerti! Did you hear that? We are going to be going home!" I cried, grabbing her into a tight hug and twirling her around, her slight frame feeling even more diminished once I lifted her off her feet. She was skin and bones... but, we were going home. Oma would see that she had decent meals again.

"You get to see Oma and Opa, Gerti! Imagine that! They will be so happy to see you. What a wonderful birthday present that will be, huh?" I asked, noticing that her face remained unchanged at the news.

"I want my mama." she whispered. "I... just want my mama." Her eyes darted nervously across the floor and her arms hung limply at her sides. Her spirit was gone.

"I know, Gerti. I want her, too... but we get to see Oma and Opa... and Uncle Alois. Think of all the fun stories he will have for you." I tried thus in vain to lift the heavy shadow from her heart while we wandered the halls in search of Gerle.

We found him reclining in the dust and brick filled grass, leaning against what remained of the back wall of the school. His eyes were closed

177

and his hands were clasped across his very thin belly; dysentery and malnutrition had steadily eaten away at his already slight build.

"Gerle, I'm back." I said, nudging his shoulder gently.

He started and yawned, keeping his eyes closed against the warm sun baking his pale face. "Oh, good, Alfie. I hope your mother gave you a better meal than we had here." he said. "It was awful…" He opened his eyes. "Gerti!" he shouted. "Gerti! Hi! Wow, you've grown!" he cried, as he scrambled to his feet.

He grabbed Gerti's small fingers in his own, and it was then that I noticed that her hands were still covered with blood… Mother's blood. Gerle noticed too. "What's this? Gerti? … Alfie? What's going on? Why is she here?" he demanded suddenly. The situation seemed to dawn on him, for he held Gerti closer and planted a fervent kiss on her forehead.

I grabbed his arm, pulling him slightly away from my sister, who seemed fascinated by the other children in the yard. I said, "She's dead, Gerle. I saw her. It happened… just like the girl."

"Oh, God, Alfie. I'm sorry!… Where, uh… where is she?" he asked, his forehead creased with sadness.

"They took her away, Gerle. I didn't even get to follow. It was horrible." Tears twitched into the corners of my eyes, but I blinked them away quickly. "I don't even know where they took her." I finished, sadly.

"Um, Alfie, I heard some of the people here talking, and they were saying that most of them… the, um, bodies… get buried together in a big hole… and bulldozed over." he said, somberly. I turned away, refusing to picture my mother in such a grave, and Gerle, sensing my unease left it alone.

"There is some good news, though, Gerle." I said, after a lengthy pause. "We have been given permission, all three of us, to go to the camp where Oma and Opa are. From there, eventually, we will be going home… together." I exclaimed.

"That's great! When do we go?" Gerle asked, excitedly.

"As soon as we are ready. Is there any food left, Gerle? Gerti could use some—she's so thin. Hardly anything left of her. It will be good to get some of Oma's cooking into her. Mother was never very good at it. Oma, though… Oma can make the smallest things into a great meal…" I broke off suddenly, the rumbles of hunger were erupting in my stomach with too much ferocity to continue with any comfort. Also, my heart ached with longing for my grandmother's warm embrace.

"I don't think so. But, Alfie, the sooner we get out of here the better. Let's go!"

After a long walk across the town, through one destroyed street after another, and skirting lines of soldiers wandering in every direction, we arrived at the tall facade of the school building that housed my grandparents and Uncle Alois. Gerti had whimpered most of the way, stumbling along with her hand tucked up in a ball inside mine, while every few minutes pleading for her mother.

The building that held my grandparents had fared only slightly better than ours during the intense bombing. Nonetheless, the doors creaked fearfully as we pushed them open. A dank office, filled with dust still settling in the long late afternoon light, stood to our right. We entered without pause, eager to be finally reunited with what was left of our family.

A severe woman was standing behind a long counter writing intensely in some ledgers, but she looked up upon hearing our footfalls, her pen poised above some long columns of names.

"Can I help you?" she snapped.

"Um, we are here from the other camp. I'm Alfred, and this is my sister, Gertrude, and this…"

She interrupted, "Ah, yes. They are down the hall all the way to the end, then left." she said, crisply, before returning to her papers.

"Thank you." I muttered, glancing with a slight grin at Gerle, who sniggered, quietly.

"Well, that was quick." I said, after we had escaped to the hallway. "I was expecting that to take longer. I guess it is because the war is over—everyone is leaving." I continued. "Let's go." I grabbed Gerti's hand and we wandered along the dark and littered hallway, which reminded me greatly of the one we had just left behind.

A sickening smell of urine filled the air, hanging thickly throughout the narrow space. Dust and smoke swirled in through open gaps in the brick walls of the large building. Clearly, Oma and Opa had witnessed their own share of numerous assaults during the week long siege of the city.

We tiptoed carefully down the hall, skirting piles of debris that had been pushed hastily to the side to make a path for walking. We turned into the door on the left, as directed, and we found ourselves in a room filled with listless individuals, most of whom were resting miserably on filthy bunks. Hollow coughs and children's pitiful moans disturbed the uneasy stillness. We inched slowly into the dimly lit room.

Gerti cried, "Mama!", in a squeal under her nervous gasps and she hid herself behind Gerle and me. Eyes turned toward us, their faces blank and devoid of emotion. Several whispers reached my ears, as we shuffled into the room, yet the faces I so longed to see did not appear.

Gerti braved a peek from behind my sleeve and suddenly screamed, lunging forward into the outstretched arms of a hunched figure just emerging from a dark corner. Oma's sweet face materialized out of the shadows and it blossomed into a broad smile as she wrapped her warm arms around her tiny granddaughter. Gerle and I ran forward, enclosing the two in a wider hug, just as Opa appeared from around the corner of a bunk.

"My dear boys!… and Gerti! Are you ever a sight for sore eyes!" he chuckled, tears pooling in his tired eyes, which were newly engraved with red-laced lines of strain and anxiety.

We pulled reluctantly away from Oma, who remained stooped with Gerti in a tight hug. She continued to coo quietly in Gerti's ear, gently stroking my sister's blond tangled tresses, lovingly. Suddenly, Oma began to sob, silently but deeply, in gulped breaths, as she rested her chin upon Gerti's small head. Her eyes were pinched shut and large tears ran down well worn creases on her aged cheeks.

Gerti let whatever control she had acquired melt away and she cried mercilessly into her sweet grandmother's heaving bosom. Young tears and old mingled together in their embrace, their sobs creating a precious halo of linked breaths.

I turned to Opa and seized him in a tight grasp, before he clutched Gerle's shoulder and included him in the three-way hug.

"It is so good to see you both safe. And, Alfie…" he said, placing his hand on my shoulder, "… thank you for getting your sister away from that place." His eyes flickered suddenly with darkness and I realized, gratefully, that they had already heard the news of our mother's death. Gerti and I would not have to relive it in the telling.

Opa dragged his shadowed eyes away from my face, thoughtfully allowing me a moment to compose myself, and he looked fondly upon Gerle who was standing quietly by my side.

"Thank you, my boy." he said to Gerle, tousling his hair playfully with his wrinkled hand. "Thank you for sticking with Alfie. I know you two helped each other survive this. You are truly a part of this family now, Gerle." His voice faltered slightly and he pulled Gerle toward him in another warm hug.

Mother's Day dawned cloudy and gray, with a slight drizzle pattering on the roof tiles. The water trickled through the many holes pocketing the building, where it pooled in large puddles on the floor among the rows of bunks.

In spite of the unpleasant conditions made miserable by the rain, I finally felt whole again. My family was as intact as it ever was going to be and for that I was grateful. The void left by my mother's violent death was eased by the soothing presence of my grandparents. They, not my mother, had always provided the center of calm in my life. Of course, I missed my mother. Though, in truth, she had had, at best, only a fleeting touch on my upbringing. I mourned her tragic death, certainly, but I longed for her more for my sister's sake than my own.

Gerti remained in a fitful state, barely willing to acknowledge her own birthday, despite the amusing attempts to engage her in play by Uncle Alois. He had traveled with Oma and Opa across the mountains in the evacuation and had remained with them the entire way. His face was thinner than I remembered, but it only served to enhance the smile that lit his entire face at the sight of us together again.

We spent the day huddled quietly among the narrow bunks, trying to stay out of the water, which turned quickly to a slippery mud as it mixed with the piles of dust and mortar scattered across the floor.

I sat in an unoccupied corner, fingering Father's gold watch, which glistened brilliantly in the otherwise morose atmosphere of the bunk room. Images of my father, his face barely visible, danced in my head, where it lurked temptingly on the brink of remembrance. He had purchased the watch on one of his trips to Vienna. I remembered his gentle fingers as they had held it carefully up for me to inspect, my young eyes filled with wonderment and admiration.

"We will be able to head home… as soon as the trains are running." my grandfather said, his voice piercing my thoughts and driving away the murky memories. He whittled slowly on a piece of wood with his dull pocket knife, turning it carefully, as narrow strips of fragrant wood, possible remnants of some pupil's desk, spiraled to the dirty floor. "It will be good to get home. The fields should be ready to burst into bloom soon." he continued, confidently, though his forehead remained knit with seemingly permanent lines of worry.

Studying his face carefully, I twirled the smooth cold metal of the watch between my fingers, before sneaking it into the bottom of my high leather shoe. I was determined to return home with my last connection to my father intact.

We waited anxiously for several days, our spirits lifting slightly by the constant trickle of people leaving to head home. Those who had traveled from the hills around Maerisch-Schoenberg were the first to go. It was the mere matter of a long day's walk and they would be home. People left with chins raised and eyes to the future. This dogged hope remained, in spite of the probability of finding houses and valleys destroyed or, at best, tainted and stripped by the greedy fingers of the hungry enemy.

The train station swarmed with families destined for further points to the East. Limited cars were available and the engines themselves were even more scarce. The victorious Russians had commandeered many of the serviceable ones for their own needs.

As trains gradually became available, the director swept through the rooms several times each day, rattling in a toneless voice names of those grouped by town and province. The waiting, as always, quickly became agony. Conditions in the camp continued to deteriorate. Control of the facility seemed to have disappeared upon the declaration of the Reich's defeat. Germany had seen its moment of power and order. Now its citizens, as well as the refugees from surrounding lands, were forced to flounder in a shattered society surviving on nothing but eachother's despairing and fearful souls.

At last the day came when we were ordered to the station. We walked with hundreds of others to the train, each of us filled with hope, hope that we would now be heading home to resume our lives. We marched in a ragged group, Oma and Opa flanking us closely. We turned our backs, willingly, on the wretched squalor of the town that had signified a defining moment in all our lives. Smoke still rose over much of the shattered city, the very heart of which struggled for its survival.

After several hours waiting in the cramped freight cars for orders to depart, the stagnant air pressing in on us like a fetid pillow being held over our faces, we finally lurched to a crawl, and the train hissed and whined its way slowly eastward.

A faint, but welcome, breeze drifted in through the narrow slits near the top of the car and eased the throbbing in my head. My forehead was beaded with sweat, despite the chilly drizzle pattering relentlessly on the roof of the car.

Low murmurs grew more confident and soon eyes twinkled with hope. Memories of homes and loved ones left behind in the great upheaval loosened tongues, and soon forgotten smiles danced shyly across many drawn and tired faces.

The train squealed to a stop in the next city, where trains fought for priority on the heavily damaged lines. We strained our ears to hear the words of the Russian soldiers, who hastened our train onto a siding, where it was quickly relieved of its highly coveted engine.

Moods plummeted, along with the temperature. The slanting rain began to drip with a torturous rhythm through the boards in the roof. Soon the muffled cries of the children resumed, Gerti among them, as hunger and thirst eclipsed any hopeful thoughts of the future.

After we suffered through the sounds of our engine lumbering away to the east, pulling cars loaded with confiscated equipment and hard goods, we were at long last released from our dark and cold confinement only to be lined up in the mud along the tracks.

The rain continued ceaselessly, trickling down the back of my thin worn shirt. The cold groping fingers of the water clenched tightly to the aching muscles in my tired body.

Gerti whimpered at my side, her face pressed tightly against Oma's side in an attempt to block out the fearful figures in front of her.

Dozens of Russian soldiers strode casually back and forth before us, their ambivalent eyes drifting coldly from one dripping and shivering individual to the next. Occasionally their eyes would rove a little too intimately across the women, who shrank back into themselves with renewed fear and panic.

One young soldier glanced repeatedly at my feet, which were housed in boots I had acquired shortly before the evacuation of Jagerndorf. The soldier twirled his cigarette lazily between his fingers, before finally flicking it into the mud, where it hissed and sputtered. He strode toward me until his face was inches from mine. I pulled back with a start, wondering what I had done to attract his attention and his obvious displeasure. His breath reeked of stale smoke and alcohol, and he spat incomprehensible orders into my gaping face.

Opa's voice swirled into the void of anger and fear throbbing between my temples. "Just do as he asks, Alfie. We don't want any trouble."

Realizing my face echoed my feelings, I jumped, and took my eyes off the man's yellowed teeth, which were now twisting into an evil grin. "But, what did he say, Opa?" I pleaded, through clenched teeth.

"Your boots. Give him your boots." answered Opa. I could hear Oma sobbing quietly beside me, no doubt praying that I would not be harmed. The soldier's patience at my ignorance finally waned and he thrust me backward onto the track, where I struggled to remove my boots.

As I pulled them gingerly from my feet, I remembered my father's gold watch hidden deep inside one. I paused, deciding I would have to do what I could not to reward this soldier with still more spoils of war. But, he was eager to move on. He reached forward and yanked my boots roughly from my feet. In surprise, I tipped backward, which allowed the watch to slide unnoticed into my pant leg, where it remained as I toppled into the cold mud pooling between the rails.

The soldier tilted his head backward and barked a mocking laugh, clearly amused at my expense. He wrapped the laces of my boots around his fingers and strode off, displaying his prize proudly over his head.

Opa reached down and pulled me from the puddle, placing me back on my bare feet. "Just forget it, Alfie. We will be home soon. We will get you new shoes then." he said, his voice grating against the silence of the sympathetic crowd. He returned to Oma's side and placed a firm hand lovingly around her shoulder. She leaned slightly against his comforting chest, weariness plain on her face.

We shuffled uncomfortably in the cold, the rain teasing us with its persistence. My feet were already beginning to ache in the chill of the rising puddles of water, but I resisted the urge to hop in place. I did not want to give the soldier the satisfaction of seeing me suffer. While pretending to wipe mud off my pants, I retrieved the watch and thrust it quickly into my pocket.

I had been so occupied with my surreptitious activities, that I hadn't noticed the raised voices to my right, until the watch was safely secured in my pocket and I began to warm with a feeling of triumph at what the soldier had so closely missed.

I leaned around Oma to see two more soldiers angrily confronting Uncle Alois. My uncle's eyes were wide with fear and confusion as he struggled to understand the sudden attention. He staggered backward, his tongue rolling around its familiar grunts and murmurs, the only sounds he could speak.

"He can't hear you. He doesn't understand." Opa pleaded, stepping forward. The eyes of both soldiers flickered menacingly across Opa's anxious face, and for a moment I feared they would strike him. Instead, they whirled suddenly back toward Uncle Alois, their arms raised in sudden blurs of violent motion, so seamless and natural that it was clear it was common practice. The butts of their rifles cracked viciously into Uncle Alois's chest and shoulders, forcing an anguished groan from his betraying mouth.

He crumpled to the ground, moaning helplessly, yet they continued to kick and prod him incessantly with their feet and guns. Opa howled with rage and sadness, pleading and crying behind the men, as he desperately tried to explain that Uncle Alois had meant no disrespect.

When the two seemed satisfied with the effects of their actions, they lurched away, pulling cigarettes from their breast pockets and dangling them between their grinning teeth.

We huddled around the figure of my uncle, unsure of how to aid him. His eyes gaped sadly out of his ashen face and he peered up at us wordlessly for help... help none of us were able to give. A thin trickle of blood pooled at the side of his mouth and a large welt was already rising on his forehead. Clearly, his injuries were serious and we were reluctant to move him. But, even then, where would we go? We settled on easing him up out of the mud and leaning him against Gerle, who sat on the metal rail of the unused track.

"He probably has some broken ribs." Opa whispered, his voice shaking with anger. "... and God only knows what has happened to his insides." He ran his hands through his gray hair, his anxious eyes resting on the pathetic figure of his only remaining son.

Finally, in the late afternoon an aging engine was coupled to the cars, and we were herded like cattle back on board for the duration of our journey. We traveled through the bitter night, the rain never ceasing during the endless cold hours of darkness. We huddled in a corner, hopelessly trying to dodge the sheets of rain that were pouring down the saturated wooden walls of the freight car.

Several times we squealed to a halt on a siding to allow the Russians their right of way on the heavily used track. Each time the car shuddered and jolted, a faint moan rose from Uncle Alois, who lay in a pained stupor among the damp and jumbled bodies.

The night was long and uncomfortable and we fought desperately to keep fear and illness at bay. The foul air of so many filthy and unhealthy people tightened uncomfortably around us.

The first rays of daylight seemed foreign, returning from days long gone. They slanted in through the narrow slats in a valiant effort to hearten our stricken souls. We staggered to our feet while the doors were pushed noisily open and we gasped with grateful breaths at the welcome air.

Our own train station rose before us. It had been spared the worst damage, though its roof toppled precariously into the yard below, yet another reminder of the presence of the war's vast shadow.

The unpleasantly familiar smell of rotting flesh reached my nose and I gagged into my sleeve. With Gerle standing at my side, we gazed onto the landscape of our childhood, now twisted to beyond recognition... almost. The shattered ruins of the sloping roofs of downtown were enveloped in gossamer veils of mist, beyond which the beloved hills rose, tenderly cradling what was left of our town.

We stepped carefully from the railcar, our legs stiff from long hours in confinement, and we turned to help Opa lower Uncle Alois to the ground. We pulled him up between us, his head lolling from side to side as we staggered slowly away from the station. Dazed individuals shuffled silently throughout the deserted streets, their eyes fixed on the one point in the distance that mattered... their home.

Nearly every house had suffered damage, some beyond salvation. The war had hit hard here. Clearly, Gerle and I would never have survived it had we stayed. Entire blocks were reduced to piles of twisted metal and crumbling brick, the remnants of lives lost. Decomposing bodies of animals and soldiers, both friend and foe, lay in heaps in the ditches and throughout the rubble-filled streets. Their souls mingled in death in a way they had never been able to achieve during their brief lifetimes. Their lives had been put up as payment by their nations for the right to dominate or defend a people. But, in truth, they had entered, in unity, a realm only their ancestors could touch... the past.

A lump rose in my throat upon rounding the last corner before the road straightened toward the bridge and our house. A heap of concrete was all that remained of the bridge, its welcome passage to the east eliminated. Trees along the road were blasted apart, their limbs dangling like severed hands along their blackened trunks. My heart sank. I feared the worst. Could our house have survived so close to the bridge?

Gerle grabbed my arm tightly, his breath catching noisily in his throat. My gaze rested apprehensively upon the eager faces of my family, watching as their eyes traveled the length of the road to rest on... the house. It still stood, though badly damaged... it was still there. We were home. We had survived... nothing could tear us apart now. It was over.

CHAPTER 16

The peaceful sounds of chickens, now gone feral, filled our ears as we approached the house. For a moment, my mind forgot the war and the horrors I had seen, and my senses drank in the many sights, sounds, and smells of home. The air hung sweetly... once the nose had sifted through the disturbing, but familiar, stench of decay. Spring was valiantly giving birth to summer and the fields had clearly benefited from the generous rains. Greens of every shade lined the road, while delicate flowers, rippling in waves of crimson and yellow, clumped among the young plants and vegetables in Opa's garden. Birds swooped above the neglected rows, intent on the multitude of insects that had been allowed to flourish in our absence.

There were changes, of course, changes that could not be ignored. Yet, the core, the heart of that place called home, remained unscathed... it had survived. I gaped feverishly around me, drinking in everything familiar. I believed, at that moment, that we would survive, too.

The bridge, or lack there of, was the most apparent difference. The shallow water of the river was filled with the crumbled chunks of mortar that had once made up the elegant spans of the river's crossing. Stagnant water pooled in spots where it had once bubbled and danced freely. The silt of the concrete now congealed into a small dam that impeded the natural flow of the water. The Germans, in their efforts to delay the advancing enemy, had destroyed the bridge during their retreat. Although the entire city had sustained heavy damage, our neighborhood, due to its proximity to the only route east, had suffered the most.

Heaps of shattered slate roof tiles lay among Opa's prized fruit trees. Their thick verdant leaves hung in copious clusters as a result of the spring's nourishing rains. They greeted Opa's outstretched fingers as he caressed them lovingly.

Hidden beneath the thick grass were shards of glass from the windows. With Uncle Alois leaning heavily on his arm, Opa labored toward the house, the glass crunching noisily under his feet. Opa approached the front door, his eyes raised to the exposed upper floor.

"Watch out there, Alfie! You don't have shoes—best wait until Oma finds you some from inside. You'll cut your feet to pieces on this glass." Opa insisted, gasping slightly as he eased Uncle Alois's limp arm higher across his stooped shoulder. "Gerle, give me a hand with Uncle Alois. Please. Julie, find him a clean place to lie down. Come along, Gerti." Opa said, opening the front door slowly with his free hand, the muscles of his burdened arm straining through his damp shirt.

Gerle ran forward to grasp Uncle Alois's other arm and together they aided his bent and moaning frame through the doorway. Oma ran ahead, her hands smoothing her skirt as she fretted about the filthy room. She found my sandals in the hall cupboard and told Gerti to deliver them to me, where I remained standing in the yard inspecting the damaged exterior.

"Here, Alfie… your shoes." Gerti muttered in a small voice, her wide eyes trained on my face.

"Thanks, Gerti. Let's go inside, shall we?" I answered, desperate to find something to make my sister smile.

Gerle and Opa had settled my uncle carefully onto his bed, which, surprisingly, remained untouched. While Gerle lifted my uncle's legs onto the coverlet, Uncle Alois groaned loudly. Then, he rolled over toward the wall, clenching his stomach tightly and pulling his knees up close to his chest.

"Will he be all right, Reinhard?" Oma asked in a trembling whisper, forgetting that her words would not be heard by her wounded son.

Opa kneaded his lower back with his hands before running his fingers through his hair. "I don't know, Julie… I just don't know." He turned wearily away from the bed, his face tight with worry. "We are home now, Julie… let's hope that is enough to bring him around." he sighed.

A warm breeze rustled through the open window, where glass fragments framed the blue sky and viridescent hills like a bold etching. The blankets hung heavily against the sill; the rain had been saturating them for weeks.

I returned to the open front door and gazed out into the littered yard. A sudden movement near the edge of the house caused me to start, until I realized it was my sister. She was walking slowly toward me, her head bent solemnly over something clutched gently in her hands. Her braids dangled down, swinging to and fro as they tickled her cheeks.

"What do you have, Gerti?" I asked, wondering what could have distracted my sister from her stupor. I walked toward her, treading lightly across the shards of glass. My worn sandals felt soft and comfortable under my tired feet, but I knew they provided little protection against the dangerous layers of sparkling glass slivers.

Gerti opened her hands slowly, holding them slightly away from her body, and she whispered softly, "A baby." Inside her cupped hands sat a brilliantly yellow chick, its oversized feet askew as it tried to find a level perch on my sister's soft skin. A small sound issued from its open beak and its black eyes blinked up into mine.

"That's wonderful, Gerti. That means the chickens are still here, and we will have eggs… and meat." My heart soared at the thought of the meals Oma could create from a few good eggs, and I placed my arm fondly across my sister's shoulders.

"It's good to be home, don't you think?" I sighed, happily. The hungry chirps of the innocent chick filled me with a sudden warmth. Its presence spoke of promise, and it awoke in me a delightful awareness that such a small thing had survived such terrible days.

Gerti stared blankly up into my face, her small brow knit with doubt, then she said, "There are bunnies too. Lots of them. Come see."

I followed my sister around to the back of the house where the small rabbit hutch had been built against the animal shed. I watched Gerti place the chick carefully near its mother, one of several hens scratching in the dirt, then I glanced into the darkness in the hutch. Deep in the shadows squirmed several small bodies, their sable-brown fur sleek and dark against the pale straw.

"Now isn't that a welcome sight!" cried Opa from my shoulder. "Fine little runts, too. They did pretty well without us, I must admit." he added, smiling, his fingers twirling the gray ends of his mustache. "Alfie, Oma would like you to get her some water. Here is the bucket." He handed me the old battered bucket and said, "You may need to give it a few tries before the water runs clear. I'm going to check the house around back." he finished, walking off beyond the shed.

I watched him go, noticing sadly, that he walked with a new stiffness in his strong old legs. I knew life in the camp had been difficult for my grandparents, yet I felt sure that it was the inactivity that had been one of the hardest parts of what my active grandfather had had to bear.

I turned toward the front of the house, relishing the feeling of the familiar bucket as it thumped against my leg. Behind me I heard Gerti talking in a soothing tone to the small pile of rabbits now nestled in her lap.

Gerle greeted me as I turned the corner, a wide smile covering his face. "Oma is digging through the cellar. Looks like we might actually eat tonight, Alfie! Wow! I can't wait for some of her cooking." He rubbed his stomach, longingly, and headed past me, saying over his shoulder, "Oma wants me to get Opa to check the chimney. She wants to light a fire. I'll be right back."

I set the bucket down in the tall weeds below the pump, proudly aware that they were soon to be beaten back by my industrious grandfather, who had always kept a very fastidious garden. The pump creaked in protest when I raised the handle, but it soon responded with bubbles and gurgles as the air filling its throat burst forth. Brown water followed, splattering into the unchecked brambles below. After several more pulls on the well, the water ran clearly. I raised the bucket, rested it on my knee, and allowed the neglected water to flow once more.

"Well, Opa says the chimney is ready to go. The roof has some problems, though. Remember that day?" Gerle's voice trailed off as he recalled the nights we had spent alone in the bombed house. He leaned against the fence and watched the water splashing noisily into the rapidly filling bucket. "It is so great to see clean water." he added.

"I know. I can't wait to eat. What's Gerti doing?" I asked, slopping the full bucket to my side with a lurch. The cool water felt clean and refreshing on my hot and dirty skin.

"She's still playing with the little creatures. You know, it's good she has something like that to keep her busy. She's been so down." Gerle answered, frowning.

"I know. I hope being home will help. Oh, Gerle! It does feel good to be back, doesn't it?" I exclaimed, fervently.

"Yeah! I guess we will be starting school again in the fall, won't we? It will be so great to see the others... I hope they fared all right." he said, suddenly standing upright, his brow knit with concern. "I hope they are all ok."

"We should see them any day now, I guess." I answered, trying not to allow any dark thoughts to destroy my good spirits.

We walked together into the kitchen, which already glistened and smelled fresh. Oma had been busy. A pile of potatoes from the cellar sat in a bowl in the sink, ready to be washed and several dusty jars of preserves were lined up upon the counter.

"Oh good, Alfie." Oma said behind me. She had entered from the hall, having been in to visit Uncle Alois. "Put the bucket in the sink, please. Gerle. Tell Gerti to search out some eggs. We can have some tonight."

"How is Uncle Alois, Oma?" I asked, grunting slightly, my weakened muscles straining to raise the heavy bucket into the sink. Gerle had turned to go, but at my words paused to hear her answer.

"Oh, Alfie... I wish I knew. He looks so pale. Of course, we all do, I expect. If only he could tell me where it ails him, I could do more to help him." she sighed, mopping her sweating brow with a linen towel from the sink. "I will take him some of that water, then I'll make him something to eat."

We bustled around for another hour before washing thoroughly with the clear water, which Oma heated in the washroom. As the layers of grime peeled from my skin, red from the scrub brush, I felt another burden lift from my shoulders. The lice fled at the touch of the scalding water, which Oma laced with pungent oils from the cellar.

Rubbing my hair clean with a dry towel, I followed Gerle and Gerti, both also fresh from the bath, into the kitchen for our first real meal in many long weeks. We sat around the table, silent in our awe of the significant moment. Oma's eyes slowly passed possessively across each of our faces, before she tilted her head forward in a lingering prayer of thanks.

"Here, Alfie. You serve everyone. I'm going to take something into Alois." Oma said, upon completion of her devotions. "He must be included in this first meal home." she added.

The foods I had once thought so simple and basic had never tasted better. The eggs lay like open golden flowers upon the steaming piles of potatoes, surrounded by young garden greens Oma had dug out from between the weeds. Beets and onions sent their fragrant juices into the fluffy potatoes like an enthusiastic painter mixing colors upon a fresh canvas. Silence hung over the table. It was not an uncomfortable silence, but one born of a desire to record every delightful sensation into the memory bank for possible future hours of need.

When Oma returned from Uncle Alois's room, she surprised us with a small bowl of cherries, a forgotten treasure hidden in the far corner of the cellar. We lingered over their sweet flavor, eating each one slowly, while Oma brewed a large pot of tea, made from fragrant lavender and sage gathered from beneath the lilac bushes.

Opa left the table suddenly and shuffled quietly into the parlor, where we heard him cranking the spring on the old grandfather clock. Soon the soothing rhythm of the clock filled the room, as the seconds steadily dissolved into eternity.

I woke with a smile on my face, in spite of the bugs already resting on my cover from their morning forage through the open window. We had found fresh straw still piled in the corner of the shed, and we had made fast use of its clean softness for lining our beds. This had resulted in the best night's sleep in many weary days.

Opa's voice drifted in through the window. He stood outside talking with Oma, gesturing emphatically with his hands at the roof.

"We can fix it, Julie. I'll have us closed in properly before the weather turns." he said, smiling confidently before moving off towards the back of the house. "We will fix the wash room roof first. That will go quickly." His words faded as he rounded the corner, and I returned my attention to my rumbling stomach.

An hour later I was wandering behind Opa in the hall of the upstairs, most of which was exposed to the sky, now thankfully clear blue and free of rain clouds. A grenade or shell had entered through the upper wall and had exploded on the opposite side of the room, destroying most of the second floor.

The continued heavy explosions around the house had weakened some of the roof beams and separated them slightly from the outside walls, which were lined in places with traces of large cracks. Opa spent most of the next few days strengthening the foundation and the supporting walls with extra lumber he had left stacked behind the shed.

Meanwhile, the rest of us continued busily mending the torn yard and house, like frantic ants shoring up their holes after being trod upon by a large foot. Oma bustled about her kitchen, once more restoring it to its proper place as the axis of the house. She counted and sorted the many root vegetables she had hidden carefully in the sand box at the back of the cellar, and she instructed Gerti on how to retrieve the bountiful crop of peaches and plums hanging heavily upon the branches of the precious fruit trees.

Gerti worked steadily, though her spirits never lifted. She was often found leaning against the house for a rest, tears falling in large drops upon the dusty soil at her feet. In spite of the nourishing food, prepared so carefully by Oma, Gerti's face remained pale and her eyes vacant.

"Let's hope she snaps out of it soon." Opa said sadly one evening, after Gerti had shuffled off to her small bed at the foot of mine. "The sunshine and activity should help her this summer. She will be starting school in the fall and will need to be healthy first."

"She's pining for her Mama, Reinhard. It's not easy to recover from what she saw... not easy for anyone, let alone a child." Oma sighed, her eyes blinking furiously as she fought back bitter tears.

"I know, I know, Julie. But, life must go on. She's so withdrawn from it. All she does is sit with her animals." he answered, shaking his head.

"She needs to get there in her own way, Reinhard. We can't force her to recover faster than she's able. Being home will be the thing that finally cures her. I just wish I could say the same for Alois. We need a doctor, Reinhard." she insisted.

"I've looked everywhere, Julie! There is just nothing in town. The entire city is in a state of disorder and chaos. We must care for him the best we can." Opa replied, sullenly.

Uncle Alois had moved little since he had been placed on his bed a week prior. He groaned incessantly, his eyes boring silently into his mother's for relief she couldn't offer. Oma sat for hours at his bedside, mopping his sweating body with a damp towel and spooning thin vegetable broth between his cracked lips. He left his room only for the washroom. He shuffled slowly, his muscles tight in his face, once so ready to smile. Now it twitched convulsively as he battled with the pain of his unhealed injuries.

Oma washed the lice from his hair, dressed him in clean clothes, which hung like rags on his spent frame, and she tucked him into a bed lined with clean straw and fresh sheets.

Oma worked tirelessly to return the house to normalcy. Every room had been plundered savagely by both armies as they ebbed and flowed along the front. Dressers were dismantled, their contents strewn around the rooms, any valuables missing. The money Opa had hidden under the mattress was gone, forgotten by Gerle and me in our haste to leave. Gerle and I never admitted to the destruction of Oma's china, convinced she would not understand our motives. Nonetheless, we agreed with each other, that it felt good to know that our recklessly defiant gesture had deprived the soldiers of another chance to destroy our home.

Opa mourned the loss of his treasured sword, a relic from the era of the Kaiser. Oma's jewelry box had been flung to the ground, a few worthless baubles broken across the floor, the rest taken by a greedy soldier to hang on some tavern girl's throat.

All salvageable pieces of furniture were returned to their proper places, anything else was broken down and burned in the stove, hungry from disuse. The long summer evenings were filled with repairs inside amidst candlelight, since the electricity had not yet been restored. As far as Opa could tell, no infrastructure remained to return the city to its prewar functions.

The neighborhood returned slowly to activity, with intermittent trickles of refugees returning to begin their lives anew. Gerle and I traveled the streets regularly to see if any of our friends had returned, but we were met with only unknown faces.

Between hours spent repairing the toppled roof, we sat quietly in the comforting grass near the edge of the river, trying to recreate the aura of innocence so long buried in our minds. Fish darted in and out of the newly formed pools, their depths expanded since the collapse of the bridge.

"I wonder when they will repair the bridge." Gerle mused. He twirled a stem of sweet grass between his teeth, his untidy brown hair laying heavily on his brow.

"It seems like no one is trying to fix anything in this town. It's as if we have been abandoned... every one of us for himself. I can't imagine how the school building will be ready in time." I reasoned, secretly hoping it was not a priority of the overtaxed authorities. Indeed, there seemed to be very little order or authority in the region at all. Store doors were open, but the dusty shelves remained empty.

"We better get back up there." Gerle said, gesturing with his chin toward the house, now bright in the midday sun.

"Let's get some water first." I said, stretching my tired arms over my head and easing myself to my feet. We drank deeply at the pump, grateful as ever for the fresh water that flowed across our dusty sunburned faces.

"l will head up; you get some more tiles." I said, water dripping onto my sweat-stained shirt. I carefully climbed the ladder, first shifting my small cloth nail apron more tightly upon my waist. The slender hammer thudded against my hip while I climbed to the top, where I returned to my task of renailing loose tiles.

I eased myself carefully onto the sloping roof and paused to look across the yard below me. I watched for a moment as Oma supported Uncle Alois on his way to the wash room. From such a height, my dear uncle seemed very diminished. The spark that had enabled him to endure the many hardships in his life seemed to flicker helplessly. I feared it would be extinguished if he didn't receive help soon.

They walked passed Gerti where she sat in the tall grass near the shed, her hands caressing the soft fur of a small tame rabbit. The sun lit the rim of her fine blond hair like a delicate finger tracing a pattern in the finest, palest sand. Her forehead bore the deep furrows of trouble, unnatural on such a young face.

Opa's trilling whistle danced on the gentle breeze, which cooled the tired muscles beneath my shirt. He was busy weeding the small patch of herbs near the fence, his mind absorbed in a long list of restorative projects.

"Here, Alfie." Gerle groaned behind me, clambering up the narrow ladder at my feet. Over one shoulder was a small pile of slate tiles, retrieved by him from the trampled grass below. He wobbled slightly, one hand clutching tightly to the ladder, the other wrapped firmly around the slippery tiles.

Opa had been thrilled upon discovering a small bundle of extra tiles in a bin in the shed. "For a rainy day!" he laughed. We had made fast use of the new discovery; there were many holes to fill. Rain had fallen several times since our return, so we were anxious to close in the house.

"Thanks, Gerle." I said. I peered across the roof, counting the spaces left to fill, and I noticed some movement beyond on the road. "Someone's coming." I said, squinting my eyes against the bright sun. "Maybe it's someone we know."

Gerle shrugged his shoulders uncomfortably and said, irritably, "Can you take these already?"

"Oh, yeah, sorry." I answered, sheepishly, tearing my eyes away from the activity on the road below. My heart fluttered. It did not look like neighbors returning. I grabbed the tiles, resting them gently in the gutter, until I had need of them. I glanced sharply back toward the road, aware now that two large army trucks were pulling up not far from our gate. "Um, Gerle, we better go down." I said, nervously.

"What is it, Alfie?" Gerle asked.

Before I could answer, a loud voice filled the air, echoing shrilly off the house beyond. "Everyone! On to the street! Quickly! Quickly!" An officer stood upon the open tailgate of the truck, one hand clasped around an upraised megaphone, the other fondling a machine gun draped across his chest. Around him soldiers were leaping skillfully to the ground, their guns poised and ready as they stood in formation along the side of the road.

"You have ten minutes! Quickly! Now!" yelled the man, peering up and down the narrow lanes running perpendicular to the main road.

"Go, Gerle! Get down! Now! It's the Russians." I gasped, backing quickly onto the shaking ladder. "Oh, God, Gerle. What do they want with us now?"

The ladder trembled violently as Gerle scrambled recklessly down the remaining rungs, before stumbling to the ground in his haste. "Where is Opa?" he asked, his breath fast and uneven.

"Never mind. Help Oma with Uncle Alois. I'll get Gerti." I ran toward the shed, my heart pounding miserably in my throat, as the thought of what might lay ahead raced through my mind. "Gerti!" I shouted, my eyes darting toward the vacant spot near the hutch. Several rabbits browsed aimlessly among the sweet clover, but my sister was nowhere to be found.

A soft creaking reached my ears and in the corner of my eye I caught the motion of the shed door swinging shut. "Gerti!" I whispered frantically. I tiptoed toward the door, vaguely aware that the yells from the road had grown more intense.

"Gerti." I whispered. "I know you are in there. You must come out. We need to stay together. Everything will be all right." I pulled the door open and my sister jumped back like a startled animal, the sun pouring in upon her tear-streaked face. "Come on, Gerti. We must go." I said, holding my hand out toward her. "Come with me."

"Mama! I want my mama! Don't let them take me, Alfie! Don't let them touch me." she sobbed, her lower lip white between her clenched teeth.

"Oh, Gerti! You'll be all right. We have to go, though, sweetie. Come on." She offered no resistance as I lifted her into my arms, but she buried her face against my chest, her hands clutching tightly around my neck. I ran awkwardly to the front of the house, where I bumped into Gerle rounding the corner.

"Oma sent me to find you and Gerti. She'll handle Uncle Alois. Opa is in the house with her." he said. "Oh, Alfie... what do you think they will do to us?" he asked nervously. Gerti whimpered against my shoulder and I held my finger to my lips, shaking my head slowly at Gerle's question. I needed to keep Gerti calm. I had no answer for him, anyway.

We met Oma at the door, her arm cradling Uncle Alois, who swayed unsteadily on his feet. He looked feverish and pale, his eyes only vaguely aware of his surroundings.

"I have to get some papers, Julie. Wait here!" Opa insisted, poking his head out the door. Unbridled fear was written on his face and my heart leapt at the sight. If Opa was scared...

We stood in a tight huddle, our backs to each other, anxiously awaiting our fate. Opa returned quickly, stuffing papers into his shirt front, before taking his place at the front, gesturing over his shoulder with his hand.

"Let's go." he said.

I reached down and untied the small cloth nail apron, Gerti's thin arms still tightly gripping my neck. The tool belt fell to the ground with a thud. I stepped across it, leaving it where it had fallen.

We walked slowly toward the gate, not in haste to face the Russians, who still gripped their guns menacingly across their chests.

"What papers are you carrying, Reinhard? I need to know." Oma whispered, her lips barely moving.

Opa glanced suddenly backward, his eyes hard and intense, then he nodded his head slowly and answered, "The birth certificates, the deed to the house, the insurance and bank notes. I didn't dare take more." he sighed, patting his shirt front carefully. The bundle was small enough to keep hidden.

Suddenly, he bolted to my side, pulling a small pile of the papers back out from his shirt. "Maybe you better hide some of these, Alfie… just in case." he whispered. "Quickly, now!" I grabbed the papers and stuffed them into my pocket.

We joined the fearful crowd milling about the street, their faces as nervous as ours. The megaphone twisted to and fro above us, the man counting the time remaining with alarming accuracy. "Three minutes! Everyone, quickly!"

He decided, suddenly, that time was up, and he gestured to the soldiers below him to enclose us in their ranks. They shuffled quickly into place, earning slight gasps and screams from the crowd, as the fear became palpable.

"March!" the officer yelled. The lead soldier echoed his cry, and we began our slow descent into the hell of the unknown.

CHAPTER 17

My head buzzed uncomfortably with the many questions filling my troubled thoughts. Gerti continued to cling to my neck, which was slippery now with thin rivulets of sweat. The townsfolk were walking as closely together as possible without stepping on each other; the primitive instinct to herd the weakest to the center had taken effect. Opa and Gerle struggled to drag Uncle Alois, whose arms were stretched limply across both their shoulders. His head lolled from side to side and tears streamed silently down his anguished face.

Oma walked beside me, rubbing Gerti's back soothingly with her hand. The other hand toyed anxiously with the delicate cross hanging about her neck.

"Move! Quickly! No talking!" barked the officer, his gritty voice hideously amplified by the megaphone. I stumbled slightly and Oma's hand moved to my wrist. She grasped it tightly, an unnaturally strong hold for her gentle nature. I glanced into her face, which was damp with perspiration. Her eyes glistened with tears, poised to trace the too familiar route along her soft cheek. My throat clenched suddenly with anger as I thought of the days since our return.

Hope had finally seemed worth having; life had been full of promise again. I had even heard Oma humming one of her beloved operettas, her hands deep in soap suds, vigorously scrubbing the bedding clean with lye. My head had finally stopped itching. The population of lice had finally admitted defeat upon Oma's diligent attention to our daily toilet. The work to rebuild the house had been exhausting, but we had worked willingly and with pride. Most importantly, the time spent with each other, in peace and renewed hope, had been all the more precious, for its juxtaposition to what innocence we had lost.

I curled my fingers around Oma's hand and squeezed it lightly. Her lip quivered as her eyes darted upward to Gerti, whose chin rested somberly on my shoulder. Gerti seemed in shock. Her body was unresponsive when I shifted her weight, slight as she was, to my other shoulder. I needed to pace myself for our walk, the distance of which I was uncertain.

We headed through town, encountering other large clusters of people being aggressively shepherded along. I gazed ahead, barely able to see beyond the rows of bedraggled heads before me. A painfully familiar sight caught my eye. The lovely white church, its stout steeple tickling the sky, danced across my vision, and the small mountain upon which it perched came into view.

Every morning of my childhood, I had checked the condition of the day upon the side of that church from my bedroom window. I had rejoiced when the sun had set its steep angles into sharp relief, because it foretold fine weather for our many adventures. Likewise, I had cursed the clouds that left a dull gray sheen across the otherwise white facade of the soothing structure.

Now, the sight of it filled me with dread, because I knew what lay slightly below it—the Arbeits Lager—the work camp. It had been built by the German military machine for the Russian prisoners—now it was to be used by the Russian victors for housing and controlling those who they deemed to be the pathetic masses. As we filed slowly upward, the road to town fell away behind us. I glanced quickly over my shoulder and stifled a cry. At least several hundred figures shuffled slowly behind us, rippling like a supple snake slithering toward it hole. The entire town was being methodically emptied.

I turned forward and gulped, trying to suppress the feeling of panic rising into my tight chest. Similar sounds of fear and worry spread across the crowd, the realization of our destination dawning across many of the faces.

We walked beneath the camp's broad iron gate, its tall curving lines looming fearfully over our heads. We found ourselves in a wide stark courtyard, the earth beneath our feet patterned with the footprints of several hundred miserable souls.

"Women, over here! Men, over there!" spat the officer, his knuckles white upon the handle of the black megaphone. He pointed to various sides of the square yard, directing everyone to line up in rows along the brick walls of the barracks. "Children under ten are to accompany the women. Boys line up over there." he continued, his icy dark eyes surveying the terrified faces with grim satisfaction.

Oma gasped loudly at my side, her fingers rising to her throat. "Reinhard, they can't separate us. They can't... not now, not after all this!" she whispered in a voice laden with tears.

"Alfie... give Gerti to Oma." said Opa, in reply, his voice choked into a hoarse whisper. "There you go, dear. You'll be with your Oma." he added soothingly. His hand trembled upon Gerti's soft hair.

I gripped Gerti firmly under her arms and pulled her away from my chest. Her little hands clenched tightly at my shirt, her nails digging into my sunburned neck. She screamed loudly, her breath coming in sharp gasps.

"Mama! I want Mama! Nooo! Don't let them take me! I want Alfie. I want to stay with Alfie!" she cried, her sobs fragmenting her words. "Don't let them take me, Alfie!" she pleaded, her eyes boring into my heart like a dagger.

Opa grasped her closely, leaving Uncle Alois to slump on Gerle's small shoulder. Opa hugged Gerti tightly and whispered in her ear, "We will be here, Gerti, dear. Oma will be with you. No one will hurt you." His voice shook, but he persisted in handing my struggling sister to my grandmother, who grabbed her tightly, tucking the small blond head against her warm comforting bosom. Opa rested his hand firmly on Oma's shoulder and stared intently into her eyes. He then turned back to attend to my uncle, who had dropped to his knees with a groan.

"Opa, can you handle Uncle Alois on your own?" Gerle asked, hugging Oma closely.

"Don't worry. Everything will be all right. They can't keep us here forever—the war is over, after all. This will just take some sorting out." Opa answered. "You two just stay out of trouble." he added, looking sternly at us. "Go line up." he finished gruffly, hugging us each tightly. His face felt damp against my cheek, and I realized, with a sinking heart that his eyes were full of tears.

I kissed Oma hastily and watched her wander reluctantly to the huddle of women and girls, the fear visible in her retreating back. Opa grasped Uncle Alois firmly by the elbow and steered him slowly toward the small crowd of men, the rare few present who had been too old or too useless to die on the front.

"Come on." I said, placing my shaking hand on Gerle's arm. We walked into the midst of approximately forty boys, all of whom were over the ten year old mark, but all still children, all still petrified. Their older siblings had not yet returned from their stint as men on the front lines—most likely they never would.

A vague splattering, as of water, bounced audibly upon the parched dirt next to me, and I glanced down along the knobby legs of a small boy to my right. He seemed barely tall enough to pass for ten and he was shaking like a leaf. I realized with a great wave of pity, that the boy had wet himself. A dark damp stain ran down his pant leg, ending in a pool of urine. I turned away, closing my eyes. I was not ready to face what lay ahead. But I was, once again, thankful that I had Gerle at my side.

A loud voice bellowed, "Boys, forward!" We shuffled three abreast through a dank hallway, our noses tingling with the all too familiar stench of human excrement and disease. Mold grew thickly upon the damp walls and dark puddles littered with rat feces filled the corners. Clearly, the place had seen much use. The camp that had housed Russian prisoners would now be the holding place of the vanquished.

I clung closely to Gerle, my mind racing with the reality of what was before us. Salvation had been plucked from our aching and tired hands, just as the future was beginning to open back up for us. We faced another stretch of deprivation and despair, with no reprieve in sight. Home had just begun to feel secure again; my sleep had finally been somewhat free of bad dreams. Now, we were going to be living a nightmare, again… and it made me want to scream.

The bunk room was filled to capacity with beds stacked three high. They lined every wall like shelves, more suitable for storing dry goods than human beings. All forty of us paused in the doorway, uncertain of what to do next. A stout woman entered, shoving her way toward the front with her broad hand, while she sniffed disgustedly at the lost faces around her.

"You pick a bunk! Hurry now! No fighting." she said, her speech clipped and heavy with a Russian accent. A murmur rippled through the crowd of boys as the larger ones used their size to jostle for the best spots.

I noticed the small boy from the yard had remained frozen in the doorway, his wide eyes darting nervously around the room.

"Come on." Gerle whispered, pulling on my arm. We maneuvered slowly between several boys and found ourselves in a corner of the room where a row of unclaimed beds remained. I climbed nimbly to the top and crawled onto a narrow strip only two feet below the ceiling. Gerle swung into the bunk adjacent to mine and I heard him grunt in disapproval at the hard and foul straw mattress he was expected to call home.

From my perch above the room, I watched the small boy inch his way forward until he found the only remaining bunk, a low shelf below the window. He sat dejectedly upon the mattress, which sent puffs of dust up into the hazy sunlight.

Through the grimy window I could see rows of people shuffling slowly into their barracks. I tried in vain to spot the familiar shapes of my family, but the dirt and fog on the window flattened the view beyond, distorting their identities beyond recognition. I shuddered suddenly, my heart filling with an unexplainable dread, as I looked out upon the faceless forms to which my loved ones had been diminished.

I gripped the edge of the bunk, my head swimming into blackness. The anger and panic rose into my being like an uncontrollable flood. My life had been shattered again. We had worked so hard to survive... and we had survived so much, only to be back where we had started. The burden of unexplainable guilt returned, flooding through me as I struggled to reason with the feelings of responsibility. What had I done to deserve this war? What had I done to deserve such suffering, and to have to watch those close to me suffer... to suffer until they died? What had I done?

I had lost my parents, seen my sister reduced to a shell of her former self, been forced to stand by while my uncle was beaten, been deprived of basic human dignities... all to ultimately be driven a second time from my home like a stray dog, only good enough to be housed in a kennel with the rest of the mutts and mongrels. This war was not our war; it was not our burden, but we were paying the price—like all the other victims of all the wars that had come before us. Thus, it had always been.

A single dim light bulb hung on a cord in the middle of the room and I gazed at it intently, desperate to squelch the nausea that was rising in my throat. Beneath me the straw rustled and crackled, its sweetness long since replaced by the sour stench of urine and sweat. My skin crawled with the very thought of the lice that my grandmother had finally banished from our bodies. It would now have a fine breeding ground upon which to mount its revenge.

The room overseer, her stern dislike of us never wavering, pointed out the camp's latrine and the camp's only water source through one of the windows, which ran along the rear wall of the barrack. Beyond the yard, the entire camp was wreathed with a tall and menacing barb wire fence, its top reaching, with groping talons of looped wire, toward the sky.

The latrine consisted of a long ditch, which was at least several meters deep. It was covered with randomly placed narrow planks of filth encrusted wood. One was expected to slither along the splinter-filled beams upon one's exposed backside. Meanwhile, with one hand braced against teetering into the muck below, one dealt with the unpleasant results of the inadequate food. The other hand gripped one's pants to keep them from being sacrificed to the filth only a short distance below one's feet.

My head swam with sickness as I wobbled precariously over the dark waste below me. Flies buzzed fiercely around my head, their small feet tickling my nose and ears. My eyes dimmed with disgust and I prayed vainly that the inevitable dysentery and other afflictions of the bowel would not return. There was no toilet paper available and not a blade of grass grew in the yard to be used as a replacement.

Typhoid and cholera soon ran rampant throughout the camp, tackling the already weakened systems of the refugees. Only one pump provided water for everyone, so there was little chance to stay clean. Water was intended solely for drinking; we relied on luck to keep our disease ridden hands from infecting us.

Gerle and I confided to each other our worries about our family, especially Gerti and Uncle Alois. We sat on our bunks, shivering in our sweat stained shirts and bitterly contemplated our futures. We were greatly vexed when we observed that contact between the barracks was limited. Chance encounters in the yard, at the latrine or the water pump, were our only hope, and as time went on that seemed increasingly unlikely. The women were housed in a barrack that ran parallel to ours, across the wide yard, and the men's barrack, the smallest, sat upon a low rise up the slope of the hill. In spite of this proximity, it was left to pure chance for a meeting to occur; the number of people in the camp had swelled alarmingly.

As each day passed without word from Oma and Opa, we sank further and further into depression. We spent hours lying on our bunks, trying to find sleep that wouldn't come. Instead, we traced the paths of filth on the ceiling that the flies traveled, their feet coated in the waste from the open pit of the latrine.

Lights were put out at nine o'clock and everyone tried vainly to sleep in the smelly and cold room, under the insufficient blanket. Many nights passed among the sounds of soft crying, as one boy after another tried to come to terms with his lonely situation. Sleep came slowly. My eyes struggled with the darkness and the sudden flashes of white upon the length of the wall, where the search light explored with its probing fingers along the perimeter of the camp.

One night, after I had struggled with sleep for several hours, I awoke with a start to the sound of loud crying from the small forlorn boy whose bed was beneath the window. I rolled onto my stomach, straining my eyes through the darkness in an attempt to see his face more clearly.

I was startled by the sudden appearance of the overseer at the door, her fat hand brandishing a large wooden shoe. She flung it madly across the room toward the noise, yelling, "Silence! Go to sleep!" It clanked against the wall below the window, toppling onto the boy's covers. The cries ceased.

Bodies around me shifted and stirred as nearly everyone awoke with a jolt. Soft whispers and questions were halted upon the arrival of the other shoe, with a thud, into the middle of the room. The door slammed loudly upon her hoarse voice yelling from the hall, "Silence! Now!"

My body returned slowly to the world of dreams, the muffled sobs of the boy grating on my nerves. Suddenly, a series of sharp gun shots burst through the darkness, sending every boy scrambling to the window. The silhouette of a human figure hung limply against the fence, like a rag doll hung out to dry.

The overseer stomped noisily down the hall, yelling as she went, "Go back to bed! Now!" We bolted to our bunks, none of us wanting to receive a bruise from another of her projectiles. We quickly lay down, though few of us slept. The image of the woman's body, lifeless against the sharp claws of the fence, danced into my fitful dreams for the rest of the short night.

The morning dawned dimly and I rolled over slowly, unwilling to welcome what promised to be another grim day. I glanced down toward the bunk under the window and I saw the boy was awake. He was sitting up and nursing several bloody gashes along his spindly shins and thighs. I gasped audibly and the boy's head jerked around. He noticed me peering down upon him, shock and disbelief clear on my face, and he said through his tears, "… Rats. There were rats… chewing on me." He gulped loudly and buried his face in his blanket, sobbing quietly.

"Wow." croaked Gerle beside me. "I guess we can be thankful for a top bunk. We just get the flies."

We hurried outside, preferring to steer clear of the angry overseer. Instead, we ate our meal of stale bread. The only sign of any occurrence the night before was a small stain of reddish brown in the dirt near the fence, but the guards quickly shuffled over it with their dusty boots, their eyes glaring threateningly at anyone who wandered too close.

The sunlight felt warm on our faces, which we trained skyward with our eyes closed to soak in the heat. My bones ached from the cold and damp that seemed to pervade the barracks. Although it was high summer beyond the walls, the soothing heat never seemed to permeate the darkness of the interior.

"What do you think happened?" whispered Gerle, opening his eyes.

"I don't know." I answered, shaking my head.

Almost in answer to my question, a loud panicked scream erupted from the women's quarters. A thin woman, her hands clutching a torn dress, bolted from the door, knocking over an elderly lady who stood in her path.

Instead of stopping to assist the old woman, she darted past the latrine, which ran near the fence at the end of the yard. Her eyes were wide with terror and a large purple bruise was already rising on her forehead.

Behind her, two guards strolled casually out of the woman's barrack, one of them sneering as he buckled his belt slowly. He whispered something to his friend and they laughed heartily, their faces widening into fearful grimaces of mirth.

The woman glanced behind her, spotted her pursuers, and headed desperately toward the fence, her hands clutching at the sharp wires in a frantic, but futile, attempt to escape.

The soldiers both raised their guns in a lazy fashion, their shoulders still shaking with laughter. They fired. The shots echoed across the camp. The woman's scream died in her throat. Her head slammed against the wooden pole of the fence and her body dropped backward in a heap, the blood already making a fresh stain in the dirt.

Silence filled the yard. Gerle and I backed slowly into the boys' barrack, hoping not to attract attention. I crawled into my bunk, where I curled into a tight ball and pressed my eyes shut, in a hopeless attempt to erase the terrible visions crowding into my head.

Several more women were shot that day, as the guards went on a lusty rampage through the women's barracks. As if in sport, the guards watched one young woman try to earn her freedom, by allowing her to crawl skillfully under the fence, which dug deeply into her bleeding back. They chortled and joked as she raised herself excitedly on the other side. But, just as she made her first step forward she disappeared in a loud explosion as her foot triggered a small buried land mine. The guards slapped their knees in amusement and walked away shaking their heads.

One refugee, a sickly man with sallow skin and greasy hair, shook his fist in anger at the guards, yelling profanities and insults at their retreating backs. The guards turned back, lunging fiercely at the stooped man. They both thrust the ends of their machine guns roughly into his soft stomach and forced him to the ground, where he lay moaning and pleading, his hands raised anxiously in front of his face.

The two guards then proceeded to bash their guns into every inch of his body, until it flopped lifelessly from side to side with the impacts. Blood tricked slowly from his many open gashes and his hands twitched in a last effort to grasp his escaping soul. The guards shouldered their guns, grabbed the man roughly by the arms and legs and threw his tattered body into the stinking latrine, where it hit with a loud splash and floated grotesquely among the disturbed flies.

Several hours later, his hand still twitched occasionally, reflexes being the only thing left of his defiant self. His face stared blankly up at the blue sky above, though the flies soon obscured it from his unseeing eyes as he sank slowly into his fluid-filled tomb.

Gerle and I spent the day huddled in a corner of the yard, shock and despair painting blank expressions on our gaunt and pale faces. The pathetic food offerings sent my stomach rebelling, while the day's horrors swam continuously through my mind. I longed for Oma's touch, and I forced myself to believe that she and Gerti were all right and unharmed.

"Alfie!" yelled a soft voice, breaking my daydream of Oma's soothing hugs. My eyes flew open, searching frantically around the yard. It was a voice right out of my dream! I looked for Oma's sweet face. "Alfie! Over here." she cried hoarsely, struggling to keep her voice from carrying to the ears of the guards.

"There!" Gerle pointed, his eyes wide with delight. "Oh! She looks so sad." moaned Gerle. He pushed his bangs out of his eyes and we walked slowly toward her, still unsure what contact between barracks was allowed.

"That's close enough, Alfie. Frau T. was struck by a guard yesterday for trying to talk to her husband." Oma said, stopping ten feet away from us, her hands clenching her skirt tightly. "Lord knows I want to hold you both..." she said, her tears flowing freely now.

"How are you, Oma? ... How's Gerti? Have you seen Opa? Is he ok?... Uncle Alois?" I gushed, suddenly needing every question answered at once. Gerle sighed loudly at my side, stuffing his hands into his pockets.

"I'm fine, child. I'm fine." Oma said, raising her hand slightly toward me, her fingers curved in a familiar caress. I could almost feel their soft touch on my cheek, and I had to force myself not to raise my own hand to my face. "Gerti cries all the time. I'm worried about her, Alfie.... she doesn't eat, she just sits in her dark bed and cries." she continued, sadly.

Guards began to mill about the yard, summoning everyone back to their bunks for curfew, and we waved furtively to Oma, who had begun to move away at the first sight of a guard. I was grateful that she knew not to draw attention to herself, but my heart clenched at what I knew she and my sister had been forced to see in their rooms.

We walked back to our bunks, Gerle muttering incoherently under his tight breaths. At the door we turned to look behind us, anxious for Oma's safe return to Gerti, and we saw that she had already gone in. Instead, we watched for a moment as the sun dipped over the town into deepening shades of rose and purple, colors that seemed too pure for such a terrible day.

"The house is just over there... see?" pointed Gerle. "Where that sparkle of light is. That's the roof tiles on the house next door. It's not too far... we know these woods like the backs of our hands." he insisted. I smiled sadly at these words, remembering bitterly the many thrilling games of cowboys and Indians in the cool woods flanking the camp.

"Your sister needs food, Alfie." he said suddenly. He glanced into my face, his eyes probing to see if I understood. He leaned over and whispered, "We can get out, Alfie... I know we can."

CHAPTER 18

Gerle and I agonized over our decision to escape for days. The images of Gerti's thin sad face tormented our minds. Yet, the thought of the ring of plate-sized land mines filled us with an overwhelming fear. Death would be sudden, but certainly not clean. Several more mines had exploded in a hideous shower of dust, twisted metal, and charred scraps of human flesh. The desperation of the inhabitants, especially the women, had increased.

We scanned the yard every day, hoping for another word with Oma. It seemed as though the entire population of the city had been brought to the camp, yet no familiar face greeted us amidst the seething mass of humanity present in the overcrowded yard. Our thoughts wandered to our friends and we hoped they were safe somewhere far away, where the aftermath of the war was filled with legitimate peace and deserved renewal.

Life flowed interminably forward, the line between survival and utter defeat blurring painfully. We gazed longingly upon the flowing hills and meadows beyond the barrier of the fence, until the pain in our hearts consumed us. We daydreamed at length about the cellar of food sitting unclaimed at home.

Finally, the pull of the outside world overcame our fear and we decided upon a nighttime escape. We fixed the path of the search light into our minds and counted the lengths of the intervals of sheltering darkness between the blinding ferocity of the piercing light.

The following evening we struggled to stomach our dinner, which consisted of a thin flavorless broth, void of any satisfying or nourishing morsels. My head whirled with the anticipation of the coming endeavor and my jagged-edged soup tin sat forgotten in the dust at my side. Rows of boys and men surrounded the long rickety table of the field kitchen, each one of them waiting for their daily dollop of food. I scanned the crowd for Opa or my uncle, but, as usual, I found no familiar face among the masses. Meals were scattered throughout the long day to accommodate the high volume of people housed in the camp. My eyes traveled slowly along the lines of miserable souls, beyond their heads to the end of the yard. I eyed the fence nervously, mindful of the humps and newly formed craters that loomed beyond it like an impenetrable labyrinth.

"We need to follow the path of the craters, Alfie…" Gerle said quietly, interrupting my reverie. "… the ones that have already… um, blown." He grimaced and I thought, with a shudder, of the many fragments of bodies we would encounter along the way. But, the only path of possibility lay between those exploded mines. Nonetheless, the thought of a hidden, yet untouched surprise made my hands sweat.

We followed the other boys back to the bunk room and rested stiffly on our beds until lights out was announced. We waited for the nightly sobs of the boys to diminish into the even sighs of sleep, then we scrambled silently down the frame of the shelves to the cold floor.

We paused momentarily, our breaths catching in our throats while several boys murmured and squirmed in their restless sleep. Calm descended once again and we tiptoed toward the door, carrying our shoes.

It was not unusual for people to be awake at night. Diarrhea and other ailments were so pervasive throughout the camp that the latrine was rarely deserted. I longed to be free of its revolting odors, yet I felt thankful for its existence at the moment, as it provided a perfect cover.

Once outside, we paused to observe the location of the search light. It traced the fence perimeter slowly, its long arm reaching menacingly into random crevasses of the camp. We flattened our backs to the wall of the barrack and sidled along to the corner, pausing with our breaths held as the icy light scoured the knobby wall inches above our heads. Ahead of us loomed the barb wire, reaching toward us with its clawed hands, bidding us to come nearer.

"Now!" I whispered hoarsely. We dashed forward and our stomachs slammed into the dirt, which was still slightly sticky with congealed blood. I spat the dirt from my mouth, my stomach turning over in revulsion. The images of the mangled bodies being dragged away swam before me while I forced myself blindly onward toward the fence.

Gerle's hand suddenly smashed firmly into the back of my head, returning my face to the foul dirt. I sputtered angrily, ready to hiss reproaches at him, until I felt the cold chill of the hair on the back of my neck tingling with fear. The pulsing light swept rapidly over our flattened bodies. I shrank into the soil. In spite of my thin build I suddenly felt very visible and I wanted desperately to disappear into the earth.

I sensed more than heard Gerle's small sigh of relief as the search light passed on without raising any alarm. I lifted my head from the dirt and blinked the sweat from my eyes. We continued forward, words unnecessary adornments for the urgency of the moment. We carefully lifted the wire, the clatter of which seemed amplified in the stillness of the late hour. The month of minimal nourishment finally paid off as we slithered, unscathed, through the small gap beneath the fence.

Before us lay the perilous path to freedom, boldly trodden by our predecessors as they had vainly attempted to escape to a better existence. Deep pits lay scattered about, leaving the path clear before us. Gerle moved slowly, remaining slightly behind me. His eyes continued to scan the camp for the location of the search light.

I took a deep breath and dust prickled my nose. I fought, with rising panic, to suppress a sneeze. The slightest noise would draw the attention of the white light. I groped cautiously before me, my fingers testing the ground for raised dirt mounds beneath the grass. The blown mines had made our job easier and I uttered a heartfelt lament for those who had gone before us.

The gentle night breeze ruffled my hair and I paused, only briefly, to relish the fresh air that enveloped us as the wind shifted, clearing the foul cloud that hung over the camp. The darkness of the cool woods rose before me and I was engulfed by a wave of nostalgia. My mind darted joyfully back to the familiar paths our feet had taken during our forages for berries and our involved games of cowboys and Indians so many years before, when life had been so full of promise.

I continued to inch forward, remembering to be careful not to raise my head too high above the grass. I remained prostrate even as the field began to give way to prickly juniper and tangy-smelling pine needles. Not until I was clear of the reach of the light did I feel confident to lift my head above the forest floor.

The lights from camp seemed miles away and I searched the grass nervously for Gerle. He soon appeared, having been forced to mold himself into the ground several times as the light crept across the long blades of grass like a lioness on the prowl.

The forest felt cool and inviting, its murky depths no longer filled with the sights and sounds that had made it seem menacing to me as a young child. Now, it breathed of life and freedom, reflecting a world beyond the reach of man's evil potential to destroy.

"Wow! That was amazing!" whispered Gerle, raising himself from the ground and dusting his front with his hands. "I don't know when I've ever been more scared! Though, lately..." He allowed his words to trail off and he peered silently into the dark branches, the ends of which waved and sighed in the soft summer air. "It feels great to be out of that hell hole." he said, tears of happiness streaking down his beaming face.

"Gerle... remember, we have to go back. We can't leave them in there to... Well, we just have to go back." I finished, awkwardly.

"I know, Alfie. I didn't mean that. It just feels good to be out here." Gerle defended, gesturing dramatically with his hands at the circle of woods around us. "We better take it easy from here, Alfie. There might be patrols around. We don't want to get caught." Gerle continued, nervously. He tiptoed into the trees, the shadows of which lengthened boldly in the rising moonlight.

The soothing sounds of a summer night danced around us as we hurried silently toward town. We had donned our shoes on the edge of the woods, though reluctantly, as the fresh grass felt soothing and cool beneath our dusty and calloused feet.

The vacant dark windows of the houses rose before us when we left the safety of the woods. A surreal air hung over the shapes of the buildings, every other one of which bore the evidence of the beginnings of repair—repair that had been interrupted, and for many, repair that might never be completed. The townsfolk had been plucked from their attempts at rebuilding their shattered lives. Now, the empty houses, many with ladders and paint cans still leaning against the walls, stood as a last testament to the dogged resiliency and tenacity of their owners.

We avoided the center of town, skirting instead along the train tracks, which were lined in places with thick brush, providing us ample coverage from any roving machine guns. Several times we were startled by an indistinct sound and we flung ourselves into a ditch along the rails. We retraced our route of departure many months ago and soon found ourselves staring down into the blackness of the long trench in which we had spent the night.

Decaying bodies of soldiers felled in battle were still draped among the toppled sandbags and equipment boxes. Clearly, many had not retreated far enough to spare them a violent death. We turned our backs on the ghastly faces staring up at us from vacant eyes, now picked hollow by scavengers, and we headed for the river and the home that lay beyond.

We stumbled through the water, trying to step carefully among the slippery rocks in the darkness. The water tingled like a gentle caress upon our dirt-caked feet and legs, and my heart rose for the first time in weeks.

"Almost there." whispered Gerle. "Do you think it's locked?" he asked.

"I don't remember seeing Opa lock it." I answered, clambering up the damp riverbank toward the house. We opened the gate slowly, suddenly conscious that its hinges needed oil. The door of the house gave way silently and easily, as if welcoming us like an old friend, and we tiptoed into the familiar halls. The stillness inside felt inviting and invigorating after the constant sobs, moans, and depressed talk of the camp.

"Let's get food first." I said, groping my way forward to the cellar. "Ouch!" I cried, stubbing my toe on something in the hall. It clanked sharply against my foot and I hopped about in pain, clenching my toe. As the pain subsided, I realized it was the small metal box that Opa usually kept under his bed. He had rummaged through it hastily on the day of our departure and I guessed that it had contained the valuable papers he had hidden in his shirt.

I wondered, while kicking the empty box to the side, whether Opa's papers were still safe upon his body, and I wondered, worriedly, what Opa's thoughts would be if he knew Gerle and I had sneaked out. A wave of guilt swept across me as I imagined my grandparents grief if we failed to return.

With my elation at being home now somewhat dulled by these thoughts, I continued into the cellar, which felt cool and inviting after the relentless heat of the camp courtyard. The reassuring smell of rich appetizing foods wafted before me and I staggered down the dark narrow staircase. Hunger enveloped me, the fragrances of many the delicious items overwhelming my patience.

I rummaged roughly through Oma's specially designed sandbox, pulling carrots and radishes from their forced hibernation. I gnawed on a carrot, which was still crisp with freshness, and my teeth tingled at the unusual demand to chew. Thin flavorless broth had been our staple for so long.

Gerle, who had followed me into the darkness, ran his hands along the dark walls, toppling jars and bottles in his eagerness to land upon something tasty. He wrenched a jar open, grunting audibly with the strain on his wasted muscles. He crawled toward me with the conquered jar of peaches in his outstretched hand.

"Oh, that's so good!" he gasped, between sticky breaths.

I eased a slippery peach out of its heavy syrup and relished the sweet tang of the fruit as it rolled around in my ecstatic mouth. My eyes watered with delight at the long-forgotten taste and I reached quickly for another one.

"Let's take some upstairs." muttered Gerle, his mouth brimming with juicy peaches.

"Here's some dried fruit, I think. Let's take this back for Gerti." I said. My hand had landed on a small linen sack tied up tightly with twine. Tucking the rough sack into my shirt, we wandered back upstairs, our stomachs rumbling noisily at the unexpected meal. We explored the kitchen carefully, hoping for a surprising morsel, but remembered sadly that we had barely been settled in the house before the Russians had torn us away from it again.

"I can't wait to sleep without rats crawling around below." Gerle muttered, barely suppressing a wide yawn. He ruffled his messy hair with his hands and led the way to our room. A cool night breeze shook the blanket, which hung loosely over the clinging remains of the glass shards that still framed the window. Glass to repair the windows had not been available. Everyone had been forced to wait, thankful that it was yet summer.

I flopped happily onto my soft bed, the slight feeling of guilt returning as I remembered Oma's long labors at the washbasin getting our linens clean of lice and dirt. I knew my grimy hands and tattered remnants of clothes were leaving unsightly marks on the soft, snow-white coverlet. But, my exhaustion forced any feeling of concern to the back of my thoughts, and I fell instantly into an undisturbed slumber.

I was having a pleasant dream. The gently drifting clouds, clustered in soothing masses of billowing down, were reflected perfectly in the crystal clear water of the river. I was floating above the water, simultaneously gazing at the sky above and its reflection below. A bewitching calm lay over the land and no indication of the massive destruction of the war was present to disturb the scene.

Suddenly a ripple fanned out across the pristine water and a familiar voice called, "Alfie!", from far away. My body shook upon its perch in the air and the voice prodded further. I opened my eyes and saw, in the half-light of the predawn, that Gerle stood over me, his hands gently jiggling my shoulders.

"Alfie!" he urged. "Wake up!" He ceased shaking me, having noticed that my eyes were finally open, if not yet focused. He rubbed his own eyes and added, "We better get back to camp before it gets too light."

I roused myself quickly, though I was disappointed to have to shake off the lingering effects of the wonderful dream. I stuffed the small sack of dried fruit back down the front of my shirt, and after a last glance back at our house, and a couple snatched apples from the trees in the yard, we retraced our steps.

We trotted along toward the woods, skirting with averted eyes the trench filled with corpses. We felt the renewed energy of a good night's sleep and decent food in our stomachs. The trees lining the city limits stirred with the sounds of small animals scurrying about for their last attempts at a meal, before they settled down for a peaceful rest in an old log or stump. Occasionally, a bird twittered above us, its sleep disturbed momentarily by our passing.

Soon, the camp emerged from the edge of the wood, and we dropped to our knees to slither through the dew-laden grass, which tickled and cooled our sweating faces. The soft glow of dawn made the mounds of the unexploded mines easier to identify and we reached the fence without delay. The search light had been retired with the approach of morning, so our return under the wires went unnoticed.

I couldn't help feeling a pang of disgust as I felt the stiffness of the wire slide across my calves behind me—the free world had been mine for a few hours, but I had willingly turned my back on it. Then, Gerti's sad face swam into view, and I carefully shifted the precious bundle of dried fruit to a less conspicuous spot inside my shirt; I hoped I would see Oma again soon.

We rose slowly near the latrine, and on the chance we were being observed, we toyed with the buttons on our shorts as if we had been relieving ourselves. Gerle glanced longingly back at the woods, which now glowed with the first hints of day. The sun was just striking the clouds of mist hanging loosely over the valley, while the courtyard of the camp still lay hidden beneath a cool mantle of shadow. The filth and odor seemed slightly diminished, without the intense rays of the sun adding heat to the toxic stew of the latrine.

"Let's get back inside, Gerle. I want to lie down a little." I said quietly. The sudden activity and the unusually rich food from the night before had unsettled my stomach.

"Yes... Let's." Gerle answered. The smell of the latrine had us both slightly pale after the reprieve of the fresh forest air.

We wandered slowly into the barrack, which remained calm with slumber, although several boys lay moaning and crying with their nightly infliction of rat bites. No one stirred as we clambered slowly and quietly back up to our bunks. I tried not to think about the soft mattress at home as I stretched out awkwardly on the lumpy hard straw of the bed. We slept for another hour, then rose to face the long wait of the breakfast line, in hopes of encountering Oma.

"Do you think she will be here? We haven't seen her every time." Gerle wondered. "I wish we could see Opa. I wonder how Uncle Alois is doing?" he continued. We followed several bunk mates out into the hazy sunshine of a warm midmorning and queued up behind a long row of hungry and restless boys. The sun warmed the air quickly, stirring the flies into their daily frenzy. Most people had long since given up brushing the relentless insects away, and the flies took every opportunity to partake in the meager meals.

The line inched slowly forward, each person fingering their small soiled can for their shallow ladle of soup.

"There!" cried Gerle, pointing excitedly across the yard to another line of hungry people. In the sinuous row of women, we spotted my grandmother, her tired eyes peering anxiously around for what we guessed was a sign of Opa.

"Wait until we get our food, then we can get closer." I answered. I shifted the warm sack of dried fruit beneath my shirt, then I began to think of what we should tell Oma. We shuffled forward, holding our cans out for the small sampling of the day's offering.

Our cans half full of tepid broth, we continued onward, in hopes of attracting Oma's attention. We watched her carefully, ready to signal when her eyes passed over us. She looked worn and nervous; her face was pale and her hair was knotted and tousled with neglect. A lump formed in my throat, as I longed to run toward her and fold her into my arms. I shook the feeling off and concentrated on getting as close to her as possible without attracting the attention of the guards, who milled about threateningly.

"Come on." I whispered sideways to Gerle. I stared at Oma, willing her to turn her head. She stood morosely to the side of the line of women, her hands holding two small cans of broth. Gerti was nowhere in sight. Her eyes traveled aimlessly over the somber faces about her… and they passed directly across us without a glimmer of recognition.

A yell rose into my throat, but I forced it back down. I noticed her start and finally focus her eyes lovingly upon Gerle and me. She raised her hand slightly, the can tipping precariously. I gestured for her to walk forward and we headed toward the tightest clump of people, hoping to hide in its midst.

"Oma! Here, this is for Gerti." I said, quickly, handing her the linen sack from beneath my shirt. She glanced up at me in surprise and a question formed on her lips. "Make sure she gets it." I added. "Take care." We moved forward, the cover of the crowd having broken apart. I peered behind me and watched her stuff the sack into her apron pocket. Her gaze lingered on my face, anguish and pride mingling upon her strained features. Saddened, I turned and walked away.

CHAPTER 19

We rested fitfully in our bunks, the heat of the day reaching an unbearable level in the stifling courtyard. A little before noon, we braved the sun and wandered aimlessly into the dust, hopeful for a spot in the shade. A loud rumble echoed against the rough walls of the barracks and the tall gate swung forward, admitting a large Russian truck. Its empty hold was lined with crude slats of wood. The truck bounced and belched into the middle of the yard, its brakes screeching fiercely to a stop.

The camp commander, a fleshy man with lipid circles beneath his dark eyes, emerged from his small office at the end of one of the buildings. Leaning against the frame of the door, he peered casually into the crowd making way for the vehicle. In one hand he twirled a cigarette, the ashes dangling precariously close to his drab green uniform. His other hand held a bottle of vodka, its contents nearly gone.

His broad face widened into a sickening grin, as he watched the truck grind a narrow turn until its front grill faced the gate and the valley beyond. He flicked his cigarette forcefully to the ground, grinding it finely with the toe of his polished black boot. Then, he strode purposefully into the shadows of his office.

He returned immediately with a machine gun hoisted onto his wide shoulder, its barrel pointing menacingly toward the blue sky. I heard Gerle's gasp beside me, and I turned to see his pale face directed toward a row of women who seemed filled with a sudden panic.

"No!" I whispered, through gritted teeth, knowing now the purpose of the truck. I let my head tilt back against the wall behind me and, closing my eyes, I willed the truck to disappear. A sudden spattering of gunfire returned me to the moment and I opened my eyes to see the commander firing an entire round of ammunition into the air. He laughed maniacally, throwing his other arm up into the air with joy. The vodka bottle crashed to the ground, its meager contents disappearing into the dust beneath the beating sun.

In response, several young soldiers jumped awkwardly out of the truck, their feet struggling to keep their liquor-saturated bodies upright. They lurched forward and propped themselves against the railing of the commander's porch.

"I don't like the way this looks." Gerle muttered. "Let's go inside." he added. I nodded, dumbly, but we both remained rooted to the spot, dread having planted our feet into the dust.

The men seemed to be enjoying a private joke with the commander, who slapped them heartily on their shoulders with a loud guffaw. He then turned back to his office and spoke to someone inside, before returning to his friends to continue their jest. A small man shuffled from the room and we recognized him as the interpreter, whose job it was to ensure that any miscommunications between guards and guarded, did not go uncorrected.

The commander gestured pompously to the man, who leaned in reluctantly to hear his instructions. The interpreter flinched and stared questioningly into the commander's watery eyes, where he received an emphatic answer to any thoughts of defiance. The man cleared his throat and walked forward, glancing several times back at his superior, who continued to watch him with a mixture of contempt and amusement.

"Women... All of you, line up! Double file! Hurry up!" he yelled, his voice cracking with effort. He stared about, the color rising uncomfortably upon his narrow face, as he continued, "Right now! All of you."

Instantly, sobbing and hysterics commenced among the women, their worst fears staring them in the face. The lucky ones today would be the ones who had returned to their bunks for a rest. I prayed Oma and Gerti were among them. The women in the yard numbered at least several dozen. They now tentatively shuffled forward, clutching each other tightly. Their hands caressed the heads of the younger girls, the most vulnerable. These they encircled in the middle of the group, while the older ladies elevated their chins, instinctively proud and determined to go into this hell with grace and honor.

The interpreter proceeded to organize the petrified women into two lines, leaving a wide path between the rows. The rest of the people milling about had gone silent, pressing themselves against the walls of the barracks, but otherwise too shocked to move. The only sounds were the trees being rustled by the hot wind, and the muffled sobs of the dozens of women huddles together in reckless rows.

The commander barked something to his friends and they stumbled forward, the effects of their drunken excess clear on their sweaty faces and in the odor of their fetid breaths. They wandered between the lines of women, leering cruelly at the frightened faces.

"You!" grunted one of the soldiers, and he thrust his hand into the chest of one young women. Her hands nervously clenched a tattered sweater tightly against her throat. He grabbed the collar of the sweater, and with a sharp tug, he pulled her toward him. The suddenness of it sent her sprawling into the dirt.

A fair young woman next to her was holding a baby, an infant so new he had to have been born in the camp. The small fists squirmed and jostled from within a soiled blanket, but no sound could be heard. The soldier seemed particularly fascinated by the child, curious that the youngster seemed so quiet. Suddenly, he grabbed the baby from the woman and thrust him roughly into the feeble arms of a small elderly woman who was cowering nearby. The mother began to sob, her hands reaching desperately for the child… and the baby's cries began. At the sound of her baby's distress, the mother screamed and sank to her knees, her hands clutching the soldier's legs in a desperate plea for mercy.

The soldier kicked her brutally, sending blood rising from her lip. He hauled her to her feet by the hair and pushed her with the other woman toward the truck. Two other soldiers grabbed them as them slumped near the wheels of the truck and flung them into the hard back of the vehicle.

"My baby!" screamed the mother, clambering to her knees in the bed of the truck. "Someone, please, take care of my baby! His name is Friedrich. Oh, God! Please, my baby!" Several women attempted to respond, but they were silenced quickly by the back of a soldier's hand.

The men proceeded to select at least ten more women, before nodding to the commander with merciless sneers. They were satisfied… for now. They loaded their treasure, most of whom were still screaming and sobbing, into the bed of the truck. The women huddled in a corner, some calling in vain for their loved ones. Two of the soldiers clambered into the truck bed with the women and began fondling the ones closest to them, their guns held threateningly in their free hands.

The truck rumbled to a start and headed slowly out of the gate. The screams of the women continued, their bodies just visible where they were in a heap, their arms flailing before them to fend off the brutal advances of the men. It seemed the men did not want to wait to share their prize with their comrades.

In the center of the yard, the women who had been spared clung to each other in a grateful embrace. They were strangers no more. They would forever share the memory of this dreadful moment, just as they would forever share the guilt that inevitably accompanies such lucky twists of fate. They had stood and watched the others go, secretly grateful that they had been overlooked.

The orphaned infant had been passed to the center of the comforting circle. His pitiful cries rose into the air, as though his immature soul was already able to sense the loss of his mother.

The resulting mood in the camp was one of heightened fear and suppressed anger. Were death and despair to be the fates of us all?

The departure of the women was followed the next day by another group, equal in size and as miserable as the first. Gerle and I tried to fade into the shadows, our thoughts constantly on Oma and Gerti. As much as we would have liked to see them, it was better that they had remained inside. The soldiers had not only selected the women in full bloom.

"I want to go again tonight, Alfie." Gerle murmured one afternoon in the dark bunk room. He looked fixedly at me, his big brown eyes red and puffy from mounting emotions and sleepless nights. His face was pale in the low light, his skin thin and transparent over his bones. "I have to get out of here." he grimaced, sadly, his small shoulders shuddering slightly.

"Ok." I answered, though I felt there would be little reprieve from the deep depression into which I had sunk. What would our futures hold? Would we all die in the camp, forced to watch painfully as those around us sank slowly into a starved stupor? Life seemed to hold little hope, whether we were inside or outside of the barb wire.

Nonetheless, we resolved to brave again the maze of mines outside the fence, their numbers having diminished by the day. We repeated our successful routine of the first night, now more confident with the outcome. I reminded myself to stay alert; the slightest mistake would be my last. I slithered quickly beneath the wire, marveling at how much thinner I seemed after just a few days.

The latest bomb explosions had been carelessly triggered and the soldiers didn't care to brave the mines themselves to clean up. This meant that severed and bloody limbs lay scattered among the gaping craters of soil. I gagged and swallowed hard, pausing for a brief reprieve with my eyes closed. But, I forced myself to open them again. I respected the danger enough to know that I had to overlook the gore while on the move. I also knew that I had to keep moving.

We reached the safety of the woods. This time a light drizzle cooled our heated faces. We lay on our backs for several moments, relishing the clear untainted water, which washed away the weeks of grime caking our sunburned skin.

"I hate this!" Gerle suddenly complained, fervently. "I don't ever want to go back in there! Ever!" He paused, sobbing slightly. Roughly brushing his hand across his damp face, he continued, heatedly, "I know, Alfie. You don't have to remind me. That's what makes it so awful." His fist slammed angrily into the damp soil. "We have to go back."

I sighed loudly and said softly, "Let's go, Gerle. Let's make the most of our time." I eased my tired limbs to standing and we tiptoed through the damp forest. All around us the rain dripped soothingly off the sodden branches. The drizzle persisted, increasing to a slight downpour, but the trees sheltered us from the worst. Darkness lay about, broken only by pools of mist hanging in the hidden hollows of the hillside.

We reached our house quickly. The rain lost its appeal after several minutes and we expended precious energy to run the rest of the way. The water pattered loudly on the newly repaired tiles and I smiled slightly to know that my efforts on the tall ladder, which was still leaning against the house, had not been in vain. At least the house would be dry.

With our hunger mounting, we dashed for the cellar. We easily located the jars we had jostled about on our previous visit and we set to work emptying many of them. This time, I gathered several carrots beneath my shirt in the hopes of giving them to Oma. Time passed quickly and, once again, our stomachs rebelled at the assault of rich food. I stumbled uncomfortably to the latrine in the washroom, returning several minutes later to find Gerle already asleep in his bed. His face wore a contented smile, though it did little to mask the strain of the last few months. I eased the fluffy coverlet to his chin and crawled into my own cool and inviting bed. My clothes felt damp against the sheets and once again I apologized wordlessly to Oma for my momentary disregard for her efforts at cleanliness. My head sank into the thick pillow and I fell instantly into a peaceful slumber.

This time my dreams departed before I awoke, leaving me refreshed and ready to face the coming day. The night still lingered, though the pale lavender and gray of the sky reminded us that morning was not too far off. We paused at Opa's precious trees and filled our pockets with the abundance of fruit which now had only the birds to admire them.

We wandered steadily upward, staying close to the path of our initial escape from the city. The tart plums felt refreshing and sweet in our parched mouths, but they caused me to regret not having stopped for a longer drink at the pump in the front yard.

We soon arrived at the perimeter of the camp, its shadows occasionally sliced by the thin sliver of the search light as it swept its way mercilessly across the vast yard. We lingered in the forest until the light turned off with a loud thud. Now was our chance to make a safe return. I braced myself for the sights in the minefield and whispered a farewell, one more time, to my precious freedom.

We tiptoed cautiously into the barrack, a slight feeling of guilt darkening our moods. Moans of pain and discomfort echoed from the dark trench of the latrine. I stood in the doorway and glanced backward. The early morning light was rising shamelessly upon the trembling figure of an old man, who sat teetering upon his weak frame over the frothing waste below. He moaned again, his gaunt face raised imploringly to his chosen maker.

I sighed guiltily and thanked the stars that I had not recognized my grandfather's face in that pathetic figure in the fading darkness. I shuffled silently behind Gerle, who stifled a yawn behind his hand, and we cautiously entered our bunk room. Our companions in our daily existence were all sleeping soundly, the rats having taken a rest from their nocturnal forages among the sickly flesh of the youngest boys near the floor.

We returned to our beds, the thin blankets still bundled in heaps to resemble our sleeping forms, and we dozed until morning crept over the camp in earnest.

We were roused by the summons of the interpreter's sniveling voice over the loud speaker. "Attention, entire camp to assemble in the yard. Immediately! Line up in an orderly fashion, grouped by barrack. Now!" The speaker crackled, whistled slightly, and went silent.

The boys sat up nervously in their beds, their wide eyes asking unanswerable questions of their bunk mates. The barrack guard, the lady with the accurate aim with a wooden shoe, entered suddenly, yelling hoarsely, "You heard him! All of you, move out! Now! No stopping." Her German had improved over the course of time and she had no doubt her orders would be obeyed. To emphasize her confidence in her ability to intimidate, she only scowled slightly before returning to her small office near the door.

Every boy in the room leapt to the floor, clambering to be seen obeying her authority. She had quickly earned a reputation for punishing those who seemed more reluctant to be anything but absolutely compliant. Gerle and I followed grimly, convinced that any summons to the yard had to be laced with trouble.

Our fears were not unfounded. The wave of people who littered the yard was vast and diverse, though it was clear the number of women had dramatically decreased. A high pitched wailing reminded us of the newest orphan in our midst and I caught a glimpse of the red contorted face of the baby who had lost his mother. He had been forced to survive on water and spooned broth, instead of the life-giving nourishment of her milk.

There was a loud squeal of brakes as another large truck rumbled in and idled noisily just inside the entrance to the camp. The gates remained open, making it clear that the truck was planning a rapid departure.

Among the many nervous faces, Gerle and I searched for our grandparents. I longed for a sight of my sweet sister, her pleas for me still pounding in my head. I had sworn to myself to protect her and now I had all I could do just to keep myself alive.

The interpreter's voice cracked brusquely over the murmurs of the crowd and he said, "Line up as you are selected. Stay quiet!"

A ripple of silent, yet palatable panic swept over the rows of people, each one hoping the person next to him would be chosen first. Guards strode stiffly between the trembling masses, selecting individuals to satisfy the required number. After several minutes, broken by scattered sobs of protest, as families were cruelly separated on either side of us, the interpreter's voice rose once more to remind us that any more audible disturbances would be punished.

Gerle and I leaned tightly toward each other, twining our hands firmly together. I peered worriedly about, scanning the frightened faces, continuing to search for our loved ones. They were nowhere in sight.

Suddenly, a scuffle broke out from the midst of the swarm and three women bolted through the open gate toward the woods. They ran through the low shrubs, heedless of the thorns gouging their thin legs. A rapid succession of gun fire followed them, sending them sprawling limply across the damp grass at the edge of the wood.

I gasped sadly. I realized one young lady lay slumped beneath the very tree that had dripped sweet water into my tired face the night before. Now, a pool of blood replaced the puddle of clear water. Her eyes gazed lifelessly up at the very sky that had held comforting stars on one of our previous escapes.

Those who had been selected knew it was folly to do anything but cooperate. They shuffled sadly aboard the truck, aiding the elderly and blowing sad kisses to their loved ones who remained behind.

Finally, the gates shuddered closed, the backs of the unfortunate people disappearing beyond it around a bend in the road. For a moment nobody moved or spoke; only the sobs of the grieving broke the stillness. But, soon a line formed at the field kitchen, as hungry stomachs smelled the first whiffs of our daily offering of food. Gerle and I moved in behind some old men, hopeful for a sight of Opa.

"Siberia... that's where they are going. You mark my words." grunted a shriveled man with a thin bald head. "Better alive in here then dying up there in the snow in the north." he continued, staggering forward with his shaking hand clenched around his tin soup can. Its jagged rim glistened in the sun, which was now beating down mercilessly upon the heads of the people being driven away from their lifelong home to some feared destination to the east.

Each day we watched with trepidation, as several more large clusters of prisoners, their faces tight with dread, were led out of the camp. The stress of our uncertain futures mounted rapidly and Gerle and I soon found ourselves craving another night in our own beds.

I had failed to make contact with Oma, so the carrots shriveled for days beneath my pillow, before Gerle and I gnawed on them fitfully late one night. Over our stolen meal, we decided we would brave the minefield the following night. The camp was emptying rapidly and we were determined to have one more glimpse of our home before the inevitable happened. It never occurred to us to leave permanently; our bond with Oma and Opa, though we hadn't seen them for weeks, was very strong and reuniting with them filled our every thought.

We forced ourselves to remain confident that our futures beyond the camp would include our family. We had been through too much for it to be otherwise.

So, we resolved to attempt one more journey home, this time to retrieve something truly special for Gerti to eat—an egg. I remembered the tiny chick Gerti had cupped gently in her hand upon our return and I felt sure that the hens had not yet strayed too far from the house.

We tolerated another day of watching the camp's population dwindle. Loved ones were torn from eachother's arms and the occasional overlooked female was dragged off in an officer's private jeep, her screams of terror sending flocks of birds scattering from the canopy of nearby trees.

After a stressful day full of anticipation, evening finally settled over a somber camp. Only a few hundred prisoners remained, a mere fraction of the original number. We had watched the soldiers load each truck carefully and were fairly certain that our family, as yet, remained intact. Rumors of where everyone was being led swirled among the elders, each of them offering a more gruesome scenario than the last.

We waited in our bunks, the time inching slowly toward the cover of darkness. When at long last all was quiet, I grabbed my rucksack and we followed our regular path, tightly along the outside of the barrack wall and to the fence beyond the latrine.

"You go first this time, Gerle." I whispered, gesturing with my hand.

He glanced at me nervously, his eyes barely visible in the darkness, but he answered, "Ok. Just keep track of that light, Alfie."

228

I nodded and fell to my stomach, raising the fence slightly for Gerle to pass beneath. We slithered quickly forward, pausing with our faces to the dirt to allow for the light to skim the sparse blades of grass inches above our heads. We reached the shadows of the woods easily and without a backward glance we rose to our feet and headed home.

I scrambled about the familiar cellar, determined to find a morsel of food decent enough to surprise Gerti. The hens had been clever and had taken to hiding their eggs somewhere away from the house. We startled several fluffy brown hens on their perches in the coop, but not an egg could be found. I decided on a small jar of cherries, their crimson juices glistening in the slanting moonlight shining through the kitchen window.

I glanced at the beautiful round moon, rising as a perfect golden sphere over the church on the hill. The silhouette of the church's onion-shaped domes pierced the moon proudly, as if hoping to lasso itself for a trip up to heaven. The peace of the scene was too painful to bear; I knew that just below that church lay the camp.

Instead of sleeping, we contented ourselves with clambering about the house, reacquainting ourselves fondly with all its treasured corners. I ran my hand over the smooth walls of the Kachelofen, delighting in the coolness of the deep green tile. Gerle busied himself with winding the grandfather clock, rattling its long chains as he shuffled around its insides trying to reach the crank.

A reckless joy overcame us. The uncertainty that surrounded our lives at camp made our time at home seem all the more precious and fleeting. We laughed and joked, digging through old clothes stuffed beneath a bench in the hall. We found my old skis leaning against the shed in the yard and I buckled them around my thin shoes. I lurched dramatically across the yard, sending Gerle to the latrine with overzealous fits of laughter. The hens clucked with indignation, their slumber rudely disturbed.

Still chuckling, we cleared the plum tree of its plump black fruit; most of them had fallen unpicked to the ground. We then forced ourselves to swallow our mirth, knowing silence and caution were required for the return to camp. The moon had traced a long path across the sky during our adventures and it now prepared itself for slumber and for the arrival of the sun.

We quickened our pace, realizing that we had cut the margin of safety rather closely. The tall posts of the fence rose above us between the trees, but suddenly and inexplicably, I felt a tingle of panic rise on my back.

"Something is not right." Gerle whispered, nervously, at my elbow. I nodded, not sure exactly what he felt was missing, but he was right. The usual smoky smell from the field kitchen that lingered above the camp was absent.

We inched forward, our hands tightly entwined. We gasped as a bright light shone suddenly upon us. Staring back into the shadows, I struggled to discern its source. The intensity of the light sent a stab of pain across my forehead, while my eyes struggled to adjust.

Beyond the ring of light, I noticed a growing swarm of figures. They were all holding machine guns, each of which was aimed directly at us. I felt Gerle's arm trembling beneath mine and his knees seemed to sag. I pulled at his elbow, willing him to stay upright. I feared if he moved, they might shoot us.

In truth, I knew that they would shoot us anyway. The memory of the women running toward the woods, their blood splattering across the green grass, filled my throbbing head. Was this, too, to be our fate? Even if I had wanted to run, my legs would not have supported me. I determined to stand and face my fate alongside my friend. There was some consolation in knowing that we would die together, here, side by side.

The light was flicked off and a lone soldier advanced slowly, his eyes wide with surprise. Clearly, they had not expected anyone to be sneaking into camp. Behind him lay the empty yard. Everyone was gone. The troops had swept through during the hours prior to dawn and taken every last soul with them, including our family... our beloved grandparents... once again, leaving us behind.

The soldier raised his gun inches from our faces, his mouth twisted into a sneer of diabolical fury, and he yelled, "Stoi! Stoi! Hands up, or I'll shoot!"

CHAPTER 20

Finally, our luck seemed to have run out. We stood together, our arms in the air, while dark barrels of guns materialized all around us in the lifting gloom. Several soldiers, roused by the sudden disturbance, wandered, disheveled from the commander's office, suspenders hanging loosely about their waists.

Heated discussions followed, the guns jostling precariously inches from our faces. The shocked soldiers finally decided that the commander's office was the best place for us, until they determined our fates. We huddled nervously in the corner, the rich foods of the night before playing havoc with our heaving stomachs.

One soldier was assigned to guard us, a duty he seemed to feel was beneath him. He sat casually in a chair, leaning it awkwardly against the wall, which was splattered recklessly with chipping green paint. His hands toyed absently with the straps on his gun, though its barrel remained positioned on our slumped forms. We prayed he wouldn't kill us out of sheer boredom.

The commander strode in from an adjoining room, which, from the state of his clothing, we determined must be his sleeping quarters. He scowled angrily beneath his bushy dark eyebrows, the folds under his eyes puffier than normal. He was furious that his slumber had been disturbed; it was clear he was nursing a fair hangover.

He winced whenever a door banged loudly, which happened often, as officers bustled in and out, busy with their tasks of dismantling the camp. We were obviously an encumbrance to their allotted duties, and no one seemed to be able to say where we should fit in. This uncertainty left us forgotten in the dank corner for several hours, our legs growing stiff in their cramped positions. I longed to talk with Gerle and express the turbulent emotions overwhelming me at that moment, but every time one of us opened his mouth, the officer left to guard us would snarl incomprehensibly, yet convincingly, and he would thrust his weapon closer to our faces.

The stillness of the camp felt unnatural; there had always been a hum of voices from the throats of the hundreds of people housed in such close quarters. Now, only barked orders and the appropriate staccato responses echoed between the empty shells of the barracks.

A small bonfire smoked in the middle of the camp, fed with the forgotten treasures of the prisoners. Any sign of the masses of people who had huddled together, suffering, for so many weeks, had disappeared with the last puffs of dust from their ragged shoes, as they were led away. Only the smell from the latrine lingered to remind us that humanity, although denigrated and demoralized to the state of animals... humanity had once existed here.

We sat for several hours, ample time to fill our heads with terrible thoughts and images of what had become of our family. Once again, I was overcome with an overwhelming sense of guilt. I felt I had to have done something wrong to someone in the world to justify the continuous assault of the horrific twists of fate upon my tattered life. My thoughts went sadly back to my mother. I remembered her indifference and anger after I had struggled for days to reach her, all my hopes resting in her hands... and she had thrown them back in my face.

My throat clenched tightly, a complex mixture of sadness, fear, hunger, and exhaustion. The laughter of the sleepless night seemed so remote, so distant. Gerle shuddered silently beside me, his small shoulders leaning into my back, seeking comfort I could not give. The messy brown hair, once so playful and thick, now hung in dull, stringy masses against his gaunt face. He had never fully recovered from dysentery and I feared what we would face ahead without better food for my dear friend.

The desire for water became unbearable, as the sun rose into a clear sky, lending added heat to the already stifling room. It wasn't until the sun had almost reached the apex of its journey across the ambivalent heavens, that we were roused from a fitful dozing by rough kicks from the commander's highly polished boots.

The arrival of several supply trucks into the center of camp seemed to have provided a sudden solution to the question of our fate. After moments of further heated discussions among the guards, we were hoisted firmly to our feet and ushered to the bed of the vehicle, which was already being loaded with equipment and crates of food. Gerle and I were shoved between large stacks of wooden boxes, where we were ordered to sit still. But, a sudden urgent need to urinate made it very difficult for me to comply. Gerle sensed my unease and his eyes darted questioningly in my direction. At last the noise of the engine grinding to a start allowed me a cover with which to answer.

"I have to pee, Gerle. Keep a look out, ok?" I groaned, raising myself awkwardly to my knees. I tried to wedge my shoulders between several boxes to keep myself upright, as the truck began to move with a jolt. The truck lurched aggressively along the rain-pitted road, and I strained to relieve myself quickly in a dark corner before we arrived at our destination.

Two soldiers had been selected to guard us, but they ignored us completely, clearly convinced we would cause no trouble. I settled back down next to Gerle, taking little comfort in his familiar shoulders slumped against mine.

We watched, worriedly, as well-known sites in our town flashed past us. The truck thundered noisily through the deserted streets of the city. Piles of rubble remained where houses had once stood; clearly no one had had time to do much repair before they were swept out of their homes again, this time by the occupying victors.

Russian flags hung from several upper stories, the bold red with its golden hammer and sickle, replacing the vivid and cruel swastika of the defeated Third Reich. To us, the result was the same, a terrifying void in which we were left with no control over our own lives. It didn't seem to matter what color the flag was; we were still just as sick, just as hungry, and just as alone.

We reached the center of the city. The large and ornate towers of the city hall loomed over us as we lurched across the damaged cobblestones of the assembly square. I recalled, bitterly, the day many years before, when the crowd of jubilant townspeople had welcomed Adolf Hitler into their lives as the answer to their unsettled problems. I remembered the disturbing feelings of hatred I had felt toward the soldier as he had filled me with my first taste of deep humiliation, which as a six year old I had never experienced so profoundly before. I remembered too, the tears that had pricked angrily at the insides of my eyelids, and the kind words of encouragement Opa had spoken to me as he tried to guide me safely along the unknown path that lay before us.

Now, I faced the postwar future with only my young friend at my side. Opa and Oma were out there somewhere, and I prayed, my heart full of anguish, that they would be able to provide Gerti and Uncle Alois with some chance at an untroubled life. Where had they gone? Where had the rest of the city gone? It seemed very surreal to be the only ones left. We were the only ones left to whom the jumble of streets meant anything, anything beyond another jurisdiction to resettle with people meeting approved ethnic profiles.

We circled behind the city hall, the truck barely squeezing between several tall narrow buildings that had once housed offices and apartments. Now the alleyway led to a crudely built compound that encompassed the old city jail. Hastily installed barb wire fencing enclosed the small yard, one side of which was protected by the tall building.

We were unloaded into the dusty shadowed square and pushed, with as equal force as the deposited crates, against the brick wall. Gerle stumbled as the soldier's large hand thrust him effortlessly against the rough shell-pocketed bricks. I reached out automatically to help my friend regain his feet and he turned toward me with eyes filled with fear.

We leaned against the wall, grateful for its solidity, as our empty stomachs sent waves of dizziness through our tired bodies. Around us, the soldiers bustled to unload some of the equipment from the truck, while the rest of the supplies remained aboard to rumble away to another destination to the east.

"Look!" I whispered to Gerle, through a throat so dry that my voice was nothing more than a croak. I jabbed my chin sharply across the narrow yard toward several men lying upon the dusty cobbles.

Clearly, they were German soldiers. They were still in their uniforms, which were torn, and on some, caked with dried blood. Beyond them lay a few more men, civilian men who had been too old to put themselves forth to die for the Fatherland. Somehow, though, they had managed to receive wounds, many of them severe enough to imperil their lives. All the men were filthy and had apparently been living as prisoners for some time. Their clothes were ragged and their stomachs concave, but they lounged in the yard as if they were familiar with a long-practiced daily routine. Most of them wore the vacant expressions of individuals who had seen so much suffering and experienced so much pain, that they had lost the ability to process the continuing traumas in their battered lives.

They observed our arrival with little expression. The few who had them puffed on their small stubs of cigarettes, as though willing the putrid smoke of the stale and reused tobacco to fill their empty stomachs.

We waited with bated breath for almost an hour, the intense sun making our hollow insides turn somersaults. A stillness seemed to descend over the yard while the afternoon inched forward into evening. We dozed fitfully against the cool wall. It had fallen into shadow as the sun traced a path over the rooftops.

Finally, the dozens of men seemed to stir restlessly, like a singular massive organism with a sudden eager anticipation of an expected occurrence. We hoped desperately that it was something that involved food; we had not eaten since the night before. Guards began to amble about the yard, hauling scraps of lumber to a heap in the middle of the dusty cobblestones. What had once been carefully painted shutters on beautiful stucco-sided villas, now became fuel for a meager, but welcome, meal.

Soon, the guards had a large pot of fragrant cabbage soup steaming over the open flames. A thin ripple of smoke drifted upward between the neighboring buildings, while the prisoners huddled close, expectantly. An elderly man, his hands gnarled into pained fists, gestured at us sullenly with a scrap of wood he used as a walking stick.

We glanced at each other, reluctant to leave the safety of the wall. But, after several minutes, Gerle said, "Alfie, I can't stand it anymore. I'm so hungry! They can shoot me if they want to. I need food."

My mouth watered suddenly and I nodded in response. We raised ourselves slowly to our numb feet and paused, our ears bracing for a reprimand from the guards. None came, so we hobbled forward, the blood pounding into our tingling limbs. The elderly man who had beckoned to us, nodded his head silently and his lower jaw worked mysteriously over teeth long since lost.

Only a few heads turned as we entered the ragged circle that encompassed the crackling fire. The warmth from the flames was inviting, although my head still pounded from the heat of the day. A wave of guilt poured over me, as I realized I was enjoying the soothing ambiance of the

235

remnants of my fellow townspeople's homes, parts of which now rose as hot sparks into the fading rose-colored light.

The presence of welcome food drove the feeling away and we soon found ourselves grasping two small warm cups of soup that appeared from outstretched hands before us. With the soup came a thin crust of hard bread, which sent my stomach into fits of uncomfortable anticipation.

I held my cup eagerly to my nose and inhaled deeply. The sour smell of the cabbage prickled the inside of my nostrils and tears rose to my eyes. Gerle followed me to a spot slightly outside the circle of men and we quickly ate the sparse meal. Only the sounds of hunger, barely satisfied, surrounded us. The men ate in religious silence, with only the clanks of empty metal cups against the cobblestones echoing among the hungry group.

Roughly, the guards shoved aside two of the men and threw handfuls of broken chair rails onto the dying fire. They laughed heartily among themselves and one of them pulled the familiar obligatory vodka bottle from inside his unbuttoned coat. His eyes were shining with the excess of drink that had already been consumed, but he took a sloppy swig from the rapidly emptying bottle. He scratched, with filthy finger nails, the hairs of his chest where they poked through the buttons of his uniform, and he spat into the fire. It hissed in protest and the guard strode insolently into the shadows between the buildings, where we heard the splattering, as of water, into the dirt. In this way, we determined where the lavatory was, which became vital knowledge as the cabbage ripped a rapid path through our traumatized digestive systems.

Gerle and I were soon moaning uncomfortably in a corner, trying desperately to alleviate the pressure on our bloating stomachs. The prisoners chuckled, knowingly, their own stomachs barely hardened against the debilitating effects of dysentery and malnutrition. Only the guards seemed unfazed by the thin cabbage soup. Perhaps the level of alcohol in their systems limited any attacks by foreign parasites.

As the evening wore on, the air grew refreshingly cool and we wormed our way closer to the comforting glow of the fire, which was kept continuously ablaze by the slow, but steady dismantling of the city's finer wooden structures. All the while, the bottles of vodka were passed among the jovial, trouble-free Russians.

I sat with Gerle, watching enviously as the commradery among the guards was displayed in rousing songs. The words tumbled from their sodden tongues in an incomprehensible, yet beautiful flow of patriotic tunes from their homeland.

Gerle and I sank into a stupor, forgotten in our shadowed corner, where we watched from beneath tired eyelids. The excitement among the guards mounted as the vodka bottles continued to make the rounds. The fire danced merrily to the joyful tunes and the flames taunted the feet of the Russians, licking at their heels as they jumped over the fire in boisterous cossack dances.

The lighthearted mood of the Russians stood out as such a heartless contrast to our misery. We watched their pleasure increase, matched only by our downward spiral into despair. What we had lost seemed so much more poignant now that we saw that others were so blissfully ignorant of our plight.

What would become of us? Were our grandparents sitting in some similarly forlorn corner with my sister and uncle? Were they trying to imagine our fates amidst the chaos that now swirled throughout the once peaceful valleys of our home?

Late in the night we were prodded awake by the elderly man we had encountered at the evening meal. He said nothing, but gestured for us to follow him. He shuffled slowly toward a dark doorway and disappeared into the gloom.

"We actually get a bed?" whispered Gerle, his voice thick with sleep. I shrugged and stepped through the opening in the side of the narrow building, trying to follow the sounds of the man's thudding cane. We tiptoed along a short hallway and wandered into a small room, lined along each wall with several dozen narrow cots. The beds creaked and wobbled as the wounded German soldiers tried to find comfort on the stiff frames of the folding beds.

We glanced around, acknowledging the awful, yet familiar, stench of stale sweat and urine that mingled in the warm tainted air of the room. Only one small cot remained, so we wound our way through the tangle of reclining bodies to where it rested against the wall.

"Do you want the inside or the outside?" I asked, quietly.

"It doesn't matter, Alfie. I don't think I can sleep anyway. I don't feel very well." Gerle muttered, his face damp with perspiration.

"Then, why don't you take the outside… in case you have to get up." I added. I crawled awkwardly to the far end of the cot, trying to shake it as little as possible in my attempts to stretch out. The bed seemed ready to collapse, so I held my breath while Gerle lay down, twisting himself stiffly sideways to find enough room.

We both lay as still as possible, trying hard to return to the numbing comfort of sleep, but the groans and sighs of the men surrounding us reminded me of our new position in the world. I couldn't sleep. Oma's face floated before my eyes, my lids weighing heavily in an attempt to shield me, in sleep, from the pain of my thoughts. Night passed slowly. Gerle shifted constantly during the night; clearly he was awake as well.

I finally drifted into a tepid slumber near dawn, only to be jostled awake by Gerle's hasty dash to the makeshift latrine behind the building. I remained on the cot, unsure of what was expected of us for the day. It seemed the men were prepared for more endless hours of boredom. They slumped over their knees, their hands kneading together as their restless eyes echoed their tormented thoughts.

It had been two days since we had seen Oma and my heart ached knowing she was no longer next door. We had had so little contact with her in the camp and none with the others, yet I had sensed their presence and it had provided me with a reason to go on… a reason to remain positive.

Now, I felt adrift in a vast sea, with no sight of the shore. As if shrouded in a heavy mist, while a dreadful sense of foreboding loomed sightlessly over me, I drifted helplessly toward a giant whirlpool, the only possible fate being to be sucked downward into oblivion. So many of my neighbors, friends, and family members had disappeared thus, without a trace, almost without proof that they had ever existed. Was this to be my fate, as well?

Gerle returned, rousing me from my depressing thoughts. His face was pale with glittering sweat beneath the morning sun that slanted in through the thin strip of dirty windows along the east wall.

"Are you all right?" I asked, sitting up slowly to keep the shudders of the bed at a minimum.

"I guess. That soup tasted good and it felt good to eat something… but, my goodness, what a night!" he sighed, heavily, pushing his damp hair away from his puffy eyes.

"I didn't sleep either." I lied, realizing that my several moments of calm in the morning were probably much more than Gerle had enjoyed.

We walked out into the yard, eager to clear our heads of the musty air of the small overcrowded room. It seemed food was to be served; the men had begun to pace expectantly. I glanced at Gerle, wondering if he could handle another meal so soon. I knew in my heart that he desperately needed it.

"Let's just hope it is something easier on the stomach." I muttered.

We wandered forward, trying to avoid too much attention. Somehow, the presence of the soldiers of the two competing forces unsettled us. These men, who had once been ordered to seek each other out for the sole purpose of elimination, now shared a very small corner of the world—each of them trying to fulfill some vague expectations of their roles, now that the war was officially over.

The wounded Germans huddled in a bunch, avoiding the sneering grins of the Russian guards. Any truce that existed was clearly forced. One young guard, his face less hardened then the others, leaned against the wall of the office. He stared at us for several moments, making us feel so uncomfortable we ceased our conversation.

He turned suddenly into the room behind him, just as other officers began tossing handfuls of small gnarled potatoes into the laps of the prisoners. We moved away from the wall, hoping to get a potato or two of our own. Instead, the young officer returned, muttering something to the man who held the remaining tubers. The food was handed over to the Russian and our hearts sank. We feared we were being overlooked.

Then my heart jumped anew; the officer approached us slowly, his hand thrust deeply into his coat, a thin smile playing across his youthful features. Were we to be shot? Did he have a gun in his pocket?

Instead, to our astonishment, he pulled two small bottles of something from a dirty bag and thrust them toward us, along with a small cluster of pale new potatoes. We nodded our thanks, unsure of what else to say. We peered nervously into the bottles, trying to determine what we had just been handed. A deep red liquid glittered darkly through the glass and, twisting off the cap, I took a tiny sip. A cool, sweet, fruity taste met my parched mouth and I gulped down the welcome richness of the juice… raspberries… something I had not experienced for so many months.

My mind darted back to the previous summer, when my hands had been stained daily by the dark berries that had grown along the lanes throughout the valley. Now, the tang of the sweet fruit felt foreign and strong on my abandoned palette.

I glanced up suddenly, noticing the officer was still standing over us. He laughed deeply at my sullen face and strolled off to his comrades, still chuckling happily.

"Is that just the best thing you have ever tasted?" groaned Gerle, tilting his head back to allow the last few drops of the jewel-toned liquid to splash into his opened mouth.

I nodded, my mouth too full of potatoes to answer properly. We completed our meager, but tasty, meal and leaned against the wall to allow the food to settle in our rumbling stomachs.

The day inched forward; nothing stirred in the warm yard. Everyone seemed to be waiting for something unexpected. This couldn't possibly be all we had to look forward to—an endless drone of hours, with no change in sight, I thought, hopelessly.

We were convinced that this was all our future had in store for us, until early one morning on the third day. We were roused from a restless doze, the night having proved sleepless once again. A tall dark officer, his German broken and sporadic, ordered us all to assemble in the yard. It took several minutes for the more wounded of the men to gather themselves to join us and we formed a pathetic cluster of humanity, representing all whom the Russians had managed to strain out of the remnants of the town now under their jurisdiction.

The guards hoisted their weapons, reminding us of their control, and Gerle and I shifted our bodies closer to each other, each clearly hoping to find strength from the other. A previously unseen officer arrived from around a corner, followed by two fellows dressed as civilians. They stood back several paces and discussed with each other, amidst exuberant gestures and glances, something concerning the prisoners.

Gerle and I glanced nervously at each other, realizing from snatched words that the civilians with the officer were Czech, not Russian. I wondered silently what bearing this might have on our fates, but hesitated to voice my concerns to my friend. As I struggled with these worries in my mind, the three men began to pace slowly back and forth before us, their eyes gazing appraisingly across each of us in turn.

The silence of the tense moment was broken by the officer pointing his finger at three men, all of whom stood to our right.

"Forward! You! ... Yes, and you, too!" the officer barked, poking one of the nervous men in the chest with his gloved hand. The men stepped forward, trembling upon their weak legs, and they were herded into a row. The men peered around with fear in their eyes, yet their faces still harbored a blankness born from the intensity of their continuous suffering.

"March!" yelled the officer and he nodded to a guard to lead them down the street, with one of the Czech civilians slowly following. As the echoes of their footsteps faded into the jumble of city streets, Gerle and I glanced cautiously at one another. The other prisoners also seemed to feel the level of fearful anticipation that hovered threateningly like a black cloud over all of us. We feared that our worries were not quite over.

As everyone shifted restlessly upon their tired limbs, a large bald man, the remaining Czech civilian, strolled languidly among the clustered group. The Germans stood with their shoulders slumped and their eyes trained nervously on the ground, fearing the worst. The penetrating gaze of the beefy man took in the state of each individual carefully. He seemed to be looking for something in particular. Without a word, he flicked a single finger at a young soldier, who aside from a shoulder covered with filthy bandages, appeared healthier than the others.

The soldier stepped forward, his chin raised in a sudden attempt at pride and bravery. The Czech man chuckled slightly, his face barely cracking into a smile, and he walked onward, finally pausing in front of Gerle and me.

I felt Gerle's fingernails dig sharply into my forearm and my knees began to tremble. I found myself thinking, "Please, just let us be together. Whatever you want, just don't let me lose Gerle." Beads of sweat rose upon my forehead, and, though I longed to look away, I gazed doggedly back into the cold eyes of our future.

As if in slow motion, the man raised his large fat finger. It hovered for a moment, a moment that, to me, seemed an eternity. Then, it pointed at... me... only me. Gerle's legs sagged beside me and he clung desperately to my arm. His sobs burst forth in a lurching flood and my heart plummeted as I glanced at his tearstained face.

"No...!" he sobbed, trying to clutch at my sleeve, as I was gestured forward again, the man having ignored Gerle's pleas completely.

241

"Step forward, boy!" said the nearby officer and I tried to comply, but Gerle refused to let go.

"It's ok, Gerle." I whispered bravely, over my shoulder. "We will find each other soon."

"Shut up!" growled the officer and I closed my mouth, fearing the torrential flood of grief that I would emit if I tried to speak again. I stepped forward, first gently prying Gerle's hand from my sleeve. I gave his trembling hand a tight squeeze before dropping it. I stepped away, closing my eyes against the dreadful ache in my heart. The guards were already moving forward with the bandaged soldier, the only other one, besides me, who had been chosen.

I opened my eyes and looked up at the sky, which was now a bright blue, with the sun just shimmering golden off the tiled rooftops. Everything blurred before me, but I forced the tears away. I wanted to be able to see my dear friend through clear eyes one last time. I glanced back at him. He stood, shaking violently upon his thin legs, and I rose my tingling fingers from my side in a feeble wave.

I turned away, fearing my emotions if I continued to gaze upon my friend. The wrenching sounds of Gerle's loud sobs followed me along the streets and I heard them still as they echoed loudly across the large plaza in front of the city hall. I tried to block his sadness from my mind; the pain it caused was too great. I dreaded the possibility of never seeing my sweet little "brother" again. Somehow… I had to steel myself to the fact… somehow, I had to accept that now I was truly alone.

CHAPTER 21

Istumbled along behind the German soldier, who walked briskly forward in spite of his wound. We weaved among the piles of debris that still littered every street throughout the city. Heaps of bricks and roof tiles were scattered among the torn fragments of people's lives. In the dusty street, curtains and pieces of clothing whirled and danced, their delicate flowers and patterns faded and fouled in the dirt and sun.

The soldier and I managed to keep up with the large man, in spite of the fact that we had been living off meager rations for so long. It seemed we had been chosen because we appeared more able-bodied than many of the others we had left behind.

I forced the thought of Gerle from my mind, though the memory of his tearstained face was seared permanently upon my heart. I knew he suffered greatly from illness and malnutrition and I prayed that now, at the very least, he would receive my few helpings of food during meal time.

The large shoulders of the man bobbed and weaved before us. He had our uncertain futures in his oversized hands. He strolled easily along, obviously free of the fear that hung over me like a terrible toxic cloud. There it sat, poised and ready to swoop down and engulf me beneath its increasingly oppressive weight.

My ears were ringing with a repressed shock that released itself in uncontrollable waves across my befuddled brain. I barely heard the warm breeze of the mounting summer day as it swept through the tops of the trees that bordered the long winding street. We had left the center square and were following the river toward the floor of the valley. Across the way lay my home, the house in which I had been born and the land that rooted me to my true self. The rustling leaves of the trees, many now ready to relax into autumn slumber, blocked my eyes from seeing the road that led to the remains of the bridge and my yard.

I imagined the many men who had found their final resting place in those fields around my house. I wondered after their families, who would never be able to bury their loved ones in the place where their lives had begun. They lay instead with the carcasses of horses and cows, the beasts of burden for the hearty souls who had once inhabited this silent forgotten city.

Now, it only housed ghosts. The hearts of man and beast lay together, mingling in the rich black soil... and hundreds of years from now would humanity remember the terrible legacies of this war? What would my legacy be? Would I survive to go on? Would I ever return to where my cradle had rocked? Would all the people who had made up my world as a child... would any of them survive to go on in this life?

My heart lamented thus, to the tune of the twittering birds, as they hopped about in the undergrowth of the neglected rose bushes in the front gardens of people's empty homes. I lurched onward, simply not caring anymore where I would end up.

It appeared, finally, that the man did have a destination in mind. We snaked our way through the torn streets of my town, while I tried, desperately, to block the visions of Gerle. He appeared in my mind's eye, his small figure standing on every familiar street corner. We arrived at the train station, its long red roof pockmarked with bullet holes and bomb blasts.

Turning to us, the man addressed us for the first time since selecting us from the bedraggled group of prisoners. His accent was familiar, as if he belonged here, as well. I wondered if he had once been from the land... my land, that now existed only through the selective mercy of the Russians.

"You will work." he stated, simply. "There is a large farm... a collective." He paused, staring intently at each of us, in turn. "You will have food and a bed, as long as you work hard and do as I tell you." he finished. He turned away to lean against a platform wall and began to talk in hushed tones with several guards who had been patrolling along the waiting train.

The soldier and I looked at each other for the first time, both of us with our own private fears playing across our faces. He was young, though perhaps old enough to have a wife and family waiting for him somewhere.

It seemed as if he doubted he would ever see them again; our futures looked like a guaranteed dead end. His eyes trailed sadly to the dirt along the tracks and I watched with pity as he rotated his wounded shoulder in an effort to find some comfort.

We waited for what seemed an interminable stretch of time before we finally boarded a rickety freight car, in which our overseer found us a dry corner to inhabit for the duration of the journey. Several other forlorn-looking people stared out at us from their own dark corners and I glanced around eagerly in the instinctive hope of finding a familiar face. As so many times before, vacant eyes looked back at me, revealing hearts laid bare with grief and fear. I saw no one I knew.

Our new guardian slid the large door closed, apparently to pass his own journey in more hospitable surroundings. Darkness engulfed us, broken only by narrow shafts of dusty light where it filtered through the jagged chinks in the planks of the freight car's walls.

Again, I had time to dwell on my sad predicament. I was utterly alone now. These faces surrounding me in the gloom were as miserable as I, yet, I sensed there was no space in their own troubled worlds for any concern for me. At this thought my depression deepened. No one had room left for empathy. I had to be strong for myself. I had to make myself go on, in the hopes of someday finding the family that had always meant so much to me. They had been my world—my grandparents, Gerti, Uncle Alois, and of course my dear friend, Gerle, who had shared so many wonderful, as well as terrible, experiences with me. Now, my world was void of any compassion and I agonized, once again, about what I must have done to earn such an existence.

I found myself dreaming, hovering in that soothing world that exists trapped beneath the blanket of a very shallow sleep. I was leaning against the brittle planks of the freight car, the lulling motion of the train easing me into a troubled slumber. I felt it roll me farther away from my home, from the one place I had ever truly belonged.

The memories of my childhood flooded through my mind, in such an uncontrollable torrent of images, so powerful in their meaning that I awoke with bitter tears in my eyes. I blinked them away, reminding myself that I had to be strong.

We were rocking to a stop, the pistons on the aged engine hissing angrily as the train eased itself into a dark station. The air felt damp and oppressive and I sat forward, anxious for the fresh air that would pour in when the doors were opened.

Coughs of sickness filled the darkness and I held my breath for a moment before I realized it was futile to try to avoid the waves of illnesses that pervaded this ravaged population of refugees. The mass of people grew restless as the doors remained closed. Although we all knew only a little of what lay in store for us, the endless waiting in the stale air of the train car was torture.

After many agonizing minutes, the large doors shuddered noisily open and the hot sun of late afternoon beat upon our pale faces. I squinted my eyes tightly against the rays and struggled to focus on the flurry of activity that was taking place in the immediate space around the tracks. The unfamiliar words of the Czech partisans filled the station, and people were sorted into their work groups. There seemed to be a great deal of new collective farms in the area; many long-neglected fields now needed attention. The fall harvest was around the corner and the victors in the horrible war clearly didn't want to wait one moment to take advantage of the many rich resources our demoralized country had to provide.

The displaced farmers who had struggled and toiled before the war had placed their meager earnings in trust in the rolling meadows of crops, which had yet to grow and return a bounty. None of the original farmers remained to realize the reward of their many long years of work. Most of them had died on the Front, fighting for a regime in which they didn't believe. Many more lay rotting in some dreadful camp, a forgotten statistic in the aftermath of the war. Still others lay rotting in their very own fields, fertilizer to crops they would never gather.

The soldier and I were met on the platform by our overseer. His eyes bore into mine with a curious mixture of contempt and pity. I wondered what his story was. How had his life been affected by the war? Where along the way had he chosen to align himself with those who sought nothing better than to reap what others had sown? Did he have a home waiting for him somewhere, or had he been willing to give it up? Had he been willing to betray the very culture that had once been his own?

There was an abundance of confusion in the station, as people tried to sort out where they needed to be. We followed the man into the relative calm of the small town's streets and he allowed us a moment each in the outhouse near the station.

We were ushered onward and my stomach began rumbling painfully in protest. Soon, daylight faded without any food to mark its passing. I wondered, with strong misgivings twisting in my chest, how far we would be made to walk. I felt the pull of home very strongly, knowing that I was far away from it. I felt in my heart that I would not be back for a long time. What would become of our house? Would it simply sit empty until it fell into ruin or would strangers move in and make our personal things their own?

We wandered in silence for several kilometers along a narrow road that wound between hedge rows of thick brush. These bordered long stretches of farm land, the rows of crops dense with weeds and with plants left to flounder about on their own. It was clear we had a great deal of work ahead of us, but, at least, I reminded myself, I would not be locked behind a barb wire fence—or so I hoped.

The evening sun slanted across the wide valley, tinting the fields a golden hue. I felt the heat of its soothing rays kissing my cheek in a bittersweet greeting, as we made our way slowly toward a long row of barns in the distance. The deep brown of the old wood of the outbuildings showed that these had been family farms for many long years.

Now, we were directed to our new home and our new existence on someone else's soil. The soldier was told to head to a long shack, which appeared to house several dozen men of varying ages. He glanced silently at the overseer, not mouthing the many questions that seemed to be dancing across his troubled face. Then, he walked away without a single glance in my direction.

I remained rooted to the ground in front of the large man, uncertain as to what his expectations were. Finally, he spoke, "There is a place for you to sleep in the barn." he said, slowly. "You will tend the animals. You will find all that you need in the back room, near the stables." He pointed casually with his beefy finger toward an aging barn on the edge of a vast field. "There will be a meal shortly. The latrine is over there." His hand swung in a small arc to point at a cluster of thin trees beside a narrow house. "You will eat with the others over by the bunk house." His eyes softened slightly and he added, "If you work hard, you need not worry. You will not be mistreated." His gaze remained even but he coughed slightly. Then he turned away, leaving me standing awkwardly in the dust of the yard.

I blinked. The contrast of my situation from the morning seemed suddenly unnerving. I forced the thoughts of my family from my mind, burying them deeply into a special place in my heart, where I could attend to them when I felt stronger. My head whirled with uncertainty. I was alone, on the edge of a large field, no more barb wire restricting my movement… yet, I felt more trapped than ever. I was miles from home; I didn't even know in which direction home lay. Where would I go?

Before I could think upon it further, I turned toward the large mass of the barn, which loomed darkly against the shadows of the rolling hills beyond. I let out a great sigh. The gentle breeze of the coming evening echoed my breath and it played coolly against my heated cheek. I made the decision to trust to fate and I walked toward my new life… a life in which I would have to face all coming trials on my own.

I reached the vast wooden doors and eased open a smaller door nestled within the larger. It creaked loudly on its hinges and the sounds of stamping hooves could be heard from within. I stepped through the door into the darkness. The heady smell of manure and hay swirled through my nostrils and I struggled to suppress a mighty sneeze. The shadows were cool and inviting and the noise of the animals stirring in their stalls was strangely comforting.

A restless whinny met my ears and I peered around a corner to determine its source. Coal black eyes looked passively back at me from a spot quite a bit higher than my head. Two massive draft horses stood before me, each seeming too large for his narrow stall. Their strong neck muscles rippled as they threw their heads nervously toward the hidden hayloft above.

I shuddered slightly at the thought of having to care for such powerful creatures and I backed away slowly. I decided I would approach them for the first time after I had had a chance to settle my nerves with a meal. My stomach rumbled audibly and I longed for some water to rid my throat of the dust from the train.

Several stalls away from the horses was a narrow cubicle that had been converted into a cot to house the stable boy. I realized, with a start, that that was now me. I noticed that at least the straw was fresh and there was plenty more to replace it with when needed. I scratched my head sadly, remembering the brief reprieve from the lice. They had now returned in full force during the grim conditions in the camp. I wondered what other creatures I would be sharing my nights with… a barn seemed like a prime place for vermin of all sorts.

My hunger began to overwhelm my thoughts. Retracing my steps out of the barn, I headed toward where I had been told I could receive a meal. My mind wandered over all the wonderful possibilities I might be offered; the man had said we would be well treated.

Upon reaching the kitchen, a low shack tacked to the side of one of the bunk houses, I was met with disappointment. A tepid cup of tasteless cabbage soup was thrust into my waiting hands. Only through my excessive hunger did I manage to find solace in the pathetic trappings of this first meal and, after downing it quickly, I shuffled quietly back to my bed without speaking to a soul.

The overseer roused me early in the morning, his large hand engulfing my thin shoulder like a vast net, as he shook it roughly. "You must feed and water the horses each morning—the creek is out back." he said, gesturing over his shoulder. He paused while I sat up, rubbed my eyes wearily, and picked some stiff straw from my tangled hair. "Tie them out to the post for the workers to take them to the field. In the evening you must water and feed them again. Mind you…" His voice grew stern, "Brush them well." He paused, studying my shocked face in the low light of the morning. I swallowed sullenly, thinking bitterly to myself that the animals seemed to receive better treatment than the humans.

"After you take them out, you may eat." He smiled briefly, as if allowing me to receive nourishment was a special treat. "You can work the fields during the day—there is a great deal to be done." He turned away suddenly, clearly finished with his planned instructions, then he turned back, saying, "Best put on some other shoes… you might slip in those. We don't want you falling down beneath those beasts, do we now?" he said, with the smile returning. I noticed that it never reached his eyes.

He saw me try to answer and in anticipation, he added, "There is a pair of clogs in the tack box by the door. Try those on." He turned suddenly and left, the door clattering stiffly on its crooked hinges. The barn sank back into its cool darkness.

I sat for several moments, my head in my hands and my knees drawn up beneath me, and I tried to focus on all he had said. I had never dealt with such large animals before. Opa's timid goats had been the most I had managed. I shook my head sadly, aware that I would need to learn as I went. But, I suddenly felt anxious to begin. I forced myself to focus on the food I would be offered once I completed my task. The thought emboldened me and I strode bravely out of my stall toward the horses, ready to show them who was boss.

They looked at me from the gloom, their eyes glittering fiercely from the darkness. I whistled, forcing myself to remain calm, and I filled their bins with fresh hay. This was followed by a large scoop of oats, which they gobbled noisily, their yellow teeth playing into sneers as their lips twisted and turned around their food.

I gazed at them, a tinge of envy washing over me, as I realized the horses would be getting food more often than I would. This seemed so ridiculously unfair I began to laugh, an unnatural hollow laugh, that, nonetheless, made the horses start. They raised their massive heads and their ears flattened with bristling unease.

While they settled their nerves, I rummaged through the tack box for the promised shoes and I pulled out a dusty pair of large wooden clogs, covered with tangles of old cobwebs. The underside of each was covered with small rubber strips, which I imagined were to keep me upright in the muck alongside the beasts while I cleaned their stalls.

I dusted the shoes off and put them on, alarmed at how they engulfed my feet. I shook my head and turned to stomp back to the horses.

I paused before opening their gates, wondering how I was going to manage harnessing them when their necks loomed so far above me. My eyes rested on a small crate, which I dragged through the hay to the edge of their stalls. Climbing up on it, I was high enough to carefully settle the harnesses over their noses, one by one. Then, jumping down, I gathered their long reins between my fingers. I led them out through the large doors, which shuddered and squeaked loudly as I slid them open. The beasts stomped loudly and pulled at their reins, the morning air tempting them. I headed the horses in the direction of the stream, where they would take their daily water and I would have a chance to wash the dust of the barn off my face.

I left the horses to drink downstream and I shuffled in the awkward clogs to the edge of the stream. As I raised my dripping head, tingling from the cold water, I glanced around at my new home. The sun was beginning to tickle the tree tops and the heavy mantle of night was slowly lifting. I could make out long tangled rows of crops bursting in the overgrown fields and I imagined the many delicious foods that must be rotting in the hot sun without enough hands to retrieve them.

Even while I entertained these thoughts, I saw the silhouettes of several figures making their way slowly into the meadow, which still hung heavy with mist. I wondered if one of them was my soldier, now the only connection with my home. I told myself that, realistically, he must have been from somewhere else. But, I was still curious where he had been placed, his wounded shoulder potentially slowing his work output.

The horses seemed ready to graze placidly, but I was eager to get some food for myself, so I led them back toward the barn, their hooves clopping loudly on the dirt behind me. My ragged clothes hung damply against my pale skin and I wondered how I would fare when the weather began to turn. My clothes were the very same I had worn so many months before when we had been torn from our home by the Russians. The long woolen socks would provide a little cover for my bare knees, though they were beneath short pants that only came to the middle of my thigh. The cloth, itself, had become so threadbare from the constant dirt and sweat, that I wondered if it would disintegrate entirely before winter even arrived.

I secured the horses where I had been instructed to and they immediately began munching complacently on the tall grass that grew near the post. I wiggled my toes uncomfortably inside the vast wooden shoes, convincing myself I could get used to their bulk. I was determined to wear out someone else's shoes besides my own. I stumbled forward, painfully aware that my toes were the only things holding the clogs upon my feet. Awkwardly, I made my way across the dew-laden path to the bunkhouse.

Smoke already rose from the cook house and I struggled to quicken my pace in the oversized shoes. When I rounded the corner, several faces turned toward me, then returned to the small morsels clutched in their hands... potatoes. That was what I had hurried through my chores for... small wrinkled potatoes... the only thing offered to us from the vast fields that suddenly seemed to taunt me with their forbidden delicacies.

I soon held my own piece of the brown root and I tried hard to eat it slowly, forcing it down my clenched throat. I distracted myself with looking around at my surroundings, anxious to find a friendly face. The yard was full of workers coming or going between their chores. Very few laid eyes on me at all. Those who did met my stares with a level gaze, noncommittal and uninviting. Everyone seemed absorbed in his or her own world, a world comprised of a profound effort to survive the endless series of horrors I felt sure they had all seen.

Most of the people were men, German soldiers who had been abandoned due to their wounds. It was apparent that many had never completely healed. Some were elderly men who had displayed enough energy left in them in the camps to be taken away... only to be sapped of every ounce of life that remained in their tired aged bodies.

A handful of women milled about as well, though they were clearly at a disadvantage because of their sex. They were spared the heavy work in the fields, for the most part, but the many overseers seemed to want to keep them close by—in case they had need of them for other uses. The women wore constant masks of fear and sadness, as their household duties were interrupted regularly whenever one of the governing men or guards had an urge that needed satisfying.

I seemed to fit nowhere into this grim jumble of people, so I found myself alone most of my days. The horses became my confidantes. Their comforting warm breath soothed me as I leaned against their muscular flanks and ran the rough brush firmly across their gleaming coats. The weather turned slowly toward autumn and I talked to the animals endlessly, half expecting them to answer. I felt as though I were slowly losing my mind. In my troubled thoughts, it seemed to me that if I opened up only to the animals, I would protect myself from the potential harm the rest of society could inflict on me. They never passed judgment; they never yelled an order. The beasts soon comprised the one world in which I had any control and that was, of course, only on their terms.

One of the horses, his coat a pale gray, was old and ornery and he seemed on the verge of nipping me whenever I turned my back. The second fairly young one was auburn brown, with a bold white streak along his soft nose. He soon began to expect my arrival at his side in the mornings and he would whicker gently while I brushed the dust and mites from his glowing reddish hair.

At their meal times I had to perform a dangerous sort of dance to put their oats near their muzzles. I had been instructed to place the horses in stalls farther away from the door in anticipation of the coming winter, so to reach their feed troughs I had to squeeze between the wall and their huge bellies. More often then not, it was the old grump who decided to make my passage a difficult one. With seemingly vindictive cunning, he would wait until I was at the thinnest part of the space and then he would shift his weight to the side with a loud snort, all but crushing me against the rails of the wall.

While the horses and other animals on the farm were coddled and pampered for the coming winter, the people were worked to the breaking point in order to complete the harvests before the first snowflakes fell. The sky turned a brilliant blue and the leaves began to exude the sweet and pungent odor of decay. The summer's rains were over and everything pointed to an abundant yield. The fields swelled with the carefully rescued produce. They had been returned to a delicately cultivated state by the toil and sweat of so many forced laborers, myself included.

In spite of the prolific return in the fields, our meals remained as sparse as they had when I had arrived at the height of the summer. Potatoes continued to make up the bulk of our meals and soup from cabbages or beets comprised our one hot serving each day.

The poultry yards stirred noisily with many hens and their strutting mates, yet we never received the many eggs that we had to collect in the mornings. I found myself daydreaming about the succulent crispy meat that could be peeled off one particularly fat bird and I had to force myself to walk away without wringing her neck. I satisfied myself instead by cracking an egg open behind the shed and slurping the sticky yolk from between the fragments of the shell.

As the weather continued to grow colder and the fallen leaves blanketed the paths with a thin layer of auburn and gold, I craved a richer diet in a desperate and primitive attempt to put some more insulation on my thin frame.

September drew to a close and the overseer gave me a thin worn coat to help keep me warm on the frosty autumn mornings. I wondered, grimly, what poor lad had died to free up this item for my use. The back had been painted with a large yellow letter "N", to identify me as a German, though I reminded myself sadly, that Austria, not Germany, had been my home. Others wore varying letters or signs on their clothes, depending on their nation of origin, and it startled me to see so many people such a distance from their homes.

Even with the extra layer with which to cover myself, I felt my body growing weaker, as the added toil during the days depleted my already meager store of energy. I took advantage of free moments by the stream where I took the horses twice each day. The winding path of water ran up against a small orchard, the trees of which were heavily laden with apples of many varieties and colors. I found it easy to retrieve the occasional windfall from the russet grass below the old trees, yet they only eased my hunger slightly. I found out the hard way what my stomach thought when I consumed too many.

I discovered also, to my advantage, that the milking of cows usually happened under the cover of dawn's leaden light. There were many cows, each one having been retrieved from a local abandoned farm and brought here to be utilized for the collective. There simply were not enough laborers to milk all the beasts, so many of them suffered horribly from disease and infections in their udders. The milk would run yellow in a foul stream of rotten cream, before the fresh milk bubbled forth, relieving the cow of her uncomfortable burden. Thus, I felt no remorse when I leaned in under the hot, bursting nipples and drank deeply of the rich, slightly sour milk. My stomach, on these days, felt less empty and I soon began to look forward to the early morning milking.

The big harvest meant the horses were worked constantly and it was my duty to keep them clean and well-fed. I shared my precious apples with them; even the old gray was grateful enough at these moments not to try to bite my fingers while I held out the sweet fruit for him on my dirty hands.

I never felt completely clean, although I braved the freezing water of the stream in the mornings to wash my face. A layer of grime soon coated my clothes and my skin, and I smelled of the barn and its contents. The conditions on the farm were extremely unsanitary. None of the overseers seemed too concerned with hygiene, as long as productivity was high and the resulting yield was significant. The guards, themselves garbed in filthy torn uniforms, spent most of their time lying about in their own foul drunkenness. They roused themselves only long enough to haul off one of the poor women to an abandoned farm house for some group activities with their comrades.

The women would stagger back, ashen-faced and bruised, only to be beckoned forth again the next day. I was amazed that more of them didn't disappear each night—the vast fields were surrounded by dark forests that would have provided ample cover for escape. Perhaps, the alternative seemed too grim; the coming winter meant survival away from civilization was very slim.

My mind wandered sadly to my own family. Would they find sufficient shelter to protect them through the harsh winter? Had Uncle Alois recovered from his wounds or had he succumbed to them through the lack of a doctor to aid him? And Gerle!... I was convinced he was in peril. It tore me to pieces, knowing I could not help him anymore. We had always looked out for one another, and now he was out there somewhere... as alone as I was.

I forced myself to ignore the dread that kept quelling up inside my head... Was he even alive? Were any of them still alive? Was it possible to feel any more alone? Waking up to face another day beneath the pale gray sky of the coming winter, I shivered and pushed away the terrible nagging thought that I might be the only one of us still alive.

CHAPTER 22

I awoke, twisting my stiff neck painfully from side to side, and I shivered into a tight huddle under my thin, moth-eaten blanket. The early spring light was thin and still and my breath rose in a silvery mist against the sheen of frost that lay along the dark sill of the stall in which my bed was nestled.

It was April, 1946, and I had spent the seemingly endless months of the previous fall and winter being cold and miserable. The year of 1945 was forever marked in my memory as the year my life had exploded and rapidly descended into the fires of hell. It had ended without any fanfare for me or for my fellow laborers.

We had been too busy trying to cover our ears against the endless zealous festivities that the guards had initiated for marking the season. This ambivalence to the passing of the holidays, what had once been precious milestones in our lives, was all eclipsed by the primitive attempt to rest our weary and overtaxed bodies in our chilly beds, whenever a rare moment of leisure presented itself.

These celebrations amongst the men who lorded over us in their various capacities had, of course, involved the women of the farm, who were a continuous valuable commodity for the guards and the overseers. The poor women were slowly wasting away to brittle bones, thinly covered by sallow hanging flesh, as they marked the precious hours or, if lucky, days, between the assaults by the men on their tormented bodies. They had been reduced to mere shells of their former selves through regular abuse, neglect, and the loss of all their rightful human dignities.

Thus, each of us met the New Year with his own sense of resignation as to what the future had in store, and this intense despair resulted in many faces that lacked any spark of hope or vitality. The farm worked and hummed as ever, but it soon became stagnant with people's emotions stifled and repressed. Everyone was losing heart.

The spring had decided to come late, leaving us with a protracted visit by the rancorous grip of winter. It continued to taunt us in the weary hours before the warming sun of spring met the icy tendrils of dawn. I had suffered through many long months of a lonely, labor-filled autumn, only to be blasted by the particularly bitter cold season. My pathetic bed did little to provide me with needed comfort, yet the barn remained my only haven from the uncertain road ahead.

My thoughts wandered hopelessly to my family, whose faces, in my mind, drifted between painfully vivid clarity and agonizingly opaque obscurity. I had spent the past few months thriving on memories. I had learned to feed off them as my only source of substantial sustenance. My body had wasted away from its already thin frame; it had been overworked and underfed for so long. I no longer knew what reality was. The world around me had become so surreal. I withdrew into the protective cocoon I had manufactured in my mind—the only realm in which I felt I had any remaining control.

I stubbornly resisted the nagging voice in my head, which reasoned that there was little hope of ever seeing my family again. That hope, however unrealistic, was my only motivation to continue forward each day. It was hope that made it possible for me to plod onward down yet another row of crops that disappeared into the setting sun. It was hope that allowed me to gulp down another cup of tepid slime called soup. And it was hope that led me to dare to dream away another night in my little hollow in the barn... and to mark another birthday gone, my fourteenth... without a celebration, except a bitter acknowledgment that I was alive.

My physical life on the farm had become a monotonous challenge to survive. The hours spent with the horses became routine and I soon learned to manage them well enough. But, the work in the fields was exhausting and isolating. Alone, toiling awkwardly in a long even row of potatoes, I felt the world around me slipping away. The wind rushed loudly in my ears and my intense hunger throbbed relentlessly and interminably in my throat. The distant shapes of my fellow workers felt remote and removed and the hours stretched before me in an indistinguishable labyrinth of sweat, dirt, and loneliness.

It was on one such evening, as I leaned against my hoe and wiped the grime and dust on my tattered shirt tails, that I glanced up into the lengthening light and saw the silhouette of an approaching figure. The spring's first flies and aphids swarmed up as the thin outline of a woman stepped gingerly across my neatly tended rows of freshly planted seeds. I watched her approach with an unsettling blend of hope and anxiety, as any significant interaction with my fellow workers felt unnatural to me now.

The late day sun filtered through the hanging dust in a golden halo behind her, and I noticed, sadly, how wasted her limbs appeared through the fraying fabric of her faded skirt. As she reached the row opposite my own, she stopped and brushed some graying wind-blown hairs out of her intense blue eyes.

Her voice shook slightly as she spoke, "Alfie?"

I nodded, though reluctantly, and she continued, "Your overseer would like to see you in his office, please." She paused and peered anxiously up and down the rows, as if uncertain how much she was supposed to say. "Now, if you please." she added, slightly breathlessly. She turned and quietly began retracing her ambling route back toward the path to the farm.

I paused uncertainly. Then, deciding it would be best not to anger my overseer, I followed the woman, using my hoe as a walking stick to help navigate the wider spots of the rows.

By the time I reached the long yard of the main farm, the woman was already disappearing into the kitchen of the largest house. Most of the women spent their days cooking and cleaning for the many overseers and guards, and they were rarely seen in the fields. I paused for a moment in the dust of the yard, trying to prepare myself for whatever the summons might entail. I shook my head worriedly, convinced that any interaction with the various local authorities seemed, more often than not, to bring me nothing but trouble.

I shuffled slowly to the door of the long farmhouse, a large decrepit structure that had been selected for the headquarters of the collective. I leaned my hoe against the wide wall, the rough planks of which glowed with the deep ruby tinge of the setting sun. I entered noiselessly through the narrow door.

My eyes adjusted quickly to the dim light of the narrow hall. The daylight was now almost abed and the small light bulbs in the hall buzzed with an eerie, swinging wreath of undefined light upon the dusty floor. I had never been to the overseer's office before, but I gauged its location by the hum of voices behind a wide door to my right. The booming words of the large man vibrated through the wood, though the details of his loud utterances were strangely muffled by their own intense volume.

I reached the door and forced myself to take a deep calming breath before pushing it ajar. My hand grasped the edge of the door and I eased it slowly open. I began to worry that perhaps I was to have waited in the hall. It was too late. I peered nervously around the door into the smoky room beyond.

The overseer sat behind a large battered desk, which was thoroughly littered with papers and empty coffee cups. I had just a moment to observe that it lacked the requisite vodka bottles I had come to expect as an accompaniment to any figure of authority, before I realized, with a start, that there was someone else present in the room.

A small elderly man, his sparse white beard skimming the grimy collar of his buttoned shirt, stood, with a slightly stooped back, to one side of the desk. His gnarled hands quivered gently upon a thin walking stick as he stared back at me out of surprisingly kind eyes. They were rimmed with deep wrinkles, hinting at a wealth of mirth and wisdom beneath his feeble-looking frame. He wore a thin brown jacket, also buttoned neatly to his collar. It was clearly emblazoned upon its left breast with a large yellow star, identifying him as a Jew.

His slightly watery blue eyes twinkled for a moment at me. I peered intently at him, my mind racing with curiosity. This was more than slightly mingled with tinges of sadness at the thought of my own grandfather somewhere out in the world. Opa's eyes had always twinkled, too.

I gulped and pulled my gaze reluctantly back to my boss, who sat silently behind his desk, puffing contentedly upon an ugly fat cigar. I fought the temptation to flee; the sour smell burned my dry throat, and it had me longing for fresh air. The man watched me with amusement playing across his broad pale features and he gazed thoughtfully between the old man and myself, clearly weighing his coming words. His fat fingers drummed monotonously upon his vast belly, which was encased beneath generous folds of an official-looking jacket.

He chewed for a moment on the end of the cigar, which responded by sending a great plume of smoke belching up to the ceiling. Then, he spoke, saying matter-of-factly, "This is Jacov, Alfie. As you can see he is Jewish." He gestured toward the man with his broad hand, the wide fingers of which were still curled around the fat cigar like a python twining itself around its prey.

I stepped forward clumsily and shook the old man's outstretched fingers. They were cold and bony, but he squeezed my hand warmly. I returned to my place by the desk, confused as to where all these introductions were leading.

"Jacov seems to have a grandson, a boy about your age, perhaps—I don't know. It also seems that he has never seen him. Is that right, Jacov?" The man turned his gaze to Jacov and cracked a shallow smile.

Jacov nodded slowly, his eyes shifting suddenly to mine. Excitement danced across his weathered features, making his aged face come alive.

"The boy and his mother live near Nurnburg, in Bavaria. Since he is Jewish, we can allow him to travel. Before this, of course, that would have been impossible." The man paused and stared at me carefully, apparently deciding if I was worthy of hearing more. "You might not be aware of it, but Bavaria is quite far from here, actually, and Jacov would find navigating the borders, most of which are closed, rather... difficult, given his... age." He smiled more kindly upon the old man, then he returned his steady gaze to me, crossing his fingers into a tent in front of his many chins.

"I'm sorry, sir. Where do I come into this?" I asked slowly, anxious not to appear too dim.

"Well, he needs someone to travel with him, doesn't he? And... as I have been ordered to send any German nationals now under my care to work in the coal mines in Moravia Ostrava, I thought we could, instead, just make you... disappear." His eyes darkened suddenly and he scowled, adding, "You wouldn't last long in the mines."

The old man shook his head and clucked his tongue sullenly against the roof of his mouth. I realized I was gaping with my own mouth wide open, so I snapped it quickly shut.

"Why me... uh, sir?" I stammered, visions of my family swarming before my eyes. The thought of leaving the wretched farm filled me with excitement, but Bavaria! I was quite aware that that was far away from home... far away from my family. The chances of finding them would diminish greatly. But, had I truly had any hope, anyway? Or, had I only been living off the dispersing vapors of a very tenuous dream?

"Well," he said, thoughtfully, "Let me just say, you remind me of a boy I once knew, a boy I wouldn't have liked to see in the mines. The mines are a wretched place, Alfie. The Germans blew them up as they retreated. Now most of them are filled with water—prime places for breeding foul diseases. Most people waste away fairly quickly." He shuddered and shook his head. "Let the stronger ones do your work. The two of you would soon be just corpses, getting in the way." His thoughts seemed to turn inward and his deep voice faded to a coarse whisper, rumbling in his chest.

His head jerked up, as he emerged from his reverie and he said, brightly, "So! Here is some money." He stood up brusquely and tipped a few coins into my hand. He dropped several more into Jacov's and continued, seemingly unaware of my shocked stare. "You need this paper, Jacov, to identify yourself." He handed a folded sheet to Jacov. "And here are two train tickets... for as far west as I could manage. Best of luck to both of you."

He sat back into his large chair, which creaked beneath his immense bulk, and he returned his attention to his momentarily neglected cigar. I stared, dumbfounded, at the few coins in my hand. It was the most money I had ever had the pleasure to hold. I felt rich, beyond measure.

Jacov hastily stuffed his share of the money into a pocket on the inside of his overcoat. I began to copy him, deciding it was indeed best to hide such wealth, then he spoke to me, his dialect ringing pleasantly nostalgic of home. "Wait. Take your coat off and turn it inside out. It will look better." He smiled warmly and the merry twinkle returned to his blue eyes. "We best be going, before the boss changes his mind!" he added, playfully, smiling kindly at the overseer, who remained in his large armchair behind his desk.

The boss chuckled jovially, his large belly rolling in undulating waves and he said, "Just stop by the kitchen; there is a little lady there who will be expecting you. I think you saw her in the fields." He winked, thrusting his chin in my direction. "She has a few items set aside for you both. Best get moving. You will want to catch the next train out of here." He scowled again, saying, "A trainload to the mines is scheduled to head out in the morning." He gazed at me significantly, as if trying to quell any second thoughts I might be having about leaving. "Wouldn't want to have to put you on that one instead." he muttered, soberly.

"Thank you, sir." I stammered, realizing instantly that he was a man who expected to be listened to and obeyed. I turned and opened the door, waiting for Jacov, as he shook the overseer's vast hand with his own frail one. Jacov followed me from the room and we walked quietly, side-by-side, down the hall to the kitchen.

My mind buzzed with the sudden drastic change in my life. I would soon be traveling away, farther from my homeland than I had ever been. My thoughts darted to my father, who had seen much of the world in his short life, and I wondered if I would be stepping on cobbles that had once held his footprint. In turn, I wondered if my own feet would ever touch the soil of home again, or if my future, the one I had been so morosely pondering, would finally be unfolding... unfolding into a world unlike anything I had ever known.

We reached the kitchen without exchanging any words. It felt strange to have suddenly acquired a traveling mate, with whom I would undoubtedly share many long and possibly dangerous hours... and we had yet to speak to each other. The only sound was the steady echo of Jacov's walking stick upon the wooden floor, as he methodically maneuvered his aged body forward.

The kitchen was hot and stuffy and it bustled noisily with several women hurrying about in the narrow space trying to prepare meals for their very demanding overseers. They had limited resources with which to work. Supplies still seemed at a premium and the goods the farm produced were shipped off immediately without ever being extensively sampled on site.

I recognized the frail woman among the others and she seemed to have been anticipating our eventual arrival. She glanced calmly in our direction and continued to carefully tie up a small cloth bundle. At a glance, I could tell it contained some crusts of hard bread as well as a couple of small slabs of smoked bacon. The sudden sight of food made my stomach rumble and I sensed that Jacov felt the same. His eyes darted excitedly around the kitchen, taking in all the sights, and lingering across the wafting fragrances that mingled with the spring breezes sifting through the open window.

She handed the bundle to Jacov, deciding, with a deprecating look in my direction, that he was the obvious leader of our coming adventure. She smiled, sadly, as he planted a delicate kiss on her pale cheek. "Good Luck." he muttered and I followed him from the room.

"If you have anything in your bed that you want to take, best get it now." he said, as we left the delicious smells of the kitchen behind. "We should get to the station. It will take a little time with these old legs of mine." he said, twisting his hands upon the knob of his walking stick.

"Oh… yes, I'll be right back." I answered, breathlessly. I ran back to the barn, stumbling slightly on the damp cobbles outside the door. The horses whinnied in greeting, so I gave the gentle one a quick pat on the nose… the old gray I left alone. My heart was racing with the unexpected exertion and I was forced to lean over to calm a nagging stitch that had emerged in my side. I retrieved my battered old rucksack from beneath my mattress and a quick grope inside it revealed mostly room to spare. There was the small stack of papers Opa had entrusted me to keep, beneath which lay my long forgotten slingshot. I had stubbornly carried it with me throughout my many journeys with Gerle.

I closed my eyes, remembering, with a sudden satisfaction, the looks of outrage on the faces of the neighborhood girls as Franz had pelted them with the thick wet sand from the banks of the Gold Oppa. My slingshot had certainly never been used for such devious means, but I recalled, with a pang, that Opa had never discovered it in my possession or he most certainly would have confiscated it. Now, I thought, I would give anything to be able to hand it to him in person… no penance was too great to have him, and Oma, my sister, and Uncle Alois back in my life. Once again, I suppressed all thoughts of Gerle… that pain was still to fresh.

I shouldered my sack, not surprised that I had to adjust the straps to fit my thin back. With a sigh, I glanced sadly down at myself. I imagined that I must look a fright. My clothes had been hanging on my bones for almost a year—the same light summer clothes I had been wearing on the day I had been replacing bombed out roof tiles… on the day the Russians had come and changed my life forever.

My shorts reached only a short way down my thighs; I had neglected the passage of time enough not to realize that I had grown, in spite of the horrendous food. My shirt was threadbare and was stiff with caked-on dirt and sweat. It occurred to me that I must stink, but my senses had become so immune to the torrent of foul odors, that I was unaware of just how much. Over my shirt I wore the thin jacket that I had turned inside out on Jacov's instruction and I decided, with a sullen frown, that it looked only marginally better than my shirt. My long socks no longer reached all the way to my shorts, so my legs were always cold. The thin fabric of the socks all but stuck to my feet, which were peeling and cracked beneath layers of grime. I still wore the wooden shoes I had found in the barn and over time they had become easier to manage. I had outgrown my original shoes anyway. So, with my clogs still perched across my strengthened toes, I clumped my way out of the dark barn, my limp backpack across my back. With dogged determination I refused to look behind me as I closed the door. Jacov's stooped figure was lit by the newly risen moon, which glowed brightly upon his upturned face. Full of curiosity about my new companion, I studied his features as I approached.

"Good. You can carry the food." he muttered with a grin, having spotted my sack. I marveled at the trust this old man maintained for those around him. He moved so slowly; I could easily abandon him, taking the vital food with me. He was Jewish and as far as he knew, I was German. Yet, he handed me the precious bundle without any hesitation and I felt a sudden and overwhelming fondness for this man, about whom I knew nothing.

The smell of the bread drifted through the thin cloth and I forced myself to swallow my hunger, knowing we would have to make our supplies last—Bavaria was, after all, a long way away. I eased the backpack off my shoulder and stuffed the food into the cavernous space atop my small slingshot. After lacing it shut, I had to trot to catch up with Jacov, who seemed very eager to be on the move.

"We can still make the last train if we move quickly." he gasped, his breath coming in short bursts that made me unsure about his endurance. But, we made steady progress. The train station was in the small village in the valley below and we soon found ourselves waiting on the quiet platform, Jacov fingering the tickets as if they were gold.

After only a brief moment, the train hissed into the station and we backed up as the large billow of steam rose eerily across the softly lit space. Only one man stepped off further along the platform, so we boarded quickly, anxious for a seat and a good rest. The train was nearly empty; only a few foreign nationals and some Russian guards wandered the aisles. We remained undisturbed, though several people eyed us with curiosity, which faded upon sight of the star on Jacov's chest. I wondered if Jacov had had other reasons for wanting my jacket turned inside out—the "N" proclaiming me as a German was now conveniently hidden. We would have made an unusual pair, one possibly warranting awkward questioning.

The train made regular stops as it transported us slowly westward and I wondered how we were to navigate our way to our final destination. The train creaked to a final halt long past midnight and we stepped out into a chilly damp air that had me longing for my cubicle in the barn. I was asleep on my feet and I was relieved to see that Jacov looked rather weary as well.

We had shared a heel of the bread on the train, deciding to save the meat for farther into our journey. My stomach had grown used to the soothing meal of soup, no matter how thin or tasteless it had been, and I found myself longing for a bowl of something warm.

"Let's find a place for the night. We can't be too far from a decent haystack." muttered Jacov, shaking his graying head somberly, while his bright blue eyes peered about him into the gloom. A cloud floated gently away from the moon and we used the brief moment of brightness to look around.

We soon had ourselves encased in a thick layer of hay and I sent up a thanks to the clouds for remaining dry. My eyes were leaden with fatigue, but my heart raced with anxiety as I listened to the even breathing of my sleeping companion. My head filled with the memories of similar nights shared with my dear friend, Gerle, and with a familiar dull ache in my chest, I hoped for his safe keeping, wherever he might be.

The morning came too soon, my dreams having swarmed around my boyhood days with my friends. It took me several minutes to shake the cobwebs from my thoughts and remember where I was. Jacov still slept at my side, his chin glistening with a new thin layer of a silvery beard.

We roused ourselves quickly and scrambled across the fields to the next village, in hopes of finding a train heading in the proper direction. I almost felt a physical pull from behind as we moved ever further away from home... from those I had set all my dreams and hopes on finding. I swallowed the lump that seemed determined to rise into my clenched throat and I tried, instead, to focus on the path ahead. Jacov seemed to have a general idea of where we needed to go, for which I was grateful. I sank into a stupor, not caring where we ended up, knowing only that we were going away.

"Where are we going, exactly, Jacov?" I ventured, finally, after another switch of trains in another forgettable village. I peered nervously around the car, as a tall and surly-looking man approached us, his bulk menacing in his uniform.

Jacov shushed me with a glance and I retreated in my seat toward the window, which retained its old blackout curtain from the days of the war. I pulled it around my head, allowing it to obscure my face from view. I hoped it would appear as though I were only gazing out into the night.

Jacov's calm voice reached my ears beneath the thick blanket where I remained hidden and I heard him shuffling for his papers, presumably the ones given to him by the overseer. The official seemed satisfied and moved on, greeting the next passenger in a brisk tone.

"He's gone." whispered Jacov, pulling the blanket away from my face. "You need not fret so much. They won't trouble with a small lad like you. Besides, I just told him you were my grandson." He smiled kindly and patted me on the shoulder.

I returned the smile, though halfheartedly. I ventured forth again with my interrupted question. "Jacov, how do you know where we are heading?" As I asked it, I realized that it mattered very little to me what his answer would be. It all meant the same to me—somewhere unknown, somewhere that was not home, somewhere where I would continue to be alone.

"We take the train as far west as possible, then..." He paused, his wrinkled hands rubbing his stiff knees. "... Then, we walk." He suddenly looked very tired and slightly pale, as though he were going to be sick, and I found myself doubting again whether he would manage such a strenuous journey.

We each settled into our own thoughts. Often, I gazed at his face. His mouth was hanging open and his closed eyes were flickering through a dream of better days. I wondered what his story was. We had never asked each other how we had ended up on the work farm; there were many variations of the same miserable story and I respected his need for privacy.

I was aware, through my own fragmented memories and observances, that the Jews had suffered an unusual fate during the war, and I wasn't sure I could handle the details. Somehow, the world now tiptoed around Jacov, because he was Jewish. But, I felt certain, that at one point he, like so many others, had paid a great price for his faith and heritage.

Overall, we sank into a numbing routine. The jolts and wobbles of the train set the mind on a meditative path. Thus, I decided, after much thought, that I was in a better place than on the farm with a heavy basket of potatoes in my arms.

Even though I now had a kind and generous companion at my side, I continued to struggle to keep the loneliness at bay. It reared its head at moments when I was most vulnerable, sending images into my mind that pained me to the roots of my being. I felt adrift in a friendless world, with nothing familiar in sight. I was heading into a black tunnel, a tunnel similar to the endless ones the trains whistled through on their relentless paths westward.

CHAPTER 23

The answer to how far the trains would carry us came the following afternoon. We had successfully boarded another small passenger car, though it was pulled by a massive engine that seemed oversized for the job. At the next village, the train halted unexpectedly and a flurry of activity on the platform raised our anxiety.

Several dozen Russian troops stood beside a long row of aged freight cars that were laden with large confiscated tanks and other military hardware. The flat cars languored on a siding, missing the all-important and highly coveted engine. Beside me, Jacov shook his head and muttered sadly, under his breath, "This is the end of the free ride, son. They are taking this engine. The train is done." He stood up slowly and stretched his stooped back laboriously, trying to ease the many kinks left by the hours of immobility. "Let's go." he said, emphatically, glancing about the dimly lit cabin for the nearest door.

We slipped quietly off of the train, Jacov groaning slightly as he jumped down from the high metal step. We darted surreptitiously between the rusted cars to the dense bushes beyond the small platform. The presence of such a large contingency of Russian soldiers made us decidedly nervous. Once clear of the rails, Jacov beckoned me to stay low. We hastily skirted the short length of the village, keeping just within the shadow of the trees.

The afternoon light stretched its long fingers into the boundaries of the impenetrable undergrowth, but we were very careful to stay within the rim of small saplings well beyond the sun's reach. Jacov's breathing soon became ragged and shallow, his strength diminishing as we kept to our swift pace. Finally, he slumped to the mossy ground, where it was still damp in the opaque corners of the thick woods.

"I... must... rest!" he wheezed, rubbing his coat sleeve across his sweaty brow. I lowered myself to the ground beside him, grateful for the forced reprieve. We both sat in silence for several minutes, allowing our taxed lungs to replenish their stores of oxygen.

"We should cut through these woods to the next village west, I think." said Jacov. "This seems too active a place for us to find safety so close to the train tracks." He coughed loudly and, with a belabored groan, he raised himself slightly off his bent elbow. He peered around at the darkening forest just beyond our bed of last year's autumn leaves, almost as though he expected Russians to materialize out of the shadows.

I began to grow anxious. Jacov's unsettled mood was contagious. I asked, "Which way do we head? How are you sure there is a village on the other side of this wood?" My imagination formed a vision in my head of a vast expanse of trees, the narrow trunks outlining a labyrinth that was both thick and dark, blocking our view of the sky and the life-giving rays of the sun. In my mind, we might as well have been on the moon; the world no longer held any familiarity for me.

He answered, "There are little villages scattered all over these hills, my boy." He smiled reassuringly, adding, "There will be a village on the other side... not to worry."

Following a quick refreshing sip of some clear cold water that trickled peacefully from beneath a lichen-coated rock, we headed in Jacov's chosen direction. As we limped along, I struggled with the notion of committing my future to someone who remained a virtual stranger.

We stumbled upon a small clearing after several hours of awkward scrambling among slippery moss-coated rocks and brittle fallen trees, whose gnarled limbs reached toward our frayed clothes like the fingers of forgotten graveyard ghouls. The sunlight failed to enter the center of the open space. Instead, it now grazed only the tips of the tall trees, as the mantle of darkness inched ever closer.

In the growing gloom of the clearing we made out the shape of a small abandoned forester's cabin, long-since left in disrepair. Shutters hung at toppled angles over windows that were laced with panes of cracked glass. Torn and faded strips of fabric that had once framed the view as curtains, now rustled sadly in the wafts of the breeze that drifted from out of the forest.

The roof rested as a crumpled heap upon the frame of the house, which, valiantly, continued in its attempt to hold it up. Sections of the roof were missing entirely. The resulting holes were rimmed with beams that had been charred to an ebony sheen by what must have once been raging flames.

The rising wind of the evening whistled eerily through the gaps between the shutters, the glass no longer providing a welcome barrier to the elements. The air had cooled rapidly with the setting of the sun; winter was continuing to be stubborn about giving way to a much needed spring. Piles of dead leaves that had blown against the sides of the cabin during the long and rough cold season, now whirled and twirled in a clattering macabre dance. We shuffled wearily through them toward the lopsided door.

I shuddered unintentionally as Jacov pushed the creaking door open on its uneven hinges. Shivers of unexplained unease rippled across my skin, raising the fine hairs upon the back of my neck. I shook my head numbly, telling myself that the long day of eluding the Russian authorities had made me skittish and filled with the oppressive feeling of being hunted.

The darkness of the small cabin interior rose before us, its corners hidden in shadows and undisturbed cobwebs. A massive shape loomed in the deepest corner of the cabin, its bulk partly concealed behind heaps of rubbish and twisted beams that had fallen from the shattered roof. A tantalizing thrill coursed through my frazzled nerves, massaging my battered soul. I recognized the familiar outlines of an intact Kachelofen.

I rushed forward, letting out a clenched cry of excitement, and I nearly tripped headlong over a pile of tumbled bricks and overturned scraps of furniture. I caught myself against the twisted frame of what once must have been a bed. I stepped the remaining few feet more carefully and leaned against the cool smooth surface of the oven. Its reassuringly familiar green glaze was partly hidden beneath many layers of thick dust, but the sight of it warmed my heart, as thoroughly as any soothing flame would have done. Nothing remained of the chimney that would have taken the heat up through the nonexistent rafters. Nonetheless, I stretched my cold and dirty fingers across the cast iron cooking plate that sat upon the surface of the stove.

I squeezed my eyes tightly closed and let myself go to the imagined sensation of heat. My head whirled with the ecstasy of once faded, yet suddenly vivid, memories. In an instant, I stood in Oma's warm kitchen, the scent of crackling sap from the newly lit fire drifting beneath my nose, mingling with the intoxicating aromas of Oma's delicious cooking. The clean fragrance of Oma's fresh soap flickered through my crowded mind and I found my head nestled against her warm bosom, her arms folded tightly around me in a loving embrace... a hug that drove all fear and trepidation from my tormented heart. A soothing wave of unbelievable comfort flowed through me and my body shook with the overdue release of emotions. Peace and joy coursed through my body, as my senses overwhelmed me with the fabled reality.

Behind me a crunching sound crashed through my cocoon of dreams and I opened my eyes with a start. Jacov had entered the cabin, his wooden shoes grinding the scattered shards of glass into a fine powder. I ran my hand across my eyes, determined to cloak my private memories from anyone's eyes—even Jacov's. They were mine alone... all the more precious for their fleeting essence.

Jacov was too preoccupied with his own thoughts to notice my brooding face. "We must rest here, Alfie." he sighed, his voice coming in starts between shallow breaths that only marginally cloaked his obvious discomfort. His face was pale and damp with sweat, though the air outside had grown decidedly cool, and he staggered into the cabin with a limp that could not be concealed through use of his walking stick. He slumped onto a pile of rubble, shifting himself painfully into a bearable position.

"Are you all right, Jacov?" I asked distractedly, still reeling pleasantly from my brush with sensations of better days.

He shook his head sadly, leaning closely over his knees, "You go on without me. I can't carry on with this leg. It will be the death of me." he muttered, an unusual tone of anger creeping into his normally gentle voice.

"No! Jacov, no!" I insisted, my head jerking up at his words. "You just need some rest. Tonight we'll stay in here where it is warmer. We can go on in the morning." I stammered, determined to hold on to the one person who had become my new anchor. Suddenly, the thought of being alone again terrified me.

"I'll just slow you down, Alfie. You know that." he sighed. "They'll most likely shoot us if they spot us. This is a restricted area for civilians. We are close to the border, now. You will have a better chance without me."

He moaned loudly as he shifted his weight around on his uncomfortable perch.

"Jacov," I interrupted, angrily. "Without you, I would be on my way to the coal mines!" I paced the length of the room, which was difficult, given the amount of rubble in the small space. "Let's just get you some rest." I paused in front of him and placed my hand on his shoulder. "We will stay out of sight. I'll go at whatever pace you need me to, Jacov. I won't leave you." I finished, emphatically.

A brief smile played across his pale lips and he muttered, "Who would have thought, a young German boy and an old Jew... who would have thought."

"I'm not German!" I cried, vehemently. "I'm... I'm... I don't know what I am anymore! I just know I want my family back. Whatever country my city lies in now, I don't care! I just want to be able to go home. That's all."

"Ok, son, Ok. I want to find a home someday too." he said, soothingly. "It's just that I don't think I have one to go back to. I hope you do, though... I really do."

We sat in silence for several minutes, each of us pondering our futures... and our pasts, as we allowed the sudden flurry of words to fade into the emptiness of the room.

The sounds of the forest's creatures coming alive filled the void and a lonely owl's call drifted towards us on the wind, which also carried with it new noises, less soothing noises... the grinding hum of motors. I ran to the crumbled wall, keeping my head low, and I peered over the jagged glass of a former window. I stared out into the twilight, my heart pounding loudly against my chest.

Jacov appeared incredibly silently beside me, his aching leg forgotten for the moment. The gray sky fell away into blackness beyond the ring of trees around the clearing, but a line of movement slowly materialized in the distance.

"Damn!" Jacov hissed. "We have to stay hidden!" he whispered. "The Russians will not treat us kindly if they find us here." He pushed my head down and hunched closely beside me, his panicked breathing hot against my ear.

Time inched forward and I tried to remain still. My stiff muscles cramped and tingled all the more as I tried to ignore them. Untapped adrenaline tore through my body, setting my nerves on edge. The cold mist that settled in over the house did little to improve the conditions. Jacov groaned slightly, his legs twisted uncomfortably beneath him against the damp earthen floor. The steady rumble of heavy armored vehicles continued for several hours and we feared to make any movement.

The moon rose mockingly into the clear sky, bathing the forest in a cold blue light. My stomach roared with hunger and my throat clenched with dryness; I longed to soothe both. Suddenly I remembered that my forgotten sack lay beneath me like a crumpled pillow. I eased it slowly off of my shoulders, careful to keep my head below the sill of the shattered window, which I noticed, grimly, was exceptionally low.

"Easy, Alfie." whispered Jacov. "Take it slowly. You never know where they might be looking."

I carefully unlaced the flap, fumbling over the stiff strings with my cold fingers. I pulled out the very diminished bundle of food and laid it open on the ground beside me. Only two narrow strips of bacon remained; the bread had disappeared by the second day. I stared at it for a moment, realizing that the salty meat would only increase my awful thirst. But my exceptional hunger won out, and handing one piece to Jacov, I stuffed the other one into my eager mouth.

I regretted my haste immediately, as the dry lumps of fat clung to my throat, and I retched clumsily into the dirt beside me, nearly choking in my effort to remain quiet. Jacov simply placed his hand soothingly on my shoulder and continued to nibble slowly on his own piece of bacon.

The activity in the woods seemed to diminish as the night stretched on toward morning, so we risked possible discovery to slither across the floor to the dark corner near the Kachelofen, further away from the numbing cold of the window. Jacov's walking stick poked into my side several times as we navigated the larger heaps of rubble, but our chilled bodies were only slightly heated after the awkward exertion of trying to stay so low to the ground.

"Here, Alfie. Move closer. It will be a cold night." Jacov said, grunting as he pulled a broken bed rail toward us to lean against. I moved in next to him, tugging a long strip of rotten curtain fabric over our legs in a vain attempt to gain some warmth in our stiff limbs.

The night passed slowly. Sleep came in tantalizing, but restless, intervals. Jacov stirred constantly, moaning and shifting his weight uncomfortably against the cold floor. The mist grew heavier as morning approached and it held a bitter dampness that dug into my body like a slowly grinding drill. It seemed an eternity until dawn would arrive; with every moment the cold deepened. The higher altitude meant winter still reigned in the early hours.

Morning arrived to find Jacov shivering beside me, his face wet with perspiration that had no benign cause to be there, given how cold it was. My heart turned to ice at the thought of what I would have to do if he became too sick to travel. I couldn't abandon him; I also knew I wasn't strong enough to carry him.

His head jerked up with an anguished cough and I jumped, kicking our pathetic blanket off of our cold toes. "Alfie." he whispered, his voice thin and reedy, as if he spoke through a sieve. "Alfie, you go, boy… you go." He shook his head, seeing the ready argument playing across my features. "I just can't make it. We are close to the border, Alfie. I can feel it. You just go." He coughed again loudly, leaning his head against the wall, pressing his eyes closed to hide his pain.

"Jacov…" I pleaded, pausing to consider my words, before finally choosing a tact I knew he would find hard to resist. "Jacov, I would never make it on my own. I have no idea where we are. You have to go…. Please!" With a groan, he sat up, his vivid blue eyes gazing with concern into my face. I had won. I had chosen the one thing to say to make him keep going. "I need you, Jacov." I continued, determined to get him up off the floor. "Please, if you help me find the border… I'll help you get there."

He nodded slowly, returning his head to the wall. I busied myself with retying my sack and by scrambling to the window to check the state of the forest, which now appeared peaceful and undisturbed beneath its thick blanket of fog. The movement of the previous night had ceased; the troops had moved on… for the moment.

"We should go now, Jacov, before the fog lifts. Besides, I need to find some water." I stood up and crossed to the corner where Jacov sat slumped against the wall. I held my hand out to him, trying hard to keep it still; waves of hunger were causing it to shake with uncontrollable tremors. Jacov peered up at me from beneath limp eyelids, his bloodshot eyes full of sadness and an alarming sense of fatalism. He shook his head, as if he were ridding his mind of the annoying voice of reason, pelting him with easy excuses to give up and succumb to his fate.

For a moment, I thought that he would falter and that the despair ringing through his thoughts would win out, but finally he raised his own aged hand and placed it firmly in mine. I pulled with what little strength I had remaining and he stumbled to his feet.

"We will go only as quickly as you are able, Jacov." I muttered quietly, reinforcing my determination to help the old man. He nodded dumbly and we headed for the door, the search for water our first order of business.

We soon wandered upon a stream, its cold water deep and clean from the long winter snows. We both drank at length and I longed to be able to carry some with me; we might not find such fresh water further on. But, without a bottle, we were forced to leave our thirst behind. We headed slowly westward, staying far clear of the route taken the night before by the Russians.

The day wore ponderously away, warming only slightly to ease our chilled bones. We soon found a steady rhythm, stopping every few minutes to allow Jacov to rest his legs and catch his breath. I didn't mind the breaks, as the lack of food was beginning to make me decidedly weak and dizzy. I scanned the underbrush on a regular basis for any early berries, but the bushes had barely begun to bud, the altitude being so high.

There seemed to be water everywhere, spring rains had followed on top of the brutal winter and it had left the ground soggy and thick with moss. Although my feet remained cold from treading in many puddles, the moisture did have one advantage—mushrooms.

Most were to be avoided, the fabled toadstool being one of them, its brilliant red skin and stark white spots shouting poison loudly. But, after several minutes of careful inspection, I found a delicious variety I had been familiar with from my days in the woods with Opa. I kicked them gently with my wooden shoe, allowing the dusty spores to settle before lifting the mushrooms delicately and wrapping them in the empty cloth from the farm kitchen.

Jacov clapped me on the back with delight at the sight of the unexpected meal. My spirit lifted to see a twinkle had returned to his blue eyes. "You have a good nose, my boy. Those will go down quite well. We best keep moving, though." he said, peering anxiously around him, the hunted look returning to his shadowed eyes.

We found a clear pool of water in which to wash our meager treasure, and we ate the heady mushrooms rapturously; with eyes closed it felt like the finest meal.

The disorienting feeling of dizziness now temporarily at bay, we stumbled onward, although I grew increasingly unsure of the day's particular goal. Jacov continued to insist that the border with Germany must be near, but we saw no signs to reinforce his conviction. We proceeded with caution, nonetheless, aware that security would be tightest near the border.

Finally, we reached the rim of a wide strip of land that had been cleared of all trees. Where the sun had been able to reach, a thick tangle of underbrush had taken root. The strip encompassed a hill, with a narrow stream dividing it into halves in the hollow. Nearer to the water, thick grasses grew, their arms waving toward the sky, searching for the sun, which had spent the day dancing in and out of low hanging clouds.

"There!" Jacov whispered at my side, his voice heavy with fatigue and nervous excitement. "There is the border... I'm sure of it." He pointed to the opposite crest of the steep hill. "This strip represents 'no man's land'. It's not far now, Alfie, but we best wait to see what is moving."

I found myself doubting him—this place seemed too calm and too quiet to be an official border between nations. Nothing moved but the gentle wind through the tall trees to our rear, stirring the damp mist that persisted over the highest limbs. I shuddered upon realizing the sounds that had kept us company in the forest had ceased; not a twitter or a squeak could be heard. This was indeed a place where man, not beast, reigned.

As if to reinforce my sudden unease, I became aware of a tall brown watchtower that had eluded my attention before. If I had not known we were in a former war zone, and on the verge of a recently contested border, I would have guessed it belonged to local hunters, a hidden retreat in which to wait for an unsuspecting four-legged victim. But, in this case, the hunters were sure to be armed guards, and the prey, if we were unlucky, would be us.

I peered into the distance to my left, as well as to my right, being careful to keep my head hidden within the thick bush behind which we were huddled. My eyes were forced to squint against the rays of the sun, which had chosen now to peek through the clouds and skim the tree tops on its gradual descent into bed. The clearing, about one hundred meters wide at its narrowest, stretched to the left into the horizon, which rose slightly where another hill folded the land. To the right lay a similar view, though the row of thick brush next to us curved slightly, leaving much of what I sought in question.

At the very navel of the clearing, parallel to the stream, but on our side, ran a winding dirt path, Just as I was pondering where it might lead, an approaching figure appeared in the hazy distance. I gasped in spite of myself and felt Jacov's knobby fingers dig warningly into the flesh of my arm.

A machine gun cradled ready in his arms, the guard led a large German Shepherd on a thin chain, its links straining under the massive strength of the animal, who seemed to be wound as tightly as a coiled spring. The guard's gaze appeared to be directed forward along the path, and we turned our heads reluctantly away from him to what might be capturing his interest.

From the other direction came yet another guard, with an equally intimidating dog at his side. The men walked toward each other, apparently preparing to exchange reports of their separate patrols. As they slowly approached one another, the dogs began snarling and pulling against their leads. My heart grew cold at the thought of having to try to help Jacov outrun one, or both, of the ferocious beasts.

Directly below our hidden position, the guards met, pulling the chains of their dogs tightly to restrain the snarling and snapping teeth of the high-strung animals. The taut muscles in the hindquarters of the nearest dog quivered with nervous, unused energy, and I closed my eyes for a moment to block the image of his bared teeth. My neck tingled nastily, as the horror of our possible fates played itself out in my mind's eye.

When I dared to look again, the men had managed to prop their machine guns under their arms and were nonchalantly exchanging cigarettes. They chatted for a moment, seemingly oblivious to the deathly power that stood beside each of them. Both beasts pulsated with a loosely contained, profound desire to kill.

Finally, after the cold sweat of fear had risen on my forehead, the guards passed on to continue their monitoring of the border—for I was now without any doubt that we had indeed reached the partition between the two lines of control, and that our goal lay on the other side of this last, but daunting and terrifying, hurdle.

Jacov drew in a deep breath through clenched teeth and I realized that he was as overwhelmed as I was with the significance of the task ahead. "We must stay here until morning, Alfie. They must never find us." he said, fervently. "I don't want to die like that." he whispered, his voice littered with fear and revulsion at his own horrific thoughts, which must have been similar to my own.

I stared into his darkening eyes; they were wide with anxiety and pain, which I knew had been mounting during the long day. I nodded in agreement and said quietly, but with determination, in case he doubted my resolve to help him, "We will cross in the morning, then."

We passed the terrible night in an agonizingly slow blur. The cramping of hunger in my empty stomach was only intensified by the nausea that crept over me as the images of the dogs persisted in forcing their way into every corner of my mind. They haunted me like spectres from a grave, their gnashing teeth flashing brightly before my clenched eyes.

The cold had intensified to such a point that I worried if Jacov would survive until morning. We huddled as closely to each other as possible, but neither of us had sufficient clothing, or insulating body weight, to retain any heat we managed to generate. By dawn a thick layer of dew had settled upon our shivering forms and we were entirely soaked to the skin.

My mind was in such a fog that I barely noticed the lightening sky, but Jacov's whispered moans roused me immediately. With his head flailing sadly from side to side, he croaked, "You go on, my boy. I'm as good as dead already. I don't think I can even stand on this leg. It's killing me!" He sobbed violently into his hands, which he threw over his face in an attempt to muffle his uncontrollable cries.

"No, Jacov!" I hissed fiercely, glancing behind me at the empty path near the stream. I grabbed him by the shoulders and shook him gently, but persistently. "No! I will not let you give up! Not after we have come this far. I will not go on alone!" I insisted. "They will just have to shoot both of us. I'm not leaving you here."

He continued to sob into one of his hands, his other fingers massaging his aching leg.

"Besides," I continued, trying to smile, "You have a grandson to find. He is looking forward to meeting his grandfather." My voice faltered slightly as I added, "You will be a wonderful grandfather... give him the chance to know you." Opa's face swam painfully before my eyes.

He took his hand away from his face, which seemed much older than the night before. He placed his hand on my shoulder and, squeezing lightly, he whispered, "I hope he is just like you, my boy. Then I will die a proud man." I smiled and looked away. When I looked back, the manic twinkle had returned to his eyes. He peered eagerly toward the opposite hill, muttering, "Ok, let's do it!"

Soon, the distant barks of the dogs could be heard, and I braced myself for their arrival. The guards had their weapons as ready as the day before, and the dogs seemed to us more menacing, if at all possible, now that the hour for action was at hand. We had agreed to watch several passes of the guards, and to carefully count the length of the brief intervals when they were out of sight.

Initially, it seemed an agonizingly long wait, but once we were resolved to act, the time became terrifyingly short. "When he rounds the bushes, Jacov…" I said, my voice quivering with fear, "… we go… Now!" I cried, seizing Jacov's arm and hauling him out of the bush. I knew we had very little time and I was desperate to keep my new friend with me.

The heavy dew on the grass was slippery and we slid recklessly down the hill, flailing our arms to remain upright, as we stumbled ever closer to our goal. Jacov huffed and puffed at my side, but his eyes had hardened with a fierce determination. We crossed the narrow path and I forced myself not to look about for the guards, but, instead, to stay focused on the distance remaining—we were now at the point of no return, committed to our fate.

Only the stream and the gradual rise lay before us, so I plunged blindly into the icy water, my hand tightly clutching a gasping Jacov. Suddenly, behind us a wild barking commenced and I caught my breath with fear. "Come on, Jacov! Don't look back! We will not die!" I yelled, as much to convince myself as to invigorate my companion. My legs ached in the cold water and I stumbled on the slippery rocks, but miraculously, Jacov had found a reserve of energy and kept his footing. Now, it was his turn to pull me forward.

Shouts began behind us. Then, the rhythmic crackling of shots being fired sent fear pouring over me like a wave of ice, colder than the water in which we were floundering so slowly forward. We reached the opposite bank and my wooden shoes almost slipped off my feet in my attempt to mount the steeper opposite bank. I glanced over my shoulder to where Jacov was laboring forward. Beyond the water, which was still settling from our frantic crossing, I spotted the two guards, their guns raised to deliver another round of bullets.

Jacov scrambled frantically up the bank, his hands clawing at the thin wisps of grass, which continued to slide through his fingers. His wheezing breath caught roughly as he made agonizingly slow progress forward on the damp grass. I reached for a bush in front of me to help haul us up and I turned back to Jacov.

"Here! Grab my hand!" I cried, clutching the thin branch of the bush more tightly in preparation. He lunged valiantly and I caught his brittle fingers between my own. His terrified face peered up into mine as the yelling increased behind us. For the first time, I felt that we might not make it—this was going to be the end. I would die an orphan on a unknown stretch of one of the most infamous borders on the world, with only a kind old man at my side to know that I had passed on.

"No!" I cried out angrily, pulling at the bush with all my strength, and I hauled us to the crest of the hill, shots still whizzing all around us. I scrambled for my life through the tall grass, gasping for air. As I brushed my hair away from my eyes, I looked up through the grass in front of me, eager for my first sight of Germany. Instead, I found myself staring into the long black barrel of a machine gun.

CHAPTER 24

M y insides turned to ice. The barrel of the gun quivered only inches from my ashen face, so close I could smell the foul taint of its cold black metal. A withering gasp rose behind me as Jacov cleared the crest of the hill and also found himself staring directly into the cruel leaden eyes of death.

My heart was struggling between pounding its way out of my chest through my throat and stopping entirely. My mind thudded painfully with thoughts of the mocking and untimely irony of having successfully cleared the gauntlet of the border, only to be confronted by a possible bullet through the head.

"I'm dead!" I thought, the overwhelming panic being replaced by an eerily ringing hum of numbness and powerlessness, which roared through my body like a runaway freight train. Voices swirled in the air over my head, sounding distant, as though resonating through churning water. I tried to focus on their content, dimly aware that Jacov's pleading words were among them. But, the deep chasm of fear into which I had fallen sent spots of blackness playing across my eyes. I closed them tightly and placed my hands over my head, burying it deeply into the damp grass in front of me. The earth smelled sweet and calming, and it eased the waves of nausea and dizziness that threatened to engulf me.

Out of the fog in which I was floundering, came Jacov's excited voice. I forced my mind to open enough to raise my head and I peered over at him. He was slightly behind me, to my left, and on his knees. His trembling hands were grasping at the large dark green boots of a soldier.

281

The soldier looked at me, a disconcerting grin of amusement on his young fair face. I realized, with a start, that he was different from any soldier I had ever seen before.

A helmet in a muddy green color sat like a bowl upon his blond head, and although his hands were wrapped around a familiar sight, a cocked and very deadly machine gun, he managed to make it look unalarming. His uniform was the color of sand and his pants were tucked neatly into his low boots, very unlike the high shiny black knee-high boots I had become familiar with from my association with the Germans and the Russians. The intimidation I had become accustomed to with soldiers seemed to melt the longer I gazed at him. Suddenly and unexplainably, in his presence, I felt safe.

As I absorbed this new and unnatural feeling, I raised myself to my knees, and I brushed my sodden bangs out of my eyes. Jacov seemed very much at ease at my side, though he was still breathing heavily after our frantic dash to what we had hoped would be safety. I was still unsure of our success; the prospect of what this unusual soldier had in store for us remained very much in question. The more I peered about, though, the more I sensed the lightened mood, most of it generating, to my continued surprise, from Jacov and the young soldier.

Across the creek, behind us, the Russians had ceased their shooting and were busy calming the restless dogs, who persisted in barking madly, undoubtedly enraged by their failure to nab their prey. The Russians shook their fists in our direction, but did little else in the form of pursuit. Clearly, Jacov and I had surprised them on this hidden stretch of the border, and we had caused quite a stir in our crossing. For It seemed clear to me now, that we had managed to cross the border. But, then, just who had we stumbled upon? Who was this man... and was he a friend or a foe?

As I puzzled this in my head, he spoke, in a barely understandable tangle of words that, under normal circumstances, would have frightened me except for the eager smile on his face. "Well, my friend, that was quite a dash! You are safe, now." he said, his smile broadening.

I marveled at his brilliant teeth. I remembered suddenly, stories I had heard about my heroes in America—they all had had beautiful clothes and big, straight teeth. Everything in America was supposed to be grand and different. Was this man an American—someone right out of my favorite tales of the great country across the ocean? It dawned on me that if such were the case, it would mean we had succeeded... we were indeed free at last!

Jacov stood up, clapped one of his hands kindly on my shoulder, and held the other one out for me to grab. He hauled me to my feet, and I gasped loudly at his surprising strength. His eyes were full of delight and tears sparkled in the corners, increasing the jolly twinkle that danced across their watery blue surfaces.

"We did it, my boy! We did it!" he cried, grabbing me in a tight embrace, then holding my sagging shoulders in his two hands. "This is the American sector. We are free!" He gulped the last words, profound happiness trickling from every breath. He turned me toward the waiting soldier, one arm still across my shoulder, where I hoped it would remain, as my knees had suddenly turned to jelly.

It was over! I was free! A surge of relief swept over me, overwhelming the stagnant feeling of fear with which I had lived for so long. My ordeal was far from over—I was painfully aware of that. I was still separated from everyone I knew and loved... but I was alive... at the very least, I was alive! I hastily convinced myself to believe that the Americans would help me find my family. I would not be alone for much longer.

It seemed as though time had ceased to exist. I stumbled along in a daze, as we were led back to the American camp. There we were met by several other soldiers who all seemed equally pleased to see us and genuinely concerned about our welfare. One fellow with sable brown hair, his teeth clamped tightly around a thin smoldering cigarette despite his broad grin, wrapped each of us in dry warm blankets. It was then I remembered that we were both still soaking wet from the long damp night and the brief and frantic drenching in the stream.

Suitably warm and at last beginning to dry, we were ushered, with much ado, into a small open jeep, similar to ones I had seen many times overturned along the roadside. The thought of riding in one unpleasantly rejuvenated my relaxed nerves, and I climbed in with more than a little trepidation. As we bounced recklessly along the pitted roads, the noise of the engine seemed to rumble from the very pit of my hollow stomach. I clenched my fingers tightly to the sides of the vehicle, hoping our ride would be a short one.

Jacov seemed to be on the verge of collapse. His skin was pale and clammy, and I wondered if he would become sick from the movement of the jeep. But, he managed a small smile, albeit a rather sheepish one, and he returned his proud and happy gaze toward the east, the direction in which all our past troubles lay. Now, in the east lay the sun, tripping playfully along the tips of the trees as we jostled westward along the winding road. I felt my own wave of pride pound through me as it dawned on me just what we had accomplished. We had defied the odds, which had been stacked heavily against our survival, and we had soundly defeated them.

As I pondered, with awe, life's complexities, the jeep slowed to a jiggling amble. We rolled into a small village, which was tucked cozily against a long bank of undulating hills. A seemingly well established American base was now housed in the once elegant center square of the village. The sparse and scattered, war-torn, stucco houses appeared out of place among the tidy tent rows of military order.

I stared around with amazement. The number of soldiers made the skin on my scalp crawl uncontrollably; I had been conditioned to fear such a concentration of military-backed testosterone and fire power. As though he could read my mind, Jacov's comforting hand patted me on the back before he was helped from the back of the jeep. We were led to a large brown mess tent, its wide flaps tied open to allow the smoke and heat produced from the constant preparation of food to escape.

I stumbled forward eagerly, faced with the imminent possibility of a proper meal. Jacov and I had survived with only the meager fare that had been in my sack and, when that had quickly dwindled, we had made do with what little the forest had had to offer. The days had seemed endless; I had soon given up counting. But, now I tried to puzzle it out, finally deciding we had been on the move for at least a week… a very long and miserable week.

Passing beneath the awning of the tent, I was met with smells that threatened to engulf my neglected senses with their fabulous and enticing aromas. A young woman, her uniform as neat and trim as the others, smiled kindly at me, and the lump of ice that had sat on my heart for so long gingerly began to give way.

It seemed that here, finally, we were going to be treated like human beings, like individuals who had suffered great hardships, and who deserved a sign of kindness, however small and seemingly insignificant. The simple gestures, which I had once taken for granted… a reassuring smile or an encouraging pat on the back, now filled me with a profound warmth of spirit and a sincere and renewed hope for humanity. I smiled shyly in return, aware suddenly that I was most definitely a frightful sight, and I hastened to take the large mug she was holding patiently out to me.

My gaze turned with uncontrollable relish to the offering, the fragrance of which was swirling pleasantly before my nose. It was a hot cup of soup like those buried in my oldest and most treasured memories of Oma's cooking. Large chunks of meat floated in a thick and piquant broth, which also revealed cubes of golden potatoes and brilliantly vibrant carrots.

"Here." the woman said, smiling her wonderful smile at me again, and I marveled, for a second time, at the brilliance of the teeth of Americans. I tore my eyes away from her face, only dimly remembering Oma's words that staring was rude. Instead, I stared equally intently at her hands, which held out to me an entire plate of delicacies—some of which I had only read about in books.

Shifting my hot mug, I took the plate from her, managing to mumble, "Thank you.", as I backed away. I nearly tripped over Jacov, who was holding a plate with a similarly amazing array of foods. Upon both our plates there were several pieces of white bread formed into neat squares, very much like my favorite bread that Oma had always baked for our special Sunday dinners. Next to the bread was a pile of fruit—including, among other things, bananas, and apples as shiny as everyone's teeth, and beautiful red tomatoes.

"Well, Alfie! What do you think? This is more food than we have seen these many months, eh?" chortled a delighted Jacov. I followed him to a quiet corner, and after maneuvering ourselves into comfortable places among some stacked sandbags, we began to feast. I started slowly, eager to enjoy the many new flavors. But, after the first sampling of the soup, my desperate hunger overtook me, and I began to shovel large dripping spoonfuls into my salivating mouth.

As we ate, we realized we had become somewhat of a source of curiosity to the inhabitants of the camp. I paused to look up and spotted a tall man studying us with a very concerned frown. When my eyes met his, the frown dissolved into a smile, though the air of concern lingered about his eyes. He stepped eagerly forward, obviously wanting to speak. I glanced nervously at Jacov, who had also noticed the approach of the soldier, and he now sat with his loaded spoon poised on its path to his mouth.

What was I going to say to this man if he spoke to me in English? I knew only several phrases from my books, things unsuitable for this setting. It dawned on me, at that moment, that I had been away from learning anything from a book or a school for such a long time. The war and its horrible aftermath had severed the paths of my life in so many ways, I wondered if I would ever find normalcy again.

Upon hearing the man speak, I knew my alarm had been unfounded. "Eat slowly, slowly." he said, in clipped, but tolerable, German, and he smiled again, patting me gently on the shoulder. "Take your time. We don't want you to be sick."

Moments later, as though cursed by his untimely premonition, my stomach began to churn. I threw myself toward the back of the tent, burying my head in a corner behind another row of sandbags. The delicious food tore its way out of my distressed and overwhelmed stomach, which had tried so valiantly to adjust to the unexpected assault of the many new and rich foods.

"Well!" said the man, chuckling kindly as I reemerged, my face beaded with sweat. "Well, I think now would be a good time for a shower for you both." I shook my head, rattling his words through my brain… had he actually said we could bathe?

Jacov grinned at me. I knew his thoughts reflected mine—I had not washed properly for almost a year. The thought of finally being able to remove the foul film that had encased my skin beneath several deep immovable layers of grime served to distract me from the rumbles still threatening to escape from the recesses of my innards.

Setting our plates aside for later, we followed the soldier to a large barrack, the interior of which was divided into many small rooms. Here we were ushered to undress and my clothes came off with a cloud of dust, the fabric having almost disintegrated after so long on my filthy body. My bones poked out where my clothing had hung so loosely and I longed to scratch my flaking skin. I realized, with a shudder, that some parts of me had not seen daylight for a very long time.

As I stood beneath the hot water, my skin tingled with delight, a sensation that had been forgotten for so long beneath the thick coating of dirt and the formidable stench. I stepped from beneath the water very reluctantly and found myself confronted by a medic with a large and menacing spray can. Thankfully, Jacov stepped at that moment from the shower to my right.

He noticed the fear and distrust in my eyes and he said quickly, "Alfie, it's ok. They explained it to me—they will spray you with some chemical, called DDT. It will kill the lice and any other nasty vermin." I shuddered visibly, wondering what sort of strength this killer spray had... could it really rid me of the one constant, however unwelcome, companion that had stuck with me during all my travels?

I closed my eyes, spread my arms, and waited for the stinging blast of the spray. Instead, soft puffs of a very pungent powder were distributed gently across my body, and images of parachuting lice danced through my head. I suppressed a laugh, delighted that I would finally be rid of the itching and the scabbing that had been a result of their infestation.

When I opened my eyes I stared before me through the lingering puffs of the magical cloud, and I watched with fascination as the medic repeated the procedure on Jacov. Jacov's shriveled limbs trembled slightly as the cool powder landed on his head and shoulders like the first gentle snow of winter. As I watched the procedure, I thanked the many lucky chances that had brought us to safety just in time. Jacov's body was so wasted and so frail, I knew he would not have lasted many more days.

We were told to stay still to allow the chemicals ample time to settle onto our slightly damp skin. In a few minutes we would be given a new set of clothes. I glanced at the pile of our discarded items and wondered, with amazement how they had managed to remain on our bodies for so long. The simple act of removing them had all but turned the cloth to dust; only a few clinging fibers remained.

My wooden shoes lay in a heap near the clothes, and I wondered what plans our hosts had in store for those. For so long, my feet had been molded into a begrudging acceptance of the awkward and cumbersome clogs; I could scarcely even imagine the relative freedom of regular shoes.

I nodded a farewell, smiling slightly, as Jacov was led away to the hospital tent, with only a towel around his middle. I hoped the care the Americans could provide would help Jacov regain the strength he needed to match his greatly deserved dignity.

Shortly after I was left alone, the soldier who had warned me of the imminent unrest in my stomach appeared at the door, holding a small bundle of army issue attire.

"I hope these will fit you. I looked for the smallest size we have." he said, handing me the clothes. "Oh... and here are some new shoes. It's about

287

time you got rid of those." He grimaced, pointing to the wooden clogs in the corner. "You know your old clothes will need to be burned, also anything else you were carrying that cannot be sterilized."

"I know… it's ok… I have nothing with me, really… nothing." I answered, sadly running through my scant belongings in my head. The handmade slingshot had survived as a token of my innocent carefree days, and I vowed to keep it with me as a reminder of what had once been. Also, the small bundle of papers that Opa had given me before the Russians had herded us into the camp, remained folded tightly in the bottom of one of the pockets of my rucksack. The proof of my birth was included. Even though it had remained unopened during the past dreadful year, it had served as a soothing reminder that I had, indeed, once had parents after all.

He handed me the clothes and left with another smile, saying, "Check back at the mess tent—they will tell you where you will bunk tonight."

"Thank you… really, very much. Everyone has been so kind… thank you." I stammered in reply, setting my new clothes on the bench beside me. I remained motionless for a moment, listening to the man's retreating footsteps on the floor in the hall. I took a few deep breaths, forcing myself to slow down the speeding train on which I had been so suddenly placed. I glanced at the clothes at my side, turning them over in my hand, amazed at their spotlessness.

I stood, allowing the damp towel to fall from my waist, and I held up the shirt in front of me. It, too, was the color of sand, and it looked wonderful. I pulled it over my head, amused with the sudden thought that Gerle and the other boys would not believe that I now stood dressed in clothes from America. The thought of Gerle quickly turned from delight to pain, as I was forced to ponder his fate, yet again, just as at countless times during the past year. Had he, too, been rescued by the Allies, or had his path been even more troubled than mine? Perhaps he had traveled East—to the coal mines… I couldn't see my small, frail friend surviving long in those dark pits beneath the earth. I tore my mind away from the dreadful images forming in my mind, forcing my thoughts to what I hoped would be a better path.

And what of the others… my partners in the many adventures as a young boy? Perhaps, the inhabitants of Jagerndorf… at least, the ones who had been fortunate enough to survive, were now scattered across the vastness of Europe, each of them adrift in a purgatory of postwar chaos, indifference, and homelessness.

With familiar sadness now marring my brief delight at the clothes, I shook my head, trying to focus on the task before me. Somehow, I needed to accommodate my withered frame into a significant pair of long trousers.

The fabric hung in loose folds around my thin ankles, mocking my desperate conviction that I had indeed grown in the past year. I had been in shorts for so long, it felt strange to have the weight of cloth near my feet, so I rolled each pant leg up several times until they grazed my calves only slightly below my knees.

With renewed eagerness, I turned my attention to my new shoes, the article of clothing I had been most anticipating. Replacing the large stiff wooden clogs were two shiny black leather boots, each with several glistening silver buckles to be clasped across the ankle. I pulled them on, relishing in the softness of the leather. My feet swam in the vast interiors, so I took them off and wandered around the vacant room peering into corners and cupboards until I found something suitable. Wadding some small discovered rags into balls, I crammed these first into the toes of the boots, then eased my feet back in for another attempt.

I sighed with pleasure at the wonderful idea of painless mobility, and I proceeded to stomp around the room, awed at the ease with which I was able to move. As my body warmed up with the sudden motion, I realized that I was hungry again. Determined to eat more slowly this time, I prepared to return to the mess tent, grabbing the last remaining article of clothing, a jacket with all official insignia removed.

For once it felt good to be anonymous. I could leave behind my torn jacket with the sewn-on label, a demoralizing symbol of a nationality I had been assigned. I was now embarking on a new future, one in which, I hoped, my country of origin would be irrelevant. I was simply one of those who had lived… one of those who needed to pick up the many torn threads of his life and move forward.

As I strolled down the dark and quiet hallway, I grinned with pleasure, amazed at my own luck. It was May, yet it felt like the most opulent Christmas ever. My shoes squeaked beneath me with newness, and my clothes felt clean and cool against my freshly scrubbed skin. The last Christmas had passed without any celebration, except for a silent prayer in my bed at night that all my loved ones were safe and well.

It had been three long years since a joyful holiday. It had been 1943, a time that seemed so much more distant than it really was. I had been surrounded by my family—including both my mother and my father; we had been together and we had been happy. The war had still been something we acknowledged in the abstract sense, something I had barely understood. But, it had not yet slithered its cruel clawed fingers around our lives. Food had been abundant and delicious, as it always had been at my grandparents' home, and the mood had been light and festive.

The passage of time that had separated my happy life—the carefree life of a child from the life turned horribly wrong, had been so very brief. Standing in the hall, warm and dry in my American clothes, I struggled to define exactly when my life had begun to cave in, but the many instances of fate and design had served to build a complex web of occurrences, all of which had had a profound effect on where I stood at this very moment.

Would my future prove to be as intricate a maze of events, as untraceable to my roots as my past appeared to me now? Would I live the rest of my life in this new part of Germany? Was I meant to make my way on my own? Was I ready for such a life… the loneliness and the responsibilities that a life alone would entail? Was time on my side? Would I find my family… or did fate yet have some nasty card in reserve, with which it was waiting in the shadows to deal out to me… me alone? Only time would tell.

CHAPTER 25

I woke early. The sun was still abed, and I listened to the comfortable breathing of the soldiers around me. My bunk was in a quiet corner of a long barrack, similar to the many I had slept in before, except for one very significant thing. Unlike the many camps, the mood, during the week that I had been with the Americans, had been light and cheerful. It had lacked the ominous air of despair and fear that had hung over everyone like a toxic vapor, threatening to tear us all down and engulf us, one by one.

Not everything in my new surroundings had been perfect, of course. I still longed daily for my family, and I felt like an inadequate boat adrift in a turbulent sea. Also, in spite of, or, as the medic insisted, because of, the improved food, I had been quite sick for several days. I was eager to enjoy the burgeoning array of fine edibles, but my body had decided that it needed more time to adjust to the increased intake. I was forced to refrain from overzealousness and was constantly reminded to take things slowly.

Jacov spent these same days holed up in the medical tent, recuperating his much needed strength. I missed his merry smile and the kind twinkle in his blue eyes. I realized, by the third day, that I had grown quite fond of the old man, and I longed for his familiar company as a comforting substitute for those individuals I had lost.

On this particular morning, I had been told to stay in bed and rest, the medic having deemed that my ailments simply needed time and quiet. I tried, unsuccessfully, to doze as the soldiers woke and began to bustle about, setting themselves in proper order. Soon the buzz of activity swirled

291

to a low murmur, as the men dispersed to attend to their various duties, and I sank gratefully back into a deep sleep.

Later, I was roused again by the bright light streaming in through the long windows, and I lay in my bunk watching the sun warm the walls of the room through the half-closed lids of my eyes. A fly buzzed lazily against one of the windows, and its clattering drone had a soporific effect upon my tired senses. It felt so good to be finally clean, rested, and well-fed... so well-fed, in fact, that my body could not properly handle it yet. But, I reveled in the peace and quiet that surrounded me.

The slamming of the door to the hall alerted my senses only slightly; I knew it must be a soldier returning for a forgotten item. But, as the footsteps approached my bunk, I felt inclined to stir, and I looked up, squinting my eyes against the midday sun. Jacov stood before me, his face beaming with happiness and health beneath a neatly trimmed beard.

"How's my boy?" he exclaimed, enthusiastically. "You are looking a little green, Alfie... Are you still trying to eat the entire mess tent?" he asked, winking merrily. I eased myself up onto my elbows and continued to blink in disbelief at his jovial face.

"You're looking better, Jacov." I croaked, my throat suddenly craving water. He truly did appear transformed. His skin had regained some of its healthy coloring and he wore clean clothes that no longer smelled of stale sweat and urine. Seeing him so altered made me hope that my appearance had improved as well. Then remembering his greeting, I asked, "Do I really look that sick, Jacov?"

"No... no, not at all. I was just teasing, my boy. Word has it that you can't seem to eat everything you want to, that's all." He smiled and shook his head. "A little rest and you will be heading off same as I am."

"What?!" I stammered, sitting up straight. "What do you mean—heading off? Are you leaving? Where are you going?"

"They have provided me with the means to finish my journey." he said proudly, then he paused, seeing the confusion on my face. "... To see my daughter in Nurnberg, remember? I have a grandson I would like to meet."

Of course, I had known all along; that had been the reason I had been asked to accompany Jacov in the first place—he had family to find, and they were expecting him. Somehow, I had buried in my mind the fact that our separation would be inevitable; it had felt refreshing to be needed by someone, and to have mattered to someone... at least for a little while.

"I'm... I'm happy for you, Jacov. Really, I am." I crawled out of bed, my feet cold on the hard floor, where the sun failed to reach. I held out my hand, determined to honor him with a proper sendoff.

"Well, thank you, Alfie." he replied, taking my hand and giving it a firm shake. He tipped his head to the side, his intense blue eyes penetrating my thoughts. "You will do just fine, Alfie. You have a good head on your shoulders, and a kind spirit. I wouldn't have made it without you. Thank you." He patted me kindly on the shoulder, adding, "I believe you have what it takes to put all of... this... behind you. Just keep your chin up, Alfie. And never stop looking for those you lost—keep them in your heart, and they will always be with you." He smiled warmly and it lit up his wise face. He jerked his head toward the door, saying, "My train is heading out soon. I expect to be on it. Take care, my boy... take care." He embraced me warmly, then he turned and left, his walking cane echoing loudly into the poignant stillness.

I simply nodded, at a loss for words, as I watched him walk proudly out the door, barely leaning on his walking stick. I remained rooted to the spot, the silence of the empty room pressing in around me. A wave of loneliness poured over me, so profound and sudden, I had to sit on the edge of my bed with my teeth clenched hard to contain my surging emotions.

"Ok." I thought fiercely, pinching my eyes tightly closed. "Ok, I'm alone... again, but I'm in a better place; the Americans will help me. If they helped Jacov, they will help me." I rubbed my tired eyes roughly with my hands, then ran my fingers through my hair which was, thankfully, finally free of tangles and lice. I was determined to remain positive. I had come so far; there had to be promise ahead.

Several days later, I had managed to retain two entire meals, and the medic finally allowed me a second helping. As I sat outside the mess tent, gnawing hungrily on a piece of toast, I looked up to see a man approaching from across the square.

His face was set and his eyes studied a slip of paper held tightly before him. He glanced up at me as he drew nearer and his concentrating features broke into an awkward smile.

"Good morning." he said, coughing slightly into his fist.

"Good morning." I replied, hesitantly. I wiped my hands on my pants, and set the remaining crust of bread onto my plate, anxious to continue my meal as soon as possible.

"Are you Alf Titze?" the man asked, his German clear and natural, his accent barely hinting of distant lands.

I blinked in surprise, then managed to stammer, "Alf?... Yes, yes, I'm... Alf." I slowly curled my tongue around the name, which rang pleasantly fitting and grown-up in my ears. "Why not?" I thought to myself. I was now alone, expected by those around me to navigate this postwar world on my own. After all, I was fourteen years old, and my future was ahead of me. "Yes, I am Alf." I repeated, staring vacantly into the man's expectant, but confused face.

"Ok." he said slowly, looking me over with a hint of concern. Then he continued, as if deciding he didn't want to puzzle out my peculiar behavior at the moment. "They have instructed me in the office to inform you that you are to be directed to an assembly camp in..." he paused, momentarily consulting the paper in his hand. "... Waldsassen, a town not far from here." he said. "There you will be processed, and your name entered into the system. The authorities there will then decide how to best proceed for your future."

I shook my head, startled, once more, by the sudden decisions being made on my behalf. "Waldsassen?" I asked, uncertainly. "Processed?" I whispered.

"It's procedure, you understand. Among other things, it is meant to help your family... any possible survivors, that is, trace you." he muttered, realizing too late that his comments might seem a trifle insensitive. But he charged on, maintaining his official demeanor to the last. "Uh, you will be provided with transportation. Across the square is the office. Please report there within the hour for your directions on how to proceed." He paused, fiddled with his stack of papers, then, pointing with his pen, he added, "It's just across the square."

I nodded, scowling slightly, and I picked up my plate, determined to complete my meal. He nodded too, though curtly, clearly reluctant to deviate from his assigned role as messenger. He wandered off, looking back at me several times. I wondered if he thought I was a bit dim; my reaction to his news had been muted, at best. But, my mind needed a moment to take in the ever changing paths of my life. I munched quietly on my toast, standing up only after I had licked every crumb from my fingers.

I crossed the narrow street, along one side of which ran the mess tent, and I rounded the corner. I stepped into the sunlit square heading for the office with a feeling of dread in my heart. The thought of being sent to another camp filled me with revulsion. But, I told myself with feigned conviction, it would certainly be better than all the others.

My thoughts were interrupted by a noisy flurry of approaching vehicles, most of them large military convoy trucks, though these were interspersed with an occasional small jeep. I paused at the edge of the sidewalk, wondering how I would navigate the loud belching trucks in my attempt to get to the office that lay diagonally across the wide square.

As I glanced up and down, debating what route would be safest, I spotted a very striking soldier standing fearfully close to the path of the oncoming vehicles. His arms were raised and he was directing the motorcade like a conductor with a baton. His skin was as black as the night and he was dressed in a dark green uniform trimmed in glaring white from head to toe. His helmet was white. It bore the letters, "MP", which identified him as a military policeman, one of the few I had seen since arriving among the Americans. His belt was also white, as was the shoulder strap that held his pistol within easy reach. In addition, he had on gloves of the same vivid color, and I marveled at how clean they were. Finally, even his shoes were encased in white wrappings. He looked, simply... incredible, like no one I had ever encountered before. Once again, I forgot Oma's mantra on politeness.

My jaw almost grazed my neck, as I gaped in awe. When the soldier's eyes met mine he gave me a smile that revealed teeth whiter and more brilliant than any I had seen all week. He chuckled to himself, sending my mouth snapping shut with embarrassment. Continuing to laugh, he rolled something around in his mouth, and I couldn't help staring, once again, out of uncontrollable childlike curiosity.

What was he eating, and how had I not seen him put it in his mouth? With one more wave at a large passing truck, he left his post in the traffic's relentless flow and walked pointedly in my direction. I gulped with sudden panic. How was I going to explain my provincial behavior? Approaching slowly, he reached into his breast pocket with one of his gloved hands and pulled out a narrow thin strip of paper.

I stepped back, wondering what mischief my curiosity had gotten me into this time. But he smiled even more widely and held the wrapped candy out for me to take. The wrapper was stiff and had the word, "Wrigley's", dancing invitingly across the length of it in bold letters.

He gestured broadly for me to open it, muttering something all the while in a very rapid English. I eased the fragrant strip into my mouth, folding it in half to fit. It was sweet and tangy, and it seemed determined to stick to my teeth as I gnawed on it with great effort. The candy refused to break apart, but as it was small enough, I swallowed it as it was, coughing slightly to push it down my throat.

Instantly, the soldier whooped a big booming laugh, and I jumped at the deep ringing bass tones that burst forth in his zeal. "No! No!" he said, shaking his head dramatically, as he indicated with his own piece that one was only supposed to chew it. He handed me another wrapped morsel and laughed again as it finally dawned on me what he had meant. I slipped the second thin strip into my mouth, this time being very careful to keep it from gravitating to the back of my tongue. My eagerness to fill my vacuous stomach made it difficult to resist the urge to swallow.

He nodded merrily. Still chuckling, he returned to his duties in the street. Catching his eye, I waved shyly. My mood lifting, I slipped through a gap between several large and slowly lumbering supply trucks. Weaving my way between the many rows of vehicles parked along the perimeter of the square, I realized, chewing happily, that the world held much for me to learn.

The place I had known as a child had done little to prepare me for the future that now lay before me. The world was changing, and the tide was sweeping the war's survivors, myself included, along for a very unpredictable ride. The nations of Europe were trying to find their places again after an upheaval that had threatened to destroy the very foundations of their civilizations. I knew, at that moment, that I would encounter, as would each and every person affected by the war, many new things along my path to adulthood. I knew that I had to approach every day with an open heart and an open mind. I gnawed the rubbery candy, mulling these thoughts over in my head, as I approached the office, ready to face my assigned future.

I received word at the office that I would be driven in two days' time to the nearby town of Waldsassen, in Bavaria. Therefore, I needed to be prepared and ready to depart at daybreak. On the appointed day, as the soldiers went about their morning rituals, I forced my weary body out of bed and plodded to the street corner on the square, my baggy, travel-worn rucksack slung upon my back.

The sun was barely toying with the treetops, and I longed to return to the relative comfort of my bunk. But, my future awaited, and I had been told that I must not be late. The Americans were kind and giving, but orders, they insisted, must be followed.

My mind whirled with the overload of information that the Americans had given me; they seemed determined to make sure I understood just how the world I was entering now stood. I had learned that Germany was seen as a broken and fouled land. Its sprawling beauty had once been the proclaimed pride and joy of Hitler, the passionate, yet diabolical dictator who had proceeded to methodically destroy the very nation he had promised to protect and enrich. Instead, they told me, he had used the desperation of Germany's downtrodden, as they strove to rejoin the world after the first World War, to advance his own twisted attempt to achieve a New World Order.

Upon his decisive defeat, Germany had been meticulously divided into four zones, each area now under the watchful control of the various victors. The inhabitants of Germany had been soundly reprimanded and criticized for their complacency and feigned ignorance during Hitler's scourging of Europe, which inevitably led to the millions of horrific atrocities, the truth of which had rapidly begun emerging upon the arrival of the Allies.

I recalled, with a shudder, the feeling of helplessness mingled with rage that had overwhelmed me at the sight of the small man, the Fuhrer. I remembered his dark mustache razing a blunt line across his weak mouth, as he spat his dreams for the land across the throbbing masses in my town. I had been so young, only six, but my untrained instincts, unknowingly, had warned me that the hysteria that had coursed through the crowd on that day, so long ago, had been something to fear. It had really been a wave of ignorance and desperation, not something driven by reason and mindfulness.

I remembered, also, the terrified faces peering out at me and my school mates from a waiting freight car, their voices rising to heaven in a plea not to be forsaken. They, too, I knew now, had been victims of Hitler's onslaught to such an extent, I acknowledged, that I could never truly comprehend.

It seemed, as I watched the golden sun rise higher into the morning's blue sky, that very few had escaped the ripple effect of the Fuhrer's attempt to achieve domination of the peoples of Europe. Ultimately, because of him, because of one demented man's greed and lust for power, I now stood alone, on a street corner, in a land I had never seen, about to embark on a journey that held little hope for me.

The guardians of this shattered country had been sworn to aid the humiliated nation as it struggled to rebuild, renew, and recover. Sending me to Waldsassen, I was told, fell under the heading of that broad authority. I was, as they graciously informed me, one of the millions of refugees swarming over the continent in search of loved ones and, subsequently, a meaningful life.

The American officers had finished by informing me, as they chuckled at my apparent good fortune, that Jacov and I had missed crossing into the zone controlled by the Russians by only several kilometers. I had had enough experience with the Russian version of renewal to know that I had most certainly had luck on my side that day… even if the Americans were now sending me away.

I stepped from the curb and headed toward my ride to my next home, Waldsassen.

The ride was indeed a short one, under an hour, and it was completed before the sun had properly heated the misty spring air. The soldier transporting me talked incessantly during the journey. Since I had yet to master English, it provided me with sufficient time for a brief rest. My good-natured companion left me at the gate of the camp, his reassuring smile only slightly boosting my resolve to step through the door to the overseer's office.

The hallway was pleasantly bright, and the windows managed to bring in some much needed fresh air, but still, the familiar taint of stale air drifted beneath my nose. The sound of voices made me pause, but I forced myself onward, heartened slightly by clearly understandable words issuing from beyond the door. I had been told very little of what to expect upon my arrival, but it was apparent that here the locals, with their Bavarian dialect very similar to my Austrian one, had been placed in control of the camps.

I wondered, as I raised my hand to knock, whether or not this would be in my favor.

I tapped firmly on the door and the conversation ceased. "Enter!" said one voice, in deep decadent tones, as though the speaker were trying out his new position of authority with great relish. I pushed the door ajar and stepped into a long cluttered office, its flaking pale green walls littered with maps and lists of names.

"Yes, what do you want?" barked a thin waspish man seated behind the large desk. Another man stood next to him and they seemed to be consulting a crumpled pile of papers. I hastily took in the disarray of the room, hoping that the man ran the camp in a more orderly fashion than he kept his office.

"Um… I am Alf Titze." I said, quietly, the new name still sounding foreign on my tongue. "Here… here is a letter." I added, stepping forward, and unfolding a paper I had been given at the American base. I held it before me, trying to keep my hand from trembling. The indifference in the man's bland face made me reluctant to continue.

He gestured to his companion to take the paper, and meanwhile, he leaned pompously back in his large chair to wait. The man, a secretary, I assumed, snatched the letter from my hand and twisted it around to place it upright in the man's outstretched and impatiently waiting fingers. I tried to remain calm, peering around the room with what I hoped appeared to be only a mild curiosity, instead of what it really was—a rising sense of dread.

"Sit down." the man drawled casually, his hand waving to me while his eyes grazed the letter slowly. "So, we have another young orphan, do we? You are from…" He consulted the paper, saying slowly, "… Jagerndorf?" He frowned, screwing up his long nose, as he peered at me over his lowered reading glasses. Instantly, I felt as though the man saw me as a nagging fly on a dish of food he was being forced to consume. "Where is that, exactly?" he managed to whine.

"It, uh… It is in the East… uh, sir. East of here, in Sudetenland." I tripped over my words, remembering that I still didn't really know where I had ended up, at least on a map.

He seemed satisfied with my vague answer, because he nodded, pursing his lips, as though trying to convince me that he understood completely. "You came by train, then?" he asked, glancing at the paper again.

"Um, not entirely." I let my voice trail off, wondering how I was going to explain the complicated sequence of events that had brought me so unexpectedly to his camp. But, he listened patiently, albeit with a slightly puzzled and incredulous expression on his face, as I floundered uncomfortably through the many turns my life had taken in the past year.

"Well," he answered, when I had completed my tale. "We will make a record of your arrival for the authorities who are in charge of networking displaced peoples. My job is to keep you fed and out of trouble. You will have a bed and ample food." He twisted his nose again, as though disgusted with something, as he continued, "There are others from your area, I believe. There are people from everywhere, really… too many of them." he muttered quietly, as he shoved my papers back across the desk. "You will be in the room at the top of the stairs. There is a family in there who will accommodate you just fine."

I stared in disbelief as his words tumbled from his mouth. This man was utterly ambivalent to my fate. I was simply a nuisance, something to be "processed" and filed away into the vast system, over which, I realized, he truly had very little control.

"That is all." he said, and his secretary pointed to the door behind me. I nodded, unable to answer. I stumbled backwards, suddenly desperate to breath some fresh air.

I leaned against the hallway wall and closed my eyes. I knew what it meant to be put with a family… instant anonymity and loneliness. I had experienced it before, but then, at least, I had had Gerle. Suppressing painful thoughts of my own family, I gritted my teeth, and I headed down the hall, deciding, if nothing else, that I could get some food. But, my week with the Americans had spoiled me. Here, the only path to a meal was a long, slowly moving line, and the reward for such patience was meager and foul.

After forcing down a thin rancid broth, I stumbled to my room, dodging sprawled legs along a dank narrow hallway. As I approached my assigned space I shuddered with the thought of having to face the stares and the taunts always reserved for a lone and unclaimed orphan. The room, instead, bustled so loudly with dozens of screaming children and wildly gesticulating adults, that my presence went fairly unnoticed. I found a vacant bunk which was at the top, where I hoped the rats, with their diseased yellow teeth and their scabby naked tails, would not bother to forage.

I slithered between the thin blankets, cursing angrily under my breath at the vermin that already seemed to be making my skin itch and tingle. "So much for the recovery of a nation." I thought bitterly. "It seems only the rodents and lice can survive a war." I rolled over to face the stained wall. Trying to block out the relentless din surrounding me, I prayed for a dreamless sleep.

CHAPTER 26

O nce again, life had become a monotonous grind. The hours of each day were consumed by long waits in food lines and lonely vigils in my miserable bunk. The school building that had been set aside for the assembly camp was large, but it was already filled beyond capacity. Additional refugees swarmed into town daily in search of a new beginning.

Languages and dialects, both familiar and foreign, whirled around me, as people from all the reaches of Europe mingled loudly in their desperate attempts to track missing loved ones. I searched among the crowds each day for anyone who hailed from the same region as I, but my efforts were met with only sad denials or blatant dead ends.

So, I sank, once more, into the numb trance that had enabled me to survive the endlessly depressing routine of the work farm. Here, at least, our time was our own.

We were not herded into fields to plant and harvest food that we would never eat. Rather, the hours stretched before us, with little choice as to how to occupy each lonely moment. But, the void this aimless and inactive existence created was almost more than I could bare. The family with whom I had been placed treated me like the many forms of vermin that crept among the hordes of countless unclean bodies—a nuisance who had to be tolerated. They spoke to me rarely, and at these moments it was only to shout at me insolently about taking up too much space.

I spent as little time as necessary, therefore, in the bunk room. Instead, I lingered near the food line, waiting, with bated breath and a rumbling stomach, until the next pathetic offering. Food, it appeared, was still scarce. It seemed, at the very least, that if more were available, very little of anything decent trickled down through the system to the refugees, who were clearly at the bottom of the very ragged and tenuous social hierarchy.

The makeup of the line for food consisted of, for the most part, patient dazed individuals, who shuffled along quietly until they were handed their small plate of tepid food. But there were also the occasional unruly loud people, who felt they deserved more than their allotted share. Scuffles often erupted among the more brazen women, many of whom had large groups of hungry children to feed. I found myself, quite often, therefore, accosted by several frantic mothers, competing for my share of the bread or cheese. It became painfully clear to me, that being alone made me more vulnerable among the group. No one ever defended me.

On one such day, I had fended off their challenges to my scant servings, and I had sat down in a corner to eat my meal. It consisted of a very dry slice of bread and a piece of pale cheese, which, to the naked eye, appeared significantly aged. Its rind was trimmed with a rim of rancid yellow slime, and furry blotches of mold were erupting from its numerous small holes. But, my hunger was such that I didn't care, so I greedily tore it into two small chunks. Instantly, nausea replaced my zeal for nourishment. The cheese reeked and all but steamed a fetid cloud of decay. The insides of the cheese crawled with small white worms, their tiny brown heads writhing and twisting blindly from being disturbed.

The deplorable condition of the cheese did little to deter the hovering women though, who sprang upon my discarded pieces as soon as I set them aside. I watched with revulsion as the women mingled together, picking the frantic worms from the crumbling remnants of my meal, just as monkeys groom each other for insects.

The camp truly had begun to resemble a colony of animals. People milled around, their restless energy lacking focus, as they eyed each other with distrust. The hierarchy in the food line became increasingly rigid. Children ran unchecked and unfettered throughout the long dark hallways, urinating in corners and howling like beasts. During their rare quiet moments, they rocked back and forth, their eyes glazed with an alarming vacancy. Clearly, they were unaccustomed to being so overwhelmed with boredom and worry.

Sleep was my only true escape. When I succeeded in shutting out my troublesome surroundings through these stolen moments of rest, I was able to visit numerous happy and sustaining memories, and the harsh realities could, for the moment, be forgotten. This assumed, of course, that I managed to navigate the many perils that lurked within my own mind, many of which were, admittedly, far from pleasant. Images swirled through my fragmented dreams, fighting for prominence. Some lulled me into a much needed state of calm, and others forced me awake, where I lay upon my narrow bunk, shivering beneath a cold sweat.

But, I quickly learned that my greatest enemy was loneliness. I soon realized that being an orphan meant that I was, for the most part, passed over with little more than a glance. I began to feel as though I had been written off as an irrelevant byproduct of the war—an individual, it seemed, not worth rescuing, and certainly not worth transferring to a location with more promise for a smooth return to society.

I had noticed that the assortment of families in my room changed often, with few staying for very long. The camp was, in effect, a holding station, where aimless souls awaited the promise of greener pastures. The authorities transferred hundreds of people to and fro every day between the dozens of camps scattered across Germany, as they attempted to achieve a grand disbursement of the millions of people displaced by the war.

At first, noble endeavors were made to reestablish a refugee in his original home in his prewar nation, but the nature of the war was such that very few places existed as they had before the fighting had begun. Entire villages had been destroyed, their only legacies being the many unidentified, rotting corpses buried hastily in mass graves along the roadsides and the silhouettes of the skeletal remains of people's homes and businesses. Enough time had passed that new families had moved in and taken the remaining houses and town squares as their own, claiming them, in a sense, as the justifiable spoils of war.

The authorities soon learned, therefore, that homes would have to be found elsewhere for the many homeless individuals now overtaxing the camp system. The locals saw the refugees as highly undesirable neighbors, envisioning them as threats to the recovery of Germany.

Nonetheless, I was aware of the steady movement of individuals and families out of the camp, and I grew hopeful that I could be sent to a more promising place, one with a better possibility of finding my lost loved ones.

Thus, I wandered into the office one afternoon with this in mind, also partly hoping for concrete news of my family. But, instead I found myself met with practiced rhetoric and marked indifference.

"You must understand, young man, that it is necessary to have a destination available in order for us to follow through on any relocation." The man's thin face appeared even more pinched and drawn then when I had arrived several weeks before, as he glared at me across his lowered glasses. "Since you do not know the location of your family, and there is no one else to… claim you, we simply cannot move you. Others take priority… others with relatives to take them in." He sneered and returned to shuffling the many papers that lay strewn across his cluttered desk.

I wondered, as I stood there, if the names of anyone I knew had gone unnoticed in that mess, but I realized that raising the point would be sheer folly. The man was clearly overwhelmed with his assigned task, with the number of desperate refugees increasing every day. Most likely, any mention of potentially overlooked names would do little to help my case.

"Thank you, sir. Just… if anything comes up, anything at all…" My voice trailed off as he pursed his lips tightly and blinked coldly. I knew then, that my pleas had fallen on deaf ears.

"Yes. You may go back to your room. You don't want to miss the meal line up, now do you?" he hissed, clearly not caring if I did.

I shuffled sadly into the corridor, not eager to return to the chaos of my room. I leaned against the cool wall, relishing the relative stillness of the hallway. I reached into my pocket and fiddled with the few coins that the overseer had given to me at the farm, wondering what use they would ever serve. Movement outside the camp was not encouraged, anyone with refugee status caught without identifying papers would find their chances at relocation severely compromised. Besides, even with a pocket full of money, there was little or nothing to buy.

Supplies were trickling very slowly across the borders, and stores had been slow to reopen, as many of the successful businesses had been run by the Jewish inhabitants of the towns. They, of course, like many others, had failed to return to their homelands; their fates more in question than any other victims of the war. Besides, stores that had managed to open had little to offer with their display cases, most often, sitting empty.

I knew, as I stood in the quiet darkness of the hallway, that few of the food provisions that had managed to find their way to the town, would end up on our small and dented tin plates. But, even with the knowledge of the camp's pathetic offerings in mind, I decided to bide the moments remaining until meal time in the food line, my brain being too rattled to find any rest in the noisy bunk room.

The school yard was warm and the air thick with the summer's first flies. The quickly rotting food attracted many small creatures, none of whom made the cramped, walled yard more inviting. I stood at the end of the line, bracing myself for yet another long wait.

After almost a month in the small town of Waldsassen, my requests for attention were acknowledged, albeit begrudgingly. I was to be sent away, much to the obvious pleasure of the overseer. As I boarded the crowded truck that was to take me to the train station, his twisted sneer widened into a genuine grin, which did little to improve the charm of his narrow, hawk-like face.

His condescending drivel played continuously in my head, as I watched his face fade into the distance. "I did everything I could for you, young man, and I will graciously accept your thanks for my prompt attention to your interests. I am sure you didn't realize I was looking out for you so well, did you?" Whoever had provided for my transfer, I didn't know, but I sincerely felt that he had had very little to do with it.

I watched the hills around the town fade into the haze of the warm afternoon, while the train trundled toward my newest hope for a future. I was headed to Weissenburg, in Bavaria, where an old fortress above the town had been converted into one of the many assembly camps. My curiosity at the possibility of living in an old castle briefly outweighed my anxiety at heading into another unknown.

We reached our goal in the late afternoon, and soon the large stone towers of the fortress, called locally, the "Wulzburg", loomed above us, as the truck slowly wound its way up the hill overlooking the city. The fortress's position above the valley had been well chosen. Travelers from bygone eras would have been spotted very quickly as they approached from afar. The many narrow windows that surrounded the tops of the tall towers provided clear views in all directions across the wide valley.

A large open arch led into a long courtyard, with several doors on either side concealing the various chambers and turrets. I followed quietly behind a chattering family of youngsters, confident I would get lost in the mix, and perhaps, as a result, win over a decent bunk… high off the floor, of course.

Once out of the warm sunlight of the courtyard, the dampness of the ancient stone walls closed in around us, wrapping our thin bodies in a penetrating chill. My mind filled suddenly with images of whirling snow and clammy stone passages, and I thanked the wheels of power that had brought me here at the height of summer. I tried not to allow myself to think of the disturbing possibility that I might still be here when the leaves began to fall, or when the biting winds of winter began to blow.

We were led up a narrow winding stairway, its stagnant air stale and thin from years of relentless moisture and the elements. The living quarters to which we were led were little better. The air was cold, and it seemed the light that blazed beyond the thin mullioned windows rarely penetrated to the room's dark interior. Several rows of straw-covered bunks had been installed along the walls of the room, and there was a sudden frenzy of activity as people rushed forward to claim the most coveted places.

This time, there seemed to be more to consider than the likelihood of rats. It was apparent to everyone that the somber chill hanging in the air would have to play a role in where one chose one's bunk. Therefore, I scrambled frantically past several small boys and nimbly climbed to a third row bed, well away from the drafty windows. Despite the prime position, the bed left little to be desired. The straw was old, the stale pieces crisp and dry, and they poked uncomfortably at my legs as I sat upon my bunk to survey my latest surroundings.

Already, I was receiving nasty stares from many of the other refugees, clearly over my success at obtaining a relatively decent spot to call home. The room filled up quickly, and I thought, with a tinge of bitterness, that the presence of so many bodies would at least serve to warm the air on the long cold nights.

The overseer, a slight and balding fellow, seemed to cower nervously in anticipation of the inevitable strife among his many charges. His voice shook anxiously as he led us to another courtyard, where several rows of small outhouses had been hastily tacked together. It seemed, at least, that we would not be faced with an open latrine.

"Meals will be in the main hall, located at the bottom of the north tower." he muttered, his frail voice barely audible over the whines of the hungry children.

Once again, I sank into the endless routine of survival, my main enemies being, as always, boredom and loneliness. Food was only marginally more satisfactory than at the previous camp, but for the time being fewer refugees were present with whom to share the rations.

The biggest worry soon became obvious. On my first night in the sleeping chamber I realized that I would have to brave the cold and dark of the winding tower staircase to make my hasty way to the latrine. Tiptoeing between the sleeping rows of bodies, my ears absorbed the many eerie sounds of the vast old building. The narrow staircase loomed darkly below as I began my careful descent. Only two small bulbs hung at great distances along the stone wall, their dim glow hissing in the dampness of the ancient space. My shadow loomed long and ghoulishly before me as I groped my way downward, marveling with every tentative step at the surprising distance to the bottom.

A sudden brush of something soft against my bare ankle sent me leaping backwards, and I stumbled several steps forward, only preventing a fall by catching my hand on a protruding stone. I struggled to focus my weary eyes on the steps below me, and to my horror, I saw several fat and fearless rats scrambling up the stairs out of the darkness directly toward me. I stepped to the wide part of the stairs, allowing a clear path for the foul beasts to go around me. They ignored me entirely, clearly set on a specific goal... "Children's ankles." I thought grimly. Their naked pink tails slapped grotesquely on each step as they wound their way upward, staying as close to the inside of the spiral as possible.

As they disappeared into the gloom, I turned and hastened onward, being careful to navigate the stairs at their widest point, which seemed to be relatively free of the nasty creatures. I was ready to return to my bed, pathetic as it was; the chill of the castle had begun to seep beneath my skin. I despaired at how little of the mild midsummer night air managed to reach the inner haunts of the fortress. It seemed the stone bastions kept out more than just intruders.

The charm of a medieval stronghold quickly wore off. The discomfort experienced in such primitive housing soon engulfed any momentary fascination I had had with my surroundings. The continuous arrival of refugees gave the relentless rats more succulent flesh from which to choose, as bunks quickly became overcrowded.

I tried to distract myself by exploring the hidden corners of the sprawling stone building, and it served to briefly occupy my time. More often than not, though, my thoughts rested on my friends; all of whom, I knew, would have enjoyed an uninterrupted romp through the many curious passages of the building. I knew that without the war to spoil its purpose, this building would have been fascinating to many a child as a place of wonder and discovery, a rare chance to sit in history's lap and contemplate its significance. But I quickly tired of the fortress's allure, and instead, saw nothing but its detriments, all monumental in making life unpleasant.

I longed for activity. My mind reeled from stagnation and lack of stimulation. So, I was mildly curious when I was summoned one morning, after a fortnight in the camp, to the overseer's office. I followed the rambling directions to the letter, and still had to ask my way twice in order to end up at his door. His office looked out upon a small private courtyard, where several large shrubs were awash with blossoms, beneath which the paths were delightfully free of crowds and litter. I gazed longingly upon its peaceful space, until I realized the overseer was quietly contemplating me.

"Oh! I'm sorry, sir… um, you asked to see me?" I queried, awkwardly, puzzling over what possible twist of fate was in store for me now.

"Yes." the overseer answered softly. The short time on his job had clearly not been enough for him to feel confident with his new authority. He still spoke as though on the verge of a heartfelt apology. I wondered what this diminutive man had made of his life before the war. Perhaps he had sold flowers, perhaps he had been a baker. But, regardless of his past, he seemed decidedly uncomfortable in his present surroundings.

"Yes." he repeated, shuffling through some neat stacks of paper on his desk. "It has come to my attention that you are an orphan. Is that correct?" He gazed at me with calm eyes and I fought to read beyond his mild detached demeanor.

"Um… yes. I am looking for my family. Have you had any news?" I blurted eagerly, approaching the desk anxiously. He seemed to start at my sudden motion, so I stopped and forced my arms to my sides.

"No, no. I'm sorry. There is nothing." he answered, his voice laden with a heavy weight, as though he felt the personal need to defend my family's absence. "No. But, I believe it would be to your advantage…" he paused, uncertainly, and consulted his papers again. "How old are you?"

"Oh. I'm fourteen, sir, fourteen last March." I answered, wondering where these questions were headed.

"Ah, yes… Fourteen. Well, you are now of the age to make your own way a little in this world." he said, then added quickly, "Oh! don't worry. You are not being expelled from the camp. Not at all. But you are of the age to begin the process of earning some money to help you return to society… while you await the results of the search for your parents."

"Grandparents. My parents are dead" I muttered, softly.

"Oh, yes, sorry… grandparents." he stuttered, clearly at a loss for words. "So!" he exclaimed, with sudden surprising zeal. "… So, you need to head to the Youth Social Office in the town, and they will provide you with a vocation that suits you."

I stared at him silently, my own words now failing me. He blinked at me quietly, then resumed the study of his papers. "Here are the directions to the office." he said, handing me a small slip of paper. "And here are the necessary papers for you to give to the office manager." He handed me another bundle of neatly tied papers.

"Sir, um… do you have any idea what kind of work they will have me do?" I asked, remembering my brief, but unpleasantly memorable stint in the brick yards at home.

"No, that is up to them. It depends, mostly, on what there is a demand for, you see." he answered, standing, finally, and awkwardly holding out his hand. "If word is found of your… grandparents, you will be contacted."

I shook his hand, muttered a hasty, "Thank you," and left. I navigated the maze back to the bunk room without truly realizing where I wandered.

Once again, I had been handed my "papers"—instructions as to what path my life was to now follow. I felt a renewal of helplessness, as though my fate continued to be decided by every force in the vast world but my own volition. Yet, I was to be handed a job, my first paying job, and the resulting money would be my own. I knew in my heart, though, that the amount would be minimal and nowhere near enough to begin a life in which I could decide my own future. I was aware that I was still quite young. This was painfully apparent each night as I forced the agonizing images of my loved ones from my mind, so I could fall into a fitful sleep.

I hastened to my bunk and, ignoring the curious stares of my neighbors, I trussed up the tie on my small trusty rucksack, and I slithered quickly back to the floor. Before leaving the crowded room, I watched several people already eyeing each other suspiciously. I was confident that my bunk would not remain vacant for long.

For the first time in the two long weeks since my arrival, I walked out the expansive front doors of the fortress and followed the route directed to me by the overseer. A wide dirt path led through the trees and pitched gradually downward toward the city in the valley. The forest smelled sweet and refreshing after the damp moldy air of the stone castle. Small animals broke the silence with busy chirps and twitters as they went about their active day of gathering and feeding.

I breathed deeply, relishing in the crispness of the afternoon air. Summer was well under way, and normally the heat in the air would have been oppressive, but I found it exhilarating and new. I glimpsed the city below me, spread out in a colorful grid at the bottom of the wide valley. Realizing my brisk pace would have me at the Youth Office very quickly, I slowed to a meander, determined to enjoy the solitude of the tree-lined path for as long as possible.

Eventually, though, despite my lingering walk, I arrived at the edge of the town, and I turned my face back toward the hill to see how far I had wandered. Only the tips of the tallest towers on the fortress were visible above the dense summer foliage, and the path disappeared into the dark woods behind me. For a moment it reminded me of the thick overgrown woods around home, the trees towering above the valley's floor.

I returned to the papers I had been given, and I consulted the small slip with the directions. The man's descriptions depended upon me knowing something about the town in the first place, and since I had only experienced it from the back of a rickety truck two weeks prior, I was at a complete loss as to which way to go. So, I headed toward what looked like the main square, convinced I would find someone there who could direct me to my destination. After encounters with two surly individuals, each of whom clearly did not want to be talking to, let alone assisting, a lowly refugee, I finally received the desired directions.

I found my way to the large city office building, its imposing metal doors revealing a rat's nest of tiny offices. I wandered through the wide halls for several minutes, in awe of the cavernous corridors, until a secretary confronted me with a scowl.

"Young man! What are you looking for?" she asked, her lips compressed tightly and her gray hair in a taut bun against her head. "The Youth Office, I imagine?"

"Uh, yes, please." I answered, trying on my sweetest smile.

"Just to the left, then the third door on right." she answered, already hastening away from me in the opposite direction, her hands busily sorting papers as she walked.

I followed the brief directions and quickly found myself outside a black door, the top half of which was covered with a frosted pane of glass. The words, "Youth Services" were scripted on a small dusty placard alongside the door, and the rusty knob shook as I knocked.

Silence answered me, though I thought I could discern the clatter of typewriter keys from the room beyond. Finally, after I inflicted several more significantly louder knocks upon the decrepit door, a deep grumbling voice barked, "Enter!"

I paused for a moment, bracing myself for what would surely be another encounter with the stiff hand of authority. Then, I carefully turned the old knob, its base wobbling precariously against the peeling wood of the door, and I entered the office.

Immediately, a large cloud of smoke engulfed me, and I coughed. The sickly smell of tobacco wafted throughout the room, coating it in layers of fresh smoke over stale. Behind a vast desk sat a man, his gray hair blending with the bland swirl of smoke encircling his head. In his hand he held a drooping cigarette; several more smoldered in an overflowing ashtray on a bookshelf behind him.

"Yes! Step forward, young man. What do you want?" he growled, puffing deeply on his cigarette, and coughing loudly into a soiled handkerchief he had clutched in his other hand. His small eyes peered at me curiously but patiently from beneath the blue haze, and he seemed ready to wait for me to come to grips with my voice, which had suddenly gone very hoarse.

"Um, yes, I was sent here by the director of the Wulzburg refugee camp. He said you would find me some… work… sir." I muttered, shifting my rucksack to the other shoulder, purely out of nervousness; it was too light too be cumbersome.

He coughed violently into the crook of his arm and muttered something I couldn't understand. Then, he stared at me intently, as though he were trying to test my metal. Suddenly, he rotated on his vast chair and sent it swiveling to a shelf behind him, where a large file box stood on a shelf.

"What do you want to be when you grow up, anyway, kid?" he muttered, his voice muffled from within the large box.

"Wh... What?" I stuttered, completely unprepared for such a question. I had spent the last few years just struggling to survive. I had given very little thought to the future beyond my goal of reuniting myself with my family and Gerle. After all, what would I be capable of handling? My school career had been grossly interrupted, as had everything else in my life, and my skills for managing the daily chores of life remained to be determined. "I, uh... I guess, perhaps a mechanic... or maybe a radio operator comes to mind, but..."

"Well, nothing along those lines today." he interrupted, his vast hand gripping several cards. "We have these openings: two gardeners, a cook, a baker, and a butcher's apprentice." He took a deep breath and erupted into another fit of coughing. When he had recovered and had wiped the spit off his chin with his sleeve, he considered me again for a moment. I felt sure my face clearly revealed my feelings about the choices he had laid out so eloquently.

"Uh, perhaps...." He rummaged some more in his box, finally pulling out one more card. This he glanced at briefly, then he handed it across the desk to me. The smoke curled languidly up beneath the card, and the motion of my hand to grasp it served to disperse the thin white wisps into the greater cloud hovering near the ceiling.

"Report there this afternoon." he said, his voice full of finality. He leaned back in his chair and commenced to puffing contentedly on his latest cigarette. "That's all. Best of luck to you." he muttered. "It is just down the road... a large stone building off the square... You can't miss it." he added, dismissively.

"Thank you." I muttered, wondering what fate he had handed me with so much indifference. I backed out the door, fingering the, as yet, unread card in my hand, as though it were a grenade about to explode. My palms had begun to sweat, and my head whirled nervously, while I closed the door upon the dizzying smoke.

313

In the hallway, I had to squeeze against the wall to allow two men to pass, and their gazes fell knowingly upon me as I stood anticipating the next cog on the turbulent track to the future. By the sickening glow of the buzzing light just above me I glanced finally at the small card that shook in my trembling hands. It read, "Brauerei Lehrling"— "Brewery Apprentice".

I stared at the words for several moments, my mind completely blank, then I laughed bitterly to myself, as I realized the man had cared little what my answer had been to his query about my future desires. I doubted he had even heard. Now, I was headed for employment in a brewery—something I had never, in my wildest dreams, considered. Frankly, I had given very little thought as to how I would earn my way as an adult… it had always seemed so far away. Today, I would face my first major test at navigating my own path in a world governed by injustice and mired with constant pitfalls. With sudden resolve, I decided that I would face it with my head held high.

CHAPTER 27

A dogged determination had replaced the nervousness and uncertainty that had shrouded my mood for most of the morning. As I wandered about the narrow streets of the old town, I fingered the stiff card that still smelled of the stale smoke from the man's office. It was midday, and there was a mounting bustle of activity as the townsfolk slowly dispersed for their luncheon hour. I felt it was too early to make my way to the brewery, so I meandered among the wandering people, each of whom was as absorbed in their own thoughts as I.

Approaching the main square, I found myself increasingly jostled and bumped by the milling crowd as they searched through the limited offerings in the dusty shop windows. A delicious smell of freshly baked bread wafted across the street on the warm summer breeze. I jerked my head eagerly about, determined to find the source of the tantalizing odor.

My hand reached for the coins still jingling temptingly in my large pocket, and I pulled them out into the pale light of the afternoon. The silver of the large Reichsmarks sparkled beneath the hazy glare of the sun, and I thought sadly of how little the grossly devalued currency would now buy me. "I should at least be able to find some of that bread." I thought, following my eager nose around the corner of a small brick building at the far end of the square. A large plate glass window revealed an admirable array of freshly baked loaves of breads, some curled and braided, some black as pitch. In the middle of the display sat a basket with several firm golden rolls remaining in the bottom.

Clearly, the proprietor of the shop was doing a brisk business, one of the few prospering in the town. "Probably bread made from wheat picked by the likes of me." I thought, bitterly. But my feelings of indignation faded as the thought of being able to make my very first purchase with my own money. My stomach rumbled noisily in agreement, and I walked into the bright interior, eyes locked on my target.

I soon emerged clutching two crusty rolls in my hands, the diminished stash of surviving coins, once again, banished back to my pocket. Eating slowly to prolong the flavor of the fresh bread, I headed finally in the direction the man had instructed. Wandering only a short distance, I easily found the imposing building of the brewery on a narrow street just off the main square. I hastened to finish my meal, my reemerging nerves making the last few bites disappointing and easily forgettable. I knew I was early for my first day, but it seemed that waiting for my new life to unfold was more of a strain than facing its inevitability.

I tapped quietly on the heavily carved oak door. After a moment, I realized I couldn't possibly have been heard through the thick wood, so I knocked again, this time more loudly. Shuffling uncomfortably on the wide landing, I stared over my shoulder at the regular stream of people strolling along the narrow street. They glanced at me in passing, their eyes full of suspicion and distrust, having successfully marked me as a lowly refugee. After seconds, which to me felt like time streamed out into eternity, the heavy lock on the door began to turn noisily, and the vast door swung away with a creak, revealing a dark and dusty hallway.

Mingling with the gloom of the passage, loomed the large figure of a man, his stooped shoulders doing little to diminish his great height. His small gray eyes glittered behind his thick glasses as he blinked from the shadows of his burrow into the sunlight of the afternoon.

"Yes, what is it? What do you want?" he asked, his voice curious but not unkind. He shielded his eyes with his large sun-spotted hand and peered down at me beneath random wisps of graying hair. He wore a long white apron over his clothes, which were covered with a pale thin dust.

"Um… um… I'm the new apprentice." I gulped, suddenly feeling very small and insignificant. I held out the card from the Youth Office, noticing with dismay that, in my anxiety, I had crumpled it slightly. I longed to make a good first impression, so I smoothed the bent creases hastily before placing it into his outstretched hand.

"That's all right." he said, a trace of amusement toying with the deep wrinkles around his eyes. He turned slightly and yelled suddenly over his shoulder, "Erna, our apprentice is here!" His loud voice grated like gravel along the hall, and I swallowed hard in spite of myself. This man was to be my boss and I had yet to take proper measure of him. He seemed kind enough, but his size was imposing, and I sensed that he demanded respect.

The hallway behind the man filled with another, slowly approaching, figure—a slight elderly woman who appeared very small beside her tall husband. Her face was gentle and round, with high cheekbones that hinted at long-faded, once youthful beauty. Emerging into the light of the crowded doorway, she hastily wiped her hands on her flowered apron, then took my hand between both of hers and gave it a warm shake.

"Welcome." she said kindly, in a voice both light and airy, reflecting refinement and a schooled knowledge of courtesies. "Please come in, young man. What is your name?"

"Alf... Frau?..." I stammered in surprise, taken aback by her politeness. I had become so accustomed to brisk tones that words of kindness felt alien to me now.

"Call me Frau Erna, dear." she replied, her smile widening, as she released my hand gently. "Alf... that's a fine name. How old are you, Alf?" she asked, glancing at the card in her husband's hand.

"I'm fourteen... fifteen next March." I answered, with a sudden desire to stick out my chest, to prove how old I really was.

"That's wonderful. You can call my husband, Herr Herman. Why don't you come in? We don't need to keep standing here in the doorway, now do we?" she asked, with a gentle laugh.

"Yes, come in, young man. Come in." said Herr Herman. He turned and headed along the passage, which grew dark for a moment, while his bulk sealed off the flow of light.

"I'm sure you must be hungry, yes?" asked Frau Erna, leading me along behind her husband. We reached the large room that was the kitchen, and I was surprised to find another old man sitting at the table. He had one hand wrapped around a large mug of frothy beer and, with the other hand, he was shoveling fragrant food into his mouth from a heaping plate.

"Um... thank you, that would be wonderful." I answered, tearing my eyes away from the new face, and more importantly, from the delicious looking food. Frau Erna was gazing at me in wonder and amusement, her face clearly full of many questions, but she thankfully spared me the interrogation, and instead introduced me to the man at the table. "This is Willhelm. He is another laborer here at the brewery. He will help you if you have any questions. This is Alf, Willhelm." she said, nodding her head at me.

"Hello." muttered Willhelm, not bothering to pause in his eating. A large drop of gravy glistened on his grizzled chin, and he wiped it casually with his sleeve. Clearly, the arrival of the new apprentice did not rank very high on his ladder of importance. I nodded in return, trying not to stare at each dripping spoonful of mouthwatering stew, as it hung, poised and ready until Willhelm cleared a space for it in his overstuffed mouth.

"Well…" said Frau Erna. "I will see about some lunch for you, Alf, then we can show you to your room."

I nodded in continued amazement, unable to find words to match my jumbled thoughts. I was to be served lunch, a meal I had gotten used to going without for so long. Then, I was going to be given a room… not just a bed or a space in some basement corner with the rats, but a real room. Life had certainly taken another unexpected turn, and I wondered, for a moment, what my family would think if they could see me now.

A small shudder of guilt trembled through me as my mind flew to Gerle. My last memory of my dear friend was the sound of his heartbreaking sobs as I had walked away from him in the town square, on that awful day so long ago. Each mournful breath of his as it had burst forth with despair had haunted me for months. Was he well? Was he even alive?… Would I ever know? Did he think of me kindly, as a brother lost, never to be forgotten, but to be found again some distant day? Or… did he remember only that I had left him crying bitterly for me, the only remaining constant in his life? Was I ready to live with that unanswered question? It had tormented me every day since we had been separated, and it tormented me now, as I sat upon my own bed in a quiet tidy room under the eaves, my stomach full of nourishing food.

Frau Erna had made sure I had received several helpings of her thick rich stew, with abundant slices of warm bread to soak up the dark gravy at the very bottom of my bowl. I had walked away from the table content and full.

As I peered about my room, a charming space near the top of the tall building, I struggled with the waves of dizziness engulfing me as I came to terms with my first encounter with beer in any significant quantity. Frau Erna had served me a large mug of ale. The sides of the gray crock had been slippery with the overflowing suds. It had been bitter, yet strangely satisfying, and as rich as any full-course meal.

Of course, I had sampled Opa's and Uncle Alois's beers many times at the tavern as a youngster, but my education had been limited to several sips at each sitting. Now, I knew, as I fought a large bubble mounting in the pit of my overfed stomach, that I would have to get used to the beer, where here, at the source of its creation, it ran as freely as water.

I rubbed my hands vigorously across my tingling face, determined to be lucid enough for my first tour of the brewery. Herr Herman had passed through the kitchen, adjusting his long apron for another busy afternoon of overseeing the meticulous process that transformed his master brew into the coveted local drink of choice. I knew I needed a clear head to take in the many instructions that would be thrown my way. Herr Herman had left me little doubt that he intended to work me hard.

"You will learn the techniques of fine beer-making, a craft that will serve you well in your promising future." he insisted, his eyes glittering with a contagious passion. I did not want to disappoint my new benefactors. A warm clean bed and regular meals to look forward to each day made me very ready to give the life as a brewery apprentice my full energy and attention.

An hour later, I stumbled along behind Herr Herman through winding passages that smelled strongly of roasted barley and sweet pungent molasses. My headache had faded slightly, but the close spaces and the heady odors revived it, as I struggled to focus on my new boss's rapid narrative.

"Now, Alf. This, too, will be one of your tasks." he said, his wide hand pointing toward the narrow staircase leading to the vast cellar system beneath the building. "The beer, of course, is stored in barrels, each of which needs proper sterilizing after it is emptied and before it can be reused." He nodded proudly, as though I should be thrilled at what was coming next. "That is where you come in. You will scrub out each barrel thoroughly, preparing it for the next batch of beer. Got that?" he asked, gesturing for me to follow.

I nodded dumbly, wondering what the inside of a beer barrel looked like. We finally returned to the kitchen, its large oven steadily burning to cook the perpetual meal that seemed always to be in the process of preparation. In spite of having eaten several servings of the delicious noontime meal, I polished off a hearty portion of the succulent roast that sizzled before us on the large oak table. Clearly, the brewmaster's high social position in the town had made such an unusually extravagant supper possible. Herr Herman and Frau Erna talked quietly between themselves, discussing the day's affairs. This left me to my thoughts, while I plowed through several servings of the delicious meat.

Supper ended peacefully, and I excused myself with many exclamations of thanks, before meandering my way to my room at the top of the two flights of stairs. The sloping walls glowed warmly beneath the soft light from the sconce near the door. I lay upon my bed, very tired, but my mind too much in flux for sleep to come. Beneath heavy eyelids, I watched the moon trip along neighboring rooftops and dance a graceful arc across the glowing night sky.

Somewhere out there, I thought, Gerle, Oma, Opa, and my baby sister were looking at the same moon… or at least I had to hope they were. Was I now the only one watching from the comfort of a real bed? Were they still suffering in subhuman conditions, while I slept in warmth and security? How had fate twisted in such a random fashion to place me here… and every one else I cared for, so far away?… Were they lying awake thinking the same thoughts as I?… It gave me a mild comfort to think that they were.

In spite of my restless night, I awoke refreshed and ready for my first day as an apprentice. Breakfast turned out to be as promising as the rest of the meals, and I took full advantage of the table's bounty. Herr Herman allowed me a second helping of eggs before reminding me that my first task as the apprentice was to sweep the rambling courtyard that was bordered by the three buildings in the large brewery complex.

"You will find the broom near the waste basin by the back door. Make sure you do a decent job." he said, though his strict words were paired with a small wink. I nodded solemnly, anxious to please on my first day— the courtyard would be spotless after I was through.

Later, just as I was leaning the broom back into its corner, Herr Herman's large shape appeared behind me, his shadow massive in the long morning light. The air was crisp and tinged with the zesty essence of autumn, but my body felt warm and invigorated from the activity. I was ready for my next chore.

"Now, Alf, I want you to restack those piles of crates." he said, pointing into a dark corner of the wide yard. "They need to be placed— neatly, mind you, into rows, three high, near the doors to the cellar, over there." he continued, his hand swinging across to the opposite side of the yard.

I glanced into the shadows, the bright light of the sun coaxing my eyes closed against its brilliance. I saw a large pile of jumbled boxes stacked recklessly almost to the roof line. I sighed quietly, realizing sadly that actual beer-making must be relegated to the bottom of the list of apprentice duties.

"Now get busy, my boy. Frau Erna will have a wonderful lunch ready soon." Herr Herman said, chuckling, as he thumped me merrily on the shoulders before heading off to the cellars for the daily inspection of the newest brews. Clearly, Herr Herman was well aware of the power of his wife's kitchen to inspire his workers.

I labored methodically, slowly transferring the crates across the wide yard. The wooden boxes were cumbersome and heavier than they had looked, and by the time Frau Erna called me for lunch, my back and arms were aching. I thought, bitterly, as I washed my hands at the pump in the yard, that months of poor conditions in the camps had reeked havoc upon my growing body. At a time when I should have been thriving and developing the strength of an adult, I was, instead, struggling to simply keep ample flesh on my weakened bones. My muscles were thin and tired, and I had limited stamina for the many hours of work.

The long day's labor wore heavily on me, and by the time I trudged up the flights of stairs to my bed, I was dead on my feet. During the night I was struck with a furious bout of diarrhea and I barely made it to the lavatory near the kitchen door. Once again, I found that I had to deal with the cruel paradox of becoming ill when finally provided with proper nourishment. Or, I thought, with a sinking heart, that perhaps the rampant waves of typhoid that had been sweeping through the camps had finally gotten their deadly claws into me, as well.

The constant flow of rich dark beer did little to relieve my ailing stomach. Herr Herman insisted, emphatically, that I had to be intimate with the product if I ever planned to be skilled at the art of beer-making. So,

I forced down the strong drinks, wishing, more often than not, for a cup of clean water instead. The resulting headaches soon became a part of my daily existence, even after I had learned to adjust to the other side effects my continuing education in proper beer consumption entailed.

The availability of decent food had its own detrimental side effects, as well—some of them as hard on the system as the diarrhea or the prolonged beer-intake. The smell of Frau Erna's rich meals sent waves of painful nostalgia flooding over me, and I would find myself frozen with a forkful of food forgotten on its way to my mouth. Frau Erna seemed to sense the sullenness that would come over me at these times and she was always very respectful.

My past was my own; my hosts seemed to care little where my young life had begun. They seemed void of the distrust and lack of respect normally directed at the many refugees crowding their city's streets. This was mostly welcome. It saved me from reliving horrendous memories, the scars of which were still too fresh to revisit. But, it did serve to isolate me in my loneliness, which manifested itself through an obsession with a renewed worry over my loved ones.

My mind wandered increasingly to my family, and as the weather turned further toward autumn, my thoughts drifted to my home and its beautiful surrounding hills. The fields would be glowing with a golden light, I thought, and the frantic flocks of swallows would be swooping among the high amber grains as they chased after the season's last insects. The water in the Gold Oppa would be reduced to almost a trickle, the reds and oranges of the turning leaves reflecting in its clear playful ripples.

Was there anyone there, now, to play alongside the water, or did the water have to play alone? Did the eyes of our lovely house stare out vacantly into an overgrown yard, or was someone tending it and making it their own? Had any of my friends and neighbors made their way back to Jagerndorf, a city devoid for so long of those who had made up its very heart and soul for generations? Would the inhabitants remember me, as I remembered them, and would they think back on the many wonderful memories along that magical riverbank?

My thoughts would torment me thus, setting up a virtual world in my mind, where life reverted back to the days before the war, when pleasures had been simple and pure. I could smell Oma's cooking wafting through the crisp autumn air, and I could hear the laughter of Gerle and Otti as they kicked a ball to each other on the road. The wind would blow down from the mountains, hinting of the coming frost, and Gerle's hair would ripple beneath the wind's teasing hands. I could see the crackling leaves swirling beneath their feet as the boys ran to and fro and the dust-covered ball wobbling into the ditch as a horse drawn cart lumbered by.

These memories chafed agonizingly along the borders of my recollection, but, oddly, they sustained me as well. They allowed me to wake each morning with a renewed hope in my heart, hope that someday I would return to those clear waters along which my life had flowed so pleasantly for a brief time. While the sun barely traced the lines of the rooftops, I would linger beneath the thick down coverlet in my small room at the top of the brewery and grasp at the last fragmented images of my nightly dreams before they dispersed into the reality of the day.

With the arrival of each new morning, I discovered sore muscles in my body that I never knew I possessed. As my intake of food increased, it seemed Herr Herman assumed that my strength did as well. He trusted me with more difficult jobs, each one testing... and ultimately sapping, my limited reserves of strength.

It was on one such day that my supposed passion for beer-making was sorely tried. Herr Herman provided many taverns across the city with his specialty beers, and they each expected prompt delivery in time for their late afternoon rush of thirsty regulars. My boss felt I was ready to undertake the responsibility for this vital mission. Therefore, I was installed behind a small wooden cart, its two rickety wheels threatening to take control as I struggled beneath the weight of several heavy barrels of beer. I grasped the two long wooden handles tightly, determined to navigate, with the utmost aplomb, the narrow cobblestone streets and hills.

The cart's cumbersome wheelbarrow-like design made any dogged attempt at nonchalance impossible. The barrels jostled and wobbled against each other, cradled as they were upon a series of shifting metal straps, and I found myself struggling to turn the easiest corners. My stomach ached from pressing against the wooden crossbar, as I heaved the cart ponderously forward across the waves and ripples of the ancient city streets.

Finally, one particularly nasty hill had me struggling to keep the cart from tipping and letting loose beer-filled projectiles on the many passersby behind me at the bottom of the long incline. Luckily, a burly youth took pity on me, albeit with much amusement playing across his pimply face. He rolled the cart to the crest of the hill, upon which, thankfully, stood my last tavern for the day.

I was late in reaching home and with significantly wounded pride. Herr Herman's confidence in me had been tested, and I had failed. As a result, I suffered through a long string of verbal admonishments. I went to bed that night with a profound desire to do better in the morning, which served to only mildly suppress a budding dislike for my new career. Also, the bitter aftertaste of supper's beer on my tongue certainly did not help to disperse that growing, nagging feeling... was this really the life I was destined to live?

The scenario was repeated for several consecutive days; Herr Herman remained confident that I would rise to the occasion and, as a result, somehow increase significant muscle mass. I managed to make the deliveries more promptly each day, but the toll on my weakened body was significant. Each night I went to bed more sore and more exhausted. In spite of the improved living conditions, I felt weaker than ever before.

Finally, Herr Herman decided my small size would be better suited for different work. This consisted mainly of cleaning the insides of the large barrels in the vast cellar, which ran like a rat's maze beneath the entire brewery. I followed my boss into the depths of the cavernous tunnels, shivering at the thought of the coming hours in the dim dampness.

"Here are the first dozen." Herr Herman grunted, peeling back the lid of one of the large oak barrels with a large crow bar. ""Your size will serve you well this time." he muttered darkly, then he continued. "Now, mind you scrub each one thoroughly. Here is the scrub brush and a bucket. There is already enough water to get you started. Remember, fresh water for each one... and make sure you drain it well when you are done." He handed me a wooden brush with large stiff bristles and a dented bucket, water splashing over its battered rim.

"Is there water somewhere down here, sir?" I asked, hoping I would not have to maneuver the heavy bucket down too many flights of stairs. But, I knew the answer as soon as the question had passed my lips.

"There is a hose near the bottling station, but that is too far. The pump in the yard will have to do." he answered, his voice almost sympathetic. He turned toward the stairs, resting his large hand on the dusty railing. "I'll send Willhelm to get you for lunch."

I nodded and watched his shadow disappear up the narrow stone steps. It took only moments for the cellar's ominous silence to engulf me. In the distance, the echo of dripping water only served to make me feel as though I had descended into an ancient catacomb. The intense odor of beer pricked at my nostrils, setting my stomach even more on edge. I forced myself to focus on the row of empty barrels, deciding the sooner I began, the sooner I could return to the sunlight.

I pulled a small stool to the side of one barrel, and teetering upon its three rickety legs, I peered down into the massive cask. It was dark and close smelling, the essence of beer overwhelming the ever-present smell of mold and decay. Steeling myself, I reached down for the brush. Dipping it in the water, I eased myself into the barrel. Instantly, the lack of fresh air overpowered me, and I poked my head back up to stop the room from spinning. Gulping the relatively clean air, I braced myself for some swift work. I lowered myself again, crouching awkwardly as I began to work.

I found it necessary to take frequent draws of air, but my headache intensified, and I felt as though I had been soaked overnight in beer. I worked frantically, taking short breaks for the dash up to the pump. The daylight in the courtyard sent black spots dancing before my eyes, and after several trips I wondered if the headaches were more of a result of the light than the fumes.

I was just completing my last barrel when Willhelm hollered down the stairs to summon me for the noontime meal; he clearly felt too put out to navigate the dark staircase unnecessarily. I unfolded my aching body from my small work space and stretched my cramped muscles. Filling my lungs with fresh air, I hoped that Frau Erna would let me forego the mandatory serving of the day's brew—even the thought of food sent my stomach swirling. Consuming beer would be out of the question.

I managed to sweat my way through lunch, taking only a small sip from the large mug at my side. Willhelm eyed me with pleasure, apparently amused that I couldn't conceal the fact that I was all but pickled from the beer fumes. I hastened through my meal, grateful that my only afternoon chore was to resweep the courtyard.

After another week of similarly long days, Frau Erna surprised me at breakfast by informing me that I would have to fend for myself at lunch.

325

She and Herr Herman, she said, would be taking the train to the next village to visit her sister, and they would not return until suppertime.

"I will leave some bread and cheese on the table for you. Of course, you can pull your own beer by yourself." she smiled brightly, as though the chance to get my own beer would be the most wonderful treat imaginable. "Willhelm will be in for the first few hours only; he will do the deliveries." she said, pursing her delicate lips. She had never approved of her husband's insistence that I could handle the heavy cart. "The barrels in the far tunnel are ready to be bottled. Do you remember what to do?" she asked, a glimmer of nervousness in her voice.

"Yes." I replied, with a brisk nod. I had watched Willhelm several times, and had been allowed a few minutes to practice on my own. The system seemed simple enough, but mostly, the fact that I wouldn't be crushed for hours inside a barrel made me feel sure I could handle the job.

After watching Herr Herman and Frau Erna disappear around the corner, I ran to the courtyard for a long draw at the water pump. I paused to gaze around at the trees peeking over the tops of the brewery's many sooty chimneys. It was a gray damp fall day, but the sheen of water on the colored leaves intensified the range of dramatic earthen hues. I breathed deeply, filling my lungs with the crisp refreshing air of the morning, prolonging the moment when I would have to face the lonely descent into the cellars.

Herr Herman had showed me, finally, how to control the large square elevator, information, I felt angrily, that should have been shared with me before my many trips with the bucket. Opa's voice whirled through my head, muttering something about "building character," but I forced that unappealing idea away.

Today, though, I could enjoy the freedom of utilizing the clever mechanical contraption, the bulk of which was maneuvered by simply pulling on a rope. As the elevator bumped to a halt, and the metal gates clattered open, I remained inside the small chamber for several moments, allowing my eyes to adjust to the dim light of the long dark tunnels. The bulbs hung from wires at infrequent intervals throughout the cellar system, but they always felt insufficient to lift the gloom. Instead, they seemed to emphasize the many shadows where the light failed to penetrate.

I quickly found the row of barrels Frau Erna had specified. They sat together in a neat row of five, their massive thousand liter bulks high above me on concrete pillars. Each barrel was equipped with a glass tube, indicating the level of beer available inside. A small wooden table stood in the corner and alongside it there was a narrow stool. I shoved both these pieces of furniture toward the first barrel, and I readied the bottles and caps to begin.

The table was a curious item. It was approximately a meter in diameter, and it had numerous indentations in its surface, each circle the proper size for a liter bottle of beer. To my left I placed a crate of waiting bottles, and to my right I put an empty box, ready to receive the filled and capped bottles. By my foot was a small box, brimming with dozens of porcelain caps, each one ringed with a rubber seal and a metal lever. Beneath the table were two pedals, each of which led to a spring, which, when hooked up to the vats, regulated the flow of the beer. The largest pedal released one of the springs, which caused the surface of the table to rotate. My job was to fill each bottle with a pre-measured liter increment of beer and, upon completion, to stack the readied crates near the elevator for Willhelm's next delivery.

Another pedal controlled the flow of the beer from the large vat above me, through a long rubber tube and into each bottle. A float in the tube regulated the output of the beer, so exactly the right amount was expelled each time. It was really very simple, though I did have to concentrate on my task, mundane as it was.

This was not always easy. The monotony of the job was enough to make the mind wander, and the eerie sound of dripping water along the distant passages sent my imagination along unpleasant paths. I knew for certain that rats dwelled in the rambling caverns of the brewery. I could hear them scratching for morsels in the shadows, and the back of my neck tingled, as though I could feel their beady black eyes peering at me above raised sniffing noses. I tried to force the images of their long yellow teeth from my mind and to concentrate, instead, on keeping the bottles moving at a steady pace.

The pedal dipped easily beneath my foot, and the process proceeded smoothly for several hours. I stopped occasionally to stretch my weary back, but I was determined to be finished before lunch. The idea of a free afternoon was motivation enough. I soon fell into a very workable rhythm, shifting the bottles steadily from left to right.

Without warning, I heard a loud grating noise, and the rotation of the table shuddered noisily to a halt. I gaped in disbelief at the furthest bottle, which should have been turning with the table away from its spot beneath

327

the tube. Instead, I realized, with my heart rising in my throat, that I must have placed it slightly askew upon its perch. Now, it was decidedly jammed beneath the tube and was filling very rapidly with beer.

With my mind wandering, I had released the pedal to commence the filling process without taking proper account of the situation. As I continued to stare, while pumping madly and uselessly on the pedal beneath the table, profound panic mounted in my tight chest. The crooked bottle didn't budge and the float monitoring the flow of the beer failed to respond. Beer began to rise in the bottle, then, suddenly, with a gurgling jolt, it gushed over the sides.

I leaped to my feet and struggled to reach the offending bottle, but the distance across the table was too far. I continued to work frantically at the pedal that controlled the rotation of the table, but it only served to tighten the position of the bottle. Already, beer had begun to dribble over the edges of the table, and it was now pooling at my feet underneath. Sidestepping the rapidly expanding puddle, I hurried around the table, searching for a better angle from which to amend the grave situation.

Bile rose in my throat as I imagined the room filling with the valuable beer. There were easily several thousand liters in the massive vat above my head. Clearly, if I didn't drown, this time I would suffer more than just a reprimand. For a crazy instant, my mind jumped to the story Oma had told me many times as a child, the story of the young wizard's apprentice who had battled with a spirited broom as it nearly consumed him beneath a sea of magically begotten well water.

I glanced around, my hands shaking with adrenaline, and my sight landed on the one thing that could save me from a similar fate. Already, the beer was wetting my shoes, the thick stone walls providing no escape for the freely flowing liquid. The small inadequate floor drain was already bubbling with the overwhelming rush of beer. Slipping and sliding across the room, I grabbed frantically for the rubber hose, intended for washing the tanks clean after they were emptied. Cranking the rusty water tap to its farthest position, I loosed a flow of water upon the suds, hoping to disperse them and enable the beer to drain away more rapidly.

Instead, to my horror, the spray of water only managed to increase the dense foam. I gasped in dismay as I recalled Herr Herman's proud words as he praised the long-lasting suds of his finest brews. Now, the same quality of foam density threatened to engulf me; my feet were already hidden beneath the rapidly burgeoning bubbles.

With an anguished cry, I turned off the water and decided, instead, to turn my attention back to the jammed bottle. Sloshing through the beer, I grabbed the stool, and I jabbed one of its long legs desperately against the bottle. It shattered instantly, sending fragments of glass flying about the room. I flinched and ducked, as I felt shards of the forest green bottles pelt my arms and hands. But, as soon as the bottle exploded, the pressure on the hose was relieved, and the float resumed its proper position. The flow of beer had stopped.

I glanced around in dismay. The bottoms of my pants clung damply about my ankles. My feet disappeared into the white froth, which rippled away from me like cascading ocean waves. All was still, except the occasional drip of beer as the remaining drops trickled from the tube. The soft hiss of popping bubbles surrounded me as the suds of the beer slowly began to disperse.

In disbelief, I stood with my hands to my forehead, angrily pulling at my wet bangs. At least five hundred liters of precious expensive beer were destined for the drain. How would I ever explain this to my boss? With my shoulders slumped and my breath coming in throbbing gulps, I stared at the slowly disappearing lake at my feet. The snakelike water hose emerged suddenly from beneath the suds, coiled where I had dropped it in my irrational panic.

A desperate idea flooded my thoughts, and a plan began to form in my mind. A sturdy mop would clear the floor of the remaining beer and glass, and neatly stacking the completed cases would distract any probing eyes. The real problem was the obvious discrepancy in the amount of beer remaining in the vat, measured against the cases of full bottles. Herr Herman would know immediately that something did not measure up—namely the missing beer.

I had always thought the beer was too strong anyway, I told myself, as I scrambled carefully up the concrete pillar, using the stool for a precarious support. With the dripping water hose in one hand, I opened the valve at the top of the vat and inserted the hose deep inside. I watched with trepidation as the level of the beer in the glass tube slowly began to rise, until it had returned to what would serve as an acceptable level.

With a rising and sickening feeling of guilt, I finished tidying the room, until I felt sure any trace of my accident had been cleared away. Knowing what I had to do, I pulled on the elevator rope with trembling hands, and I headed straight to my room. The bread and cheese remained forgotten upon the kitchen table; my appetite had faded as my resolve increased. Besides, I felt that now I had no right to it anyway. Pulling my small rucksack out of the chest of drawers next to my bed, I gathered up my few belongings, most of which still sat in the bottom of my bag.

I ran down the stairs, my heart pounding heavily in my chest. I hoped Willhelm would not return for lunch. Dashing out the front door, I pulled it firmly shut behind me. As the heavy lock crashed loudly behind me, I knew I had sealed any chance of returning to my job as an apprentice. That part of my life was now decidedly behind me.

With mounting dread, and retracing the steps of weeks before, I made my way to the path that led to the fortress upon the hill… and the camp I had hoped to forget. This time the forest canopy felt alive and intimidating, with grave voices and murmurs of judgment upon the cold wind, filling me with shame for what I had done. But, at the back of my mind a glimmer of defiance tingled. I had finally taken hold of the upheaval in my life and twisted fate in my own hands. Where that decision would lead me now, I was about to discover.

CHAPTER 28

Sun-kissed leaves drifted down around me as I approached the menacing arches of the fortress's courtyard. I had calmed down my racing heart; instead, my insides had congealed into an icy stew of tightened emotions. Uppermost in the toxic mixture was dread. I knew I would have to give a reason to the camp director for my unexpected return. The truth would undoubtedly come out and my mind rattled off numerous terrible scenarios of resulting punishments.

"I could run away!" I decided. A fantastic image formed in my mind: I was walking triumphantly back into Jagerndorf, waving to all my friends and family who had also miraculously returned. I reached into my pocket, shaking the few coins that were stuck in the bottom corner among the dusty balls of lint. Less than a handful remained. Then the beautiful bubble of fantasy faded, as the reality of the vast distance, the true significance of which I had yet to comprehend, dawned on me. Without the proper means to travel, I was stuck. At this point, in a world hostile to wanderers and those who did not belong... I had no choice but to remain.

With all my hopes vaporizing along side this depressing thought, I turned stiffly toward the castle once more. I would have to face whatever consequences the director felt were fit for my actions. I recalled the director's meek demeanor, and I hoped, fervently, that he had yet to find a backbone. Perhaps, I grimaced, continuing to plod up the long hill... perhaps, I could simply sink back into the mass of humanity crowding the camp. It saddened me to think of that possibility as a promising one.

Few familiar faces met me in the yard. In fact, only one fellow eyed me with any hint of recognition. Clearly, the number of people the fortress housed had increased significantly. But, the same vacant taciturn individuals were here; only mirrored in different faces.

There were the elderly, those who had seen so much of life and yet had been forced to finally succumb to its harsh realities amidst utter despair and the abandonment of their dreams.

Also, gazing morosely upon their broods of children, were the young mothers, their eyes filled with sadness at the upheaval in their beloveds' innocent lives… lives once full of so much promise. Scattered among the women were the men, significant in their scarcity. Few remained who had survived the war. Those who were present sat in clusters among the women, and they wore profound expressions of shock, undoubtedly filled with an anguish over the loss of their former places in the world. Most men, who counted themselves unfortunate enough to be among the refugees, were no longer able make a difference in the lives around them. They were no longer given the opportunity to be someone's provider… they were as much at the mercy of the unforgiving system as the rest.

Hardest to see, of course, were the children. The war had been particularly brutal and merciless to them… as I well knew. Each young life had seen horrors that no human of any age should ever have to witness. And each one of those young lives was struggling to make meaning of it all in a world of adults, who in their eyes, had failed them. Or perhaps, they felt as I did… they felt as though they were the cause of the downfall that had led to the wretched lives they now led. Either way, the result was the same… inert minds, traumatized hearts, sinking rapidly into a stagnant bog of self-doubt and desperation… quite a burden for those who had held so much hope for the future.

Into this sea of all too familiar hopelessness I wandered, delaying the inevitable moment when I would have to make an appearance at the director's office. I debated, for a moment, avoiding the director all together and trying, instead, to simply blend into the anonymity of the masses of people. But, I realized that I would be in more trouble once I was discovered… and I knew that, ultimately, I would be discovered. One had to register with the director's office to receive the vital bowl and spoon for meals—I shuddered to think that I truly would be sorry to miss even those pathetic offerings. I had been spoiled while in the brewmaster's care. In spite of the strenuous work, I had been well fed and, as a result, I had finally been keeping on some of my weight. I already missed the delicious food; I couldn't lose ground now.

Steeling myself, I wandered down the memorable dark hallway that led to the director's office. The continuous blend of noises became a blur in my ears, as I prepared in my head what I would say in my defense. I reached the looming door too early for my liking, but I knocked immediately, before succumbing to my nerves.

I sighed with relief, as a familiarly gentle voice said, "Come in."

I turned the knob, remaining hopeful that the camp director's voice reflected the calm demeanor I had remembered. Upon entering, I closed the door quietly behind me, anxious not to disturb the sense of peace in the room. A large clock ticked somberly in the corner, and the calm rustle of leaves sounded from beyond the narrow window behind the director's desk. Otherwise, the director himself sat quietly, staring at me in disbelief. I imagined that a refugee returning willingly to the camp was a rare sight indeed... yet here I stood.

"Uh, sir... I'm Alf..." I began, hesitantly.

"Yes, I know who you are." he interrupted, with a tinge of fatigue in his voice, as he stood up. "What I don't understand is why you are here. We sent you off at the request of the Youth Services several weeks ago." He frowned, as though puzzling how I could have circumvented the system. "We received no word of your return. This is highly unusual." He ran his fingers across his balding head and frisked rapidly through the tidy stack of papers on his desk, as though searching for an explanation among them.

I began my tale, leaving out most of what I thought was irrelevant, which meant, of course, a good deal of the episode with the bottle. Ultimately, I finished by saying that I had been... let go.

"Well, this is highly unexpected." he fretted, apparently disturbed at the disruption in his orderly management of the camp. "There simply is not room for any more people here. Did you see how crowded it is out there?" he asked, his voice rising slightly toward anger.... or perhaps panic. "How am I supposed to accommodate every boy who can't handle his job?" He slumped into his chair, peering grimly up at me from beneath his hands, which were now kneading his furrowed forehead.

I waited quietly, unsure of what to say in my defense. I was afraid any more admissions on my part would push this normally diminutive man toward the brink of madness. Clearly, any lack of control on his part over those beholden to him for their livelihoods was taken very personally, and he seemed to be truly puzzled with what to do. His hands dropped helplessly and he began toying with a slender fountain pen on his desk, the black ink rapidly staining his fingers.

"Well, I'm sorry, young man, but I have no choice but to send you back to the Youth Services Office. Perhaps they will find an answer where I cannot." He sighed, tossing the pen onto a heap of papers.

Again, it seemed he took my problem as a personal failure, and for a moment, it filled me with guilt. But, that new defiance still lingered tantalizingly close beneath the surface, so I uttered no apologies. Instead, I answered, "Thank you, sir. I will go there now. I'm sorry to have bothered you, sir." I bowed my head slightly and backed to the door.

"Please make sure I don't see you back here again, young Alf." he said, and I closed the door on his disapproving stare.

The large rambling building that housed the Youth Services Office looked even more intimidating the second time. I knew it was likely that the office would receive a more accurate account of my debacle in the cellars, but I hoped that I could pass through the system before any of it came to light. Several hours still remained until supper time, and as far as I knew, the brewmaster and his wife were still out of town.

I traced the route along the wide halls until I found myself outside the faded door of the office. A massive shadow of a man's figure passed beyond the frosted glass of the door and a muffled belch followed in its wake. I gulped, deciding it would be best to leave, and I turned to go.

Two ladies were striding purposefully down the hall toward me, deep in conversation. One of them, a tall woman with blond curls, and thin glasses pulled low across the narrow bridge of her nose, spotted me. She held up her hand to her friend, who halted her story in midstream. "Are you looking for the Youth Services Office, young man?" she asked briskly. Before I had even formed a decent reply, she had crossed the hall and opened the door to the office.

A wisp of curling blue smoke drifted out from the doorway, and "What?! What do you want?" bellowed a gruff voice from behind the haze.

"Here's a young man for you, sir." the blond purred sweetly, and seizing my shoulders with a surprisingly strong grip, she pushed me toward the voice. I managed to glare back at her retreating figure as I stumbled into the smoke-filled room, and I immediately regretted having ever come.

"Well... what do you want, young man? I don't have all day!" snarled the thick voice. Slowly the figure of the large man appeared through the smoke. He was bending over his bookshelf, on which sat a wilted plant. Several of its brown leaves were clenched in his hands.

"Damn things! Give them all the attention and they still die. Useless!" His words crackled into a gritty cough, and out came his handkerchief, which was now so filthy, I felt sure it was the same one I had seen him using weeks before.

Squinting at me more closely, I could see the recollection surfacing on his face. "What the hell are you doing back here?!" he yelled. He strode around the desk and planted himself squarely in front of me. "Just like all the rest of the good for nothings, are you?" he growled. "I knew it the moment I saw you; you would be trouble. God dammit, boys like you causing me so much grief every day... it's a wonder I don't have a heart attack." he cried, placing his hand on his chest.

I shook my head, once again demoralized into speechlessness. He stomped back to his chair, flinging the dead leaves over his shoulder into the general filth of the room. He grabbed his cigarette, one of the two perpetually smoldering in the ashtray. "What the hell am I supposed to do with you now? What did you do, you good-for-nothing? Why the hell are you spoiling my reputation like this, especially with the brew master?" He took a long puff on the cigarette, and I tried to focus on the brilliant glow of orange at its tip.

I felt an inch tall, but I had nothing decent to say in my defense, and as he really didn't seem to be expecting an answer, I remained standing dumbly as he continued to rattle out the many ways I had ruined his life. "Well, let's see what I can do? I have to put you somewhere, you troublesome kid. If only you would bother to think of the trouble you put everyone through to get away with one of your stupid antics." As he drawled on, he flipped violently through his small file box of cards. I waited with bated breath...

"Please... oh, please!" I thought. "Please make it something good."

"Ah... well." he said, with relief in his voice. He paused to read a slip of paper that lay folded up between two cards. "Yes, this is just the

335

thing. It will get you the hell out of my sight, and it will guarantee that you can't cause any more trouble to the hard working people of this town." Pulling the paper from the box, he read it again slowly, mouthing several words under his breath and nodding decisively, before he was overcome by another fit of phlegmatic coughing.

I waited anxiously, wondering what was in store for me next. He filled the already filthy handkerchief with some more grime from his congested throat and stuffed the drooping cloth back into his pocket.

"Ok. This is what we are going to do. You are going to get on a train and head for Munich." He slapped the paper decisively on his desk and stared indifferently at me, his small eyes still red and watery from his coughing.

I blinked, running his declaration around in my head. "Uh, Munich, sir?" I stuttered. "Why there, sir?" My hands gripped the sides of my trousers tightly, as I envisioned another journey farther away from my beloved home. Oh, how it pained me to keep turning my back on my homeland, and to head, instead, deeper into the unknown.

"Here, this paper will help clear things up for you, if you care at all, you little rotter!" he sneered. "They will provide you with a train ticket at the station... though, I doubt you deserve even that." he grunted. "This tag will be worn around your neck for the entire journey. Don't take it off! Do you hear me? It is more of a ticket than the train stub, actually. Without it you might be picked up by the authorities... though, that might be just what you deserve! Don't say I didn't warn you, you little troublemaker." he continued, glaring at me as though he had just scraped me off the bottom of his shoe. "I'm taking more trouble with you than I really should, you know. They don't want to bother with you at that camp of yours, either, though, do they?" he muttered, his words trailing off into a jumble of unsavory curses. I winced, as my ears took in words I had never before heard uttered.

He handed me the paper and the small placard, which I hung around my neck without reading. There would be plenty of time for that on the train, it seemed. "Now, get the hell out of here! You know where the train station is?" he snarled. I nodded. He continued, "Go, then. Show your papers; they will give you the ticket. Get out of my sight, you... you...!" he yelled, his voice breaking up with another round of coughing. I backed quickly toward the door, anxious not to hear another version of what he thought of me.

By the time I had pulled the rattling door closed behind me, he was in full wheeze mode, but I could still hear him cursing my name between gasped breaths. I hastened out into the street, where, fittingly, a cloud had wrapped its bleak hand around the sun, covering the city in a thick paste of damp gray. Rain was imminent. I knew that it would be the cold rain of autumn, and preferring to stay dry, I quickly took my bearings, and ran toward the train station.

I had yet to read the sheet of paper he had given me, but I decided that there would be plenty of time for that later. For a brief moment, I wondered if I could somehow manage to convince the ticket seller that I really needed to be going east... but, that idea faded as quickly as it had come; I had already gotten into enough trouble for one day.

My stomach rumbled loudly as I ran along, and I sadly regretted not eating the bread and cheese Frau Erna had left for me. I did not like the feeling of being hungry... and not knowing when, or if, another meal would be forthcoming.

I reached the station quickly; it was only several blocks from the Youth Services Office. I glanced around nervously, suddenly realizing that I risked the chance of encountering Herr Herman and Frau Erna. I was looking forward to disappearing without having to provide them with an explanation. I knew that Herr Herman would feel betrayed by my abandonment. He had divulged his closely held secrets of beer-making to me and had laid bare his passion for his profession. I had failed to share in his vision. Thus, I stood self-consciously in the long line, trying to keep my face hidden in case they appeared. For once, I was spared.

A kind smile greeted me at the ticket booth as I handed over my paper. The woman read it carefully, pausing to look me over curiously. I wondered, again, what was in these papers that I had yet to read. "You will want to stop at the Red Cross booth, dear. You look like you could use a meal." she said, smiling again. She handed me my paper, along with a crisp white ticket.

"Thank you." I said, smiling shyly. I stuffed the paper and ticket into my pocket and stumbled away, jostled from behind by the impatient crowd.

The line at the Red Cross booth was even longer, and it was loud and rowdy, with many small children crying for their overdue meal. I filed in patiently behind, surveying the crowd as I shuffled slowly forward. The

337

wide hall of the station was teeming with people, most of them as forlorn-looking as myself.

Where all these souls had come from, I shuddered to think, but the thought of all the empty and waiting homes that would never see their return made me ill. Would that be the fate of my own beloved house, as well? I felt cast adrift, once more, and the safety of a familiar land, as so often before, lurked painfully out of reach. In what land would I ultimately come ashore? Would I ever succeed in making it feel like home?

My journey to Munich was uneventful and brief. The soup and bread from the train station had been fresh and delicious. Although my nerves were still on edge, I had managed, nonetheless, to wipe the bowl clean with the final crusts. With a full and satisfied stomach, and finally feeling the threat of discovery by Herr Herman fading, I leaned back in my seat, and I slept. It wasn't until I awoke, hours later, and I felt the train lurching unsteadily into the outskirts of Munich, that I realized I had not yet read the paper which had such a bearing on my fate.

I pulled it out from where I had shoved it in my pocket and smoothed it out on my lap. The heading read, "Boys Town, Buchhof Jungendstadt". I blinked twice, unsure of what to make of it… was I headed for an orphanage? Would this mean my hopes at finding my family were over, sealed forever beneath the label of "orphan"? My eyes scanned the letter, which spelled out further instructions for my journey. It seemed my trip was not yet over. I would have to find my way to another train, which would take me into the high hills around Munich.

I looked up, staring out the window as the train shuddered into the large Munich station. Thick gray clouds mingled with the coming twilight, and a light rain was pattering against the window. The clouds hung low across the hills around the town, adding an appropriate mantle to the lingering destruction that still remained from the war.

As the train crept forward, I scanned my eyes along the rows of streets, which must have once been very tidy and picturesque. Now, it was rare when I spotted a street that had been spared. Munich, like so many others, had been hit directly in its very heart, leaving it with a cold and somber atmosphere, which the damp weather did little to enhance. Instinctively, I pulled the collar of my coat higher up on my neck, and I grabbed my rucksack, hoisting it onto my back. The day had been long and stressful, and I longed for the warm down comforter I had become accustomed to at the brewery.

I followed the stream of people who were exiting the train, and we joined the milling crowd that hovered beneath the cavernous ceiling of the station. There were thousands of refugees, their lost and tired faces clearly labeling them from regions far afield. Fragments of unfamiliar languages swarmed around me as we all attempted to find our ways in the chaos. Eager to reach my destination before nightfall, I struggled across the wide room, heading for an information booth.

After many minutes of waiting and only moments of questions, I learned that I would have to make the next stage of my trip on foot.

"It isn't far." she promised me. "Just head down the street to the left for six blocks. You will find the local train there— Starnberger Station. It also serves Garmisch." she prattled on.

It seemed that I would be passing the rest of my journey in the dark... and in the rain. As I navigated the many piles of crates and suitcases and people sleeping amongst their only belongings, I hoped that the walk would truly be as she had said... brief. A cold wind was blowing, and it swirled and taunted the damp leaves that blanketed both sides of the street.

In spite of the late hour, the streets were filled with people and vehicles. Clearly, Munich was a bustling and productive city that was recovering steadily after the war. There were many detours, though, as I ventured along my directed route. After walking an entire block, I discovered that I would have to backtrack and follow another street to make my way around a long row of buildings that had been completely reduced to a heap of twisted metal and brittle bricks by some carefully aimed bombs.

I blinked in amazement, as I watched another black "MP" officer direct a long row of American trucks through the narrow congested streets. My mind flashed back to an eerily parallel experience, my first encounter with a similarly clad man, so neat in his white trimmings. I had been so comfortable and safe among the Americans at the border with Jacov. I looked back fondly on those memories, a shining moment in a murky black sea of the shadows that still haunted my dreams.

"What would me sweet baby sister think of me now?" I wondered, smiling to myself. She had always been shyly captivated by any experience out of the ordinary. Well, we had both had our share of those! As I stood there on the street corner, watching a scene laced with deja vu, I hoped that she was safe and happy in some extraordinary place… or better yet, in some ordinary place, all the more special because it was home.

As I walked, I meditated on my family, recalling with grim amusement a saying Opa had often recited, "Scherben Bringen Gluck." (Broken glass brings good luck). Well, it remained to be seen if the shattered bottle of beer, and my resulting rebellion, would lead to a better fortune. But, my fate had been turned by stranger things.

I finally reached the small station, which wore the placard, "Starnberger/Garmisch-Partenkirchen", upon its long brick facade. The ticket I had originally received was sufficient to take me to my final destination, so I proceeded directly to the small platform. Only a handful of people awaited the arrival of the train on the cold evening, and I hoped the wait would not be a long one. The wind was picking up and it threatened to pull my jacket open, so I buttoned it more tightly beneath my chin.

The train arrived shortly and everyone hastened to board, eager to be out of the wind, which, although it was not yet October, had a definite wintry bite to it. I found an empty car and stretched out on the hard seat. I was tired from the long day, and I was ready for my bed. But, I was still uncertain whether I truly did have one waiting for me. I knew that I would have to forget about thick down coverlets and private attic rooms, and I would have to prepare myself, instead, for another rowdy bunk room.

It was slightly before midnight when I found myself standing on a deserted platform, in the small town of Starnberg with my rucksack hanging limply from my hand. The conductor had been kind enough to wake me just before the train had rumbled onward, and I had barely had time to exit the train before it had steamed off. I rubbed my tired eyes, trying to peer into the darkness. The rain still fell, though it had diminished to a fine mist.

I shivered, pulling my collar more tightly around my ears, and I wandered into the station's small waiting room, deciding that a wooden bench would have to do for the night. The room was warm, at least, and quiet, as very few people seemed to be traveling at such a late hour. A lone ticket seller sat behind a tall desk, waiting for passengers who failed to materialize at this late hour. No trains were leaving, but the Munich to Garmisch route seemed to be traveled frequently enough that an occasional person might get off in the small lake side town.

"Who are you, lad?" asked a soft voice behind me, after I had settled myself on a narrow bench out of the draft.

340

"Huh?" I cried, bolting up and turning around. My heart beat rapidly; I was still irrationally worried about encountering Herr Herman and the accompanying disapproval. Instead, I found myself looking upon a grizzled old man, who reminded me slightly of an older version of my Uncle Alois. He was holding a long broom, which he seemed to be using as a cane more than anything else. In fact, it seemed that if it hadn't been there to hold him up, he might fall flat on his face. His ears stuck out beneath infrequent wisps of gray, and his mouth seemed to be lacking most of its teeth. He grinned at me, revealing only several fragmented and blackened ones.

But, there was mirth in his eyes and kindness in his voice as he asked again, "Who are you, boy? Where are you headed? Awfully late to be out by yourself, isn't it?" He hobbled over to the bench, and groaning loudly, he sank slowly onto the seat beside me. "This weather is awful for my arthritis." he moaned, kneading his thigh with a very gnarled hand. "Are you one of those lads living up at the castle?" he asked, winking merrily.

"Um, castle? Uh, no... I don't think so. I'm, I'm..." I hesitated, disliking the implications of what I was going to say. "I'm an orphan." I blurted, breathlessly, and I stared down at the floor. I squeezed my eyes shut, forcing the unpleasant echo of the terrible words from my mind. Was I truly an orphan now?

"Yes. That's what I meant... the hunting castle. It's the orphanage set up by those Americans, I think." he answered, as he continued to rub his aching legs. "Mighty funny thing it is, that the Americans are making use of that building of all places, if you ask me." he chuckled quietly, shaking his head from side to side.

"Why? What is wrong with it?" I asked, growing nervous. Suddenly, I imagined a bombed out shell of a house, open to the elements and crawling with rats and lice.

"Well, it used to belong to one of Hitler's very own, wouldn't you know! His high and mighty field marshall, Goering, in fact." He pushed the broom across the floor in front of him several times and continued, "It used to be his hunting estate, I guess. Now, ironic as it is, the Americans have the run of the entire grounds. Some thirty boys or so up there, I believe. Pretty exclusive. What grand thing did you do to get yourself in that fine place?" he asked, staring at me with new interest.

341

I stared back, completely at a loss for words. The vision of a shattering bottle of beer danced through my head, splinters of emerald green glass spinning off into unforeseen directions.

CHAPTER 29

I spent the night squirming uncomfortably on the wooden bench, wishing all the while for the down bed in my room in the attic at the brewery. Herr Herman and Frau Erna had certainly returned there hours ago, and I tormented myself into an agitated wakefulness, brooding over what mess my unexplained disappearance had created in their lives. My muddled thoughts swirled with guilt-laden scenarios of the imminent discovery of my error in the cellar. But, I forced myself to remember that however present the brewmaster and his wife had been in my life, they were now a part of my past, a brief encounter amidst the continuous upheaval of my life. Still, I felt immense remorse for my actions, recalling their generous treatment of me. I had been worked hard, but I had also been treated with respect—treated as someone worthy of teaching.

Now, I had been selected, yet again, for a path I had not chosen myself. If what the old janitor said were true, it seemed as though I was going to be one of an elite group of orphans, each of whom had been rescued by the Americans from his uniquely terrible life.

I fought a stubborn refusal to succumb to my fate, which, in my mind, seemed to be an acceptance of the loss of my family. I knew that I had to remain hopeful for an eventual reunion—it was all that sustained me, all that gave me my identity. To the rest of the world I was only an unfortunate statistic. But, to my family, I knew I was much more... I mattered... and that was vital in a harsh and insensitive world. I also knew, though, that I would have to allow myself to be seen as an orphan if I wanted a place to live. I was painfully aware that the desire to find my family would never fade, but now I needed to focus on my own survival.

Morning came upon me without the accompanying calm of a good night's sleep. My back ached from lying on the hard bench, and my mind was thick with ponderous thoughts. My stomach growled in a feeble protest as I prepared myself for the next step.

A new face sat behind the desk, and the ancient janitor had been replaced by a young woman who seemed to consider me as nothing more than another piece of furniture interfering with her broom. I longed to know more about my destination, and I searched the station for the old man, but it was clear that he had gone home to his own warm bed, leaving me no choice but to head forward blindly.

The rain had left deep puddles in the dirt outside the small station, and I navigated them carefully, anxious to keep my feet dry. The air was crisp and fresh, with the scent of rain still heavy in the thick clouds that hung in clinging folds over the steep hills around the town. Occasionally, a tall peak, already laden with a blanket of snow, appeared through the clouds.

Very few people were about, as it was yet quite early, but I wandered in the direction I had been instructed by the ticket seller. He had taken kind pity on me and had handed me half of his morning roll, which I tried to eat slowly with the hope of prolonging the enjoyment.

The sun began to battle with the thick clouds for prominence in the sky, but it seemed the rain was destined to return. I marched more quickly, hoping the three kilometers mentioned had been an exaggeration. The town ran in a narrow strip along a very picturesque lake, the calm waters of which were currently reflecting the gray of the sky. Along the shore were walking paths lined with overhanging trees and quaint homes, although some had yet to recover entirely from the war.

I passed several farmers heading to their fields for an early inspection of the harvest. They all nodded kindly to me, which led me to wonder what sort of reputation the orphanage maintained among the townsfolk.

The sun was valiantly trying to dominate, though it did little more than highlight the mist of rain that was already beginning to fall. I rounded the tip of the lake, passing rows of wooden beach chairs stacked against each other like toppled dominoes. I imagined the warm golden sand that must line the shallow shores of the lake at the height of the summer, and I wondered if I would ever experience such simple pleasures again. Deciding I was getting ahead of myself thinking this way, I turned my back on the lake and headed up a sandy lane lined on both sides with a thick forest of brush and saplings.

The road was slick with wet leaves, many of which had been prematurely blown off their branches. The gravel of the drive crunched loudly into the stillness of the woods, and my anxiety returned as I drew closer to my new home. I had spent so long being alone that the thought of living so closely again with others made me rather nervous. Would I have to relive the loss of Gerle and my family to fend off the many inevitable probing questions? Would I even remember how to connect with others my own age? I had been so steeped in my loneliness and in the unnatural life I had been forced to lead, that I had forgotten all about the normalcies of adolescence.

The inside of a school no longer held the same meaning for me. The aura of stern wisdom and learning had been replaced by vivid faces of despair and the grim realities of hunger and disease. The camaraderie among boyhood friends, which had once been so effortless, had been replaced with an unhealthy isolation and a premature coming of age. I had missed some very precious rights of passage... I knew that, and I forced myself to remember, as I approached the elegant and imposing building, that most of these boys probably had missed them, too.

I rounded the last corner of the drive and nearly fell over my weary feet with shock at the magnificent sight before me. The tepid gray light of the morning glinted off a beautiful stone building, the delicate lines and angles of which were framed by a meticulously manicured garden. There were several turrets topped with graceful onion domes, and balconies framed with scrolled iron work were scattered across the castle's tidy facade. The entryway consisted of a broad porch, entirely covered by a vast balcony which was perched on four stone columns. Four double glass doors opened into a bright hallway, in which I could clearly make out the light of a glittering chandelier.

Across the front of the large balcony were carved the words, "Boys Town, Buchhof Jungenstadt". I gasped, my mouth gaping in awe and disbelief, and I shifted my flimsy rucksack needlessly to the other shoulder. I shook my head and muttered, "If they could see me now..." I walked stiffly up the wide front steps to the door.

345

"You are a very lucky young man, Alf." said Dr. Stein sternly. "Only thirty-four other lads have been admitted into this program. It is a new enterprise established by the Americans to help orphaned youngsters return to their productive places in society." He paused dramatically, allowing his grand words to sink in. I nodded solemnly, wondering what other verbose phrases he was going to throw at me. He had spent the last ten minutes eloquently expounding on the details of the community, which I had been lucky enough to join.

"You will be expected to rise to the demands of the professors and the staff, but you will be granted many privileges as well. Make sure you earn them… your space can always be given to someone else if you fail to uphold the standards expected here."

He sat with the tips of his fingers entwined beneath his chin, and he gazed upon me thoughtfully. "Everyone here has a story, Alf." He said quietly, and he smiled as I started. "But, no one is required to relive it. That is as understood as it is unspoken. Our job here is to help you move forward… not keep you dwelling on the past." He raised a hand to forestall the expected comment. "The Red Cross will have records of your arrival… if any of your family are out there—they can trace you here." He smiled again, and I nodded dumbly, as I was beginning to grow uncomfortably numb with hunger. "Now, your bed is ready for you, as well as a meal, as I am sure you are hungry."

I nodded again, this time more enthusiastically, and I managed to croak, "Thank you, sir." I backed out the door, my head swirling with an overabundance of information. I had been thrown back into a sea of normalcy, where expectations ran high, and Dr. Stein had told me that I would have to work hard not to drown. It had been years since I had sat in a classroom, years since I had done little but struggle to survive. Now, it would be a struggle to remember how to do what had once felt so natural… I would have to relearn how to live… how to live in the world of a maturing child, how to learn, and how to grow. But, oh, what a blessing that shattered bottle had been! I had been given back my future… and I vowed, at that moment, not to fail.

I awoke beneath clean sheets and a warm coverlet, refreshed after a calm night, in which I had been disturbed only by the rhythmic snores and sighs of the others around me. I had joined a small group of boys in a room that, under my previous experiences, would have held over fifty. Now, we were only seven. The beds were spread out neatly throughout the room, and there were desks and wardrobes scattered among them. This gave the room a very homey feel, something that had been lacking in my life for so long. My room in Herr Herman's attic had been a real room, but I had always felt like an intruder, a reluctant guest.

Here, I awoke to the sounds of laughter and quiet conversation and the soothing rays of warm sun on my face. A row of tall windows covered one wall of the room and the beds were spread out along the remaining sides. I rolled over lazily, too comfortable to begin what promised to be a busy day. Through the windows I could see that the rain of the previous day had finally been vanquished by the sun, which shone triumphantly against a glorious blue sky. I smiled happily, taking the sun's return as an omen of good things to come.

"Hey! You're awake!" cried a cheerful voice. It belonged to a young boy, about my own age, with an engaging smile on his face. "We were told to let you sleep in on your first day, but you missed breakfast." he said. Then noticing my disappointment, he quickly added, "But, I brought you some bread and sausage from the kitchen. I know what it can be like on your first day." He pointed to the side table, from which the enticing aroma of the food was already wafting, then he sat down on the bed opposite. He had untidy brown hair, a painful reminder of Gerle. But, unlike my friend, his face was round and healthy, his cheeks flushed with activity and happiness.

"Thank you." I said, sitting up and swinging my legs to the floor.

"Mind you, they won't let you skip a meal again… Dr. Stein is only lenient on your first day." He smiled, watching me tear eagerly at the bread, which was pleasantly crisp and fresh.

Suddenly, he stood up and put his hand out rather awkwardly. "My name is Dieter. What's yours?"

"Um,…" I sputtered, spewing crumbs, and forcing down a rather large chunk of bread. "Um, my name is Alf." I muttered, coughing slightly.

We shook hands and he nodded, smiling again. "Did Dr. Stein talk you through your schedule?" he asked, grinning mischievously. I shook my head, longing to say that Dr. Stein had talked about everything else for far too long, but he had still managed not to cover that detail. But, Dieter seemed to anticipate my thoughts, saying, "You will find that Dr. Stein has

347

quite a gift for words. But, he often gets carried away and leaves out all the important things." He laughed, a pleasant ringing sound that I had heard too rarely of late. "Don't worry. Just check in at the front desk. Fraulein Greta will tell you what to do."

"Thanks." I said again, now gnawing on the stiff casing of a fragrant sausage.

"Nice meeting you, Alf. I should run. I have soccer practice in ten minutes." Dieter said, glancing out the window at the rolling grounds. "I'm glad the sun is out!" he said, merrily. His eyes were bright with an easiness and contentment that I had forgotten could exist. I watched in silence as he and the other boys gathered their cleats and shin guards and noisily tumbled out into the hallway. Dieter waved joyfully as he closed the door behind him.

Each boy seemed to be about my age, give or take a year or two. But, none of them wore the vacant expressions of desperation that I had begun to associate with others my age. Instead, they moved with a confidence and an eagerness that I envied. Perhaps, here I would find that, too. Deciding I would have to start immediately, as to not lose my precious spot, I stood up and grabbed a set of the clothes that had been given to me the night before. They were quite similar to the ones I already had been wearing, as these too were American issues. They were dark green uniforms, and with them came a shiny new pair of shoes, which Dr. Stein had informed me needed to remain as polished as on the day they were received.

I dressed quickly, relishing in the crisp newness of the fabric and the stiff contours of the boots. As I buttoned my shirt, I crossed the room to the window, closing my eyes against the brilliance of the angled morning sun. I knew that the air outside was still cold and autumnal, but the sun filled me with a warmth that melted the bitterness surrounding my heart.

I opened a large french door and stepped out onto a grand balcony, which overlooked a vast garden in which several boys were working diligently with spades and shovels. Dr. Stein had told me that agriculture was a popular choice of study among the boys, as many of them had come from very fertile lands renowned for their rich produce.

Across the gardens lay a neatly manicured forest, with carefully maintained paths sweeping away into the shadows. Beyond these trees, across the valley, rose the snow-frosted peak of the "Zugspitze", Germany's highest and most famous mountain, and I gazed upon it in wonder. The contrasting white and black of the snow and rock stood out like an etching against the azure sky, and suddenly an intense wave of unexplainable and purely visceral longing crossed my heart.

Somehow, although I had never seen mountains on such a massive scale, I felt an instant and primitive affinity to the stark and noble lines of the monstrous peak. Its permanence could not be denied. It represented a reality that filled me with hope... hope that the world was resilient and it would, in time, recover from the terrible assault man had inflicted upon it. Perhaps, I would, too.

The grounds of the orphanage were truly magnificent and after my first two weeks I had only seen a fraction of them. I had been absorbed in meeting my roommates, navigating the halls to my classes, and renewing my ability to read and write. It felt as though rusted flood gates had been opened in my mind. I wanted to try everything, and there were many options available from which to choose. Unlike my previous experience with career opportunities—when I had unexpectedly ended up in the cellars of a brewery, here I was encouraged to try many new things.

Classes were held every day and the range of topics was tremendous. We studied the traditional curriculum, of course: chemistry, mathematics, and physics. But, there was also great emphasis placed on trade skills, such as metallurgy, agriculture, and carpentry.

The motivating force behind the establishment of the school had been to advance the democratic principles of the American sponsors. Therefore, we attended intense English classes, taught by an American officer, and we were exposed, through social studies, to the ways of life in the emerging super power across the Atlantic. Our American liaison officer, an Air Force sergeant, was a quiet man who relished the opportunity to represent the American interests with the Bavarian government.

"I was an orphan myself, though of course, my circumstances differed greatly from yours." the officer told us one day over the noontime meal. "Boys Town changed my life. I had no focus, no hope—I didn't care what happened to me. Then, I was sent to Omaha, Nebraska, of all places." He laughed, adding, "Imagine that! I was from the big city!" He shook his head, his eyes focused on some distant memory. "The program was still new, but the commitment by the teachers was just as strong as it is here for you boys." He smiled gently, his eyes lighting up with a passion that was contagious. "Never forget… this is your ticket out of the nightmares you carry around with you." The boys looked around at each other, their surprise guarded closely. "… Believe me, I know." he said, nodding. "Don't squander this chance to make the most of your lives. Anyway, working hard here will be a cake walk after all the experiences you have already endured." He peered around into the many attentive faces. "Perhaps someday, you will see my country—even live there, and you will remember your time here as priceless."

After a whirlwind month, Dieter convinced me to join the ski team, as soccer was over for the season. It seemed strange to be spending time occupied with simple pleasures again, but I dove in eagerly. The days were so filled with activities and work, that I had little time to dwell on what I had left behind. Time swept along, and my eagerness to learn and stay busy helped to lessen the pain created by the unavoidable absence in my life. Occasionally, I had to battle with a rising feeling of guilt, guilt that I had found a place to recover and thrive… when possibly my dear friend, Gerle, had not. As present as these doubts were, I didn't allow them to overwhelm me. I had been handed a world in which I believed I could truly find happiness. I had to learn to be a little selfish. I never stopped thinking of my family, but the sense of loss began to ebb as I finally allowed myself to make new friends.

Dieter, in particular, became a true companion. He was so good-natured and genuine in his manner that he made my transition into the tightly-knit group of boys very seamless. He encouraged me to join in the many activities, and he emphasized the fact that all the boys had had to face a period of metamorphosis, a painful shedding of their damaged skins. He, himself, was from the eastern part of Germany, and had been at the orphanage for almost six months. Beyond that, his past remained a mystery.

Dr. Stein had been right when he had told me that each boy had a history, each one a tale of loss and misfortune. No one ever asked or prodded, but hints at the horrors each of us carried could be witnessed during the nighttime hours, as sleep was regularly disturbed by terrible nightmares. Even the teachers, and Dr. Stein himself, bore the burden of a traumatized life. Dr. Stein was Jewish, which, by its very definition, labeled him a victim of unimaginable atrocities. But, he had chosen to overcome his past misfortunes by committing himself solely to the advancement of this now privileged group of young boys.

Many of the other teachers had spent the years following the war in and out of the various camps that had sprung up across the continent. Now, they too, took their roles as guides very seriously as they determined to assist us in our navigation toward a productive adulthood. This shared bond of parallel histories between teachers and pupils strengthened the community and made each boy more understanding of the strict guidelines of the program—for it was very strict, indeed.

Each room was to be kept spotless, and our private items had to be stored neatly in a trunk at the foot of the bed. Shoes had to be polished daily and hands had to be inspected for cleanliness before each meal. The food was excellent, as the kitchen was lorded over by a very particular German cook, who guarded his delicious recipes with great secrecy. Our introspective American liaison officer made sure the pantry stores were kept well stocked with fresh and healthy supplies, and each boy quickly made up for any lost meals from his past.

Thus, kitchen duty was a favorite among the regular chores we all had to do. Scavenged extra portions were the norm to the lad who aided the cook in his preparations and cleanup. Other, less savory, duties usually consisted of a thorough cleaning of the vast castle: polishing the wood floors until they gleamed, and washing the many rows of tall windows.

For the most part, it was done with little complaint. We all knew the value of our new home, and none of us wanted to jeopardize losing it. Also, the privileges promised to me by Dr. Stein had not been an exaggeration. We were given every opportunity to enrich our days, usually with a varied array of activities. Weekends were particularly memorable, for this was when the wives of the local American officers would come and initiate rousing games of bingo, as well as lessons in the important skills of growing up. We were taught to dance, and as an accompanying treat, we were instructed in proper table etiquette. Everyone took it in stride. Most boys had spent some of their young lives eating off trash heaps or out of rusty cans, so any chance to emphasize the finer points of living was tolerated, if not welcomed.

Often, as an added bonus on weekends, American military buses roared up the narrow lane to take us on tours of the local museums and the numerous historic castles that dotted the surrounding hills. Many of the attractions had been damaged and had yet to reopen to the public. The beautiful valleys around Garmisch and Munich became our playground, and we relished every opportunity to ski on the legendary snows of the Bavarian Alps.

So, in the midst of all the activity, the Christmas and Hanukkah holidays (many of the boys and staff were Jewish) came and went, and with it came the expected rush of emotions. The suppressed longing for my family reared again, and I found myself awake most nights imagining where they might be. Of everyone I missed, it was most painful for me to think of Gerle. I could only hope that Oma and Opa were looking out for Gerti and Uncle Alois, but I knew that Gerle's fate had been tied most intimately to mine. I had always felt responsible for him, and I couldn't shake off the feeling that, in the end, I had failed him.

I wanted so much to share my experiences with him. From a very early age we had planned to grow up together. We had imagined the many milestones we would share, and we had believed it would always be so. Now, I struggled to convince myself that my friend was even alive.

The holidays were a time when many of the boys received letters and packages, mostly from distant cousins and aunts. I looked on with poorly disguised sadness, trying to feel pleased for their good fortune, all the while not even bothering to hope that a letter might come for me. As the chances of news of my family faded with the season, I threw my energies into making a home for myself at Boys Town.

Thus, I passed another birthday, my fifteenth, and with it came new responsibilities. I was elected to the student council and I took up my place as goalie on the soccer team. Dieter and I became a force of defense to be reckoned with, and I loved the gratifying feeling of belonging to a closely-knit group of boys. Games were held at neighboring schools, where local children had also been able to get back to the busy task of growing up. My world was changing quickly, and I was frantic to keep pace.

It was spring of 1947, and I awoke in the infirmary, my entire face throbbing painfully. I raised my hands to my eyes, wondering what the bulging form looming too closely within my range of vision was. I felt the bandage. Then, I remembered. I had stopped the ball, but at the expense of my nose. My fingernails were still black with the soil from the field, where I had thrown myself on top of the soccer ball. The smell of the earth was still present in my shattered nose, or perhaps now it lingered only in my befuddled brain.

The boy's shoe had landed firmly against the bridge of my nose and he had received a penalty; I remembered that much. I longed to see Dieter, because I couldn't remember if we had won. My head swam with pain and suddenly I was looking forward more to the arrival of the nurse and her painkillers than I was to a visit from my friend. Still, when the door opened signaling her return, I winced. I knew it would slam loudly behind her.

"Well, Alf. You are awake! Your friends have been asking about you." she said, setting several bottles down on the bedside table. She busied herself with tidying the sheets, and I blushed hotly as she lifted the bed pan to see if I had made use of it. "How are you feeling?" she asked, her voice brisk with professionalism.

"I'm ok... it's just my head... it hurts." I answered, squeezing my eyes tightly together to block out the painful light of the room.

"Well, that's expected isn't it? Apparently, you took quite a kick to the nose." She patted me firmly on the shoulder, looking all the while into my eyes, searching, I supposed, for signs of dementia. "It will heal. Might be a little crooked, but it will heal. Now get some rest." she said, smiling brightly.

I tried to focus on her form as she bustled about the room, folding blankets and rolling bandages. Soon the gentle swish of her neatly pressed skirt blended with the steady sounds of my own breathing, and I slept.

It was the end of November, 1947, and the dining room was loud with boisterous celebration. We had won the final soccer match, securing the championship for the first time in the short history of the school.

"Well, Alf," Dieter cried, patting me on the back as I struggled with a brimming spoonful of hot soup.

"Hey, watch it!" I sputtered, a dribble of steaming soup landing in my lap. I smiled, though, my spirits too high to be truly annoyed.

"Next week is the first ski trip!" Dieter continued, absently handing me a napkin. "We get new skis this year—longer ones. We will absolutely sail down those trails!" He stuffed a large piece of roll in his mouth and finally paused to chew.

The time had seemed to fly along. It had been over a year since I had taken on the challenge of that box of green beer bottles... and had lost.

I had often wondered what had happened to the vat of diluted beer that I imagined had passed unnoticed for a time. Willhelm must have grumbled and cursed my name as he struggled over the heavy crates of beer that he had gotten used to leaving to me and my younger back. Had Herr Herman been forced to defend his reputation to the numerous unruly tavern owners who had undoubtedly felt cheated with the substandard product? I doubted I would ever know.

Suddenly, my thoughts were interrupted by a flurry of activity near the wide door to the dining hall. There was a murmur of voices, as Dr. Stein swept in, his face as stern as usual. The teachers regularly ate with us, but Dr. Stein was often absent, choosing to take his meals in the privacy of his office. So, his arrival caused quite a stir, and thus began the usual scramble for explanations.

"He must have found out about the broken window!" one boy whispered nervously to his companion.

"No! He is going to announce the new Student Council appointments." said another.

Everyone watched in silence as Dr. Stein walked solemnly to the front of the room, tapping a small envelope against his hand. He turned with a dramatic flourish to face us, seemingly relishing the anticipation apparent on every boy's face. Then, he smiled.

"Normally, I would leave this job to Fraulein Greta." rang his voice across the silence. "But, we have received some unexpected news today!" He paused, allowing the expectant murmurs to subside. "Our Alf, here…" he gestured with his hand to where I sat opposite him. I jumped, feeling my heart drop to my shoes. Had my crime in the cellars of the brewery been discovered? Was I to be thrown out of Boys Town?

"… Our Alf here, has been with us for about a year now, and he has made quite a fine addition to our little group." I smiled sheepishly, glancing at Dieter, who shrugged. His face was as puzzled as my own. "I must say, Alf has been quite patient, watching each of you communicate with your loved ones, while never hearing anything of his own." Dr. Stein stared at me, his eyes full of an intense shine.

I began to tremble, and my hands beaded with sweat. Dr. Stein paused again.

"A letter arrived today, though from the looks of it, it has been long in getting here." Dr. Stein continued. I blinked, shaking my head. This couldn't be happening to me... not me. "This belongs to you, Alf." said Dr. Stein, holding out the letter with a steady hand.

I stood up, my knees shaking. I reached for the letter. The paper was crisp and slightly crumpled, as though it had gotten damp and had been patted dry. Dirt stained it in several places, and a corner was torn. But, as I turned it over with a trembling hand, I noticed my name was clearly written on the front in faded ink. I stared in disbelief at the flowing script, its familiar elegance pricking at long faded memories. I fought back tears of joy. I didn't even hear the applause that erupted around me, nor did I feel the gentle squeeze of Dieter's hand on my arm as he helped ease my slumping body back into my chair.

Alf at Boys Town

CHAPTER 30

Through eyes brimming with unshed tears, I tried to focus on the fading lines of script that were struggling to remain on the thin sheet of fragile paper. Several places were smeared where water had blurred the ink, but the signature was clear. Ignoring the eager murmurs and questions billowing around me, I sat stiffly in my chair. My head swam with the possibilities contained between the lines that ran neatly across the crisp page. I read.

"My darling Alfie,

How I have searched for you all these years! It came as such blessed news to hear that you are alive and under the care of the Americans. It tore my heart apart to think that you and Gerle might have come to a foul end. I hope this letter finds you both well.

We, too, survived the camps, though from the camp above Jagerndorf, (where we lost you, my dear one!) we were taken by train to another one in the eastern zone of Germany. The constant relocating took a toll on all of us. But, I made Opa promise me that we would not give up searching for you. The persistence has finally paid off, to my great joy.

I am well, though my limbs ail me more and more each day. There are too many stairs here where I live, and I don't get out much. Unfortunately, I am alone now. Your Uncle Alois suffered greatly from his ill treatment by the Russians. By the end he was barely coherent, and he didn't recognize Opa or me. It was, I believe, for the best that he died shortly after we were transferred.

Also, it grieves me to tell you, my dearest boy, that your Opa fell ill last year, and passed away while undergoing surgery on his bladder. The conditions in the camp were hard on everyone, even one as strong as Opa. He is now at peace, reunited with his beloved boys. Be cheered to know that he spoke of you often, and that he never doubted you would prevail. You always did have a good head on your shoulders. Oh, how I long to hold you in my arms again! It would warm this old heart of mine. There has been so much sadness and pain.

For a time I struggled alone to provide for your sister, whom you must not worry about. She is well and growing into a fine young girl. Before he died, Opa was able to retrieve some of his savings from the branch of his bank here. But, the money is barely enough to provide for this small apartment. I could not continue to care properly for Gerti. These years have been hard on my health, so you must try to understand. Gerti has been placed in a very reputable orphanage, and she is better off there. I regret, though, that I do not see her as often as I would like, as I am no longer able to travel.

It warms my heart to know that she will have you when I am gone. You must take care of her—you and Gerle. I have sent news to her of your whereabouts. Take care, my darling, and be well. My best to Gerle.

Your loving Oma."

I had to read the letter several times before the significance of her news could sink in properly. The boys seemed to sense my somber mood and guessed at the nature of the letter. They backed off, allowing me time to absorb her words. I scanned the letter for the date, and I realized, with a start, that it had been written almost two months earlier.

The family was no longer together; that much cleared the filter of shock instantly. Only fragments remained, and sweet Oma was alone. My dear Opa was gone. He had taught me so much and had represented, even from afar, a sturdy anchor in my very turbulent world. It hit hard. I bit my tongue, forcing the tears away, and I glanced uncomfortably around me at the tables crowded with noisy boys.

Dieter had thoughtfully created a halo of space around me, and the boys were now absorbed in their own conversations. Occasionally, one would look over at me, catching my eye, and he would smile kindly before respectfully looking away. I remembered that each boy in the room had a true understanding of the nature of my loss, and I felt the sudden blossoming of a deeper affection for them all.

I forced myself to reread the letter again, wanting to be clear on the few details of Oma's news. Uncle Alois had never recovered; that did not come as a surprise, more as a painful reminder that others had suffered greater injustices than I. Yet through it all, his kindness toward others could never have been more genuine, his trust in others more innocent. I had always felt that he had belonged to another world, one where his unique talents would have been treasured and his unfortunate ailments, overlooked. I sighed with mournful relief as I mouthed him a silent farewell.

But, joy...! My sister was alive, and in an orphanage like I was. I turned over the paper, hoping for an address where I could send word, but it seemed I would have to wait for her to write first. Suddenly, I laughed grimly to myself. My sister was growing up and she out on her own just as I was. But, to me, she would always be the little child with the blond pigtails and the angelic smile. As it seemed Oma's health was fading, it was now up to us to continue.

I gazed greedily down the rows of the neatly penned lines from my dear Oma, and my heart sank again as I realized that Oma assumed Gerle and I were still together. I would have to write back, telling her, that to my immense sadness, it was not so. I knew at that moment, that I would have to tell her everything: how Gerle and I had been sneaking out of the camp to bring food for Gerti, how we had gotten caught, and how Gerle had cried when I had been taken away. Would I also tell her how I had not slept for weeks, hearing his wrenching sobs in my head, and wondering all the while if he had survived? Would I also have to relive the lonely year at the farm, or the blood-chilling horror of the dogs at the border?

My past swept before me in a tremendous wave of memories, each one another terrible trap in the perilous minefield of my mind. But, amidst the horrible thoughts there glimmered spectacular jewels of such clarity and beauty, images so vivid that I could almost smell Oma's delicate perfume. I could feel her soft skin as her warm hand rested on my cheek. I could hear the delicate lilt of her voice as she hummed her beloved arias.

That night I wrote her a letter. I told her everything. For the first time, I allowed myself to remember... and to feel it all.

My letter was sent off the next morning, neatly tucked into the leather satchel of the postman. I watched his small cart trundle noisily away from the castle. Already, I was eager for his return. Yet, I knew my letter would take weeks to reach Oma. The mail trains were regularly held up at the borders, and the Russians were notorious for confiscating even the most benign-looking letters. I tried to force the image of my grandmother from my mind, though I couldn't help but imagine her sweet face breaking into a smile upon receiving what I guessed must be a rare correspondence.

Meanwhile, I threw myself into my studies with renewed vigor. I dreamed nightly of valiantly returning to Oma with tales of indispensable and pleasurable employment, a large wallet of money in my pocket and my sister on my arm. The days flew by and the school work became more challenging. Skiing was a joyous distraction and I became increasingly enraptured and comfortable in the dramatic mountain ranges surrounding the small town.

Nevertheless, filling my days with activities did little to take my mind off the letter. I greeted each noon time meal with my stomach in turmoil. This was the time Fraulein Greta would sweep into the room, winking playfully at the boys through her long lashes as she distributed the mail with a dramatic flourish.

Fraulein Greta was, in essence, the house mother, though truthfully most boys saw her as anyone but a maternal figure. She was young and friendly, with a pretty, doll-like face, and she made a point of knowing everyone by name.

Often, as she passed around letters she would remark on something uniquely special to each boy. We were all secretly in love with her, and she, in turn, was fiercely protective of her young charges.

I, like all the others, waited every day for that moment when Fraulein Greta would cross the room, the long-anticipated letter in her hand.

"Come on, Alf. You'll hear something one of these days." said Dieter on one such day, noticing my frequent glances toward the door. He shoveled another dripping spoonful of fragrant stew into his mouth and proceeded to dip his bread into the thick brown gravy coating the bottom of his bowl. "Once, Manfred didn't get a letter back for three months. It all depends where it's coming from." he mumbled, his mouth full of crumbs. I nodded, frowning, as I picked absently at my food. I was getting increasingly discouraged. It was the middle of December and my letter had been sent almost two months earlier. "Oh, finish up, Alf, we have to get to class." Dieter groaned, clearly tired of my despondent and unresponsive mood.

At that moment a murmur of voices near the door signaled the arrival of Fraulein Greta. "Good afternoon, dears! Mail time!" she cried in a cheerful voice as she glided into the room, her gray skirt twirling about her legs. She maneuvered lithely between the tables handing about the letters.

"Oh, Helmut, your cousin sends her love again, you lucky boy!" she teased. Her eyes twinkled playfully, and she laughed merrily. Helmut, a capricious boy with thick waves of brown hair above a narrow face, blushed furiously, but his laughter joined hers as she tapped him on the head with his letter before placing it in his outstretched hand.

I glanced at Dieter, who was watching me intently, and I bowed my head, shaking it with sad resignation.

"Alf!" Fraulein Greta cried. My head shot up, and I turned in my seat, almost toppling my chair. Her eyes were focused on a letter on the top of the diminishing pile, and she was biting the corner of her lower lip with her teeth. She looked up, the twinkle suddenly gone from her large blue eyes. She shook her head grimly and moved forward, the boys instinctively clearing a path for her through the chairs.

She bent closely to my ear and said in a quavering whisper, "I'm so sorry, my dear... so sorry." She placed the letter in my hands and gave my shoulder a tight squeeze. I could hear her skirt rustle behind me as she moved away, but my eyes were locked on the faded envelope in my hand.

It was my own... the very letter I had sent to my grandmother with such high hopes so many weeks before. Across Oma's name, in bright red ink, was the stamp, "Empfanger Verstorben: Individual Deceased."

I could sense Dieter's closeness as he read the words over my shoulder. I heard the sharp intake of his breath, but he didn't speak. He thoughtfully let me be. I stared at the letter in shock, clenching it so tightly that the corners curled in on themselves. As they did so, I could feel the protective cocoon similarly reforming itself around me, sealing in the pain and the emotions that I had finally been ready to release into the soothing gentle arms of my Oma.

In my hands I held the outpourings of my heart's most secret places. I had sent them out into the world to be taken in hand by my sweet grandmother, the one person who would not judge, but who would help me move forward beyond the dreadful memories. But, now it was not to be so.

I rolled the letter into a ball, wrapping my fingers painfully around it. I stood up. Dieter nodded, his mouth tight with concern; I knew he would clear my plate for me. "I'll see you at class." I croaked, my words getting lost in my tight throat.

I returned to my room, grateful to find it vacant. I had only minutes until my next class, but I wanted to collect my thoughts before returning to the company of my friends. I didn't doubt that Dieter would warn the others and hence spare me the ordeal of having to explain my lack of concentration.

I sat on the edge of my bed, my eyes pinched shut, and I held the two letters in my hands—the one from Oma, now a most treasured possession, and the crumpled remnants of my own emotional response. I sighed deeply, forcing down the lump that threatened to rise in my throat. Now, only Gerti and I remained... or perhaps, I hoped, Gerle still did, too.

I had been separate from my grandparents for so long that, in a practical sense, their loss changed little in my daily life. In truth, throughout all the terrible events of the years spent alone, their mere presence in the world had made all the difference. The realization that the soothing halo of their influence could no longer be felt made the sudden void that had opened up around my heart all the more painful to bear.

Now, it seemed, I would have to rethink my path for the future. I could no longer focus my dreams on returning to my interrupted life in Jagerndorf; it seemed there was truly no one left to link me to that place. My sister had always seemed a diaphanous being flitting about the solid permanence of my grandparents; she was now as much a stranger to our home as I was. But, she remained among the few important elements I carried in my heart. My sister was as adrift as I, and as much in search of an anchor of stability as I. The question remained, would we ever find that anchor?

With a sudden determination, I decided that since my future was now wide open; it would have to be whatever I was willing to make of it. Boys Town was my home now, and I would allow my heart to make room for the scenic valleys and mountains that had begun to have such a pull on me. I would never let go of Jagerndorf or its many happy memories, but for now they were to be locked away, precious treasures in the alcoves of my heart and mind.

Christmas descended upon the castle while I was distracted with my thoughts, and I barely acknowledged its arrival... until the day the next letter came. I had wrapped my mind around my work at school to such an extent, that its arrival filled me with a momentary glow of pleasant surprise. It was written in a childish but tidy hand, and it warmed my heart to read the youthful optimism of Gerti's simple words.

She would be nine years old in May, and as I held the small picture she had included in the letter, I smiled. It seemed right that she still wore her hair in braids, and I was relieved to see that, though she wasn't smiling, the horrors of our shared experiences had left no traces of bitterness on her sweet face; it still glowed with innocence and hope.

"Dear Alfie,

Oma sent me your address so I could write. She can't visit me anymore—she is with Opa and Mama. I miss her, and Mama, and everyone. I like it here, though. I am happy and I have some friends. But, I hope we can see each other soon. I miss you and Gerle, too. Please write back. Have a Merry Christmas.

Your loving sister, Gerti."

I wrote immediately, this time confident I would get a response. Therefore, I was able to suspend my anticipation and focus my energies on the increasing demands of my daily life. There were student council meetings to attend, as well as lengthy writing assignments in both German and English. The goal of the Boys Town program had always been to return the boys to society, and for many that included the possibility of immigration to America.

Now that my family was dissolving before my very eyes, I began to consider this option for the first time. I borrowed books from the American liaison officer, and thus a vision of glorious opportunities began to form in my mind. My future would truly be a clean slate. Distance would make the memories fade, and the freshness of a land untainted by war would soothe my cynical spirit. With these ideas swirling about me, filling the chasm of emptiness left by the sudden loss of so many of my loved ones, I went to Dr. Stein, confident that he could direct me on how best to proceed.

"Well, Alf." Dr. Stein considered, his brows furrowed in serious thought. "There is no doubt that immigration to America is the perfect path for many of you young boys. The possibilities there are limitless."

"But, sir?" I asked, "What exactly do I need to do to make it a happen? And my sister... can I arrange for my sister to join me?"

"Most important, of course, Alf, is that you complete your studies. You have two more years here, I believe?" he asked, his fingers twined together beneath his chin. I nodded, sighing heavily; I had been hoping to be spared one of his infamously lengthy explanations. "You must earn some practical training, depending, of course, what your chosen field will be." he continued. "Have you given that proper consideration?" he asked, his stern voice riddled with doubt.

"Yes, sir. I believe that I would like to continue in metallurgy, and I am also interested in construction." I answered.

"Ah, yes, well that is good. America is growing at a brisk pace. Those skills will certainly be in demand there... as they will be anywhere, of course. Goodness knows most of Europe needs young men with those skills." he muttered, shaking his head. "Now, your sister... how old is she, did you say?" he asked.

"She is nine... almost, anyway." I answered, my thoughts flickering to the small photograph tucked in among my most precious belongings in the trunk at the foot of my bed.

"Well, I'm sure you understand, Alf, that she will not be eligible for immigration until she is of age, meaning eighteen... unless she is accompanied by her legal guardian, which, I am sorry to say, you are not."

"Oh." I said, my shoulders slumping noticeably.

"But..." said Dr. Stein, quickly, sensing my sinking spirits. "But, you can certainly keep in touch with her and start the immigration proceedings as soon as her time approaches." He stood up, signaling the completion of our conversation. "So, best put your mind to your work."

The years moved ever forward, and I was blessed to have regular communication with my sister. I watched her evolve through her letters, blossoming into a young woman. Her childish block letters began to be replaced by a graceful and elegant script. Letters arrived regularly for the holidays, Christmas and Easter, as well as my birthday. I marveled at her growing maturity and strength and her ability to adapt to the continuous changes that had made up most of her young life. Also, I treasured the chance to rekindle the family bond that I had never been truly able to have with her. Her childhood had been overshadowed by the monumental events of the war, as well as the ecliptic protectiveness of our mother. I had lost most of my family, and my home, and whatever legacy that would normally have entailed. In spite of it all, I had gained a sister.

Meanwhile, I grew into a man, secure in the hands that had saved me from a miserable future. Boys Town became my family, a safety net that did its utmost to fill in the many gaps that the war and its aftermath had left in my life. Before I knew it, the decade that would be known henceforth as the Holocaust had ended, and so, too, did my time as a student. I was now an adult. Though, in truth, I had been thrust into an adult world many years before… on the day that Gerle and I had pedaled my mother's decrepit old bike away from our home in search of a few morsels of food.

I never forgot Gerle. The pain of our separation never truly healed, and I secretly hoped for news of his whereabouts. But, eventually weeks and months passed when I managed to forget… not him, never him… but the anxiety that always accompanied thoughts of him. But, his unexplained loss soon became harder to bear than the knowledge of my family's tragic fate. Not knowing meant never being able to forget.

New friends came and went, and true bonds were formed with many of my "brothers" at Boys Town. However, I still struggled to shed the anger and bitterness that I realized I still harbored for a faceless perpetrator, the likely targets being elusive and vague… Hitler, the Russians, or perhaps humanity, for having allowed it to happen. I felt as though my troubled past was a cumbersome ballast restraining me from finally moving my life forward. So, I focused my energies on my goal, grand as it was. Finally, upon completion of my studies at Boys Town, I proudly submitted my application for immigration to the United States. Now, all I had to do was wait.

CHAPTER 31

Soothed by a regular correspondence with my dear sister, I began
a new life on my own. Throughout the transition, Boys Town
hovered with a reassuring presence. Dr. Stein was determined to remain
committed to each of us until we found our own niches in the slowly
emerging frameworks of the post war society.

The goals of the graduating orphans were diverse and numerous.
Many, like myself, longed to travel to America, the land of wide open
spaces and the coveted breeding ground for lofty dreams. Others, the Jewish
boys who had been among the fortunate survivors of the Holocaust, felt the
call of their forefathers, and they were heading to the newly formed state
of Israel. Still, there remained some who were determined to return to the
homes from which they had been driven so forcefully, those many long
years before, as the flood of Hitler's greed swept across Europe.

Of all the choices available to us, this posed the most unique challenge.
Hitler's evil had been eradicated. But, now there lurked a new menace—one
which made that hopeful homecoming a fearful prospect. Hitler's fascism
had been replaced by the oppressive doctrines of communism, and the
shadow of this flawed and strict ideological system now loomed over most
of Eastern Europe. To my dismay, I realized that this meant my hopes of
finally seeing my darling sister would not soon be met. The orphanage was
clearly in the lands controlled by the Russians, and for now, it seemed, we
would have to remain apart.

We doggedly continued writing to each other, and I was both thrilled
and dismayed to find my sister maturing before my very eyes through her

letters. I longed to see her face just once; I feared that soon, I would no longer recognize her. It occurred to me, with a shock, that I remembered her only as a tiny six year old girl, her gaunt face filled with pained eyes— eyes that I feared, since our separation, had seen few moments of joy. So, resigned to reacquainting ourselves with each other through the painfully slow postal system, at holidays and birthdays, we were destined to pursue our own separate lives—at least for the time being.

Determined, though, to make a future for myself, and eventually, hoping to provide for my sister, I moved to Munich, along with several of my friends. There we pursued various tracks of employment. We were allotted student housing by the Bavarian government, and thus, we were able to concentrate our attentions on acquiring as many diverse skills as we were allowed. I worked diligently, eager to learn as much as possible in the metal industry, confident that my knowledge would make me a more valuable asset when, and if, my time came to head to America. In preparation for my transition to America, I immersed myself in as much of its culture as I could. I reacquainted myself with the many favorite stories of my childhood, western tales that spoke of faraway places too glorious and wild to even imagine.

The presence of the Allies could still be felt throughout Germany, and nowhere was this more apparent than on the many air bases scattered across the country. The defense of the newly formed democratic leadership was a priority for the powerful western alliance, so good work could be found throughout the area.

I soon found temporary employment at the two local American air bases. My focus shifted from the idyllic parameters of a rigorous school setting to intense and backbreaking labor. I worked hard. My job consisted of constructing updated air installations and dismantling unused and outdated aircraft remaining from the war, an era that had barely faded to beneath the skin of consciousness. This sour taint of the war could still be felt everywhere; many of the major cities remained mortally wounded, their hearts and infrastructures facing decades of repair and reconstruction.

Munich, once an elegant cosmopolitan paradise, was now a maze of toppled history, its medieval streets filled with destroyed and condemned houses. As a result, honest money was to be made in aiding the local government in its rebuilding, so I was grateful to have acquired skills in this field. I saved my money diligently, banking on the hope that my immigration papers would be processed soon.

I had been on my own for over a year, and still I waited for my papers. I watched, with a sinking heart, as those around me made their plans for their futures and methodically followed through. But, some, like me, began to lose hope. Dieter found himself struggling with his limited options. He had also pursued the numerous opportunities available in the metal industry, and he longed to return with his newly acquired, lucrative skills to his home in East Germany, where some of his family remained. Unfortunately, travel eastward was severely restricted, and once there, he could not be guaranteed a decent life. So, for the time being, Munich was going to have to be good enough, its torn streets providing endless long hours of work for both of us.

It was on one such day that I struggled with aching muscles up the narrow flight of stairs to the flat I shared with Dieter and his brother, Gunther. It was one of a series of apartments made available in an old building that had been set aside for students by the government. The rooms were dark and small, hidden as they were among the eaves of the old building. But, they were warm and clean, and, for now, they were home.

I stifled a yawn, fumbling for the door. I was nearly knocked to the floor by both my friends who swarmed into me as soon as I crossed the threshold.

"Alf!" shouted Dieter, grasping my shoulders tightly. His eyes were beaming with delight above a brilliant smile that lit up his broad face. "We were expecting you hours ago. Whew! Glad you didn't come any later. We have been dying to tell you!" He looked at his brother with a conspiratorial grin, as he steered me into the cramped room.

Navigating the small space, I stubbed my toe on the table leg. "Ouch!" I yelped. Hopping up and down and clutching my foot, I cried, "What's going on? Why all the excitement?" I plopped back onto a worn chair, still rubbing my foot, and I scowled crossly at them from tired eyes. It had been a long day on the streets.

Munich's basic systems, like those of so many cities, had had to be rebuilt from the ground up, and it was exhausting and dirty work. I was ready for a wash and a meal, not some foolish guessing game with my friends. "Can't this wait until I clean up?" I groaned, as I rose to head for the bathroom in the hall.

Gunther laughed behind his hand, and whispered, "Give it to him, Dieter!" I looked from Gunther to his brother, wondering what could possibly warrant such excitement. Dieter suddenly whipped his hand out from behind his back, a narrow envelope grasped tightly between his fingers.

"This came for you… delivered right to the door." Dieter said, his voice full of breathless anticipation, his smile never wavering. His eyes twinkled merrily, as he stared into my astonished face. In his hands was a crisp, neat envelope from the Department of Immigration. My papers had finally arrived!

"Looks like you are going to America, my friend!" cried Dieter, his voice shaking slightly. He seemed, suddenly, to realize just what that would mean, and he patted me on the shoulder to hide the surge of his own emotions.

I stared hungrily at the official stamps and markings on the envelope, satisfying myself that it was real and not some glorious fabrication of my imagination. Inside there were pages of instructions for the commencement of my journey. I was to proceed to a camp (Oh, horror!), where I was to receive intense drilling in English, and after a thorough health exam and numerous inoculations against the many diseases that had reemerged during the war, I would finally be allowed to embark on my voyage. A position would be waiting for me upon arrival in America, details for which I would be receiving upon the docking of the ship in New York. New York!… the largest modern city in the world, its pinnacles of steel piercing the sky, separating endless rows of canyon-like streets. This was where I was headed!

"What does it say?" Gunther asked, excitedly, after several minutes of impatient silence.

"I leave for an IRO camp in one week. That means International Refugee Organization, it says." I explained, noticing his puzzled expression. "Oh my God, I'm going to America… I'm really going!" I cried, my voice shaking now, too. I realized, with a start, that it was from nerves and the reemergence of vague doubts, more than anything else. That which I had been anticipating for so long was finally about to happen. But, had I truly considered the consequences? I would be turning my back on Gerti, my only remaining family, and I would be putting behind me an era of such pain and emotion, that I wondered if there would be anything left of me without it.

Who would I be when I reached the bountiful shores of America? Would I be able to crawl out from beneath the heavy mantle of horrendous memories that had molded itself to my very skin, seeping into my subconsciousness, making up the very essence of who I had become? Could I face the fact that leaving the shores of Europe would, in essence, mean leaving behind any hope of ever finding the other half of me that I had lost—Gerle? His childhood and his fate had been tied up with mine for so long, that turning away from him, even now, after all this time, felt like the cruelest form of abandonment.

Dieter, noticing my sudden somber face and tense eyes, seemed to sense where my mind had gone. "Alf," he said, quietly, "You will do well there... and you will be back. This is the best thing you could possibly be doing for your future—and your sister's future, too."

"I know, Dieter, I know." I said, suddenly miserable. "It's just, well... why do I deserve such a chance, while so many... others did not?" I sighed, running my hands through my hair. I stared at the monumental lines on the page. "It's just... I'm going alone. I guess that I never thought it would be only me. I guess I had always hoped..."

I stopped, wondering what I really had been hoping all these years. All my family was dead, except my sister, and they, as well as Gerle, had faded into a luminous shadow in the deepest corners of my mind. In a sense, I would carry them with me always, no matter how far away I roamed. The axis of my heart would always be bound to them, and to my childhood home, nestled in the faraway rolling hills of Jagerndorf.

The day of departure arrived before I was truly ready, and Dieter and Gunther kindly accompanied me to the train station, the same one I had arrived at so many years before. It seemed smaller and more familiar, its wide platforms comparatively free of stranded refugees. We milled about, waiting for the last moment when the departing whistle sounded, none of us wanting to be the first to say goodbye.

"You will have to write us, Alf." Gunther said. "Tell us everything." He nodded enthusiastically, his eyes wide with visions of the fabled nation so far away.

"I will. As soon as I get there, I will." I answered, clapping him on the shoulder with one hand, while I hoisted my old rucksack over my shoulder with the other. It had really become too small for me, but I saved it solely for sentimental reasons. It had been with me through so many experiences, had carried my few treasured items, and it housed them still—precious photographs, my birth certificate, forgotten and still unread all these years.

Along side these was Oma's last letter, its neat script continuing to fade with age, as well as my own returned letter, the red stamp of finality brandished across its dulling surface. I also carried an old suitcase, with the few clothes, books, and photographs I had acquired during my life in Boys' Town. This was it… the few fragments of permanency that proved I had ever existed as one of the millions of souls who struggled to survive during the foulest of eras. I carried with me much more, but it was all in the form of buried memories, many of them still unwrapped.

The train whistle sounded again, and a muffled voice on a scratchy loudspeaker announced the imminent departure of my ride. "You better go." Dieter said, his voice edgy with emotion. "Take care, Alf… take care." We shook hands briefly, then fell into a brotherly embrace. I hugged Gunther quickly, then barely looking behind me, I boarded the already moving train.

"I'll write!" I called, my voice drowned out by the roar of the belching engine. "Good luck!" I cried. I waved, then ran through the lurching hall to the nearest car, where I leaned out of a grimy window to wave some more. The brothers stood silently side by side, their hands raised in a farewell, their round faces fading into the rising clouds of steam.

The serpentine tracks that had carried me to so many places across Europe were, once again, taking me away from the meager life I had managed to carve out for myself. Behind me lay my friends and all things familiar. I was about to embark on the greatest adventure of all, but this time it was to be of my choosing… and that, I knew, made all the difference.

The familiar unsettling rumble in my stomach had returned, but this time not from fear, but rather from excitement. In a few moments I would be traveling to the busy port of the city of Bremerhafen, on the outskirts of which was the "IRO" camp. There, I would board a vast ship and turn my back on the only home I had ever known.

For now though, I would have to reacquaint myself with the crowded conditions and impersonal environment of camp life. I hoped that, at the very least, hygiene and nourishment would be improved over many of my previous experiences. After all, the Americans wanted everyone to be healthy before beginning the long sea voyage.

So, it was with great relief, as I shuffled along amidst a long row of other immigrants through the gates of the camp, that I was met with fresh clean air, thankfully devoid of the toxic odor that accompanied an untended latrine. Everything was in proper order and kept carefully sterilized, including the people. The sole purpose of the camp was to prepare each potential immigrant for the most seamless absorption into American society. This included detailed medical exams and regular applications of powerful chemicals, as well as shots with terrifyingly large needles to prevent any future outbreaks of disease once we arrived at our destination. This was all meant to guarantee that no one would be bringing illnesses of epidemic proportions into the host nation.

On a more pleasant note, we received intensive English lessons on a daily basis, designed to expose each of us to the everyday situations that we might be faced with upon arrival. Thus, I learned how to order fried chicken, how to hail a taxi cab, and how to recite the Pledge of Allegiance with conviction.

I grew eager for the departure, the date of which remained vague. Large ships passed in and out of the busy ports along the northern coast of Germany each day, the vessels filled with an enormous array of goods, most of which Europeans had not seen for many long years. Also on these ships came fresh American troops, ready to relieve those who had completed their assigned roles in the rebuilding and governing of the collapsed and demoralized nation.

Thus, limited space was available on each return voyage, and there were many individuals and families eager to make the journey. A lottery system was put into place, taking into account each person's health and subsequent length of stay in the camp. I wrote to Gerti immediately, informing her of my plans, and I told her I would send her my address as soon as I was settled. It felt strange to be turning so willingly away from her, but, I knew that it would be years before I could retrieve her from the orphanage. I vowed to myself that I would indeed return for her one day... when I had more of a future to offer her.

Months passed, and soon the cold damp winds of autumn were blowing across the turbulent waters of the North Sea. I grew restless in the camp, longing to stretch my legs and flex my muscles. I had grown unaccustomed to the inactivity of camp life, the hours stretching endlessly forward, punctuated only by mind-numbing lessons and periodic health checks.

Finally, my turn arrived! My name was posted in the mess hall, alongside those of hundreds of others. We were instructed to board the camp train that would head for the dock on the following day. In preparation we were given one final medical check and a last minute delousing. Early the next morning, as the tingling dust still settled about my ears, I boarded the crowded train. The pitch of excitement was high with anticipation for the coming journey.

The day was gray and cold, typical of the coastal weather for the season. It was the beginning of November, 1951, and the damp dreariness hung over what was to be my last sight of European soil for a long time. A hum of silence rose up around me as I settled into my seat, my ears ringing numbly with unspent adrenaline. My mood seemed to be contagious, as the general furor in the car seemed to dull to a muffled drone, punctuated only by an occasional child already overwhelmed by the unexpected activity.

The smell of salt spray and pungent fish filled the air at the vast harbor. I was thrust along with the crowd, as it massed like a swarm of bees about to descend upon its hive. I searched for the ship that was scheduled to depart at noon, but there seemed to be endless rows of massive steamers docked at the quay. The noise was deafening. Everyone seemed to be shouting and laughing, and occasionally the deep sonorous boom of a foghorn would erupt, blocking out all other noise.

The long arms of large cranes swung to and fro, lifting dozens of crates of supplies onto the dock. The dock men shoved the crowds aside restlessly as they worked to maneuver the loads from the many ships before they departed that day. Slate gray water slapped noisily against the pilings; everything hung in a taut balance. I walked with my mouth open and was jostled aimlessly about by the mass of people, who ebbed and flowed as though a reflection of the restless water. Everyone else seemed as awed as I was by the presence of so many enormous ships; I watched numerous vacant faces pass alongside mine. Finally, anxious to board with sufficient time to spare, I interrupted a young American officer assisting an elderly woman.

"Excuse me, please, the midday boat to New York, please?" I asked, trying to pronounce the unfamiliar English words carefully.

"Over there, buddy." he answered, pointing to two enormous ships docked to his left. I gasped, and he laughed. "No, no. The second one—it's between those two." He turned away, still chuckling, leaving me with my mouth gaping at the multistoried ships in front of me. Black smoke belched from their large smoke stacks, and the crowds along the railings seemed to be waving at anyone who would notice.

I wandered a little forward, slightly beyond the first ship, and then I noticed it. Nestled between its two companions, like a sheltered child between two domineering parents, was a third ship. It was much smaller, overwhelmed, in fact, by its neighbors. I sighed in relief. Its scale seemed much more appropriate for the voyage I had had in mind. I couldn't imagine one of the other bigger vessels staying afloat over the deep cold ocean.

On second glance though, I wondered why the ship I was destined to board seemed to be about the size of one of the larger ones' lifeboats. I shook the troublesome thought away, chastising myself for allowing my nerves to run rampant through my reason.

I hurried aboard, stumbling slightly on the long gangplank that hung out over the black water alongside the ship. My eyes were as wide as those of the youngsters around me, as I breathlessly took it all in. I had never been on a ship before, nor had I ever seen the shore from the waterside. Suddenly, I felt that I was a part of something tremendous, something monumental— an Atlantic crossing to the New World.

I had an hour until departure time, but I knew my passage was being funded partly by my own labors while on board, so I hastened to check in with the mess sergeant. There were to be no idle hands among the passengers; every refugee had been assigned a task to defray the great expense of the journey. My task seemed simple enough.

"You just punch everyone's meal card, kid." said the mess sergeant, his broad hand scratching the hazy shadow of stubble already emerging on his chin. "One punch, per card, per meal—no exceptions. You got that?" He stared, trying to appear menacing, but his dark eyes twinkled playfully beneath his bushy black eyebrows.

"Yes, sir." I stuttered. My hopes of receiving extra food dwindled at his threat, but I nodded vigorously, nonetheless.

"But, hey, you look like you could use a few square meals, eh?" he chuckled. "You are skin and bones. Come on." He gestured over his shoulder and maneuvered his ample body through the narrow galley kitchen into the mess hall, itself. "We are just setting up for the departure feast—bit of a festive time for most people, really. Their first trip to America, and all." he said, sweeping his hand grandly toward a long table mounded with an amazing array of delectable foods. He grabbed a tray, thrust it into my hands, and said, "Well, eat up, son. One of the perks of working in the kitchens, eh?" He laughed merrily and pulled me by the elbow toward the table.

"Really, sir?" I stuttered. "You mean I can taste just a little?"

"A little! Heck, son, have as much as you like, no one will know the difference, except you." He winked and nodded decisively, glancing at his watch. "Better tuck in though, ship sails in twenty minutes."

I stared after him in surprise as he waddled back to the kitchen, his wide bulk barely clearing the edges of the narrow door. I turned back to the food, wondering where to begin; it all looked so wonderful. I piled my tray as high as I dared, knowing I had only a little time; I wanted to be on deck as the ship raised anchor. I ate quickly, wanting to sample as many of the unique offerings as I could.

There was a variety of tropical fruits, elegant puff pastries stuffed with meats and vegetables, and delicate breads of every shape. Before I knew it, the faint sound of a tuba and an accordion could be heard through the sound-dulling metal of the ship. The familiar melody, "Auf Wiedersehen" wafted across the air, as I stuffed down a few more mouthfuls of the delicious food.

Suddenly, the room gave a lurch and my tray slid across the table, thudded into the deep rim of the table edge, and slid back in front of me. A loud roar from the crowd on deck drowned out the roar of my stomach as it turned over with the violent motion of the ship. I lurched to my feet, stifling a burp that threatened to explode in my throat. I groaned miserably, suddenly wanting to be as far away from the food as possible. I stumbled for the door, but only made it as far as a nearby trash can, where I relieved myself of my gluttonous meal.

Wiping my mouth with a shaking hand, I closed my eyes, but the world around me still rocked violently. I felt my forehead in surprise, wondering what had made me so ill—until another jolt of the ship made my stomach rise into my throat again. It wasn't me! It was the ship! We were moving. We had barely moved away from the dock, and I had already experienced my first bout with seasickness.

I no longer cared to be on deck for the farewell. I hastened to find my cabin, as I was desperate to lie down. But, no matter what hallway I turned down, I was still faced with the same turbulence. Several more times I had to pause at nearby trash cans and relieve my churning stomach of its contents, until only bitter bile was rising into my stinging throat. I longed for a sip of water, but did not want to go anywhere near the mess hall again.

Giving up on the maze of hallways, I ran up to the deck, hoping the cold air would loosen the grip on my insides. Instead, the first sight of the rolling waves as they lashed against the steep sides of the ship, sent me hurtling to the edge, my eyes closed to the swirling water below, my sides heaving with the renewed strain on my stomach.

"Oh, God!" I moaned. "Three weeks of this hell!" I leaned heavily on the railing, trying to allow the cold sea spray to wash away the layer of sweat that had erupted on my face. It was going to be a long voyage. But, I told myself, I had lived through much worse, and besides, I would certainly grow accustomed to it in a few days.

A week later I had become reduced to a quivering mess. I had failed to appear twice for my required duty, but the mess sergeant, upon finding me prostrate on my bunk with a stinking bucket at my side, took pity on me when he saw the putrid color of my face.

"Whew!" he groaned. "Mighty green, aren't you? Not been on the water much, have you, son?" he asked, though kindness had crept into his words.

I shook my head, trying to keep my eyes open, but it only sent my dark and narrow room swirling anew. A tepid light drifted in through the small round porthole, casting an eerie glow across the mess sergeant's stubbly face.

"Ain't the greatest feelin' is it, son?" he whispered. "Well, it will pass. You come back to work when you are able. No problem. Ship's sailin' whether you are working or not, right?" He grimaced as the odor of the bucket wafted through the room. "You just make sure that bucket gets emptied every once in a while. Have to think of your poor roommates, after all."

I had been too sick to care much about my roommates, and though I knew there were several, I had said little to any of them. Understandably, they seemed to spend most of the day out of the cramped space; I couldn't really blame them. I had hardly moved, except to lean over the bucket next to my bed.

After another week, I was very weak and thought, perhaps, that I might not make it to New York to fulfill my dream. The irony of it was not lost on me, as I lay in my bed one night, marveling at the cruel twists of fate that twine themselves around our lives. How was it possible for me to have survived the terrors of such a horrific war with so little food, yet, here, on a simple ocean crossing, I was not able to enjoy the piles of plentiful food made available by the portly mess sergeant?

That night, as I struggled to sleep amidst the continuous upheaval of the room, I was jolted awake by a shrill whistle just outside the cabin door. Everyone sat up, wondering what could be amiss, for it was clear that something was not right. There was a deafening roar of wind outside the ship, and the water hissed violently against the small porthole between our beds. The whistle stopped, but it was followed by the crackling voice of the captain over the speaker system.

He said, "Attention! Attention! All passengers proceed immediately to your designated lifeboat and await further orders. Life vests are under your bunks. Assist all children and elderly first. Stay calm, but move quickly! Luggage will not be accepted on the lifeboats."

Several different languages erupted around me in the darkness, and there was a flurry of activity to get to the door. I stood up with a groan. The brightness of the lit hallway sent stabs of pain through my swimming head, as I struggled to put on my shoes. I was jostled and pushed as the other men from my room fought to enter the swarming mass of frantic people already filling the narrow hallways. Screams and panicked yells echoed throughout the ship, as everyone tried to struggle up the ladder steps to the floors above.

I grabbed the bunk to stay upright, but I was thrown against the wall as a particularly nasty wave blasted the side of the ship, and my empty stomach rose in revolt once again. I could hear those already in the hall being sick as well, though from seasickness or from fear, I wasn't sure. Grabbing my lifejacket, I joined the throng of people. I realized with a jolt of desperation, that it would be a long wait. An elderly lady had fainted in the middle of the stairs, and she was now being awkwardly hoisted upward, her lolling head banging dangerously on the metal railing.

The ship rolled and groaned menacingly, its seams stretched to their breaking points, but still the crew fought against the elements. Storms were a regular part of an Atlantic crossing, autumn being a particularly rough season. The captain was an experienced seaman, and he certainly had sailed successfully through many such storms… or so I hoped.

By the time I reached the deck, the winds had subsided slightly, and the rolling of the ship had become more regular, sending the waves rippling away into the horizon. The water was opaque and cold, its crests tipped with an angry froth of white. But, the danger seemed to have passed, for the lifeboats remained mounted on their brackets. The passengers began to grow restless, moaning about the long wait in the bitter Arctic air that was blowing in from the north.

The captain gave the "all clear", and it was, once again, a mad dash down the treacherous stairs to the relative warmth of the lower decks. It wasn't until the pale hours before dawn when the sky finally glowed with a blanket of stars, that we knew the danger had passed. The sea had lost its sheen of ominous black, and the waves had settled back into a gentle rhythm, ready to caress the mottled sun as it rose behind us.

I hurried back to my bunk, anxious to return to a prone position, for, in spite of the calmer seas, my knees were still trembling and my stomach was still in knots.

Later that day, the mess sergeant stopped in to check on me, gently pressuring me to venture a trip to the mess hall. "You need to eat more, son. That's your problem. You're getting weak." I stared at him in horror; the very thought of food turned my stomach upside down. "Well," he muttered, catching the panic in my eyes, "Well, perhaps I should call the doctor down here to check you out. Don't want you landing in New York looking like that—you'll scare all the ladies away!" he chuckled.

"Thank you, sir." I groaned. "I'm sorry that I have not been up to help too often in the kitchen."

"Well, that's all right, son. That's all right." he muttered, his mood suddenly somber.

The doctor arrived shortly after the mess sergeant had left, and he shook his head bitterly at the sight of my ashen face. "You should have come to me sooner. You young ones, thinking you can ride it out. Best nip things in the bud, so you can get back on your feet. That's my motto. Nip it in the bud." he said briskly, scowling. He had sparse brown hair splattered with gray, and his eyes were strained with overwork as they peered at me through the small spectacles that were perched precariously on his nose. "Now, I want you drinking fresh water regularly. Slowly, mind you—little sips." He raised his eyebrows, waiting for me to nod in agreement. "The mess sergeant told me you have been like this from day one— don't know when I've ever seen it last so long, staying this severe." He placed a small decanter of water next to my bed and turned toward the door. With his hand on the latch, he turned back, saying, with a parting glance. "Only a few more days, my boy... then you'll be on dry land again."

Those days seemed to go on for ever, and still the endless blanket of rippling gray water spread out in every direction. I longed for colors— the hues of autumn that I had always taken for granted, the dark greens of the pine forests that wrapped around the hills surrounding Munich, the red geraniums brilliant against white stucco walls.

Finally, after twenty-two days on the rocking ship, when I could have been thrown overboard numerous times and would never have been the wiser, the announcement rang out clearly over the speaker. "We will be arriving in New York City in about three hours."

America was only hours away—the ordeal was nearing its end; stable ground would never feel more precious to me then at the moment I touched the solid land. I was determined to rouse myself before we arrived. I could not land in my new home, while lying in my own vomit. I struggled upon weak legs to the bathroom. Clenching my jaws against the foul smell of the small untidy room, which threatened to begin the cycle of sickness again, I washed for the first time in weeks. Layers of sweat and grime dripped away, and I felt slightly reenergized. I knew the harbor would pose its own turbulent problems, but the knowledge that land was imminent made all the difference.

I packed my few belongings slowly, stalling the moment when I would have to go up on deck and face the motion of the water. Finally, I could put it off no longer, and I staggered to the deck, gasping as the cold winter air hit my face. The deck was already swarming with curious refugees, restless from the prolonged weeks of inactivity. The dreams of many had been steeping for so long; the pent up excitement ran like electricity through the milling crowd.

At first it appeared like a pale line in the distance, then slowly the details began to emerge. I gasped in awe, as what I had thought were a series of low hills began to coalesce into tall buildings, each one unique from its neighbor, each one with thousands of glass windows reflecting the long veiled sun of the short winter day.

Hovering like a beacon at the heart of the harbor was the Statue of Liberty, her long graceful arm raised with confidence, and her face filled with a strength that was invigorating. We sailed directly beneath her, and I struggled against an overwhelming dizziness as I tried to keep my eyes on her glorious golden flame. I was staring into the very soul of America, and she was gazing down on me with welcoming eyes, inviting me to her shores, free to recover, to live, and to dream.

The flutter of excitement mingled with the hollow space in my aggrieved stomach, and I began to grow eager for when the boat would dock. Instead, the captain dropped anchor, well out in the harbor, out of the path of ships, but away from land. We were to be quarantined until the health inspectors had a chance to check the ship over. Any sign of disease, and we would be turned away.

I leaned on the railing in despair, wondering how much longer I would have to remain aboard. My eye caught a movement against the relative calm of the water of the harbor. Peering more closely, I watched in horror as a large furry bundle scrambled nimbly up one of the massive ropes tied to the floating buoys. Jerking upright, I gasped audibly.

"Them's just water rats, kid." chuckled a fellow next to me, the ashes from his cigarette trickling into the water below.

Rats! Suddenly, my mind transported me back to the camps—the screams of the children, their legs gnawed viciously by the horrid yellow teeth, the coal black eyes glittering in the shadows just beyond the precious candlelight. Was it going to be just the same after all? It couldn't be.

As I struggled with this new fear, I wondered if I had made a mistake. Would America really be the place I would finally find a home? Could I ever truly replace what I had lost; could I even truly forget?

It wasn't until the following morning that the captain was finally allowed to hoist the gangplank and invite the restless passengers to disembark. Everyone seemed tired and overwhelmed by the long experience. Children were quieter, their eyes round saucers, reflecting the light from the sky as they gazed up at the dizzying buildings. Even after my feet were reunited with stable land, I still felt as though I were spinning. New York was an awesome sight, indeed!

Now the long waits in the lines began, as each immigrant was processed through the many sieves that made up Ellis Island. Hunger had finally caught up with me, but I forced myself to nibble on a few handfuls of peanuts I had found in my jacket pocket. I had had enough experience with hasty eating to know that, in most cases, haste definitely led to waste.

Hours later I emerged into the daylight, having faced a barrage of questions and papers. I had the name and address of my sponsor in my pocket, and I had legs finally ready to set forth onto my new road. I stepped off the crowded bus that delivered endless loads of starry-eyed refugees into the bustling, buxom lap of the world, and I stopped.

At my feet was a shiny copper penny, my first American money... a treasure indeed. Quickly, I leaned down to pick it up. I glanced around, ignoring the prods and pushes from behind me, and I turned the coin slowly around in my hand. With a grin, I spit on the glimmering russet prize, rubbed it between my fingers, and thrust it into my pocket. Maybe, just maybe, there was luck out there for me after all.

CHAPTER 32

The years passed quickly. The task of adjusting to the United States and its very different lifestyle filled my every waking hour. I soon came to regard it as home, something that had been lacking in my life for so long. But, as preoccupied as I was with my new and fulfilling life, my thoughts were never very far away from those I had left behind, both living and deceased.

I continued to communicate regularly with my sister, alerting her to my changes of address as I moved slowly westward, while I tried out various jobs in the defense industry. Korea was looming large on the minds of the nation, and employment in this area was now a vital part of what drove the economy. The thought of another war, even in a very distant land, brought forward horrible memories I had tried so doggedly to forget.

My sister fought continuous battles with her own memories, too. She blossomed into an adult, lamenting the portion of her childhood that was so cruelly lost to the war and to the resulting lonely years in the isolated orphanage. Several times opportunities arose for her to join a foster family, but each chance dissolved prematurely, and she found herself back in the orphanage, now the home in which she had spent the most years. We often wondered together, through our many letters, what might have happened to Gerle, as well as to all of our other childhood friends. I struggled with the depressing thought that my past had never happened; few now remained to remember it.

Meanwhile, Gerti's situation became more precarious. East Germany had slipped entirely beneath the Soviet Union's menacing control, and she feared for her future in such a repressive society. I was determined to share the benefits of living in the west with her; I had to find a way to get her out from behind the Iron Curtain.

Over the years I had pursued one of the few leads Oma had made available to me in a subsequent letter that had found me long after her death. In it she had relayed information regarding the whereabouts of a cousin of my father, named Rudi. Rudi's sister, Walli, had, in fact, been in contact with my sister, having received information on the orphanage from Oma before she passed away. Walli, like so many others, had been struggling for years just to get by. She was still living in crude refugee housing in West Germany, although it was now more than ten years after the end of the war.

As I muddled over how best to introduce myself to Tante Walli, and thereafter to inform her of my plan for Gerti's removal from the East, I continued to move ever westward. America, in all its vastness, had awed me from the start. Its open spaces could not have been imagined accurately from the tidy close villages of Europe. There existed a reckless freedom that I found refreshing, especially after the chaos and containment of the war. But, as the novelty of my journey began to pale, and I felt increasingly at home in my surroundings, I felt again the pull of the mountains.

The cradling hand of the rolling hills around my home town had always soothed me and made me feel safe. The war destroyed my sense of well-being, but the comfort of that nest of mountains remained, albeit hidden at times, buried deeply in my heart and mind. On the wide prairies of the Midwest a vulnerability, as well as an isolation from the natural world around me, seeped into my consciousness, and I realized that I needed to move on.

Finally, after researching the opportunities in my field, which had broadened significantly with almost a decade of experience under my belt, I set my sights on Colorado. Denver was a rapidly growing city, in a state that had found a secure niche in tourism. The beauty of the surrounding mountains attracted many others like myself who wanted to renew that vital connection to the land.

By 1960, I found a steady job making dentist tools at a laboratory in Denver, only an hour from one of the most stunning mountain ranges in the world. Life was good. Soon, I rediscovered the joys of skiing, and I found myself spending most weekends on the many glorious trails across the Colorado Rockies.

With a pang of guilt, I sent Gerti my new address. I imagined her still stuck in the small childish world of the orphanage, as she read about my many opportunities and travels. But, soon her next letter arrived, and with it came a surprise and a possible answer to her problems.

"Dear Alf,

I hope this finds you well. Please do not send word to the orphanage again. I will no longer be there. Soon, I will be traveling west. There is a chance to go to Berlin, and I must not pass this up. There is to be a conference of religious studies, and for this opportunity I will be allowed travel papers. But, with your help, I hope not to return. I will communicate with Tante Walli—perhaps you can arrange something through her, as she is our best contact.

My fondest regards, your loving sister, Gerti."

I stared at the letter, my anxiety growing, as I imagined the risk my sister was taking. The idea of assisting Gerti out of the East had been an abstract idea, one I had not considered fully. But, now I needed to act. She was a young woman, willing to travel to a strange city on her own, with the hope of making a new life away from the repression and deprivation of East Germany. I wrote immediately to Tante Walli, with very exact instructions for communicating and meeting up with Gerti. I also sent money.

I had come a long way from my first shiny penny on the streets of New York City; it was time for me to share some of that luck with my sister. I cursed every day when the mailman failed to deliver the expected response from Tante Walli, or better yet, from my sister, who I hoped was by now safely out of harm's way. Terrible images pelted my mind, my sister's sad face always at the center.

After an agonizing wait, word came. It was 1961, and my sister's first letter from the West arrived. She had traveled safely and had ultimately made contact with Tante Walli. But, my sister reported, my money had already been spent.

"But, dear Alf, please do not be angry with Tante Walli. She has meant well. She was very much in need of many of the essentials, and she used the money for those reasons. She really is a sweet lady and willingly shares her space with me. Perhaps, if you are able, you could send some more, as we are now two mouths to feed. And, since I am now in West Germany, don't you think it is about time we see each other? I want to see your face, see how it has changed. Will I even recognize you? Yours… with curiosity, Gerti."

It was 1963, and I was about to see my sister for the first time since 1945. My heart was already in turmoil even without the added novelty of flying. My first… and last, Atlantic passage, by boat, twelve years earlier, had convinced me that crossing water in any device was deeply mired with problems. It seemed impossible that an airplane would provide smoother sailing than the ship had on that awful journey… I was right. But, at least the misery was relatively brief.

A long and turbulent day later I found myself in Luxembourg, a short distance from the German border and the town of Moers, where Gerti, recently married, now lived with her husband. She had settled quickly into the new freedoms permitted to her in the West, and she had found companionship, which was something that I envied a great deal. My ability to connect with another person deeply enough to make such a lasting commitment was something I was still struggling to overcome. My life in that area had been a series of failed relationships, none of them destined for the permanence I had always admired in my grandparents.

I pondered these heavy thoughts as I made my way ever closer to the one person that I had wanted to bond with for most of my life. Now was my chance to create a relationship with my sister that until this time had continuously been challenged by outside forces, whether it was my mother, the war, or our separation thereafter.

I rented a small car and headed out onto the Autobahn; I was awed at every turn by the ease of mobility. I had left the shores of Europe from a massive refugee camp filled with downtrodden but ambitious souls, and now I was returning as an American citizen, able to travel about at will.

My sister had constantly seemed stunned by this fact. Her letters were filled with endless questions about America, the land that to many Europeans still epitomized freedom and opportunity. We had spent so much of our lives apart, that it seemed sadly fitting that I now hailed from another land.

At the heart of it, though, we both felt the pull of our homeland, its sights and smells as ingrained as a newborn's memory of his mother's voice. It would always be a part of whom we had both become, whether we lived nearby, or halfway around the world.

I approached Gerti's small apartment with great trepidation. I was pleased to see that the money I had sent had made it possible for Tante Walli to move out of the refugee housing and into some nearby rooms of her own. The steadily increasing amounts that I had included in my letters had also helped Gerti find her way to happiness. She had met Joseph, a highly educated interpreter, who had found steady work for the many new companies growing in the country.

The dull gray stucco of their old building absorbed the static light of the cloudy day, but a flash of color could be seen in the row of potted red geraniums on the tidy window sill by the door. It warmed my heart to see that people's fondness for flowers had not been stamped out by the vice grip of the war and its chaotic aftermath. Some beauty had survived.

Moers was an industrial town, one of dozens flecking the Rhein-Ruhr corridor. The war had left little in the area to salvage, so the intrepid German people, with the help of the Marshall Plan, had dedicated the flatlands along the mighty rivers to becoming the backbone of their newly tapped industrial might. The town left little to be desired, but it held everything I hoped to see... my sister. Also, I would be meeting my brother-in-law, as well as a small young niece. Gerti had not waited a moment to fill in the gaps in a life that had for so long been devoid of love and happiness.

I knocked softly, my keys clattering in my pocket. I began to tremble with nerves. What was I expecting to see? I had grown into an adult, and I knew, in my mind, that Gerti had, too. But, in my heart she would always be the little child, so frail and vulnerable, yet so strong for all she had survived.

More importantly, what was she hoping to see in me? Were there expectations yet unfulfilled... blame that needed a shoulder upon which to fall? Had I done everything I could have, back then? I had been a child too, but I had been her big brother... someone who had failed to protect her. Gerle and I had promised her... forever and always. Ah, Gerle. Was he somewhere near? Was he anywhere at all?

After waiting with these questions in my head for several moments, the door finally creaked slowly open. There she stood.

How could I have forgotten that smile, those dimples that seemed to erupt with mirth at the slightest coaxing? I was so pleased to see that she had not lost the ability to smile. Her hair was cut short, and it lay in womanly curls about her head. She was shorter than I, but not by much, and I could see both my mother and my father reflected in her face.

"Alfie!" she cried, flinging her arms tightly around my neck. The intensity of her greeting sent me staggering back into the hallway with startled delight.

"Oh my, Gerti!" I laughed, taking her by the shoulders and holding her at arms length, so I could look into her eyes. The delighted blue eyes of my six year old sister stared back at me, the long years of separation suddenly melting away.

"Come in! Come in!" she said, the familiar dialect of home emerging naturally upon her tongue. We had both been exposed to so many variations on the language with which we had grown up, but the lilts and inflections from home seemed latent and always ready beneath the surface.

Joe greeted me next, his hand shake firm and engulfing around my smaller fingers. He was a large man, with a ready smile, and a polished skill at communication. He was from Yugoslavia, so German came to him as a second language, albeit a thoroughly mastered one. But, he seemed comfortable enough to merely listen as Gerti began the many questions she had been waiting for so long to ask.

"What is America like, Alf?" she asked, rather breathlessly. "Is Colorado like home? How are the mountains?" She paused for only a moment, then added, "Do you miss it?" She stared intently at me, her hands still tightly wrapped around my arm. I knew she meant Jagerndorf, not Colorado, my new home. She seemed to be boring into my soul with her eyes, wondering what treasured memories remained, wondering if they mirrored hers.

"I will bring you to visit someday, Gerti... you and Joe, and little Marianna, of course." I answered, slightly disconcerted by her intense gaze. I was not quite ready to talk about the past. Confronted by my sister's presence, I knew that I was facing a window onto my youth, a time I had struggled to bury for so long. To mask my discomfort, I turned to look at the little youngster peeking out from behind Joe's leg. Marianna's cherubic face wore the same dimpled smile as her mother's, and for a flickering instant

I was back in Jagerndorf, my own little sister peeking at me from around Oma's skirt.

We spent the day together, recalling many moments from our past, both pleasant and painful. Finally, my emotions sapped and my mind weary, I excused myself, promising to return for breakfast the next morning. I had limited time before my flight left again for the United States, and I wanted to include a visit to Tante Walli, as well as meet her brother, Uncle Rudi, who lived in the south near Stuttgart.

Gerti clung tightly to me as we walked together to my car. "You haven't changed, Alf. Well, you have and you haven't." she added, smiling. "Remind me tomorrow—I have some things that Oma wanted you to have."

"Get some rest, Gerti. We will talk again tomorrow." I said, hugging her one last time, before slumping, with profound mental exhaustion, into the front seat of my car. I watched her wave, her small figure silhouetted against the afternoon sky, as I drove slowly away. She stood next to her husband and child, one arm wrapped protectively around each of them. In them she had found her happiness, and finally, we had found each other.

The night was restless and filled with many vivid dreams, each one recalling a particularly powerful moment Gerti and I had shared together. I sat up, discouraged, well before dawn, after waking for the second time with the glassy eyes of my mother staring at me from the top of the cart of dead bodies in Maerisch-Schoenberg. The cries of my sister reverberated still, even as I rubbed the tiredness out of my puffy eyes.

I did not want to return to that world in my sleep. I got up, hoping a hot shower would clear my head of the clinging cobwebs that had been disturbed by my reunion with Gerti the day before.

I spent the morning relaxing in my room, trying to avoid the memories that threatened to engulf me again. Gerti seemed very happy; she had found a life for herself, and she had found someone with whom to share it. The horrors of her past would never disappear, as we are all, indeed, a product of our times. But she had found a way to relieve the strain. I finally felt free… free to go home… home to America. My sister would be all right.

Once the sun had risen above the trees, and it proved to be a mild spring day, I drove back to her apartment, ready to make my farewells. Gerti seemed to have come to terms with my presence, and she spent less time clutching at my arm. Sometimes her fingers would reach out and pat my hand, as though to remind herself I was real.

Breakfast was delicious. Gerti had clearly carried on Oma's ability to turn meager provisions into a full meal. Marianna had finally grown brave enough to sit on my lap, and it warmed my heart to know that I now had some lasting connection into the next generation in Europe. A new branch of the tree was ready to place down roots, perhaps someday in the home we had been forced to leave.

"This is for you." Gerti said softly, as we stood in the doorway, my coat already buttoned against the light drizzle that had blown in along the river. She handed me a small package of wrinkled wax paper, its edges frayed and torn. But, my name was still clear beneath the rubber band tying it together.

"Opa took it from the house... that day, when the Russians came." she said, her voice faltering. "He made Oma tell me where it was. Said it had to get to you." She wiped a tear from her cheek. "He never stopped believing we would find you... never. He told me before he died... that I was to somehow, someday, get this to you." Her voice gave way and she buried her head on my shoulder. Her shoulders shook, and then she continued, her words muffled against my coat, "I never thought I would actually get to give it to you, Alf. It feels so good, finally doing something that Opa asked me to do so long ago. It has been a burden, not knowing if I could carry out one of his last wishes. It feels good to finally let it go."

"Thank you, Gerti, thank you." I answered, pulling her into a tight hug, my throat constricting in the familiar attempt to shield myself against the flood of overwhelming emotions. "I will visit again soon." I said, clearing my throat, and changing the subject. "Please send pictures of little Marianna, and the next one, of course, when it arrives." Gerti had told me the day before that she and Joe were expecting their second child.

I drove away from Moers, my mind replaying the many conversations we had shared in the short time we had spent together. The next visit would be longer, but for now we needed time to absorb the intense experience of the reunion.

In a daze, I braved the nerve-racking German Autobahn and headed south, ready now to complete my trip. Suddenly, going home to Colorado seemed very important. Here, I realized with a sobering start, I was just a visitor.

Uncle Rudi was a delightful man, full of quick humor and thoughtful words. We spent my brief visit pleasantly free of ponderous conversations about the past. Rather, we tested each other on our abilities to consume significant quantities of beer.

So, it was with a lighter heart and a slightly lighter head, that I left his house, confident that I had resumed a family bond that would survive a lifetime. Rudi had informed me that a great-aunt of mine lived nearby, so I proceeded with great eagerness to her small apartment.

Tante Anna, now a frail woman in her eighties, lived alone, tended daily by her kind neighbor. Anna had lost most of her sight and relied mostly on touch to navigate her way through the world. So, I sat calmly while her gentle wrinkled hands traced the curves and outlines of my face. Her soft touch was mesmerizing, and I marveled at the sensitivity that was apparent on her face, as her mind took in all the information that her hands fed to her so carefully.

Finally, she spoke. "You look just like your father, my boy." Her face broke into a smile, as though she could picture my startled face in her mind. "Yes, you remind me of him. He was a handsome man... so young, so young."

She shook her head sadly, a cloud passing over her sightless eyes. "You were famous, my boy." she said suddenly, and I jerked my head up, wondering to whom she was speaking.

"Uh, sorry, Tante Anna. Were you talking to me?" I asked.

She nodded, groping across the couch for my hand. "You were the boy who got the jam." She paused, apparently waiting for some kind of answer. "... In Maerisch-Schoenberg. You ran across the street to get the jam and cheese. I was there, too."

I gasped, stunned that one of my family had been so close, and I had not known it. "You were there?" I stuttered.

"After you left, my dear, after you left." she said, nodding again. "But, the word was out about Alfie and his young friend. Whatever happened to your friend, anyway? Gerle, was that his name?" she asked, her round face pinching into a frown.

"I... I don't know. We, uh, we... were separated." My mind was filled again with the sounds of shelling and the whine of bullets flying around me, as I navigated the rubble in the street outside the camp. I could feel the warm sting of blood on my neck. I felt again the cold indifference of the women as they snatched my prize away from me.

"There, there." she said, patting my hand again with hers. "So many lost... so many."

Tante Anna had tired quickly, and I left her resting quietly on her couch, her ample frame spilling pleasantly over the sides. I felt it was time to go. The memories had flooded back in waves, continuous since I had set foot off the plane. I was weary and ready to go home.

I slept most of the way on the plane, relieved that my exhaustion seemed to defray some of the motion sickness that clearly was destined to be a part of my travels.

As I unpacked my suitcase on my bed at my apartment in Denver, I finally sat down to open the package my sister had so carefully kept for me for so many years. The wax paper crinkled noisily as I unwrapped it, before it gave way to reveal more glimpses into the past.

Opa's last will and testament lay on top, and I set this aside to read later, knowing that Opa had had nothing left to pass on to his loved ones. The war had consumed it all. The home and the grounds he had cared for so lovingly had been abandoned, waiting for someone else to discover the stories it held in its old walls.

Beneath his will was a small stack of the few report cards I had brought home from school before the war had taken that, too. My name appeared at the top of each one, printed neatly in the severe style of our professors. I shuffled through these, the faces of my many friends drifting through my mind. Next came the deed to the house, something that now had little more than sentimental value. Millions of people had been displaced and property lines had been redrawn. It was not fair, but thus it had always been, and thus it remained, as the legacy and spoils of war.

I set this paper aside, taking up in its place several birth certificates, Opa's included. It warmed my heart to think that Opa had wanted me, the only surviving male in the family, to have these papers, each of them a fading link to the past, a time that had all but been erased by the war.

I set these aside gently, aware that several of them were almost a century old and in need of delicate care. The last paper in the pile was an official document, stamped with the embossed seal of the high court of Brno, the county seat. At first glance, I thought Opa had confused someone else's papers with one of his; it made no sense as I began to read. Then, my mouth dropped open, and the paper fell from my hand, drifting to the floor at my feet.

I snatched it quickly back up and sat down, my head suddenly feeling light with shock. The paper was an official statement from the court, declaring that my father had received an annulment of his marriage and had subsequently remarried. The reason for the annulment was due to adultery on the part of his first wife, who abandoned the marriage for another man only a year after giving birth to... me.

That meant... the mother I had spent my life with had, in fact... not been my mother at all. She had been only a stepmother, reluctant in her role, and she had been related to me in no other way but proximity to my father.

The paper continued to state that the offspring from that marriage... again me, was decreed to live with the grandparents of said child... Opa and Oma.

I sat in silence for several moments, the words blurring together before my unseeing eyes. I was replaying my past again, the ever-present painful parade of images. But this time, at the center was my mother... or the woman I had always believed to have been my mother. Now, I understood. I understood the indifference, the lack of concern for my well-being, her protectiveness over Gerti... the unexplainable distance that had always been there... the distance that I had always believed had been my fault.

Anger began to well into my throat, anger at everyone for the years of lies. Anger at the dead for explanations that had died with them. Anger at the mother who had turned away from me, her first born, for another man.

Then, another sensation appeared... wonderment... curiosity. What had my real mother been like? She was most undoubtedly deceased by now. How old would she have been, anyway?

I needed answers, answers to more questions than I could even begin to ask. The childhood that had always felt so elusive, the peaceful time before the war, had floated in my consciousness like a translucent dream that had never truly existed. It felt even more ethereal now. Just what had been real? What had been lies? Could I even trust my own memories? And most importantly, was there a memory of her somewhere, deep in my heart, that mother's voice... the voice a newborn never forgets? Suddenly, I longed to remember... and to find out.

CHAPTER 33

A shadowy chasm had opened before me, a pit so dark, so mysterious, that I feared going in. Yet, I was compelled; I had to know. Who was I? How much of my childhood had been lies? How many people had known, watching from their secret places as I stumbled through the awkward trials of growing up, wondering all the while at the unexplainable distance between myself and the woman I believed to have been my mother?

My childhood had been a sham, a fabrication of carefully maintained glass pillars of lies and half-truths. These lofty pillars had held up my castle in the sky, a dreamlike existence, one that now seemed to evaporate with each passing thought. Gerti was my half-sister, not entirely of my blood... but, I told myself with conviction, just as much my sister. Did I now love her any less, knowing our true relationship? No. She was all I had left, and for whatever that bond was worth, it meant everything. Just what had it meant, though, having a mother? I had seen the dead body of the woman whom I had believed was my mother. Since then, I had berated myself for not erupting in an emotional volcano upon the sight of her limp and mangled form. For years I had torn at my heart, wondering what kind of son did not feel passionate about his mother's gruesome demise. Now, I realized, she had never been my mother. Somewhere, deep inside me... I must have known. Her death had moved me and horrified me, of course, but the void that I had expected to follow such a loss never materialized. After all, the emptiness had always existed.

Now, I was desperate to fill that void. The millions of persons displaced by the war had scattered far and wide; millions more had died. The task to trace any of those I had known would be daunting. I would be searching for someone about whom I knew nothing, except that she had once held me to her breast.

The first step would be to head back to Europe, which meant braving the bumpy skies. Archives were being unearthed, though many had been damaged or lost, and regional reunions were beginning to become a regular event, as the population of Europe emerged from its hibernation of shock.

Meanwhile, my life at home had taken a more pleasant turn. My passion for the mountains took me regularly to the high country around Denver, and I realized that I belonged in the hills more than anywhere else. A small ski area provided the perfect retreat for me to work and ski, as well as a soulful spot for me to lick my many emotional wounds.

And like Gerti, I too had finally found someone with whom to share my life. It was here that I met the woman who would become my wife, someone as equally bound to the beauty of the mountains as myself. She accepted my turbulent past without question, acknowledging the baggage that accompanied that part of my life, and together we strove to learn more.

Trips overseas became regular occurrences. Often I would go alone, but many times my wife, Sunni, would accompany me. Memmingen, Germany had become the gathering place of those displaced from my region of Austria—Sudetenland, and especially, Jagerndorf, a land that now belonged to Czechoslovakia. I attended several times, tirelessly giving my name and those of my family to anyone who would listen. I milled about the aging crowd, longing for a familiar smile lurking beneath the wrinkled masks of time.

The medieval streets of the the quaint town of Memmingen seemed to hold in their timeless grasp the halted lives of so many, their names reduced to whispered breaths on the mouths of the survivors. After many repeated trips, all of them fruitless and unfulfilling, I finally found news of someone I had sought after for so long.

"He was so young." she began, her wrinkled hand grasping my sleeve, as I stared at her in disbelief. I still did not know her name; the news she carried had eclipsed all else… Gerle was dead.

He had survived the war... though how, she did not know. "You understand, of course, that he never completely recovered." she muttered sadly. "He was always very weak and sickly. It was his heart, finally. That is what did him in. But, so young..." She nodded sadly. Patting my arm again, she seemed at a loss for more suitable words.

I worked it out in my head, which swam in a fog of disbelief and denial. Gerle, my dear friend, had been thirty-eight when he died. But, I told myself, at least he had survived... for awhile. Did that mean I could now finally let go of some of the guilt?

I prodded the woman for further details, but she muttered vaguely and moved away, anxious to blend into the anonymity of the many faces and lives that I didn't know. Therefore, I was unable to shed any further light on Gerle's life. I watched her disappear into the crowd, his story fading with her. She left me standing, as the hum of the mingling voices around me blurred into a painful continuum, accentuating the numb ringing in my ears. Had he made it after all? Would I ever know? Had there been happiness? ... Oh, please, at least let there have been happiness.

But, now I knew that he was indeed gone. In a way, it soothed me to know that he suffered no more. Perhaps, now I would stop hearing his anguished sobs in my dreams, where they lingered even after all these years.

The loss of Gerle, for the second time, pained me deeply, but slowly it faded from my mind. Yet, he stayed on in my heart, an ever present symbol of lost dreams and missed opportunities. Meanwhile, my life in America had taken a new direction, and an opportunity for a permanent life in the mountains presented itself.

My wife and I raised two children, Erik and Kari, in the high mountain community that had become our home. Life snowballed, as it should, and it became busy and full. But, the fulfillment never completely suppressed the questions that remained in my mind.

My real mother had had another child, perhaps more. Where were they? Who were they?

We returned to Europe many times, taking the children along to meet their numerous cousins. Gerti and Joe, by this time, had returned to Joe's homeland, and they lived in a small community in Yugoslavia. It was a wonderful feeling to be able to show my children a part of the world that they had never experienced before, and to allow them to meet a family that they had come so close to never knowing.

Throughout all our travels, though, something was still missing. I longed to go home, not Colorado, this time... but, home. I longed to smell the air of my youth, to feel the familiar grass beneath my feet. After discussing it with Sunni, I communicated with Gerti, encouraging her to accompany me.

She was reluctant, to say the least. Gerti had left Jagerndorf at such a young age. Her memories of home had been overwhelmed by the war, which had left only vague impressions of the place in her mind.

We both knew that the return would open wounds that had never completely healed. But, I felt that by going back, perhaps I could allow some of the more pleasant memories, memories of better days, to resurface. So, after much discussion, and a little research, we headed out.

The East was in turmoil. Gorbachev was making a very public effort to move the shadow of the old school of Soviet dominance out of Eastern Europe. It would be a nerve-wracking journey. Tensions during this chaotic transition were high, and visitors were carefully monitored. But, we had made our decision, and we couldn't turn back now.

It was May, 1987, and I met Gerti and Joe in Vienna, the beautiful jewel of Austria. They had driven from Yugoslavia in their small car, the very same that would now carry us over the border into our homeland. We drove through the rolling hills of Austria, enjoying the warm spring breeze and the calming sights of a country well-recovered from the war. The luscious green vineyards rippled out in waves along the road, and the air glistened with the dew from the night's light rain.

The tension mounted and silence fell as our small car approached the menacing border with Czechoslovakia. There were the guards, their guns drawn, their eyes distrustful and full of suspicion. The many similarities to my perilous journey forty years before were alarming, and I hovered on the verge of turning back. I glanced at Gerti. Her face was rigid with latent fear, and I knew suddenly that we had to go on; we had to close the floodgates of the unknown. We had to face the past, in order to better face the future.

I tried to smile as I handed the closest guard my papers. Several others were strutting importantly around the car, staring with curiosity at the Yugoslav license plates. With a flick of a wrist and a turn of the head, they ordered the trunk opened, and they searched it thoroughly, letting us go only after they had run a mirror under the full length of the vehicle.

We breathed a collective sigh of relief as we pulled slowly away from the line of cars to continue eastward. The route was narrow and winding, lined on either side by emerald pastures, many still filled with houses damaged from the war. Flags of deep red dripped like blood from every post and pole, as the bold lines of the Soviet Union's hammer and sickle met us at every turn.

The nationalistic May Day celebrations were being conducted across all of the Soviet Union's vast domain. Evidence of military might and power blared at us from every corner, and all the roads were dominated by bombastic parades of arsenal. Just as it had been when I had pedaled madly on my bike with Gerle those terrifying days during the war, surrounded by tanks and soldiers, thus it was again. I could not help but be moved by the ironic symbolism of the parallels.

The road in front of us was clogged with belching trucks, each of them filled with Soviet soldiers reveling in their official day of self-righteousness.

Joe inched the small car forward, not wanting to get too close to the large trucks and the rows of tanks that lumbered slowly along. I shook my head in disbelief. The memories were too vivid, as I watched it all play out again before my eyes.

Finally, after an agonizingly slow trip, we approached the outskirts of Jagerndorf, renamed Krnov by our successors. Once again, silence engulfed us. There seemed to be no words to fill such a moment. I glanced at my sister, watching her eyes dart about, as she desperately attempted to find something familiar. She had been so young, so traumatized; her memories were of another place, another time.

My own memories flooded back, crystal clear and painful, constricting my throat and blurring my vision. It was all so familiar, painfully so… yet, nothing was the same. I had left as a young boy, my family gone, my heart filled with fear. I now returned as an adult, an American with a new home. Yet, here I was, surrounded by so much to remember, so much I wanted to remember… but even more that I wanted to forget.

Joe drove slowly, sensing our need to see it all. Much remained the same, including many of the buildings that had suffered heavy bombing and mortar attacks. In some places, entire blocks of houses were gone, paved under to provide for new generations. The old center of town was intact. The ornate Rathaus still dominated the cobbled square where I had stood as a young boy with Opa.

There was the same balcony, now empty, its gray stones sparkling in the sun. He, Adolf Hitler, had stood there, laying out his strategy for a New World Order, numbing the minds of thousands, as he set about to eliminate a race of people from the Earth.

Here was where it had begun for me. Here was where Opa had told me it would all be over soon, but instead, I learned it would last a lifetime. Here was where my arm had ached, as I was forced into a salute that didn't reflect the feelings in my heart. Here was where my eyes had pricked with shame and fury. With the instinct of a child, I had sensed Hitler's evil even then, my heart filling with a nameless fear, a fear that would soon come to dominate my entire life.

Now, I stood in the same spot overwhelmed by a feeling of renewal. I had come home. Hitler had not won after all. For some of us, there would be another day.

We continued on through town, inexplicably drawn toward our ultimate destination. There was the bridge, repaired now, but smaller and lacking the grandeur I had remembered as a child. There was the water, flowing as it had for centuries from the realms of ancient lore. There was the place where the house... should have been.

It was gone now, filled instead by a small garden framing the spot where the house's sturdy foundation had once stood.

Still, Gerti remembered nothing. She gazed about helplessly as though willing herself to feel. In the end she broke down, the strain of reaching for her stolen life becoming too much. We stood together, holding tightly to each other beneath a large apple tree, one of the very ones Opa had planted so long ago. Its pink blossoms drifted down around us, welcoming us home. The soft fragrance filled my senses with a warmth that soothed the empty spot in my heart. I reached up, my eyes squinting against the sun, and I snapped off a small twig of the tree—all that remained of my legacy.

Emboldened by my successful journey home, I took the opportunity to repeat my trip in 1989. Much had happened in the region and the world during the interim. Gorbachev had revolutionized the Soviet Union, and democracy and autonomy were now spreading across the long-occupied lands. I hoped that in the new political climate the trip would be more gratifying.

This time I was accompanied by a good friend, Meta, who, prior to his immigration to the United States, had been on the Czech Olympic Ski Jumping team. He had heard of the success of my prior journey home, and he was inspired to return to his hometown as well.

When Gerti and I had been in Czechoslovakia, we had been frustrated by the difficulty to communicate, as now the language of our homeland was unknown to us. So, I decided it would be useful to travel with someone who could better handle the circumvention of the many barriers that inevitably loomed when traveling in another country.

Therefore, Meta and I decided to travel together. We made our way, first, to the home of Meta's cousin, Ed, a delightful Czech man and a successful architect. Sunni and I had met him in the United States the prior year. At Ed's home Meta and I parted company for a short time, while he revisited some of his own childhood sites, and I spent time with Ed and his family, enjoying their boundless hospitality.

Finally, after two weeks, I grew too restless to wait any longer. The familiar pull to return home was emerging once again. Meta and I were joined by an enthusiastic Ed, as well as his young son, Tomas, who I gratefully hired as a driver. I wanted to be free from the stress of navigating in an unfamiliar setting. Their presence also enabled me to overcome the difficulties that arose with the language barrier.

Unlike the journey with my sister, when we had approached Jagerndorf from the south, we now followed precisely (in reverse) the route that Gerle and I had ridden on our bike those harrowing long days in 1945. Waves of nostalgia swept over me. I noticed hills and valleys through which Gerle and I had stumbled, the Russians hovering ever closer. Now, the roads were paved and free of the heaps of twisted vehicles and rotting bodies that had littered each bank and ditch.

However, humanity had been slow to return to the shattered land. Villages along the road were sparsely inhabited, and the old homes lining the streets still showed signs of damage from the war.

The oppressive presence of Soviet domination had visibly faded. The roads were pleasantly free of tanks and other military vehicles, except for the ones that had been ordered to return to Moscow.

Upon arrival in Jagerndorf, we checked into the hotel I had arranged prior to our arrival, then we set out immediately to explore the town. I had told Meta and the others that, this time, I wanted to venture into the surrounding valleys, perhaps visiting the town of Wallstein, where I had journeyed so often with Opa. With this in mind, and fearing few available restaurants on our route, we decided upon a picnic for the next day.

The following morning we wandered into an old butcher shop, its peeling paint trimming a broad window behind which were many varieties of succulent rich sausages. I found a spot in line, feeling suddenly out of place behind the long row of women, their heads draped with colorful scarves. They eyed me curiously, clearly unaccustomed to seeing a man shopping in their midst. Meta and the others watched me with amusement, but they seemed to be content to allow me to navigate this hurdle on my own.

The air was fragrant with the heady aroma of meat: dense blood sausages, fat logs of salami, and large sides of ham. I waited patiently, enjoying the easy atmosphere of the place until it was my turn. The young lady behind the tall counter gazed at me with a smile, as I struggled to get my mouth around the guttural words labeled on the cards next to the displayed items. I ordered two pounds of cold cuts, some freshly baked rolls, and I asked for several beers and sodas from a shelf behind the counter. Our picnic was going to be a full meal.

It wasn't until the crinkling of the wax paper echoed around the room, that I realized the line of ladies had ceased their idle gossip and were now staring at me in silent awe. It occurred to me, as I self-consciously drew out a few neatly folded bills and tried to figure out the currency, that I held in my hand more money than most of these women saw in a month. I had also just ordered more food then they probably consumed in an entire week. In spite of the wide variety of fine food available, there was little money circulating with which to buy it.

I blushed with a mixture of embarrassment and bitterness, realizing with a start, the irony of the situation. Would they believe me if I told them that I had walked these very streets as a boy? Would they shudder knowing that I had slithered through the remnants of the town on my belly, navigating dead bodies to return to a wretched camp? Or, did they only see an American, juggling money with relative ease? I left the store, my shoulders prickling uncomfortably with the heat of their eyes following me.

We bustled into the car, ready to be on our way, as the day promised to be a fine one. The first stop was to be Wallstein, the small village that had been the home of many of my ancestors. The narrow winding roads were deserted; only the occasional farmer's tractor interfered with our progress. We drove through two small villages, then eyeing a familiar corner, I told Tomas to turn.

Suddenly, around the wooded bend, loomed a large sign, hastily tacked against a scraggly tree. It read, "Attention! Pozor! Achtung!" The area we had been hoping to enter was restricted. No entry, no photos—Soviet military maneuvers were underway. Tomas stopped immediately and shifted the car into reverse.

"Please, Tomas, just go a little farther. Look, the place is deserted. No one is here. Please, I've come so far." I pleaded. I began to wind my camera, determined to record what might be my last trip to the area.

"Oh, no, Alf. I can't. They can take my license. or worse." Tomas moaned, still preparing to go backwards.

His father muttered something to him from the back seat. Tomas sighed heavily, then he thrust the clutch into drive with a defiant groan. Tomas drove slowly forward, easing the car carefully around each corner. The narrow dirt road was lined heavily on each side with thick bushes, some of which were very overgrown and leaning over the road.

Tomas rolled the car slowly around another bend and slammed on the brakes with a deafening screech. A massive armored Soviet vehicle was hurtling directly at us, each of its wheels taller than our car. It advanced upon us rapidly, knowing its might would overwhelm anything in its path. It was clearly not going to stop. Tomas jerked the wheel frantically, and the car slid off the road into the wet grass, sinking into a shallow ditch.

We sat in silence, as the vehicle rumbled noisily past, inches from the rear of our car. Perched on top was a soldier, his ears covered with large headphones and his face concealed behind dark goggles. He shook his fist angrily at us, but roared away without a word. We watched while the dust settled, and the road slipped again into calm, then we got out to assess the situation.

After several minutes of shoving and rocking the car back and forth, we maneuvered it so as to face away from our original destination. Tomas was not about to go any further, and this time I doubted his father would support my wishes.

As we settled ourselves back in the car, I glanced to my right through the brush, catching the reflection of the sun off something white. A small stuccoed cabin sat alone in the bushes, an old Volkswagen camper next to its door. The sun was angled perfectly, and I could read the license plate; the car was from Germany. A short distance from the cabin was a clothes line and beside it stood a woman, meticulously folding retrieved clothes into a basket.

"Tomas, wait!" I cried, already rolling down my window. "Hello!" I yelled, slipping easily into my hometown dialect.

The woman paused, adjusting the basket under her arm. Then, she raised her free hand in greeting, and to my astonishment, answered, "Hello!" The inflection on the word was the same as mine.

"Tomas! Back up!" I cried, gesturing madly with my hand. "There. Pull into that driveway!" I said, noticing for the first time a very narrow path between the trees.

"I don't know if this is a good idea, Alf." muttered Tomas, clearly ready to go home.

"Ok, stay in here then." I said, determined to heed the tingling sensation I was feeling. Something was compelling me to remain. I got out of the car, barely waiting for Tomas to come to a complete stop.

"Good day." I said, again trying out my home dialect. "Are you from here?" I asked, pointing at the license plate.

"My husband is. Just a moment, I'll get him." she answered, smiling. "Willy!" she called, turning slightly toward the cabin. She set the cumbersome basket in the grass and brushed her hair out of her eyes. "We live in Germany now, but visit sometimes. The couple who own this cabin are kind enough to let us camp here from time to time." she added. "Ah, Willy, here is a man..." the lady said, as a man emerged from the cabin.

He walked to his wife's side, his eyes filled with curiosity. "Can I help you?" he asked.

"Are you from this area?" I asked, my voice shaking slightly, as we shook hands. I hastened to introduce my friends, who had now climbed out of the car and were standing at my side.

"My father's place was just over there... years ago." he said, gesturing with his chin and gazing lovingly across the green hills.

I began a brief explanation of the reason for my presence, and before we knew it we were spreading out the ample picnic on the warm grass in the

403

sun by the cabin. Willy explained that the cabin belonged to a elderly couple, who, as victims of the war, had been given the land upon their release from a concentration camp. Many others, Willy's father included, had not been so lucky.

"We come back here every summer. The owners are so generous. It is wonderful to have this chance to come home." Willy said. "But, Alf, if you are searching for family, you should come to the yearly reunion, specific for this region. It is held in Germany, not far from where we live, and it is held in September."

I was reluctant, not confident from my past lack of success, but I took the information. Thus followed a lengthy good bye, as we exchanged addresses. Then, Tomas finally got his wish. We returned to town, our minds filled with the adventures of the morning. The following day, I put Jagerndorf behind me once more.

It was not long after my return to America that I received word from Willy, informing me of the date and location of the next reunion. I was contemplating a trip back to Memmingen, to the reunion where I had located news of Gerle, so I decided another stop could not hurt. But, my confidence was not high; it seemed all leads had run cold.

The Memmingen reunion was held in an exhibition hall in the center of the old town. People from all over wandered about, hoping to make contact with that one special friend or family member they had lost. This time I had no expectations; time had erased the traces of so many lives.

A festive air hung about the place. There was music and the ever present availability of fine food and drink. I stood off to one side, slowly nursing a tall beer, as my eyes casually scanned the crowd. The organizer had welcomed me by name on the microphone, as I was the attendee who had journeyed the farthest to participate. So, I was not surprised when someone approached me from behind.

"Alfie?" said a low voice. I turned, and there stood a lean man. His hair was gray at the temples, and his shoulders were already slightly stooped, though he seemed to be not much older than I was.

"I'm sorry?" I stuttered, wondering what face from the past matched the voice. My mind whirled with the possibilities, but age and many difficult years had hidden any youthful signs.

"It is Karl. Though, you might remember better, Gretel, my sister. She was your age." he answered, smiling. Then, I saw it, the same narrow shoulders, the thin distinguished face, different only in that now it was framed by lines of worry and the burdens of a traumatic life. He had been a young teenager, a fellow on the verge of adulthood, when the war had come. I remembered his sister, her blond braids flitting coyly about her smiling face.

"And Gretel... is, is she here?" I asked, peering around, eagerly.

"Ah, no. She could not make it." Karl said, shaking his head sadly. "She has been frail for quite some time now, and traveling is difficult for her."

"Oh, I'm sorry." I answered, disappointed at missing the opportunity to forge another link with my past.

The memories flooded back as Karl and I recalled shared experiences and marveled at eachother's stories of survival. One thing was constant— the effects of the war had never completely gone away for any of us. There were gaps in all our lives. Karl informed me that Franz was still alive, and that they had made contact with him several years earlier. I took Karl's address, and that of his sister, and he wrote out Franz's as well. We promised to write often.

I left the reunion feeling revitalized. I was ready for a heartier search into my past. I drove the short distance to Willy's town, where the Wallstein reunion was already in full swing. Not long after I arrived, the rain swept in, pounding loudly upon the roof of the meeting hall. I paid my respects to Willy, telling him I was scheduled to meet my sister at the train station very shortly.

I milled about aimlessly for several minutes, depressed by the unknown faces upon the countless strangers. Why had I come? With my mood drooping as much as my damp clothes, I decided that the anticipation of any more unlikely success was too much. It was time to leave. After a brief visit, I navigated through the puddles back to my rental car, but was distracted by Willy's voice behind me.

"Alf!" he cried, running out to my side, his hair already damp upon his head. "Come back in. I want you to meet someone." he said eagerly.

"Oh, Willy, I can't. I really have to get to the station. Gerti will be expecting me." I replied, eyeing the sky nervously. The rain showed no signs of letting up, and I didn't fancy the idea of the Autobahn in a downpour.

"It will just take a moment. I think you will find it worth your time." he answered, hunching his shoulders against the rain. "Come."

I followed him back inside, promising myself I would only stay for several more minutes.

"This is Helmut." Willy said, his face beaming. He gestured to a man standing near a warm, smoldering fireplace.

"Pleased to meet you." said Helmut, and we shook hands. His handshake was firm and his smile was open and kindhearted.

"He is going into the East next week." said Willy. "He does research." he added with a grin.

"Yes." said Helmut. "I am from the region myself. I find there are many people from these reunions who would like to widen their searches, but they do not have the resources. If you have any names or dates, I would be happy to do some groundwork for you, as well."

"That would be great!" I answered. I glanced at my watch. "I really need to get to the train station, but let me just write down a few things for you." I said. I scribbled the first few names that popped into my head, neighbors and friends, mostly. "Thank you so much." I said, shaking his hand again.

"My pleasure." he said, glancing at the names I had written down. "Right. Ah, yes. You left your address and number, too. Good. I will contact you as soon as possible if I have any information on these names."

I said a hasty goodbye to Willy and Helmut and, with my mind already elsewhere, I raced out into the rain.

I had almost forgotten my chance meeting with Helmut, so I was very surprised to receive, several months later, a brief letter, informing me of Franz's whereabouts. It corresponded to the information I had received from Gretel, who had written a long letter shortly after my visit with Karl. I wrote back immediately, thanking Helmut for his time and consideration, then I wrote a longer letter to Franz.

Life hurried on. Sunni and I filled our days with activities in the mountains, and we watched our children grow and begin families of their own. It warmed my heart to know that I was able to provide my children with a peaceful place in which to live their lives, untroubled and untainted by the debilitating horrors of war.

In September of 1992, as my wife and I were hurrying about the house, preparing to go to the airport for a flight to New York for our son's wedding, I received a call. I hadn't heard from Helmut for quite awhile, so I was surprised to hear his voice.

"I am returning to your area to do some more research, Alf. Do you have any more names for me?" he asked. "Thanks to Gorbachev we can search more easily, now. The archives have been opened."

I had given him most of the names that represented the voids in my past, but the main and obvious one I had avoided. "Um. There is one…" I muttered. I gave him the name of my biological mother—there was a slight chance that a half-sibling might still be out there somewhere.

"I will look into this, Alf, and let you know." he said. Then, he added, "Congratulations on your son's wedding."

"Thank you. I look forward to hearing from you." I said. I hung up the phone, staring at the name I had scribbled on the pad of paper in front of me. My mother… it was the final missing link, the last key to unlocking my past. It was too much to hope… I knew that.

Retracing the escape route 1994

CHAPTER 34

It was Sunday, November 15th, 1992. I was sitting in my chair at the breakfast table, watching the snow drift slowly down onto the tall mountain peaks that surrounded my alpine home. It was bitter cold, winter having dug its claws in early. I lingered over my morning cup of tea, reluctant to begin the inevitable tour around the house with the snow plow. The phone rang shrilly, interrupting my reverie, and I rose slowly to answer it.

"Hello?" I said.

"Alf?" came the voice. "This is Helmut."

I had entirely forgotten about our last conversation, having been so occupied with our travels to our son's wedding. I answered, "Hello!" in a voice filled with utter surprise.

"How was your son's wedding?" asked Helmut.

"Uh, it was great. Really nice, thanks." I answered, puzzled. Surely, Helmut did not call just to chat about the wedding.

"Good, good." replied Helmut. "Well, Alf, I just returned from my trip… and I found some names that compared with the ones you gave me." he continued, adding quickly. "I don't know if they are the same people or not. But anyway, I think you will find one quite interesting."

"Yeah?" I said, sitting down in a nearby chair. My head felt suddenly light.

"Yes. The name of Augusta Konig… Well, I found a match, but not in Jagerndorf."

My heart began to pound. That had been my mother's name… my real mother's name. He continued, "The person in question moved to somewhere in the Schleswig-Holstein region of Germany, actually. But there is a date for her having left Jagerndorf in 1942. So, it sounds promising, but I can't be sure of a connection until I follow up with the Red Cross records. It might take some time." he said. "But, I just thought I would let you know how things are going."

"Thank you so much, Helmut. I will wait for your call." I answered, my voice trembling slightly with excitement. I hung up and stared at the phone. Could it be?

Sunni, upon hearing about the call, and seeing my excitement, made a simple, yet brilliant, suggestion. "Why not call information?" she asked, shrugging. "It is possible she is listed. Helmut gave you her full name?" I nodded. "Well, if you don't find anything then you can wait for Helmut to get back to you."

"I guess I can call international information. I don't know." I answered, suddenly panicking at the thought of possibly being on the verge of something I had dreamt of for so many years. What would I say?—"Did you know my mother?" It all sounded so impossible.

I dialed right away, my heart now thumping into my throat. The lines clicked slowly through, and I wanted to hang up, but, I couldn't. "Ah, yes, hello." I said, as the nasal voice of the international operator crackled on the other end of the line. "Um, I would like some information, please." I proceeded to explain to the operator my situation, and I gave her the name and the region of Germany in which to search.

"Without a proper address or city, it will get very expensive, sir." she answered.

I laughed nervously, saying, "Believe me, I don't care how much it costs. I've been waiting for years!"

"One moment then, please." she said, and there was a long moment of silence.

"I will connect you now, sir." she said. "Have a good day."

Amidst the static of the overseas line, the phone rang… once, twice, three times. Maybe no one would answer. My heart sank. Maybe someone would. My blood went cold. Who would pick up at the other end? I was about to hang up, deciding it had been foolish to try, when there was a faint click.

A small hesitant German voice said, "Hello. Yes?"

I gulped, wishing I had planned better what I was going to say. "Uh, yes," I answered, speaking slowly and in my most proper German. "Uh, I am looking for a Frau or Fraulein Konig, please." I said, struggling to keep my voice steady.

"This is Frau Konig." answered the smoky, rather elderly voice. "Who is this?" she asked, suspiciously.

Without thinking, I switched into the dialect of my home, and I said, "I'm sorry, but I'm looking for a Frau Konig from Jagerndorf, Austria." Suddenly, I wanted to hang up, convinced... or maybe hoping, that I had dialed the wrong number.

There was a long pause, then, "Yes."

"Um, I am calling from America. But, I grew up in Jagerndorf, as well—born in March, 1932. I was wondering..." Just what was I wondering?

For a moment, I thought the line had gone dead, then came her voice, so softly I could barely hear it. "Who are you?" she asked again.

"My name is..." I gulped and took a deep breath. "My name is Alf... Alfred."

There was an loud gasp, then a long pause. The phone crackled noisily and I feared I was losing my connection. "Hello?" I cried.

I heard several heavy labored breaths, then she whispered, in a voice thick and deep with emotion, "You... You are my baby!"

I almost toppled from the chair, and I had to grip the sides of the desk to keep the room from falling into blackness. My knuckles were turning white against the receiver. I struggled to quell the lump rising in my throat. Sunni's hand tightened on my shoulder, and I leaned against her. I whispered, "Oh my God, Sunni... it's her." Sunni raised her hand to her mouth, gasping.

After several moments of silence on both sides of the world, we talked... and talked, and talked. I was talking to my mother! I felt giddy. My mind raced with the many questions, and I had to slow my beating heart to listen to the answers. I was hungry to memorize her voice, to store it away in hopes of finding its match somewhere already in my head.

An hour later we reluctantly hung up, after I had promised her that I would call again soon. I hugged Sunni tightly, finally allowing the dam

411

of emotions that I had been holding in check to burst. It was as though the years had melted away, and I was a young child again, and that glimmer of love had been crystal clear in every breath of my mother's voice. I had heard pain, too, and remorse, and a real sense of loss. It was clear that she had had a difficult life. I did not press her on the reasons; I was not ready for that. It was enough to have found that she had not forgotten me.

After I had settled myself, I dialed up Helmut, who was startled to hear my voice so soon. He laughed in disbelief, convinced I was making a joke. But, as I read him the phone number, a listing in Kiel, Germany, he gasped in surprise. "Well, what do you know? Sometimes it goes faster to skip the bureaucracy."

"Thank you, Helmut, thank you." I said. "You have given me back my Mama."

"No thank-you needed, Alf. Congratulations!" he answered, his own voice tight with emotion.

Sunni and I walked next door to her parents' home and told them the incredible news. When we returned, there was a message on the answering machine from Helmut, saying that he had called the number himself and had talked to the "sweet old lady." She had given him the name and address of her sister, my aunt, named Gerdi, as well as her address and phone number.

In a matter of moments, I had gone from having a vacuous past, one with more holes than I could count, to a large family, overflowing with cousins and relations. Another long conversation later, I sat stunned with a head full of so much information. I talked to my aunt, discovering that she was only two years older than myself, and that we shared a birthday! We discovered, also, that we shared something else, an unforgettable experience on a pivotal day in our town's history.

Gerdi had been at Hitler's rally, too, those many years earlier, when the Fuhrer had spread his troops out through the town for display. She, too, had cringed at Hitler's fierce angry face, and she, too, had taken a child's refuge in play underneath a piano in the corner tavern. The small Gerdi, with whom I had played under the piano, the girl who had shared my hiding spot at my Uncle Fritz's tavern, had been my own aunt, and I had never known... until now.

I promised her that we would meet soon. I would book the first available flight. She said that she would arrange things with her sister—my mother, and we could all meet in Kiel, Germany.

I booked a flight that day, not caring that I paid twice the fare for the short notice. This trip, I knew, would be priceless. I called Gerdi back, letting her be the one to inform Augusta, as I knew our conversation had been difficult and tiring on my mother's nerves.

The hours inched forward, as the few days until our departure passed at a snail's pace. My head was filled with conflicting emotions. My nerves were overflowing, and I found it difficult to sleep. My life was about to change forever. I had not seen my mother since I was a year old. Just what would I find? What would I feel?

The big day arrived. We had bought a new video camera and plenty of film, ready to document the reunion that I never could have dreamed would happen. It had been over sixty years, beyond the time when I thought there was hope for any more reunions with anyone from home. But to have found my mother... it was too much to believe.

During the long flight, I found myself worrying, wondering if it had all been a dream after all, wondering if it still was. But, here we were, in the town my mother had moved to so long ago. I had traveled through Kiel many times in my life, crossing the North Sea to Scandinavia for ski trips. I had passed within several blocks of her home and had never known. Now, the moment had come to knock on her door... and suddenly, I wasn't ready.

The taxi wound slowly through the busy city streets, as the driver followed the directions Gerdi had given me. Gerdi had made the long train ride from her home in central Germany, and she was already waiting at her sister's side to lend her moral support through what was most certainly an emotional time.

The taxi pulled up outside a low row of apartment buildings, and Sunni began to film. I groaned, telling her I couldn't go on. "I can't do this. Let's go." I said, sweat rising on my palms.

"Oh no, you don't, Alf! This is sixty years of questions ready to be answered. Let's go!" she said, placing her hand firmly on my arm.

The trembling in my limbs ceased, and I nodded. We walked slowly to the door. My hands were gripped tightly around a large bunch of fragrant flowers, my meager attempt at making up for so many years of missed birthdays.

The hallway was dimly lit and smelled of delicious cooking from someone's kitchen. I breathed deeply, trying to calm my pounding heart. Gerdi had told me that my mother's door would be to the left, and I found it quickly. Too quickly. My mother's name was printed on a small tag to the right of the door.

I rang the bell. My knees were now shaking more violently than my hands. Upon hearing a small click, I started. The door was opening. A veil of mist seemed to descend over me, and the hand I returned to my side seemed to move as though under water. The door swung slowly open, and the contained excitement rose to a palpable hum hovering on the breath of us all. I could sense Sunni standing behind me, but her presence was eclipsed by the vision before me.

There she stood, a small woman with eyes wide and filled with anxious anticipation and strain. But, as soon as our gazes met, the worry left her face, and I knew she recognized me. There was no doubt... this was my mother. I could have picked her out of a row of faces. There was no mistake.

Her hair was thin and white, and it framed a face flushed with excitement and emotion. She was old, in her eighties, but the wrinkles of time could not completely hide the high cheekbones and the fairness of her faded youth. She was grasping the edge of the door tightly with her hands, and I could see that they were aged and brown, but still delicate and feminine.

Behind her and off to one side, stood a younger woman, whose eyes were red from crying, though a wide smile lit up her face. Gerdi. I answered her smile with a shaky one of my own, then I returned my enchanted gaze to my mother. Her body was trembling with anticipation; I walked forward and wrapped my arms gently around her small bent shoulders, which melted instantly with released emotion.

To stay the flood of my own feelings, I pulled back, and I handed her the flowers. Clearing my throat awkwardly, I said, "Mutti." My mother's forehead sank against my chest, and she whispered my name over and over.

I turned again to Gerdi, and we, too, fell into a tight embrace. Her joyous laughter rang in my ear and I couldn't help but gaze ardently into the smiling eyes of the now-grown child who had once looked at me in the dark beneath a piano. The brief bond we had shared on that distant day could now be reforged.

The day was delightful; the sight before me, amazing. My mother... here she sat, staring at me with a love that had clearly never gone away. She patted my hand constantly, turning my fingers over between her own as though studying every line that time had etched upon them.

Beneath the obvious pleasure at seeing me, though, I could sense something else, a lingering pain, perhaps a guilt, for all the lost years. Finally, after holding it in for so long, she let it go, sobbing deeply onto my shoulder. I said nothing, but held her tightly, simply reveling in the feeling of her closeness.

I longed to ask the question that had been in my mind for so many years... Why? She must have sensed my feelings, because suddenly, she was ready to talk.

"I was unhappy, you know. I never belonged. The family never accepted me." she said. Her voice was deep with age and with too many years of smoking, but the sigh that escaped between her breaths was deeper yet, echoing profound thoughts of sadness and an overpowering regret. She stared into my eyes, carefully considering her words. "I'm not excusing what I did, Alf... I can never make you understand, I know."

I simply placed my hand over hers, knowing at that moment that I forgave her it all. Nonetheless, she continued, "I never wanted to give you up; you must understand that. But, the courts decided.... everyone decided, that it would be best for you if I was out of the picture." She wept silently into a tissue, her eyes clenched tightly shut, as the tears dripped down her soft cheeks.

I cleared my throat, saying, with a smile, "Well, we have each other now, and how many people get a second chance?" I glanced at Sunni, who stood behind me with the camera. She smiled and nodded encouragingly. I turned back to my mother and said, "It is almost Thanksgiving—in America, it celebrates a new beginning. I think we have our own celebrating to do. I know I have a lot to be thankful for this year."

We spent a wonderful several days enjoying the simple pleasures together. We shared a delicious German-style Thanksgiving dinner with my mother and Gerdi at the wonderful restaurant in our fine hotel. We were joined by several cousins, none of whom I had known existed. Over the meal, we planned the first visit of my aunt to America, though I was saddened by my mother's reluctance to join her. But, she was in her eighties, and had yet to experience a trip on an airplane. I knew all too well how traumatic that could be. Also, her health was suffering, and the strain of Colorado's high elevations made a visit seem unlikely.

Gerdi was eager to visit, though, and she did so several times, once bringing her delightful son along for the Christmas holidays. Meanwhile, I communicated regularly with my mother and made a return trip as soon as I was able. Finding my mother had filled a void that I had always imagined to be bottomless. And even though we lived thousands of miles apart, her presence in the world soothed me just as Oma's and Opa's had when I was alone and afraid.

A link to my past had been forged anew, and I wanted to carry that link forward to generations beyond while I was still able. Thus, my daughter Kari, pregnant with her first child, was fortunate enough to meet her grandmother for the first time in 1994. It was heartwarming to see the delight in my mother's face as she gazed upon the future of her family. Kari watched in awe as she witnessed familiar gestures that I had exhibited all my life, repeated in my mother. The same tilt of the head, the same slant of the hand beneath the chin.

Kari returned to the States after her brief visit and Sunni and I, accompanied by Gerdi and Sunni's cousin, Karin, continued on for another emotional trip to our homeland. Gerdi had not been back since they had fled when she was a young girl.

We held hands tightly and wandered the familiar streets, marveling at the many twists of fate that had brought us together after so long. It seemed fitting that we would share these moments together, our lives inexplicably entwined since that poignant moment on our little shared island of calm under the piano. The storm of time and history had roared around us, ready to ensnare the helpless and unsuspecting people of the world in a most terrible war, but we had found peace as only children can.

I returned to America renewed and reborn, my whole life open in front of me with new possibilities. But, several years later, after regular contact with my darling mother, she passed away, failing to recover completely from a brutal burglary attack in her home. My mother's life had been filled with sadness, but I liked to believe that our reunion had brought her some long-needed happiness, as well as an ultimate closure on a painful time in her life. It certainly made all the difference in mine.

I sat alone one night, shortly after hearing of my mother's death, perusing the large piles of photos of the many memorable trips. I gazed at my mother's face and mine, as we stared happily at the camera, the resemblance unmistakable, the bond irreplaceable.

At the bottom of the pile, I found a photo, taken by Sunni. It recorded a stolen moment as I wandered the hills near the lands of my forefathers. The colors were muted, like a vision of the past, the grass barely disturbed by my careful step.

I never noticed Sunni take the picture; my mind was lost in a flood of memories. The sweet smell of the forest and fields around me filled my senses with such profound joy. I could almost reach up to the blue sky and touch Opa's face, his voice carried to me on the eternal wind across the trees and mountains. I could almost hear the laughter of the boys as we scampered through the gnarled undergrowth searching for the fabled cherry tree. I could almost hear the panic in Jacov's ragged breathing as we ran through the woods away from the troops along the train tracks.

It was not until Sunni and I crossed the meadow, that we realized just where we had been. We had not noticed the sign, overgrown with brush and wildflowers. It was a forgotten minefield… forgotten, but still deadly. It was filled with terrors from the past, from the infamous era of my youth, but to me it meant something more. I had finally come home. The circle was complete; I could finally remember it all. As I walked carefully away from the meadow, with my eyes closed against the sun, I could just hear the soft breath of my mother's voice upon my newborn cheek.

THE END

ABOUT THE AUTHOR

A native of Colorado, **Karina Wetherbee,** lives with her husband and three children in Columbus, Ohio. Trained as a photographer, her skills have taken her throughout Europe and the Far East. Her true inspiration, though, lies in the peaks and valleys of her childhood home, Keystone, Colorado. This is her first book.

Printed in the United States
55532LVS00004B/85-102